Borders and Margins

Guy Lachapelle
Pablo Oñate (eds.)

Borders and Margins

Federalism, Devolution and
Multi-Level Governance

Barbara Budrich Publishers
Opladen • Berlin • Toronto 2018

A CIP catalogue record for this book is available from
Die Deutsche Bibliothek (The German Library)

© 2018 by Barbara Budrich Publishers, Opladen, Berlin & Toronto
www.barbara-budrich.net

    ISBN   978-3-8474-2025-5
    eISBN 978-3-8474-1016-4

Die Deutsche Bibliothek – CIP-Einheitsaufnahme
Ein Titeldatensatz für die Publikation ist bei der Deutschen Bibliothek erhältlich.

Verlag Barbara Budrich 🅑 Barbara Budrich Publishers
Stauffenbergstr. 7. D-51379 Leverkusen Opladen, Germany

86 Delma Drive. Toronto, ON M8W 4P6 Canada
www.barbara-budrich.net

Jacket illustration by Bettina Lehfeldt, Kleinmachnow –
    www.lehfeldtgraphic.de
Picture credits: www.lehfeldtmalerei.de
Typesetting: Anja Borkam, Jena – kontakt@lektorat-borkam.de
Printed in Europe on acid-free paper by paper & tinta, Warsaw

Contents

Figures

Tables

Preface

Wyn Grant, University of Warwick

The theme of the 2012 International Political Science Congress in Madrid was "Reordering Power, Shifting Boundaries." Fast forward to Poznan, Poland, in 2014, where our theme was "Politics in a World of Inequalities." The theme of the 2018 World Congress in Brisbane, Australia – "Borders and Margins" – is meant to reflect the important changes taking place in the world. Borders in the traditional sense of secure, maintained boundaries are still needed at a time when governments are hard-pressed to control the flow of migrants; 9/11, in particular, sparked renewed calls for stricter border controls.

Nevertheless, we live in a world of greater fluidity, where old territorial formations coexist alongside new territorial spaces that are conceptualized differently. Territory and power no longer align, boundaries and borders are shifting, and governance is exercised at the local or municipal level, the subnational (nation-state) level, the regional level (especially in Europe), and the global level through a range of international organizations. These include the International Monetary Fund and the World Trade Organization, bargaining forums such as G-7 and G-20, and new arrangements designed to improve international financial regulation, among them the Financial Stability Board. It is little wonder that there is growing uncertainty, among citizens, as to who is responsible for the decisions affecting them, fuelling a sense of disempowerment.

One must be careful, of course, not to write off the nation-state as outmoded – a temptation too strong to resist for some earlier writers on globalization – through there is a greater consensus, nowadays, that globalization has altered its role, with the emergence of influential subnational entities, not necessarily under traditional federal arrangements, for example in Spain and the United Kingdom. The development of power relationships between these regional entities and their nation-states is ongoing and deserves further study.

The actual process cannot be said to be uniform from one country to the next. In Spain, for example, specific regional identities re-emerged only when the authoritarian regime was displaced. The process by which French Canadians re-identified themselves as Quebecers was a long and complex, one that spawned alternative and even contradictory narratives. The process, in essence, saw a once suppressed and even subjugated linguistic minority in Canada rediscover and reconceptualize their identity. The revival of Scottish nationalism came at a time when the UK seemed to be mired in a period of irreversible economic decline, and it also coincided with the discovery of oil in the North Sea, which further spurred Scottish confidence. In Belgium, the creation of ever-stronger regional entities was the mechanism through which the country's continued existence as a nation-state could be ensured. At one time, Catalonia was viewed as an inspirational model for new regional formations. However, much of the recent emphasis has been on Scotland, in spite of its relatively new regional government. The Scottish Government is generally acknowledged to have been both strategically visionary and tactically effective in expanding and consolidating its political space. The replacement of the term "Scottish Executive" by "Scottish Government" is one such example. The Scottish Government It has also been effective at breaking down departmental silos in decision-making processes. Like many regional political processes, however, the final destination remains uncertain, with "devolution plus'" a more likely scenario than outright independence.

The advent of the single market and other changes in Europe resulted in a transfer of powers to Brussels, which to many Europeans seemed remote, unresponsive and technocratic, in spite of efforts to strengthen the democratic component of EU decision-making through the European Parliament. A "Europe of the Regions" provided an opportunity to bring the European Union closer to its citizens and offered a promising mechanism for civic empowerment. In part, this entailed the recognition that as globalization progressed and new cosmopolitan identities emerged, there was a corresponding move to harken back to or reinvent older or more specific identities that ascribed meaning to the political space, one the average citizen could easily understand.

For cities and regional entities, there was a more pragmatic incentive. The provision of additional European regional development funds, and the willingness of the European institutions to engage directly with cities and regions, created a welcome funding opportunity as well as a new route of political influence, with cities and regions now able to engage directly with the EU. In the UK, this was referred to as the "Westminster bypass." This enhanced the status of cities and regions, which hastened to establish offices in Brussels.

The high-water mark in the "Europe of the Regions" debate has long since passed. Some areas of the EU are no longer eligible for regional development funds and have scaled back their presence in Brussels. The Committee of the Regions – the institution that came out of the debate – has proved to be something of a disappointment; tainted by an expense scandal and seemingly ineffective, quite often, it was only given consultative status. In intellectual terms, one lasting consequence is the literature on multilevel governance (MLG).

This literature represents an important attempt to assess the changes raised by the theme of the World Congress. The theme resonated to a greater extent in Europe than in North America, where it encountered resistance, particularly in the U.S. Moreover, it may not be readily applicable in Asia and Latin America, partly due to above-mentioned efforts to return to or reinvent older or more specific identities that lent meaning to the political space.

MLG is not without its critics. Among them are those who believe that more traditional formulations of federalism have continued utility and greater specificity. It would be unfortunate, in many ways, if a polarity were to develop between defenders of federalism and intellectual advocates of MLG. There are some significant new regional arrangements that are not federal in character, but may be captured by MLG; "the new regionalism" meanwhile, represents another way to view them. More generally, the debate on MLG offers a means of renewing and enriching the debate on federalism. Federalist accounts, understandably, have focused on multilevel government and the variety of relationships between federal tiers in different settings. Some federal systems are more uniform, while others are characterized by greater diversity. Looking at the 50 states in the U.S. and how their legislatures operate, variety is consistent feature. With the exception of Nebraska, all have two chambers. But they vary considerably in size and the frequency with which they meet, the number of elected members in the legislature (contrast New Hampshire and California), and the manner in which they are paid for their services, to mention just a few dimensions.

MLG is about governance. It is less state-oriented than federalism, with sharper focus on actors. MLG, moreover, is concerned with the various ways in which modern government may operate, often involving public-private partnerships and a wide range of actors, including charities and NGOs. It is concerned not so much with vertical but with horizontal relationships. In Europe and the United States, for example, cooperative relationships develop across state boundaries.

MLG has been criticized for being narrow and too descriptive, and it has also been passed off on normative grounds, as a means to defend the status quo. For the purposes of this analysis, however, it is deployed primarily as a heuristic device, that's to say it offers a means of better understanding patterns of change in society and polity. No particular normative claims are made for it. It attempts to capture a complex, diverse and unpredictable reality that is the central challenge of social science in general, and political science in particular.

What are some of the issues worth addressing in these debates, regardless of the terminology used? One important general point concerns the need to distinguish between activity and impact. Resources can be invested and staff deployed, but reliable means are needed to measure the difference in relation to outcomes, particularly when it comes to the growing range of international activities undertaken by regional entities. It bears mentioning, however, that reduced public spending in the wake of the global financial crisis served to curb some of these activities, including by American states abroad.

Some long-standing activities – attracting foreign investment – may be relatively easy to measure. Foreign investment inflows and the number of projects successfully attracted can also be measured. However, attempts to influence foreign policy may present greater methodological challenges, as disentangling the multitude of actors involved is sure to prove difficult.

The role of elites in this process and their conceptualization is also an important consideration. To what extent do they lead, shape or even manipulate public opinion? Traditional nationalist movements that give rise to new nation-states or that wrest their independence from colonial rule have often relied upon charismatic figures who convey the essential distinctiveness of the new territorial formation to their followers.

Modern regional movements need more sophisticated forms of leadership to make effective use of the mass media to communicate messages to followers and potential converts. Beyond the individual leader, a new regional political class may be required, which has already occurred in Scotland, one can argue. Such a political class extends beyond the executive, legislature and political parties to encompass the media and non-governmental organizations. The manner in which business organizations respond to these new realities raises interesting empirical questions.

Another set of empirical questions relates to political recruitment. Traditionally, regional legislatures have been viewed as a springboard for political careers, providing an apprenticeship for national office, and allowing aspiring legislators to hone their political skills as well as build a reputation and a political base.

More complex patterns may now be emerging, however. Legislators may be satisfied with a career at the regional level, as it can offer greater opportunities for making a difference and may be less disruption to family life than working in the national capital. Some may return from the national to the regional level, having found it more challenging to build networks of influence there in an effort to bring about meaningful change. Many regional parties have limited representation at the national level, restricting the opportunities to move there. In Europe, the possibility of a career at the European level offers an additional dimension.

These complex patterns provide challenges of categorization, and require careful and thorough empirical research, which is now well underway.

Acknowledgments

This book is intended chiefly to analyze how governments and civil societies adapt to challenges from the new environment, particularly those pertaining to supra- and substate dynamics. The concept of multilevel governance gives us the elements we need to better evaluate political conflicts and outcomes across various levels of government and examine how institutions, political parties, social movements, business organizations and politicians move within this new environment.

We would first like to thank the Valencian Regional Government and the University of Valencia (Spain), where the collaborators on this book first gathered for preliminary discussions on the new forms of governance and trends observed in recent years. We also owe a debt of gratitude to Sanda Sijercic and Tristan Masson, who reviewed the chapters and provided a theoretical viewpoint on the contributions from collaborators. A special word of thanks goes out to Claude Berlinguette, who coordinated this special project sponsored by the International Political Science Association (IPSA), and Prof. Wyn Grant, who served as Chair of the Program Committee for the 22nd IPSA World Congress in Madrid 2012 and believed the issue of multilevel governance was crucial to the development of our discipline.

Introduction
Borders and Margins: Federalism, Devolution and Multilevel Governance

Guy Lachapelle and Pablo Oñate

Introduction

Multilevel governance (MLG) is the watchword in an increasing number of countries, nowadays, with multiple layers of government given a say in the adoption of political decisions and the allocation of resources. A wide variety of examples can be cited, from strong federal systems to regionally decentralized states. The final decades of the 20th century witnessed the emergence of a new kind of regionalism (*the new regionalism*) marked by a political (cultural and institutional) structure rather than economic arrangements. The terms used to summarize these factors include internationalization and globalization, reactivation or emergence of regional identities and culture, reinforcement of substate focal points (both local and regional) for economic development, and social regulation and collective action.

Various forms of new regionalism have set the stage for the emergence or reinforcement of institutions that play a part in shaping multilevel political systems, depending on the scope of substate cultural traditions and the presence of social and economic institutions and networks. These substate tiers of government differ regarding the extent of self-government and the existence of successful non-state-wide parties (or strong regional organizations of state-wide parties). Regardless of the capacity for self-government, however, regions work as relevant arenas for political decision-making, resource allocation and political debate. Many countries have turned to MLG as a way of organizing political-institutional activity thereby spawning a field for political and social research.

At its core, this book was born of our conviction that MLG is a useful concept for capturing the increasingly complex and shared nature of public decision-making in federal and non-federal systems, especially in the age of global competition. MLG also relates to the notion of asymmetrical federalism or the principle of subsidiarity, according to which political and financial responsibility is conferred on the level of government best able to meet the needs of citizens. And even if these new regionalisms go beyond a functional framework for political life, globalization and the issue of sustainable development should be perceived as an opportunity to create new partnerships between levels of government, civil society and the private sector with the goal of fostering the conditions for better investment and promoting fair and participative projects. Governments should propose treaties, trade agreements and regulations calling for better cooperation between levels of governance, therefore. In this way, MLG is viewed as a system of governance within or between states. The aim of this book, therefore, is to show readers how this concept, within its normative and empirical meanings, can offer an analytical framework for the study of intergovernmental relationships.

The collaborators herein emphasize the cooperative nature of MLG, a strong federalist or functional regional system, and the non-conflictual resolution of policy problems in concurrent political arenas. This book offers a fresh perspective on new means of governance that meet citizens' needs. The first section explores the concept of MLG and its use in multinational societies, while the second analyzes the issue of trust-mistrust and how it shapes central-regional-local relationships. The third, meanwhile, looks to a new dimension of international relations: the increasing role of substate entities in world debates and trade regulations. The fourth section looks more specifically at how globalization and MLG have reshaped the role and functions of political parties and party systems. Finally, since we are talking about the emergence of a new system of governance, the book studies its effects on the behavior and attitudes of parliamentary representatives.

I

In Chapter 1, Michael Stein and Lisa Turkewitsch provide an initial analysis of this concept, applying it to federations and decentralized unitary systems, such as those in Germany and the United Kingdom (UK). The concept of MLG, they argue, is a fairly recent one, emerging with the deepening integration of the European Union in the early 1990s, and drawing its basic structure from the ideas and institutions created in conjunction with the signing of the Maastricht Treaty in 1992. Moving from this historical context to present-day situations, Stein and Turkewitsch cite the United Kingdom and Germany as modern examples illustrating the limitations of and emerging patterns in MLG theory, first highlighting its strengths and weaknesses and comparing it to more traditional approaches, namely those of neo-functionalism, neo-institutionalism (both decentralized and multinational federalism), and centralized unitarism. They also include contributions to MLG theory that further highlight its utility as a comparative analytical tool, especially in relation to the UK and

Germany. In comparing these two EU polities – which share demographic and institutional similarities – they show that the ability to conceptualize these nations within traditional frameworks has eroded considerably. This is particularly the case for the UK, where the MLG framework, Stein and Turkewitsch suggest, may be best adapted to the British climate. And while the UK, in its political development, may require a suitable theoretical framework, Germany, for its part, has long-standing historical ties to MLG theory through the study of German federalism. MLG theory may be viewed as an extension of federalism, therefore, and may be used to analyze features of federal and decentralized unitary systems as well as the EU, as Stein and Turkewitsch note, citing the German state, which encompasses both types of MLG. Because it is better suited to analyzing the changes in these polities, both now and in the future, the flexible MLG framework, the authors believe, lends itself to a more accurate assessment of changing forms of governance than traditional comparative theories.

In his chapter on "Problems of Democratic Accountability in Network and Multilevel Governance," Yannis Papadopoulos analyzes democratic accountability in MLG systems. While MLG networks generate new and novel forms of accountability, he argues, its democratic dimension poses a problem, owing to the inherent structure of MLG networks and to issues of accountability. His chapter focuses chiefly on public and democratic forms of accountability, specifically as they pertain to the role played by actors in network governance and political problems stemming from accountability deficits. In doing so, he explains why decentralization and, increasingly, the lack of political authority in the market system generate problems for the quality of democracy in federated systems. These problems are caused by a lack of democratic accountability in the governance structure, stemming from four properties of network governance: Weak network visibility and uncoupling, leading to often informal and opaque decision-making processes; policy networks composed of actors only indirectly accountable to citizens and operating in isolation from democratic institutions; MLG, which can lead to fragmentation and compromise cooperation and (therefore) accountability; and the tendency towards peer accountability in networks, with the results that actors are primarily accountable to peer groups as opposed to the public. These network forms of governance, he suggests, give rise to a variety of problems related to accountability. Papadopoulos concludes by proposing a decision-making model for addressing accountability deficits through the use of institutional mechanisms.

Alain-G. Gagnon looks at how the concept of MLG redefines the political space. As our world grows increasingly heterogeneous, both on a societal and ideological level, theoretical frameworks used to conceptualize the space must take into account this diversity. This serves as the departure point for Gagnon's argument whereby multinational federalism reflects the changing societal and political structures of our time. Gagnon cites Canada's linguistic and cultural diversity as an example of how the central government's will can play a part in tensions between different cultural groups and thus erode the spirit of multinational federalism. While the multilevel approach highlights the role of sometimes overlooked actors and their contribution to government programs and policies, Gagnon notes that it fails to take into account their decision-making objectives, nor does it account for the dual pillars of federalism, namely the focus on the common populace and issues of governmental autonomy. In short, Gagnon suggests that the shortcomings of the multilevel approach serve to undermine democratic practices, making it particularly problematic as a framework for analyzing diverse national settings. In the belief that this approach ignores such issues as social structure, Gagnon notes that the multilevel approach is useful for analyzing efficacy and the economy in homogenous state structures, which he believes are rare in the modern world. Federalism, he argues, is capable of addressing these complexities.

II

Section 2 places the issue of trust-mistrust in institutions at the heart of the analysis, with Spain and Canada cited as the main examples. Francisco Llera Ramo explores the rise and fall of institutional trust in Spain using data from public surveys to emphasize that distrust and discontent with the political system, coupled with the erosion of institutional trust, could prove catastrophic for the functioning of the Spanish constitution. While Spain is in the midst of its longest-running period of constitutional democracy, public satisfaction with democracy and EU membership has been in decline since 2004, he notes. This mounting dissatisfaction may be partly attributed to the global financial crisis of 2007, he argues, adding that globalization is changing our democracies and the relationship between economy and politics, with citizens and parliaments becoming more and more distant from decision-making centres. This prolonged economic crisis has revealed deep and long-standing political cleavages in the Spanish system, contributing to public distrust and discontent with political parties and institutions. And while Spaniards have grown increasingly disaffected with politics, argues Francisco Llera Ramo, they also consider themselves to be well-informed politically. Despite this, Spanish protests have done little except to highlight discontent, with little or nothing in the way of concessions coming from political parties. This situation, if allowed to continue, could negatively impact Spain's constitutional system, he predicts, adversely affecting the relationship between its citizenry and politics.

Guy Laforest and Camille Brunelle-Hamann bring their attention to bear to the Canadian case and the relationship between the federal government and the provinces, more specifically Québec. The trust-mistrust scale is applied to highlight the collaborative-competitive nature of intergovernmental relations in Canada. Acknowledging that trust is dynamic and changes according to historical and political circumstances, Laforest and Brunelle-Hamann analyze the evolving relationship between the former Canadian Prime Minister Stephen Harper and Québec, drawing important lessons on the value of trust in federal democracies. Using John Locke's conceptualization of trust as consequential and revisable, Laforest and Brunelle-Hamann map the changes in Harper's perception and distrust of Québec from his politically formative years up to the present day, dividing this period into three sections. Harper's distrust of Québec began when he first joined the Reform Party in the late 1980s, they argue, and continued as Québec's increasingly statist and interventionist political culture flourished. This reality, paired with language issues inside and outside Québec, contradicted Harper's Hayekian conservative opposition to State intervention in economic and social affairs. And though Harper's understanding of federalism included independent provinces and rampant decentralization, Laforest and Brunelle-Hamann note that any special status given to Québec would run counter to his vision of a Canada marked by individual, provincial and regional equality united under Canadian law. Harper's distrust is portrayed as deep-seated and almost unwavering, yet it is worth noting that the years preceding his election as Prime Minister were marked by increased, albeit short-lived cooperation between Harper and Québec. Laforest and Brunelle-Hamann cite the example of Québec, in both an historical and present-day context, to highlight the importance, among elected leaders, of keeping promises and – in the case of Harper – the need to engage in open communication and display solidarity with provincial leaders. Finally, they conclude with a comparative perspective, stating that this type of relationship is not unique to Canada but can also be applied to the 2011 general election in Spain, where elected officials faced similar circumstances.

III

In Part 3, the new international role of the substate entity is analyzed, together with the development of a new form of paradiplomacy. With a focus on the international role of substate entities, David Criekemans presents the concept of multilevel diplomacy, examining the evolution of substate diplomacy in regions with legislative powers, specifically the character of foreign policy and representation across a number of regions and small states, including Flanders, Wallonia, Scotland, Bavaria, Catalonia, Québec, Luxembourg and Slovenia. There is a visible dilution of boundaries between diplomacy – which is generated by states – and paradiplomacy (the foreign policy of non-central governments), which is generated by regions with legislative powers. Substate diplomacy can be viewed in different waves, the first of which, in the 1980s, was characterized by an increase in the number of non-central actors attracting foreign investment on their own initiative, and the second, in the 1990s, which was marked by the creation of judicially grounded instruments for the diplomatic activities in certain substate entities in Europe. Criekemans purposes a third wave in substate diplomacy, characterized by increasing verticalization in the organizational structure of foreign affairs, the pursuit of geopolitical and functional priorities, and the wish to integrate substate foreign policy into a well-performing whole. Globalization has generated conditions that challenge the hierarchy of state-centred approaches, with the rise of autonomous substate actors, each with their own self-directed interests. Substate diplomacy is thus a burgeoning field of research. Criekemans offers a detailed examination of foreign policy and what it means to regions with legislative powers, the instruments used to pursue it, and how it affects intergovernmental relations in external affairs as well as representation abroad. He concludes by highlighting the ambiguity of substate diplomacy – specifically this third wave of paradiplomacy – and musing about whether it will lead to a multilevel diplomacy of interactions between central and regional policy levels. At the same time, he emphasizes the need to institutionalize these relations and support them through formal and informal ties.

Stéphane Paquin analyzes trade negotiations involving substate entities. Citing the recent trade agreement between Canada and Europe, Paquin makes the case for a multilevel approach to understanding international trade treaties through his Canadian case study. Noting that the end of the Second World War witnessed a rise in international multilateralism and trade agreements coinciding with an increase in federated and decentralized systems, Paquin draws on a multilevel rather than a centralized approach to understand international trade. Stating that foreign policy should not be a monopoly of the central state but should involve regional actors, he argues that the negotiation and implementation of international trade treaties involving Canada exemplifies the emerging need to consider regional levels of government at the international level. Multiple court rulings in the first half of the 20th century served to consolidate federalism in Canada and provide a growing platform for provinces to have their say in the negotiation and implementation of international treaties. These rulings have given rise to increased intergovernmental mechanisms for managing relations between the provincial and federal governments and ensuring that provinces are consulted on international treaties, specifically as they regard their legislative jurisdictions. This has proven necessary, as the federal government alone is responsible for concluding an international treaty, yet cannot enforce its implementation where it falls outside its jurisdiction, that is to say at the provincial level. This has led to discrepancies in the past, in terms of the number of treaties concluded at the federal level and implemented at the provincial level. The sovereignty of regional actors and their increased representation in international negotiations, Paquin argues, makes a multilevel approach necessary for understanding and studying international trade.

Iván Medina and Joaquim M. Molins analyze the role of business associations in the United Kingdom and Spain, more specifically their adaptation to MLG structures. They begin by dispelling Keynesian and neo-corporatist assertions put forward in previous studies, instead focusing on the effects of globalization, the European Union, regional elites and competitiveness on the gradual transformation of economic and political structures, and the resulting implications for the actors and business associations. The increasing importance of territorial politics has contributed to the rise of peripheral economies and regional institutions, elites and cultures, thus forcing business associations to adapt accordingly. The case studies of Spain and the UK highlight the different regional paths business associations can follow in response to changing structures of state territorialism. They show that business associations in Spain revolve around the sector and territory, which together form a complex network of business associations with a focus on defending an open economy and participating in collective bargaining. The UK, for its part, is far less institutionalized than Spain and shows no incidence of collective bargaining and increased competition between interest groups. These case studies present two different models – one where regional governments incorporate business association into their governance, and another where business associations adapt to newly devolved states – to show that these associations strive to achieve institutional representation as a means to meet their political objectives.

IV

Part 4 of the book focuses on the interaction between party systems and political parties in multilevel layered-out systems. Lori Thorlakson and Guy Lachapelle present the case of federal and provincial parties in Canada, while Juan Rodriguez and Astrid Barrio look at the Spanish case, and Kris Deschouwer the Belgium case. First, Lori Thorlakson argues that multilevel politics in a federal system can follow a model of second-order party competition or involve completely separate elections. The latter scenario, she demonstrates, has characterized the Canadian federal system. Thorlakson argues that provincial elections do not fit the model of second-order party competition, as there is a considerable distinction between provincial and federal politics in Canada, owing to the independence of provincial parties from their federal counterparts. This leads to incongruent voter behaviour stemming from separate voter identity at different territorial levels. Examining major political parties at the provincial and federal level, Thorlakson finds that the overwhelming majority are united only by weak or non-existent organizational linkages. Federal parties are thus allowed to associate themselves with more parties of the same political persuasion, she argues, while provincial governments pursue their own interests in light of conflicts between the different party levels. With the exception of Québec, Thorlakson shows that Canadian politics is marked by widespread party label incongruence and party system diversity due to the separation between provincial and federal levels of government. Congruence, Thorlakson notes, is the exception rather than the rule in Canada, and it is measured by the level of organizational linkages and the number of political parties at the provincial level. Strong fiscal and policy decentralization have created an incentive and competition for holding public office at a provincial level, as greater political autonomy and fiscal resources allow provincial governments to shape and respond to provincial policy demands. Canada's low level of congruence, party system nationalization, and inconsistent partisanship makes it unique in comparison to other multilevel democracies in the Americas.

Guy Lachapelle examines how a political party can be involved in international affairs and create new type of multilevel politics, citing the example of the Parti Québécois and its role in promoting the UNESCO Convention on Cultural Diversity. As policy entrepreneurs working to bring specific issues to the forefront of the public and international sphere, political parties can play a major part in shaping paradiplomatic relations undertaken by regional governments. The articulation of Québec's domestic concerns and foreign policy on the international stage represents one such example. Over the years, Québec's political parties have wavered in their interest in international relations. The lone exception, the Parti Québécois, has been more active in debating international issues at their conferences through the Comité des Relations Internationales (CRI). The CRI's objectives and actions were concerned largely with collecting information and fostering partnerships and international relations that might help Québec play a larger role on the world stage in the event that it becomes a sovereign state. After its 2003 defeat, however, debates on international issues have waned within the Parti Québécois, which has reverted back to mobilizing public opinion on the issue of cultural diversity. While cultural diversity has remained an issue for the current Québec government, the Parti Québécois provided the impetus for a widespread debate on the issue, portraying itself as the defender of cultural diversity. The Parti Québécois is thus an example of a political party within a multilevel system that furthers its own policy interests even where there is a shared jurisdiction in areas of foreign policy control. It has added its voice to the debate on cultural diversity, arguing in favour of its legal protection in the face of rampant globalization, and holding it up as a model for political parties in multilevel systems.

Juan Rodriguez and Astrid Barrio study the role of political parties in Spain. Decentralization of unitary states, such as Spain, forces political parties to adapt to the new framework in order to remain competitive in a multilevel system. Rodriguez and Barrio set out to explain how statewide political parties interact in the context of Spanish multilevel competition through the use of coalition-based strategies, and how these strategies allow them to achieve optimum electoral and institutional performance. This multilevel competition is characterized by a regionally differentiated electoral system and calendar, a regional discrepancy between nationalist and regionalist demands in several regions, a challenging position of the parties representing these demands on each level, and the existence of electorates showing different behaviour on each electoral level. As a result of this competition and newly devolved institutions, statewide parties have gradually changed their discourse and organization in order to strengthen their electoral presence in different territories. These indicators can be used to measure this adaptation: vertical integration, as evidenced in the presence of formal and informal linkages between the central office and regional organizations; influence, evidenced in the increased importance of regional leaders in national politics; and autonomy, seen in the incidence of interference by national organizations in regional affairs. Rodriguez and Barrio argue that while statewide political parties are adapting to this new decentralization and form of competition, their main challenge comes from the rising importance of non-statewide parties (NSWP) at both the regional and national level; in order to understand the dynamics of Spanish politics, these salient levels of government cannot be overlooked, they suggest. They examine the growing strength of NSWPs in the national system as well as regional subsystems and statewide coalition strategies adopted by parties before and after regional elections. While decentralization has not impacted the number of NSWPs, it has increased their salience and influence on political institutions, providing a considerable challenge to statewide parties and forcing them to change their practices and strategies in order to remain competitive on both regional and national levels.

Kris Deschower examines the recently devolved federation of Belgium and its complex political system based on two overlapping substates, regions and language communities. Once a unitary state, Belgium became a federation following constitutional reforms in 1995. These reforms led to the disintegration of statewide parties and their complete disappearance from Belgian politics. Replacing them were increasingly autonomous substate governments divided from west to east by a language border. Flemish- and French-language populations – which make up 60% and 40% of the total population, respectively – wrangled over the terms of devolution, with Flemish speakers favouring a federation based on language communities, and French speakers arguing in favour of a devolution into three major regions. Ultimately, a compromise was reached, and overlapping language communities and territorial regions were created, with the result that the Belgian federation and its political parties, to-day, are ruled by this linguistic bipolarity. This is evidenced at the federal level, where government must be made up of an equal share of French and Flemish speakers, and at the regional level, where electoral competitions are held within each language group. Political parties in Belgium are limited, in scope, to one of the two language communities and two of the three regions, and they are active on both federal and substate levels of government. This split party system produces two results, one for each language group, and ultimately denies differentiation between regional and federal elections because unilingual parties vie for the same votes at both levels, thereby causing a strong overlap. These major linguistic and regional cleavages and the divergent views of Belgium at the time of devolution are responsible for its complex institutional setup and division at regional and federal levels of government.

V

How will parliamentarians in Europe and North America respond to the emerging challenges raised by globalization and the manifold changes in multilevel politics? Pablo Oñate looks at the increasing professionalization of politics in Spain and the ensuing movement between political arenas in a multilevel system. Starting in 1977, during the country's transition to democracy, politics was simultaneously professionalized with the institutionalization of a new political system. Political elites were influenced by the very political system they set about designing, Oñate notes, drawing a close connection between institutionalization, professionalization and democratization. The old model political career ladder does not apply in Spain, as regional jurisdictions now hold greater appeal in some regards, due in part to decentralization and the advent of a broader political spectrum, both statewide and non-statewide. This has led to the creation of a large regional administration with many positions available. The changing structure of the state, as a result, has given rise to new structural opportunities, lending new directional characteristics to political careers: unidirectional, alternative, integrated, or reverse spring-board. Oñate examines how these four factors influence the structure of opportunities available to career politicians in terms of the movement between levels of government. There is no clear ladder model, he argues, but rather an integrated political class, one that remains on the same level or moves from one to the next, depending on the opportunities available, with national identity also playing a role in this movement.

In his chapter "Bringing Politicians Back In: Political Careers and Political Class in Multilevel Systems," Klaus Stolz maintains that a more complete analysis of MLG systems can be achieved by examining the simultaneous professionalization of politics and territorial reorganization. Pairing data from studies on territorial politics with career studies, Stolz examines how these new career paths shape institutional politics and, conversely, how new institutional arrangements produce differing career paths, with broad-ranging implications for decentralization, regionalization, and supranational integration. Stolz challenges the notion that regional government is a mere stepping stone to national or federal politics, arguing that movements between levels of government do not follow the traditional springboard structure and vary greatly among federalized states. While acknowledging that this structure is present in the United States, Stolz, citing the example of Canada and a number of EU member states, shows that political careers, in these states, follow no clear territorial direction. Instead, a host of factors – the federalization of unitary states, a strong sense of national identity in some regions, a rise in the number of positions to fill at the regional level, and the structure of elections and party systems – ensures that a regional career path remains a goal in its own right and may hold as much or more appeal than national politics. The reciprocal and intimately linked relationship between political professionalization and territorial reorganization, with one shaping the other and vice versa, is thus important to the study and understanding of multilevel systems.

Finally, Peverill Squire analyzes the American federal system from its inception with the Constitution in 1789 to the present day. More specifically, he looks at the combined impact of fiscal federalism and policy devolution on the shift in control of U.S. public policy from the states to Washington. While difficult to predict, there has been a trend towards giving policy control back to the states, he argues, with Republicans tending to favour greater devolution than their Democratic counterparts. The allocation of policy responsibilities is left, increasingly, to state legislatures, which vary from state to state in terms of their size, makeup, and level of professionalization—all of which influence their capacity to deal with policy decisions. The professionalization of state legislatures accounts for the biggest discrepancy in policy decisions, as it impacts behaviour among lawmakers as well as the operation of and policy decisions made by legislatures. This latter aspect is particularly important, as legislatures with higher levels of professionalization are more apt to adopt complex regulatory policies and systems, including environmental programs, strict campaign financing laws, funding increases for education and pension programs, and other innovative policies. The organization and mechanisms of each legislature also vary greatly from state to state, further contributing to discrepancies. Variance in state legislatures accounts for the inconsistency in the quality of policy-making decisions in each U.S. state, Squire argues.

This book addresses the impact new regionalism and MLG on political systems and relations, both in the international sphere as well as within specific political systems. In particular, it examines relations of trust between various political arenas, the configuration of institutions and the role and functions of political actors in compound and concurrent political and social arenas. Since MLG is here to stay, the time has come to identify better ways to organize the relationships between different political and social arenas. The analytical framework outlined in this book is meant to provide a good example for the organization of governance in political life.

Part I
The concept of Multilevel Governance

Chapter 1
An Assessment of Multilevel Governance as an Analytical Concept Applied to Federations and Decentralised Unitary Systems: Germany Versus the United Kingdom

Michael Stein, University of Toronto
Lisa Turkewitsch, University of Toronto

Introduction[1]

In two earlier papers that we presented to the 2009 Santiago IPSA Congress and the 2010 Luxembourg IPSA Conference, we argued that there appear to be broad global trends leading to the emergence of patterns of multilevel governance (MLG) in the internal intergovernmental relations of most contemporary nation-states; these apply in particular to both mature and emergent parliamentary and presidential federations, although to different degrees. We viewed these trends as a product of both contemporary forces of increasing international economic globalisation and political institutional and bureaucratic decentralisation or devolution. But in those earlier papers we did not attempt to delimit what we considered to be the fundamental defining characteristics and underlying causal or conditioning factors driving these evolving MLG trends in constitutional, institutional, cultural/attitudinal and socio-economic terms. In this paper, we propose to begin this undertaking by adopting a broad multidimensional conceptual framework and UK-German intergovernmental relations comparison presented in brief schematic form in section II below. We will apply it loosely to a comparison of two formally distinct types of political systems, one that is unitary and currently decentralised (the UK), and one that is parliamentary federal and centralised (Germany). We will also attempt to encompass these two systems within a broader typology of multi-tiered governance that views MLG as an overarching concept for both unitary systems and federal systems of different degrees of territorial diversity. If the MLG framework appears to fit better and account more accurately for evolving political conditions in both these countries than a traditional federalism

---

1   We would like to than Alana Saltzman and Ji Yin for their valuable research assistance.

approach that relies on a unitary-federal conceptual dichotomy, then we believe that there are good reasons for considering MLG to be a superior analytical framework for contemporary intergovernmental political analysis.

Case selection and similar systems comparison

We have chosen to compare the United Kingdom and Germany in terms of MLG because both are large and mature European polities of comparable population size, similar levels of industrialisation and urbanisation, and common parliamentary democratic political institutions. Both have recently (since the 1990s) adopted major constitutional and institutional reforms of their political-administrative systems to rebalance their internal territorial and political relations in the context of national/supranational (EU) power balances. Germany achieved peaceful reunification of its two formerly post-World War II components, Communist East Germany and democratic capitalist West Germany in 1992, although this event itself is generally considered by German scholars to have not constituted an important territorial constitutional or institutional political reform. In fact, later efforts to overcome some of the intergovernmental decisional weaknesses and political stagnation arising from its closely interlocked form of "joint federalism" are judged by most German political analysts to have been even more significant in their potential impact on federal power rebalancing than reunification. However, they only achieved, at best, minor political success. The United Kingdom, on the other hand, during the same period, did carry out a comprehensive constitutional and institutional territorial devolutionary reform involving Scotland, Wales and Northern Ireland after decades of failed efforts to accomplish this. But the extent to which these UK reforms actually did lead to a significant change in the internal territorial and power balance remains a highly contentious one, even after a decade of evolution and adjustment in this respect. Moreover, the extent of the disagreement among UK scholars regarding the utility and applicability of MLG in evaluating the impact of these devolutionary changes is still substantial. (See section II below.)

Overview

We will begin in section I with a theoretical overview of the literature covering what "multilevel governance" (MLG) is understood to mean and what its underlying causes are considered to be in general theoretical terms and in a broad international context. We will also review the literature evaluating the relative strengths and weaknesses of this concept in comparison to related concepts like "federalism" and "centralised unitarism" when applied to an analysis of internal intergovernmental relations. We will then examine some of the more important theoretical contributions and insights provided in recent years drawing in particular on Fritz Scharpf (2009), Simona Piattoni (2009-2010), and Theo A.J. Toonen (2010), a contributor to an edited volume by Edoardo Ongaro et al. (2010).

In section II we will compare in brief schematic form efforts at reform of internal intergovernmental relations and rebalancing of national-regional power relations in the United Kingdom and Germany since the early 1990s within the broad parameters of our summary in the preceding section of recent theoretical contributions to MLG theory. And in section III, our concluding section, we will redefine our evolving argument and position on multilevel governance theory in light of the schematic comparative empirical analysis of recent reforms in the UK and Germany conducted in the preceding section (section II) of this paper.

Pros and Cons of MLG versus other more traditional approaches to European Governance MLG versus neo-functionalism and neo-institutional intergovernmentalism: positive and negative contributions:

There has been much academic debate about the value of "multilevel governance" (MLG) as an analytical construct applied to internal intergovernmental relations, and its relative merits and shortcomings in comparison to earlier concepts and approaches to European integration such as "neo-functionalism" and "neo-institutional intergovernmentalism." The concept of "multilevel governance" was first applied descriptively in the early 1990s to the evolving political system of the European Union. Many specialists in European politics argued then that this concept and its related theoretical attributes constituted an important advance on two major earlier approaches that had been applied to European integration up to that point: neo-functionalism and neo-institutional or state intergovernmentalism. They also viewed it as a more accurate device for describing global trends in the economy and politics of advanced industrial countries in the late twentieth and early twenty-first centuries. They contended that MLG describes more realistically and precisely than its theoretical antecedents and competitors the complex and gradually evolving state/social, centre/periphery (territorial), and domestic/international relationships that have shaped European political developments, especially since the signing of the Maastricht Treaty in 1992. MLG is viewed as a more "actor-oriented" portrayal and a more "flesh and blood" representation of the causal forces underlying economic and political integration than the neo-functionalist dynamic. It is also considered to subsume more fully and depict more accurately the major role now played by non-state actors and agents in policy and

political decision-making processes in Europe than the state intergovernmentalist approach (Piattoni 2009: 3, citing Marks 1992).

Other analysts, on the other hand, have been much more critical of this concept. They claim that it is narrowly descriptive rather than broadly analytical
(Bache 1998), too generally or ambiguously defined and conceptually "overstretched beyond usefulness" (Piattoni 2009, citing Sartori 1970), and too dis-
missive or neglectful of the dominant "gate-keeping" function of national governments (Moravcik 1993). Still others complain that it is a highly complex
and multidimensional analytical device that is very difficult to use (Piattoni
2009: 7), that it exaggerates the post- and extra-constitutional nature of the
forms and processes that it encompasses (Peters 2000), and that it accepts some
highly debatable assumptions about the normative benefits that it contributes
in its political problem-solving capacity (Scharpf 1997), or in the compromises
it promotes (Pierre and Peters 2002).

MLG versus decentralised and multinational federalism and centralised unitarism (the Westminster model)

MLG versus decentralised and centralised "mature" and "emergent" federations

In an earlier paper (Stein and Turkewitsch 2008) we conducted a systematic
comparison of the analytical / empirical aspects of the concepts of "federalism"
and "multilevel governance" in terms of their origin, definition, evolution and
the major academic criticisms directed at them. We argued that these two concepts can be viewed as mutually influencing ideas that lie on a conceptual con-
tinuum. MLG can be seen as an adaptation and extension of federalism in an
age of increasingly close economic and communications globalisation. According to Marks and Hooghe (2002), these forces have tended to shift the
fulcrum of the political and policy-making process vertically upwards from the
nation-state level to the regional supranational or international level (e.g. in
environmental and foreign trade matters). They have also tended to push this
process vertically downwards to regional subnational and local levels. And
they have fostered a shift outward (or horizontally) to the private or voluntary
non-profit sectors (i.e. the "turn to governance"). As a result, MLG serves as a
more inclusive and more applicable term for political systems having multiple
tiers of autonomous decision-making than does federalism in today's complex
polycentric political decision-making world. And there has been a significant

degree of academic 'cross-pollination' between these two concepts so that "the interactive governance process that is given…a prominent place in both concepts is now regarded as a highly flexible, informal and dynamic relationship" (Stein and Turkewitsch 2008: 26).

Our subsequent contributions to this debate about the relative merits of "multilevel governance" versus "federalism" have focused specifically on the relationship between MLG and federalism as analytical tools applied comparatively to different types of federal systems outside the European Union. We compared changing patterns of intergovernmental relations in both "mature" and "emergent" parliamentary and presidential federations, and found a consistent trend, albeit to different degrees, toward the evolution and use of MLG governance patterns and networks in each. But we were unable to identify one type of federation (e.g. a parliamentary federation) as being more likely to generate these MLG patterns than another (e.g. a presidential federation). And we could not yet indicate with any precision the specific institutional, cultural and socio-economic conditions that produce and shape these MLG patterns.

MLG versus multinational federalism

In recent years, this debate has shifted somewhat to a comparison between multilevel governance and multinational federalism. The exponents of the latter (multinational federalism) view MLG as a concept which gives priority to the underlying values of efficiency and political stability rather than community or justice for its minority national groups and citizens. Therefore, as an analytical tool, MLG is viewed as biased in favour of the dominant elites and the status quo (Gagnon 2011). This critique of MLG is one which is focused on normative rather than analytical and empirical differences between the two concepts. Although important, due to lack of space, we will be unable to address these normative concerns in this paper.

In our view, "federalism" and "multilevel governance" share a number of common characteristics. They both can be understood in at least three distinct ways: 1) as descriptive terms applied to concrete political systems, 2) as analytical/empirical constructs, and 3) as normatively positive or desirable forms. With respect to the first (concrete systems) they each perform similar political functions, including that of dividing power in order to combat authoritarianism, managing conflict and promoting cooperation between internal groups, and protecting minority rights. They have also both increasingly abandoned an exclusive emphasis on territoriality in devising methods of political representation, and now opt for a combination of territorial and functional bases of representation in the performance of political decision-making tasks. There has also been a notable trend toward increased emphasis on ethical and normative concerns (or both) in decision-making, increased stress on the whole person rather than on the atomistic individual in societal action, and less attention to statist and hierarchical models of administration. However, as analytical and empirical constructs, the two concepts still have some important differences, such as: 1) federalism has a narrower and more restrictive reach than MLG, 2) federalism encourages greater formalisation of policy decisions and processes, 3) federalism fosters a broader climate of competitiveness, and 4) federalism tends to produce a more efficient, less costly and less time-consuming problem-solving governance process than MLG (Stein and Turkewitsch 2008).

MLG versus centralised unitarism (the Westminster Model)

The centralised unitary system model (or Westminster Model) refers to parliamentary unitary systems that are centred in political power terms on the national political executive or cabinet. This is the focus of a study by Bache and Flinders on Multilevel Governance and the British State (2004) with which we largely concur. They accept the point of view of most political analysts of the UK that that political system prior to 1998 can be described as a prototype of the centralised unitary system in the pattern of intergovernmental relations that operated between the national government, based in the Westminster Parliament in London, and the country's various political and bureaucratic decision-makers representing its territorial regions in England, Scotland, Wales and Northern Ireland during most of the nineteenth and twentieth centuries But their rather different argument, is that MLG works better as an analytical construct when applied to post-devolution UK intergovernmental relations since 1998. They maintain that the UK since that time has been transformed from a centralised unitary state of the "Westminster model" prototype into a decentralised unitary state in its intergovernmental relations involving Scotland, Wales and Northern Ireland (but not England) (Bache and Flinders 2004). Thus, Charlie Jeffery and Daniel Wincott refer to it after 1998 as a "lopsided state," and Hogwood et al. (2000) describe it as "asymmetrical devolution." Others described it as a "quasi-federal" system. There will be more discussion of this issue in later sections of the paper.

Other Recent Theoretical Contributions to MLG

The concept of the "joint-decision trap" revisited

In an early contribution to MLG theory in 1988 that was subsequently widely cited, Fritz Scharpf had identified stalemating commonalities between the decision-making structures of the German federation and those of the multilevel EC/EU system arising from their mutual dependence on unanimous or near-unanimous voting procedures, which he as a "joint-decision trap". In a 2006 paper (republished as a chapter in his edited 2009 volume), he continues to claim, with justification, that his original seminal analysis is "still basically valid", even though the European Union had diluted its unanimity voting requirements to that of near-unanimity in 1992. But he concedes that this analysis needs to be complemented by a similar account of non-governmental policy-making processes in the "supranational-hierarchical" modes of governance by the European Community Bank (ECB) or European Court of Justice (ECJ) in the financial and judicial policy sectors.

Scharpf (2009) also reviews some theoretical extensions and modifications that he made to his joint-decision trap thesis in recent years. He notes in particular his focus on and use of a hybrid model during this phase, containing three different modes of EU-intergovernmental relations: 1) the "intergovernmental mode" (i.e. an "applied negotiation mode") in which the "joint-decision trap" thesis readily applies and in which institutionalising national governments remain in full control at the lowest level of policy-making, 2) a combined or "mixed mode" of joint-decision-making that includes aspects of both intergovernmental negotiations and supranational centralisation) in which the "joint-decision trap" may or may not apply, and 3) a "supranational hierarchical mode" (exemplified by the European Court of Justice and the European Bank), in which the "joint-decision trap" does not apply. He also suggests ways that these impediments to efficient EU policy-making may be mitigated or overcome. He acknowledges that "the effectiveness of problem-solving in policy-making at the national as well as the European and international levels varies considerably from one policy field to another" (Scharpf 1997). And he agrees with other advocates of MLG that "the complexity of the multilevel European polity is not adequately represented by the single-level theoretical concepts of competing 'intergovernmentalist' and 'supranationalist' approaches." But he also warns that "empirical research that focuses on multilevel interaction overemphasises the uniqueness of its objects of study or attempts to create novel concepts which are likely to remain contested by Europeanists and over-isolates this area from general theory and the political science mainstream" (Scharpf 2009). These arguments are, in our opinion, well founded, and should be incorporated into an updated and current assessment of the relative strengths and weaknesses of MLG as an analytical concept.

The strengths and weaknesses of MLG

Simona Piattoni, in both her initial brief (2009) historical and conceptual over-view of multilevel governance, and in her subsequent (2010) full-length vol-ume on the conceptual, empirical and normative challenges posed by the the-ory of multilevel governance, defines MLG in broad and abstract terms as a dynamic three-dimensional concept involving 1) the relationship between the centre and periphery, 2) the relationship between state and society, and 3) the relationship between the domestic and the international. Each of these dimen-sions involves changes that occur at three analytical levels: 1) political mobi-lisation 2) policy-making and 3) policy restructuring. In this way, she claims to be able to generate a three-dimensional space within which to gauge MLG's empirical scope and desirability in normative terms (Piattoni 2009:1).

But there are several major criticisms that one can level at the MLG concept, as Piattoni, among others, also notes. First, empirically it is unclear which phe-nomena MLG encompasses, and whether it can be significantly distinguished from "governance" in general or other similarly broad concepts. Secondly, its epistemological and ontological meaning is unclear, and it is not evident where it stands on the ladder of abstraction (Piattoni 2009: 1, citing Sartori 1984). Thirdly, normatively, it is uncertain whether political decisions made through MLG are more legitimate or better than decisions made through other pro-cesses. (for example, whether MLG ensures wider and fuller participation in decision-making). Fourthly, MLG includes a wide variety of actors within its political structures, including supranational bureaucrats in Brussels, major na-tional governmental elites, and regional and local subnational authorities who have conflicting public philosophies and ideologies. This leaves the question open as to whether such a broad basis of political representation of its govern-ing elites is not more likely to aggravate conflicts within the EU. Fifthly, and most importantly, MLG rests ultimately on the notion of a "network configu-ration", rather than a "hierarchy", an idea which lacks empirical precision, and is largely metaphorical in meaning. Its analytical utility has therefore been lim-ited and open to question thus far (For example, see Piattoni 2009: 4).

But there are also several positive attributes and strengths in the multilevel governance approach, particularly in the current European context, that de-serve recognition. For example, Gary Marks, in a seminal article in 1992, first questioned the sharply dichotomous view of European integration presented by neo-functionalists and intergovernmentalists. He particularly criticised their lack of attention to 'flesh-and-blood' actors" in their theories. He thereby "asserted the autonomous explanatory force of a third paradigm, that of MLG" (Piattoni 2009: 2). Secondly, "MLG challenged the contention that non-state interests could only influence EU policy-making by operating through state representatives, and that they could not successfully challenge the 'gate-keeping' capacity of the central state" (Piattoni 2009:3). This insight was initially confined to cohesion policy, but later extended to environmental policy, agricultural policy and other important sectors of European policy. Thirdly, it is clear that the MLG concept is most appropriately applied to how the EU has actually operated since the signing of the Maastricht Treaty in 1991, and it has contributed to what may accurately be described as a new type of polity which is in fact sui generis. Fourthly, we also acknowledge the utility of the subsequent (2003) theoretical contribution of Marks and Hooghe to the initial concept of MLG in their distinction between Types I and II MLG. Type I MLG applies to at least three and up to five different levels of governance: international, supranational regional, national, subnational regional, and local. It therefore constitutes a modification and extension of the usual definition of federal systems as containing two levels of government, national and regional, with different jurisdictions and memberships. Type II MLG is also an ideal type that describes the political decision-making role of units and groups that are not part of the public sector, including private interest groups like business, labour and agriculture and non-profit voluntary or third sector groups such as charitable organisations and social assistance groups. According to Piattoni, "Type II governance normally coexists with Type I governance in the same overarching polity, and is generally embedded in Type I governance" (Piattoni 2009, citing Marks and Hooghe 2003: 238). These two types of overlapping governance structures coexist in a dynamic relationship that has been described as a "negotiated arrangement" in a new institutional order. It is considered to provide "technically superior solutions to complex collective problems [by] staying at a sufficiently small scale not to impose sacrifices on individual preferences" (Piattoni 2009. MLG, then, is a valuable "multilevel concept" that is capable of "moving across and connecting different analytical planes". It can also encompass much of the current literature on regionalism, which postulates an apparent causal correlation between increasing political devolution and growing civil society involvement in governance. (Piattoni 2009: 7).

In short, MLG is a concept that has both strengths and weaknesses, but is still very much in the process of theoretical framing and evolution. "It captures a significant number of policy processes, forms of political mobilisation, and trends towards polity restructuring to warrant its continued use in the future" (Piattoni 2010:13).

MLG in the European Union and Intergovernmental Relations in the US

There are also some valuable insights to be gained by conducting a direct comparison of the governance patterns of MLG in the European Union and the patterns of internal intergovernmental relations in American federalism. Such a comparison was made recently by Edoardo Ongaro et al., eds. in their Governance and Intergovernmental Relations in the European Union and the United States: Theoretical Perspectives (2010). In their Introductory chapter, they define "intergovernmental relations" as the pattern of relations between the federal and other levels of government within the public sector, one that is widely adopted by American practitioners and political scientists. They refer to multilevel governance as "the study of the 'crossroads of vertical (intergovernmental) and horizontal (state-society) relations," a general description that is widely embraced by European Union officials and students. Their objective is to "build a [theoretical] bridge between these two academic and practitioner communities and their respective 'cognitive maps'" (Ongaro et al., eds. 2010:1).

Is it possible to bridge the two very different streams of research into US federalism/intergovernmental relations and EU multilevel governance? Theo A.J. Toonen strongly believes that it is. He argues that the modern MLG model of internal intergovernmental relations and public administration is based on two new major approaches in this economically globalised post-modern age: 1) a focus on multidisciplinary and cross-sectional institutional clusters and 2) concentration on networked regions. MLG can foster "an ability to collaborate in a varied institutional context [by] using member-states, regional and local government institutions as partners and agents for joint policy-making and implementation." It thereby places greater emphasis on "networks" and on "governance arrangements" than on "hierarchies" and "government" (Toonen 2010: 30). Toonen proposes to combine the perspectives of MLG and IGR by "organising at least part of the European debate on the utility of systems of MLG along American lines." He proposes to incorporate the US public administration concepts of intergovernmental constitution (IGC), intergovernmental relations (IGR) and intergovernmental management (IGM) into the analysis of the internal intergovernmental relations of the EU.

Toonen also notes perceptively that the simple dichotomy and "juxtaposition of federal and unitary systems breaks down when it has to face the variety of administrative systems that need to be addressed today" (Toonen 2010: 35). "Federalism" is now generally understood to be "an abstract and multi-interpretable concept". And "unitarism" is likewise viewed as highly contentious and ambiguous in meaning. If one distinguishes the analysis of federal and unitary systems of governance and public administration – the governance perspective – from the study of actual states, then "the actual relative subsystem autonomy within a unitary state might be as large or as small as within a federal structure" (Toonen 2010: 36). He contends that "unitary states may actually operate as federalised systems from a sociological, political or administrative point of view," which he labels "sociological federalism." And he argues that "conversely, a governance and administratively-oriented 'implementation' federalism within a unitary state structure is also possible," particularly where there is an "informal, bottom-up 'participative management'" (Ibid.) In short, according to Toonen (2010:36), "the main a priori difference among unitary and federal states is that due to their different legal frameworks, the relative autonomy of subsystems has a distinctive legal expression." This may not, however, have important practical consequences. It follows, then, that it is both possible and legitimate to study federal and unitary systems from various conceptual perspectives: sovereign or power theory, network analysis or interdependency theory.

In our view, Toonen's effort to combine the theoretical perspectives of the IGR and MLG frameworks is promising in its potential contribution to the current debate about the utility of MLG as a comparative analytical tool. We shall consider in the concluding section below to what extent it may be used to gauge the value of the multilevel governance concept in the analysis of intergovernmental relations in the current economically globalised world.

A Schematic Comparison of Contemporary UK and German Intergovernmental Relations With Respect to Multilevel Governance Theory

The United Kingdom: Post-Devolution (1998 to the Present)

What do British scholars take the concept of "multilevel governance" to mean and what do they see as its underlying causes in the UK? In applying MLG in the UK context, Bache and Flinders (2004) note that the concept can be "strengthened by the insights of the concept of the 'differentiated polity"[2]. They also borrow the term "multilevel polity" from Gamble to describe the post-devolution UK state. Gamble defines this concept in rather broad terms as "a form of MLG that stresses the variety of institutions and processes through which societies are governed" (Gamble 2000: 290). Bache and

---

2   "Differentiated polity" is a term used by Rhodes in 1997 to describe the internal division and tension between the highly-centralised manner in which England as the principal UK region has been governed in the past in comparison to the more decentralised rule of the regional territories of Scotland, Wales and Northern Ireland (Bache and Flinders 2004).

Flinders offer a view of MLG that they characterise as an "organising perspective" or "framework for analysis" (Bache and Flinders 2004: 33). They contrast this perspective with what is generally called the "Westminster Model" (WM), which is the most frequently applied approach to the study of British governance. Bache and Flinders (2004) acknowledge that the WM has provided a valuable framework for academic research in the past, a useful behavioural guide for politicians, and a significant influence on public perceptions. It has also served as a meaningful normative standard. But in recent years it has shown a tendency to exaggerate the importance of the political elite, to adopt narrow and simplistic assumptions about politics, and to be too insular in its focus. Moreover, it reflects a resistance to adopting broader, foreign (non-British) approaches and methodologies and epistemological/ ontological philosophical views on political questions. MLG, on the other hand, offers an alternative approach both to the WM and the state-centric model of the intergovernmentalists.

Hogwood et al. (2000) provide a detailed nuanced view of "asymmetrical devolution," and its impact on UK EU policy-making. They emphasise more than Bache and Flinders the uneven manner in which constitutional and institutional change deriving from devolution occurs. Unlike Bache and Flinders, Hogwood et al. believe that it is important to place their analysis of UK devolution within a wider picture of reciprocal relationships between the constitutional context and the actual patterns of participation of territorial actors in multilevel governance. Therefore, they argue that the constitutional and institutional changes stemming from devolution do not take place in an even manner throughout the polity. Hogwood et al. (2000) nevertheless conclude optimistically, like Bache and Flinders, that trends to increasing manifestations of MLG will continue and ultimately dominate in UK politics.

Bulmer at al. (2006) provide an elaboration of an intermediate position between the polar extremes of the intergovernmentalists and more dogmatic MLG theorists. They point to the need to place the relationship between these UK "devolveds" into a broader context involving interactions between European subnational authorities and EU decision-makers, a "significant field of study ... [which is] generally termed multilevel governance" (Bulmer et al. 2006: 76). Within this field of study, they acknowledge the strong disagreements as to whether power is concentrated within the EU on the member state (or national) governments (as alleged by intergovernmentalist theorists), or whether it is shared by these national governments with supranational and subnational governmental authorities (as claimed by proponents of MLG theory). Bulmer et al. (2006), cite the work of Jeffery (2000) in declaring their preference for an intermediate position between these two points of view.

Gamble (2006) takes a historical and constitutional-institutional approach to devolution. He views the British state since devolution very differently from strong MLG exponents such as Bache and Finders (2004). In fact, he makes no mention of this concept, and does not cite its literature, either in the article or in his bibliography. With respect to the historical context, he notes that, "Britain has never been a pure type of unitary system, in which all power is concentrated and centralised" (Gamble 2006: 21). In this way, he separates himself from the staunch exponents of the UK state as a pure manifestation of the ideal type Westminster Model. A major reason for this is the practical constraints imposed on the central government by the "informal territorial constitution" (Gamble 2006: 22). He considers these territorial arrangements to be "at best quasi-federal", but prefers to label the UK type of quasi-federalism a "federacy". He defines it as "a large political unity to which smaller units are federated, even though the larger unit is not itself a federation." However, he concedes that, "Britain has been a multinational state rather than a single-nation state." Therefore, the UK has sometimes been described as a "union state", or "state of unions", rather than as a unitary state. For Gamble, the political and institutional context of devolution is best understood in terms of the pattern of electoral and political competition between the major political parties.

Hopkin (2003; 2009) provides a perspective on UK devolution in terms of the party system. In the earlier paper, Hopkin (2003) had argued that there is a need for party specialists to focus more on the "territorial dimension" of electoral politics, or what he calls "spatial and geographical aspects of party competition" (Hopkin 2003: 227). In his more recent work, Hopkin (2009), analyses the relationship between political devolution/decentralisation and the organisation of political parties, using the Labour Party in the UK and the Socialist Party in Spain as his comparative case examples. "party" is a significant causal factor within the matrix and multiplicity of conditioning variables that shape the emergence of MLG in mature and advanced polities.

The British state is becoming increasingly decentralised, regionalised, fragmented and polycentric, and is no longer amenable to systematic study using more traditional frameworks of analysis. In particular, the highly centralised and executive-centred Westminster Model, despite its continued widespread application to that system by both British and non-British scholars, now seems to be largely outdated and inapplicable to changing political realities. Notwithstanding its continued status as a relatively centralised unitary state in many comparative textbooks, devolution has brought some major changes to overall patterns of UK governance. At the same time, it has spawned several important efforts among scholars to fashion novel or recast earlier analytical frameworks that are better able to highlight the rapidly changing realities of the current economically globalised and politically interdependent world. The multilevel governance approach is only one of several new analytical frameworks that are currently being devised by scholars, but it is clear from our summary above that it is among those that are most frequently applied to UK politics. In fact, somewhat paradoxically, this framework may prove to be more adaptable to the British state than to many theoretically more decentralised political systems, including parliamentary and presidential federations.

Germany: Federal System Reforms (2005 to the Present)

There is an important link between the origins of the concept of multilevel governance and the German federal system. Scharpf's (1988) work on the "joint-decision trap" in the German federal system was cited as a major theoretical reference point for the concept of multilevel governance (Jachtenfuchs 2006, cited in Stein and Turkewitsch 2008: 7). In its relatively short existence, the concept of multilevel governance has therefore had important ties to German federalism. Research and theorising about German federalism has brought us important insights about multilevel governance and intergovernmental relations in the EU. The two-way interaction process between the concepts of federalism and multilevel governance has continued. Developments in the MLG literature can now be applied in a new light to the German system. We suggest that when applied to the German federal system, multilevel governance is increasingly an important conceptual tool through which scholars can analyse recent political and institutional developments.

The German system includes the local level, counties, inter-municipal bodies, the Länder, the federal level; the EU level; as well as Type II multilevel governance structures that exist at different levels, and often span these levels. However, the emergence of new forms of governance, incorporating the supranational (EU) level and expanding to include NGOs and other actors, has been controversial from the perspective of the Länder, whose governments resent the loss of policy making autonomy and perceive it as a threat to democratic legitimacy (Jeffery 2007: 24).

A number of terms, including "cooperative federalism" and "inter-locking federalism" have been used to describe the linking of federal and Länder level policy-making (Benz and Zimmer 2011: 149). Others have used the term "unitary federalism"[3] to describe the system (Moore et al 2008: 396). Scharpf suggested that the interlocking nature of the system leads to a lack of transparency in decision-making and makes it hard to tell which level of government holds the ultimate responsibility (Moore et al 2008: 396). This reasoning led Abromeit to describe Germany as a "hidden unitary state"[4] (Moore et al 2008: 396). All of these terms refer to the more unique features of the German federal system. In this sense, they have the advantage of helping us understand the

---

3   Moore et al cite Konrad Hesse as the originator of this term in his 1962 book, Der Unitarische Bundesstaat. (Moore et al 2008: 396; 406, endnote 9).
4   Moore et al cite Heidrun Abromeit's 1992 book, Der Verkappte Einheitsstaat, as the first instance this term was used (Moore et al 2008: 396; 406, endnote 12).

changing intergovernmental system in Germany, and in the case of Scharpf's work, its similarities to the EU. However, these concepts are less useful for broader comparative analysis. In contrast, the concept of MLG is valuable because it allows us to analyse features shared in common by both federal and decentralised unitary systems, as well as the EU.

As reflected in the terms "unitary federalism" and "hidden unitary state," a major concern shared by academics and politicians at the federal and Land levels is that German federalism is too centralised. There have been a number of reforms to the German federal system since its creation. However, most of these reforms did little to address concerns over the centralised nature of the federation, and even exacerbated some issues related to the "joint-decision trap" (Auel 2008). In the early years of the twenty-first century, there was a strong push for further reforms (Moore et al 2008: 396). The government set up the Federal Reform Commission in 2003 to explore ways of reducing the degree of joint-decision making in the German federal system. However, the commission's reform process failed, and instead, the Grand Coalition government, led by Angela Merkel, introduced constitutional changes that came into effect in 2006 (Moore et al 2008: 396). Overall, these reforms decentralised powers to the Länder, giving them, for example, exclusive competences in the areas of education, including post-secondary-education (Benz and Zimmer 2011: 167; Moore et al. 2008: 398).

A number of political scientists have criticised the reforms for not going far enough[5]. Auel points out that, on paper, the reforms of 2006 are the most broad-ranging changes to the Basic Law since its creation in 1949, at least in terms of the actual number of amendments (Auel 2008: 427). However, Auel suggests that the reforms may be counter-productive and do not offer any "escape" from Scharpf's "joint-decision trap" (Auel 2008: 425). Benz writes that as a result of the reforms, German governance is "neither more effective nor more democratic" and that the "federal system is in danger of losing necessary flexibility" (Benz 2008: 440). He suggests that the legislative system is still too centralised to be effective (Benz 2008: 442). Jeffery notes that one reason put forth for the fact that the reforms did not go as far as necessary is because Germany has a "unitary political culture." The country does not have the territorial cleavages that are often present in other, more decentralised, federations. Without these cleavages, the German system leans towards uniform policies across the Länder (Jeffery 2008: 589). Scharpf agrees with the general consensus that the reforms did not go far enough (Scharpf 2008: 509). In terms of the outcome of the reforms, Scharpf does not find a move away from the joint-decision trap, in the sense that "the need for compromises between the government majority and the opposition, and thus the possibility of party political blockades, remains pretty much unchanged" (Scharpf 2008: 514).

---

5   See the 2008 Special Issue of "German Politics" for a series of articles evaluating the federal reforms.

There is little discussion of Type II MLG in Germany in the federalism literature. This mirrors our findings in our earlier conference papers with respect to the literature on federalism in the United States and Latin America, and to a lesser extent, Canada. For example, in his discussion of multilevel governance in Germany and Switzerland, Braun acknowledges the existence of Type II multilevel governance, but chooses not to include an examination of this type of MLG (Braun 2011: 181, endnote 1). We suggest that political scientists studying intergovernmental relations in federal and decentralised unitary systems should increasingly take note of interactions that can be best understood through the conceptual lens of Type II MLG. We find more discussion of Type II MLG in the public policy, public administration, and local governance/urban studies literature. From a comparative and analytical perspective, an interesting form of Type II MLG that is emerging in Germany is inter-municipal cooperation (Wollmann 2010: 265). Harfst and Wurst (2011) provide another empirical example of Type II MLG in their study of environmental rehabilitation of mining regions in the former East German Länder.

In the German system, political parties, and specifically, party politics, play an important role in intergovernmental relations (Däubler and Debus 2009: 74). "[P]arties at the regional level are integrated into a coherent national party system" (Benz 2007: 432). Party politics at the Land level are intertwined with political competition and the legislative process at the federal level. This is a two-way interaction process that is "top-down from the federal to the state level and bottom-up from the state to the federal level" (Däubler and Debus 2009: 74). Political parties and interest groups have created "linkage structures" that span levels of government (Benz and Zimmer 2011: 159). These structures constitute "vertically integrated multilevel systems" in which regional associations also operate at the Land level (Benz and Zimmer 2011: 159).

Conclusions

The MLG framework fits better and accounts more accurately for changing forms of governance, political conditions and intergovernmental relations in both of these countries. There are several aspects in which an MLG approach is able to describe these two states better than a traditional federalism approach that places federal and unitary systems in separate "boxes." Our argument also appears to follow an emerging trend in the literature, as highlighted by the work of Toonen (2010), among others. German scholars in particular are quite open to studying their own federal system, as well as the EU, through the lens of MLG. As our research suggests, MLG is also an approach that is gaining ground in the study of UK devolution. Overall, we suggest that what might otherwise be seen as important institutional and constitutional differences between these two polities are less significant when they are viewed through the lens of MLG.

A typology of multilevel governance systems can be viewed to encompass different forms of federal, "quasi-federal," and unitary systems. Multilevel governance is an overarching concept, under which variation along two spectra can be subsumed. The two axes are higher and lower levels of territorial diversity, and a range from a high level of centralisation of power in the hands of the national/federal government to a high degree of decentralisation to substate units. We concur with Gagnon's (2011) view that a common flaw in MLG theorising is that it overlooks political cultural and socio-economic cleavages inherent in multinational federations. We therefore call for further empirical and theoretical work on how multi-national federalism and autonomism can add to our understanding of multilevel governance.

As a result of devolution, most observers now consider the UK to be a "quasi-federal" system (Bache and Flinders 2004), while federal Germany prior to 2005 was described as a "hidden unitary state" (Abromeit 1992, as cited in Moore et al 2008: 396; 406, endnote 12) that was too centralised. The MLG framework is the best way to understand the changes that have taken place as well as the calls for further changes in both of these states. In this sense, MLG is much more flexible, and thus better able to subsume the study of these changing forms of governance than are traditional comparative theoretical approaches. The MLG approach, in contrast to the Westminster Model and the various conceptions of federalism applied to Germany, such as "interlocking federalism" (Benz and Zimmer 2011: 149) and "unitary federalism" (Hesse, as cited by Moore et al 2008: 396; 406, endnote 9), is broader and more encompassing. Although the concept of MLG has been criticised for being too "overstretched" (Piattoni 2009), its elasticity does have benefits. While it could be argued that applying MLG to decentralised unitary states stretches the concept even further, we might also point out that the terms federal and unitary systems are themselves often considered to be problematic in meaning (Toonen 2010: 36).

An interesting point of comparison is the discussion of UK as a "lopsided state" (Jeffery and Wincott 2006:4) versus the constitutionally uniform powers of the Länder in Germany. There has been an acceptance of asymmetry in the UK versus an acceptance of a more "unitary" federal state in Germany, although the Länder with larger economies may be more influential in some regards (Scharpf 2008: 512). As a concept, multilevel governance does not specify a uniform or asymmetrical allocation of power to subnational authorities, giving it greater flexibility in its application. As illustrated in the typology, the concept of multilevel governance can encompass both symmetrical and asymmetrical federal and unitary systems.

Another area for comparison is the devolutionary reforms in the UK and federal system reforms in Germany. Both reforms brought about changes leading to more decentralised systems, and both generated questions regarding the overall outcomes of the reforms and possibilities for further changes. Toonen (2010: 39) has promoted an interesting discussion on types of system and reforms that is relevant here. He notes that, on the one hand, "legislated reform" is the most typical type of intergovernmental reform in unitary Westminster systems (Toonen 2010: 39). However, he notes that intergovernmental reform is typically different "in gradualist or consensual systems," which includes Germany (Toonen 2010: 39). In this type of system,

> "...the reform of the intergovernmental...system will most likely be conducted in an organic manner, with (framework) legislation very often following pragmatic and step by step transformations of the system. ... The organic systems are supposed to change 'from within' which often explains... the prevalence of deadlock – Reformistau – and stagnation if vested interests are unable to mutually agree on the required strategic action..." (Toonen 2010: 39-40).

Many of these points are relevant in the federal system reform process in Germany that we examined above. It also suggests that a significant area for further research is the application of the concept of MLG to a comparative analysis of institutional reforms in polities that are traditionally considered "federal" or "unitary."

Emerging governance structures best viewed through the lens of Type II MLG are also an area for comparative analysis, and one in which the two countries in our study share similarities. In Germany, the creation of inter-municipal bodies and other Type II MLG structures discussed above, pose challenges for intergovernmental relations. In the UK, "Distributed Public Governance" manifests itself in terms of the proliferation of "quasi-autonomous non-governmental organisations" ("quangos") (Bache and Flinders 2004). To what extent do such changes affect intergovernmental relations in traditionally "federal" or "unitary" MLG systems differently? This is an area for further research.

The role of political parties in multilevel systems is already an emerging area of research. With respect to our comparison, the intertwined nature of political parties and "vertically integrated multilevel systems" (Benz and Zimmer 2011:159) in both Germany and the UK would make for an interesting area of comparison. The work of Hopkin (2003; 2009) is perhaps a starting point here, particularly in the context of devolution.

The research that we have conducted for this paper has also enabled us to generate several additional areas for further research. One area that appears to be at the forefront of current writing and theorising on MLG involves normative questions such as the legitimacy of MLG systems (Piattoni 2009; 2010). While we have touched on this topic in this paper, limitations of space have prevented us from exploring the issue in greater depth here. This is an area of MLG that calls for considerably more comparative study. Normative concerns are also an important element in the work of proponents of the multinational federalism approach (Gagnon 2011), and this may be an important area of theoretical dialogue between the two approaches. It may also be advisable to extend the comparison of intergovernmental relations in North America versus Europe that was initially explored in Ongaro et al. (2010) to other geographic areas. Further analysis of unitary states in terms of MLG is also a promising area for future investigation.

References

Auel, Katrin. (2008). Still No Exit from the Joint Decision Trap: The German Federal Reform(s). German Politics, 17(4), 424-439.
Bache, Ian &Matthew Flinders. (2004). Multilevel Governance and the Study of the British State. Public Policy and Administration, 19(1), 31-51.
Benz, Arthur. (2007). Inter-Regional Competition in Co-operative Federalism: New Modes of Multilevel Governance in Germany. Regional & Federal Studies, 17 (4), 421- 436.
Benz, Arthur. (2008). From Joint Decision Traps to Over-Regulated Federalism: Adverse Effects of a Successful Constitutional Reform. German Politics, 17(4), 440-456.
Benz, Arthur & Christina Zimmer. (2011). Germany: Varieties of Democracy in a Federal System. In Loughlin, John, Frank Hendriks & Anders Lindström, eds. The Oxford Handbook of Local and Regional Democracy in Europe. Oxford: Oxford University Press, 146-172.
Braun, Dietmar. (2011). Multilevel Governance in Germany and Switzerland. in Michael Zürn, Sonja Wälti and Henrik Enderlein, eds. Handbook on Multilevel Governance. Cheltenham: Edward Elgar, 168-183.
Bulmer, Simon, et al. (2006). UK Devolution and the European Union: A Tale of Cooperative Asymmetry? Publius: The Journal of Federalism, 36(1), 75–93.
Däubler, Thomas and Debus, Marc. (2009). Government Formation and Policy Formulation in the German States. Regional & Federal Studies, 19(1), 73-95.
Gagnon, Alain-G. (2011). Gouvernance multi-niveaux et la reconfiguration de l'espace politique. Paper presented at the Conference on New Regionalism and Multilevel Governance, held in the Universidad de Valencia, Valencia, Spain, October 13-14.
Gamble, Andrew. (2000). The Constitutional Revolution in the United Kingdom. Publius: The Journal of Federalism, 36(1), 19–35.
Harfst, Jorn, and Peter Wirth. (2011). Structural Change in Former Mining Regions: Problems, Potentials and Capacities in Multilevel Governance Systems. Procedia Social and Behavioural Sciences, 36 (1), 19-35.
Hogwood, Patricia, et al. (2000). Devolution and EU Policy Making: The Territorial Challenge. Public Policy and Administration, 15(20), 81-95.
Hopkin, Jonathan. (2009). Party Matters: Devolution and Party Politics in Britain and Spain." Party Politics, 15(2), 179–198.
Hopkin, Jonathan. (2003). Political Decentralisation, Electoral Change and Party Organisational Adaptation: A Framework for Analysis. European Urban and Regional Studies 10(3), 227–237.
Jeffery, Charlie. (2008). Groundhog Day: The Non-Reform of German Federalism Again. German Politics 17 (4), 587-592.

Jeffery, Charlie. (2007). Towards a New Understanding of Multilevel Governance in Germany? The Federalism Reform Debate and European Integration. Politische Vierteljahresschrift, 48 (1), 17–27.

Jeffery, Charlie & Daniel Wincott. (2006). Devolution in the United Kingdom: Statehood and Citizenship in Transition. Publius: The Journal of Federalism, 36 (1), 3–18.

Lluch, Jaime. (2011). Autonomism and Federalism. Publius: The Journal of Federalism (forthcoming in print, online early access, published May 27).

Moore, Carolyn, Wade Jacoby & Arthur B. Gunlicks (2008). German Federalism in Transition? German Politics, 17(4), 393-407.

Moravcsik, Andrew. (1993). Preferences and Power in the European Community: A Liberal Intergovernmental Approach. Journal of Common Markets Studies 31 (4), 473-524.

Ongaro, Edoardo, et al. (2010). Governance and Intergovernmental Relations in the European Union and the United States: Theoretical Perspectives. Cheltenham: Edward Elgar.

Peters, B. Guy & Pierre, J. (2004). Multilevel Governance and Democracy: A Faustian Bargain? In Bache, Ian and Matthew Flinders, eds Multilevel Governance. Oxford: Oxford University Press. 75-92.

Piattoni, Simona. (2009). Multilevel Governance: A Historical and Conceptual Analysis. Journal of European Integration, 31(2), 163-180.

Piattoni, Simona. (2010). The Theory of Multilevel Governance: Conceptual, Empirical, and Normative Challenges. Oxford: Oxford University Press.

Scharpf, Fritz W. (2008). Community, Diversity and Autonomy: The Challenges of Reforming German Federalism, German Politics, 17(4), 509-521.

Scharpf, Fritz W. (2009). Legitimacy in the Multilevel European Polity. European Political Science Review, 1(2), 173-204.

Stein, Michael B. & Lisa Turkewitsch. (2008). The Concept of Multilevel Governance in Studies of Federalism. Paper Presented at the 2008 International Political Science Association (IPSA) International Conference International Political Science: New Theoretical and Regional Perspectives, Concordia University, Montréal, Québec, Canada on May 2. Retrieved from: www.montreal2008.info/site/images/PAPERS/section3/RC%2028-%20Stein%20Turkewit sch%203.4.pdf.

Toonen, Theo A.J. (2010). Multilevel governance and intergovernmental relations: integrating the theoretical perspectives. In Governance and Intergovernmental Relations in the European Union and the United States: Theoretical Perspectives. Cheltenham: Edward Elgar, 29-50.

Wollmann, Hellmut. (2010). Comparing two logics of Interlocal Cooperation: The Cases of France and Germany. Urban Affairs Review, 46 (2), 263-292.

Chapter 2
Problems of Democratic Accountability in Network and Multilevel Governance[*]

Yannis Papadopoulos, University of Lausanne

Introduction

Several studies focusing on different policy sectors, in diverse national and local environments, find broad convergence toward a policy-making style dominated by cooperation among government levels and between public and non-public actors. 'Governance' as a particular style of governing refers to 'sustaining co-ordination and coherence among a wide variety of actors with different purposes and objectives such as political actors and institutions, corporate interests, civil society, and transnational governments'.[1] In its 'multi-level' form, it involves 'a large number of decision-making arenas (…) differentiated along both functional and territorial lines, and (…), interlinked in a non–hierarchical way '.[2] It implies the formulation or the implementation of public policies by networks involving public actors (politicians and administrators) belonging to different decisional levels, together with non-public actors of different nature (economic agents, interest representatives and

* Research for this paper has benefited from generous funding by the Swiss federal government (Secrétariat d'Etat à la recherche). Previous versions of this paper were presented at various events organised by the 'Connex' network: the conference 'Linking European, national and subnational levels of governance: drawing lessons from structural funds, regional and environmental policy', Panteion University, Athens, May 5-7, 2005; the workshop 'Delegation and multilevel governance', Sciences Po., Paris, May 11, 2005; the workshop 'Accountability and Legitimacy in Multilevel Governance', MZES, Mannheim, November 2-3, 2005 and the follow-up workshop on 'Accountability in Multilevel Governance', University of Lausanne, June 23-24, 2006; the session 'EU-Multi Level Governance and Democracy', 20th IPSA World Congress, Fukuoka, July 9-13, 2006. I am grateful to the discussants (Rainer Schmalz-Bruns, Pasquale Pasquino, Christian Joerges, Renaud Dehousse, and John-Erik Fossum) as well as to other participants for their insightful comments. I hope that most of them have been taken into account in this published version.
1 Pierre, 'Introduction: Understanding Governance', in J. Pierre (ed.), *Debating Governance* (Oxford University Press, 2000), pp 3-4.
2 Eberlein and Kerwer, 'New Governance in the European Union: A Theoretical Perspective', (2004) 42 *Journal of Common Market Studies* 1, 128.

stakeholders, experts).[3] Deliberation, bargaining, and compromise-seeking are the rule in governance arenas, which are characterised by cooperative relations between governmental units attached to different territorial levels (subnational, national, European, etc.), and by collaboration of these units with various non-public bodies (associations, third-sector organisations, firms, etc.) instead of top down policy-making. This chapter exposes the reasons why this, at first glance promising and in all likelihood necessary, shift to less 'dirigist' forms of policy-making can generate problems with respect to the quality of our democracies. This is a largely neglected issue in a research field which is dominated by managerial concerns about governance performance: based on a survey of about 1'600 projects included in a 'Connex' database on EU governance (GOVDATA), Kohler-Koch[4] concludes that not more than 17% of them address questions of democracy or legitimacy.

Problems with respect to democracy are caused by a deficit of democratic accountability of governance structures. This deficit mainly stems from four properties of network governance: the weak presence of citizen representatives in networks, the lack of visibility and uncoupling from the democratic circuit, the multilevel aspect, and the prevalence of 'peer' forms of accountability. After explaining the accountability problems generated by each of these properties, I conclude with a model for decision-making that would be likely to alleviate the accountability deficits. Accountability can be defined as 'a relationship between an actor and a forum, in which the actor has an obligation to explain and to justify his or her conduct, the forum can pose questions and pose judgement, and the actor may face consequences'.[5] Stated somewhat differently, 'A is accountable to B when A is obliged to inform B about A's (past or future) actions and decisions, to justify them, and to suffer punishment in the case of eventual misconduct'.[6] One should note that this definition of accountability combines justification by A to B with the availability to B of sanctions vis-à-vis A. What is more, the constraint for justification depends on the availability of effective sanctions (not necessarily the utilisation of sanctions, but their 'shadow'). Such a resource in the hands of the accountability 'holder' means that the actions of the accountability 'holdee'[7] will not remain without

---

3   See the definition by Skelcher: 'Jurisdictional Integrity, Polycentrism, and the Design of Democratic Governance', (2005) 18 *Governance: An International Journal of Policy, Administration, and Institutions* 1, 90: 'Networks engage mainstream state, federal, regional, and local governments in interactions with arm's length public bodies including quasi-governmental agencies, single-purpose boards, public-private partnerships, and multi-organizational collaborations.'

4   Kohler-Koch, 'Research on EU Governance: Insight from a Stock-Taking Exercise', (2006) *Connex Newsletter* 3, 5.

5   Bovens in this issue, manuscript, 6.

6   Schedler, 'Conceptualizing Accountability', in A. Schedler et al. (eds.), *The Self-Restraining State* (Lynne Rienner Publishers, 1999), p 17.

7   R. D. Behn, *Rethinking Democratic Accountability* (The Brookings Institution, 2001).

consequences for him or for her, and that the decision about the positive or negative character of these consequences is in the hands of the accountability holder. However, the two dimensions do not need be simultaneously present: Courts for instance are compelled to provide reasons for their decisions, but they cannot be sanctioned for them,[8] while MPs can be sanctioned without being (formally) obliged to justify their decisions.

Grant and Keohane[9] are right in claiming that 'we should resist the temptation to narrow the issue of accountability to that of democratic control' and they mention several other forms of accountability (administrative, fiscal, legal, etc.). In addition, even political accountability is not necessarily democratic. In 18th century England for instance, the Parliament claimed that the ministers of the Crown should be accountable to it, even though it was not democratically elected. And even the European Parliament was not (directly) democratically elected until as late as 1979 (but it is true that its role as an accountability holder was weak). A thorough survey of accountability issues would require scrutinising who is accountable to whom, for what, through which procedures, what kind of arguments and justifications are provided by the accountability holdee, and what kind of sanctions are available to the accountability holder. Being exhaustive in that respect for complex forms of multilevel governance would go beyond the scope of this article. The article also disregards the rhetoric justifications used in the framework of accountability,[10] and focuses on the (arguably limited) role of public and democratic forms of accountability to citizens and parliaments of actors involved in network governance. In other words, it scrutinises the democratic anchorage[11] of network forms of governance, meaning by that the possibility for those affected by collectively binding decisions formulated in policy networks, and/or for those representing them, to hold participants of these networks accountable by sanctioning them. It is often argued that horizontal and cooperative decision-making procedures operate in the shadow of the hierarchy, meaning by this that the options taken by actors who cooperate are subject to state approval, which usually takes the form of parliamentary ratification. To what extent do actors participating in policy networks operate in the shadow of democratic control, and in case of limits to this control to what kind of factors are they attributable?

Possible deficits in political accountability are not only the object of normative concerns, but can generate political problems too, leading to governability

---

8   Note however that in some systems judges may not be re-elected or are even subject to recall.
9   Grant and Keohane, 'Accountability and Abuses of Power in World Politics', (2004) 99 *American Political Science Review* 1, 42.
10   Goodin distinguishes between different forms of arguments likely to be supplied by actors requested to account: on their actions, their intentions, their (sometimes unintended) results, etc. See Goodin, 'Democratic Accountability: The Distinctiveness of the Third Sector', (2003) 44 *European Journal of Sociology* 3, 364.
11   Sørensen, 'The democratic problems and potentials of network governance', (2005) *European Political Science* 4.

or legitimacy deficits. Such deficits are not only the objects of critical normative assessments, but also become the targets of anti-establishment political
'entrepreneurs'.[12] Thus accountability of decision-makers is not only a goal to
be achieved by political systems claiming to be democratic, but also a means
for their legitimation in environments where democratic values prevail. The
availability of effective accountability mechanisms forces policy-makers to anticipate the ex post control by policy-takers, and to act in the shadow of their
sanction, which produces a 'deterrent' (or disciplining) effect.[13] For accountability to be enforced in contemporary political systems where the institution of
binding mandates is no longer *au goût du jour* (see E. Burke's criticism as
early as in the 18th century), both mechanisms are necessary. The 'institutionalisation'[14] of retrospective control by the governed requires publicity in the
actions of political elites and justification of these actions by them, in other
words their 'answerability'[15], which reduces informational asymmetries between 'agents' and 'principals' due to delegation.[16] Answerability strongly induces rulers to anticipate the retrospective control by the governed.[17] The dam-
oclean sword of control fosters responsiveness to the preferences of the accountability holder: the more decision-makers feel that they act in the shadow
of possible sanctions, the more it will be rational for them to endogeneise the
preferences of their 'principal'. The idea that the citizenry should be the ultimate 'principal' is central to democratic accountability, although in reality the
mass public is not the only judge of governmental performance (think about
the role of Constitutional courts, or of external agents such as the IMF for some
countries). Political actors are accountable to a number of 'forums' which are
not their democratic 'principals'. Also, the 'harder' accountability mechanisms

12 Papadopoulos, 'Populism, the democratic question, and contemporary governance', in Y.
    Mény and Y. Surel (eds.), *Democracies and the Populist Challenge* (Palgrave-Macmillan,
    2002).
13 Behn, above note 8, pp 14-16. As Schmitter puts it, the most accountable leaders are those
    who have nothing to fear from accountability: see Schmitter, 'The Ambiguous Virtues of Ac-
    countability', (2004) 15 *Journal of Democracy* 4, 49. Mansbridge however correctly main-
    tains that, notwithstanding its current diffusion, 'anticipatory representation' based on 'antic-
    ipated reactions' does not involve accountability in its classic form: 'The representative acts
    only as entrepreneur, preparing to offer and offering a product to a *future* (emphasis added)
    buyer': see Mansbridge, 'Rethinking Representation', (2003) 97 *American Political Science
    Review* 4, 526. Anticipatory representation can only fit accountability in its classic form under
    the assumptions that voters remain the same and do not modify their preferences from one
    election to another.
14 Schmitter, ibid, p. 48.
15 Schedler, above note 7.
16 'Principal-agent' models are often used to describe accountability problems: for a recent over-
    view see Bendor, Glazer and Hammond, 'Theories of Delegation', (2001) *Annual Review of
    Political Science* IV.
17 Koenig-Archibugi, 'Transnational Corporations and Public Accountability', (2004) 39 *Gov-
    ernment and Opposition* 2, 237-238.

are,[18] the more effective we can expect them to be in ensuring responsiveness. In that sense, genuine accountability mechanisms do not rest on a 'logic of appropriateness' – rulers behave in a responsive manner because they feel they have to -, but on a logic of 'consequentiality': rulers behave in a responsive manner because they anticipate the costs of unresponsive behaviour. It should finally be added that accountability and responsiveness must be conceptually distinguished:[19] paternalistic dictators are responsive to the needs of their followers without being accountable, whereas behaving in a responsible manner and displaying 'leadership' qualities in democracies require from politicians to make decisions that may well contradict the preferences of their constituencies.

The accountability problem in network governance

It is expected that network forms of governance will lead to decisions enjoying a strong 'output' legitimacy,[20] because their content is more appropriate, or because they are better accepted by target-groups. In other words, network governance is expected to be conducive to technically more adequate and politically more realistic decisions. However, the consequences of network governance for democracy have long been neglected, as the literature originally stressed that more 'horizontal' forms of policy-making are more responsive to the concerns of policy-takers, because in governance the latter are integrated into the policy-making process, and thus appear as 'co-producers' of the collectively binding decisions that affect them.[21] However, as suggested by

18 Bovens, 'Public Accountability', in E. Ferlie, L.E. Lynne Jr. & C. Pollitt (eds.), *The Oxford Handbook of Public Management* (Oxford University Press, 2005). An example of allegedly powerful accountability forum today are the media, and it is no accident that contemporary democracies have been defined by Manin, a major theorist of representative democracy, as 'audience democracies': B. Manin, *The Principles of Representative Government* (Cambridge University Press, 1997). However, if the incumbents fail to follow the recommendations formulated by the media this does not entail any automatic sanction, so that we should speak here of a 'soft' accountability mechanism.
19 Bartolini, 'Collusion, Competition, and Democracy, Part I', (1999) 11 *Journal of Theoretical Politics* 4.
20 F. W. Scharpf, *Demokratietheorie zwischen Utopie und Anpassung* (Universitätsverlag Konstanz, 1970).
21 See for instance the European Commission's plea for 'fostering participatory democracy'. NGOs 'are held in high esteem because it is assumed that they contribute to the formation of European public opinion, they provide feedback so the Commission can adjust its policy, they contribute to managing, monitoring and evaluating EU projects, and their involvement helps to win acceptance': Kohler-Koch, 'Framing: the bottleneck of constructing legitimate institutions', (2000) 7 *Journal of European Public Policy* 4, 525.

Renate Mayntz[22] and more recently again by Mark Bevir,[23] cooperative governance is not conceived primarily in terms of its potential for democratisation of policy-making, but meant as a solution to functional problems, like the management of interdependence between various collective actors or concerns with compliance by policy-takers.[24] As several recent works point out,[25] governance by policy networks in fact generates a number of problems with respect to democratic accountability. In this article, I identify and scrutinise four of them.

The weak visibility and uncoupling of networks

Lack of visibility impedes accountability in primarily two respects. Firstly, decisional procedures in policy networks are often informal and opaque, as this is deemed to facilitate the achievement of compromise. Secondly, networks dilute responsibility among a large number of actors: this is the 'problem of many hands' or 'paradox of shared responsibility',[26] that can be viewed as the negative facet of multicentric decision-making, at least as long as guidelines for 'collaborative' accountability[27] remain 'fuzzy'.[28] Even if these problems are attenuated through provisions for access to information and good governance, the latter are no substitute for traditional accountability mechanisms that should give the opportunity to the controllers to sanction the controlled.[29]

---

22 Mayntz, 'Politische Steuerung: Aufstieg, Niedergang und Transformation einer Theorie', in R. Mayntz, *Soziale Dynamik und Politische Steuerung. Theoretische und methodologische Ueberlegungen* (Campus, 1997).

23 Bevir, 'Democratic Governance: Systems and Radical Perspectives', (2006) 66 *Public Administration Review* 3.

24 According to Wolf, 'the primary normative guideline for governance is not democracy but legitimacy': see Wolf, 'Contextualizing Normative Standards for Legitimate Governance beyond the State', in B. Gbikpi & J.R. Grote (eds.), *Participatory Governance. Political and Societal Implications* (Leske+Budrich, 2002), p 40.

25 I. Bache and M. Flinders, *Multilevel Governance* (Oxford University Press, 2004); Benz, 'Postparlamentarische Demokratie? Demokratische Legitimation im kooperativen Staat', in M. Th. Greven (ed.), *Demokratie - eine Kultur des Westens?* (Leske + Budrich, 1998); Benz and Papadopoulos, 'Actors, Institutions and Democratic Governance: Comparing Across Levels', in A. Benz and Y. Papadopoulos (eds.) *Governance and Democracy. Comparing National, European, and International Experiences* (Routledge, 2006); Papadopoulos, 'Cooperative forms of governance: problems of democratic accountability in complex environments', (2003) 42 *European Journal of Political Research* 4; Papadopoulos, 'Taking Stock of Multi-level Governance Networks', (2005) *European Political Science* 4.

26 M. Bovens, *The Quest for Responsibility* (Cambridge University Press, 1998), pp 45-52.

27 Behn, above note 8, pp 72-74.

28 Flinders, 'The Politics of Public-Private Partnerships', (2005) *British Journal of Politics and International Relations* 7, 230.

29 Héritier, 'Composite democracy in Europe: the role of transparency and access to information', (2003) 10 *Journal of European Public Policy* 5.

Transparency lacks the element of sanction: it induces the accountability holdee to provide justifications for his or her action, but if these justifications are not considered satisfactory, the accountability holder has no possibility to impose any sanctions. Publicity is a necessary condition for democratic accountability but not a sufficient one: if exposure to media scrutiny for instance induces politicians to behave in a 'responsive' (perhaps also populistic manner), this is only because negative reporting by the media can convince voters to sanction unresponsive politicians in forthcoming elections.

Also, policy networks are often uncoupled from the official representative bodies, whose capacity to exert effective oversight over such parallel decisional circuits is questionable.[30] Analytically visibility and 'coupling' should be distinguished: visibility has to do with the ability of controllers to watch and monitor behaviour, while coupling has to do with their ability to influence ex-ante the behaviour of the controlled, or to sanction it ex-post (or both). But of course, effective control is not possible in the absence of visibility, or if networks operate in remoteness from democratic institutions. In network governance, the initiative and control functions of parliaments are then in all likelihood weakened, with parliaments possibly confined to a role of ratifying bodies. True, parliaments have the formal right to overrule decisions made by policy networks.[31] The question, however, is to what extent they can be a credible menace. The capacity of representative bodies to nullify decisions prepared in networks can be questioned above all for sheer lack of expert knowledge.[32] One should 'bring the state back in' into the debate on network governance: the state is not 'hollowed-out' simply because networks require management and steering, and this is largely done by public actors.[33] However this does not solve the problem of accountability because it can be reasonably hypothesised that 'meta-governance' functions (the governance of governance networks) will rather be devolved to bureaucrats rather than be directly operated by

---

30 The concept of a 'post-parliamentary' governance has been coined to depict that phenomenon: see Andersen and Burns, 'The European Union and the Erosion of Parliamentary Democracy: A Study of Post-Parliamentary Governance', in S.S. Andersen & K.J. Eliassen (eds.), *The European Union: How Democratic Is It?* (Sage, 1996).

31 Voelzkow, 'Von der funktionalen Differenzierung zur Globalisierung: neue Herausforderungen für die Demokratietheorie', in R. Werle & U. Schimank (eds.), *Gesellschaftliche Komplexität und kollektive Handlungsfähigkeit* (Campus, 2000), pp 273-276.

32 This is clearly an empirical issue and of course institutional arrangements are of relevance too. On European matters, the competencies of the EP are not comparable to the competencies of national parliaments on national matters, which depend in turn on the system of government and on parliamentary resources. Also oversight of EU legislation by national parliaments is subject to considerable cross-country variation: Benz, 'Path-dependent Institutions and Strategic Veto-Players - National Parliaments in the European Union', (2004) *West European Politics* 29.

33 B.G. Peters, The Meta-Governance of Policy Networks: Steering at a Distance, but Still Steering, draft paper for the Conference on 'Democratic Network Governance', Roskilde, 3 November 2006.

elected bodies. In a sense, it is rational for parliamentarians to delegate some of their governance or meta-governance competencies if the information costs for their achievement are too high for them. But for parliamentarians to be able to subsequently veto proposals made by their 'agents' they need again to have access to information so the problem remains (except in cases where politicians can credibly argue and decide along strictly ideological lines).

Remoteness from parliaments and voters can be the object of deliberate institutional design (as in the case of autonomous bodies, courts, etc.), in order to make institutions less sensible and less responsive to short–term political concerns. Yet remoteness also produces – most probably unintended - cognitive limits to the capacity to correctly perceive what is indeed happening in policy arenas. MEPs for instance – for their part directly accountable to the electorate – demonstrate a lower accuracy in their perceptions of policy issues than members of national parliaments, including typically European issues such as the common currency or the abolition of national borders. As regards voters, 40 percent are not able to identify the policy positions of European transnational parties on unemployment policy, which is closely related to the familiar left-right divide, and the situation is worse for typically European issues,[34] especially as regards 'the everyday policy-making and implementation'.[35] In sum, remoteness aggravates informational asymmetries at the detriment of accountability holders, causing thus prejudice to the exercise of accountability.

There is therefore a risk that decisions will be made by actors other than those regarded as legitimate decision-makers by ordinary citizens or by members of the affected communities. Mair[36] for instance considers that the EU exemplifies this by assigning a limited role to party democracy, and goes so far as to claim that through a socialisation (or habituation) effect this can result into citizens becoming more generally accustomed to the decline of the role of representative institutions in policy-making. It has also been argued that a sphere of (problem-solving oriented) *'politique des problèmes'* – dominated by governance arrangements in 'backstage' policy-making - is to a large extent disjointed now from the 'frontstage' sphere of *'politique d'opinion'*, which is the traditional realm of party competition but seems to play merely a symbolic role.[37] The relevant actors are not the same in the two spheres, and the goals

---

34 R. Andeweg, '*De super* and *ex post*? Political Representation and Europeanisation', paper prepared for the Leiden workshop of CONNEX Research Group 2, Leiden University, March 3-4, 2005, pp 13-16.

35 Olsson, 'Democracy paradoxes in multilevel governance: theorizing on structural fund system research', (2003) 10 *Journal of European Public Policy* 2, 285.

36 P. Mair (2005) 'Popular Democracy and the European Union Polity', *EUROGOV. European Governance Papers*, C-05-03.

37 Leca, 'La „gouvernance" de la France sous la Cinquième République. Une perspective de sociologie comparative', in F. D'Arcy & L. Rouban (eds.). *De la Ve République à l'Europe* (Presses de Sciences Po, 1996), pp 345-346. The European Union is particularly emblematic

and rules of the game tend to differ too. This can raise 'coupling' problems between dissimilar logics: Lehmbruch[38] stressed for instance about Germany the lack of compatibility between the competitive logic of party politics and emphasis on negotiation and cooperation within the federalist multilevel governance arena. In addition, when the sphere of 'policies' is disjointed from the sphere of 'politics', the effectiveness of accountability procedures is undermined. The retrospective evaluation of office holders on the grounds of their policy achievements, and the prospective evaluation of candidates (incumbents and members of non-governmental parties) on the grounds of their pledges are hardly possible. The incumbent parties are held responsible for political decisions whose formulation in fact largely escapes their control. Of course, this is not new: ministerial responsibility implies for instance that ministers are considered responsible for problems of 'maladministration' even though it is unrealistic to expect from them to be aware of all actions undertaken by their subordinates. However, network governance increases the number of actors who are involved in the policy process without being democratically authorised ex ante, and without being subject to democratic control ex post. It therefore amplifies the fictitious character of political responsibility. In the more recent years governing parties have increasingly been 'punished' for their performance in office: electoral losses of incumbent parties are higher than in the past.[39] It may therefore be argued that elections are today at the same time a more drastic and a more symbolic accountability mechanism, and that this is a symptom of the disjuncture between the competitive logic of 'politics' and the cooperative logic of 'policy-making'.

The composition of policy networks

If one may criticise the fact that policy networks operate in insulation from democratic institutions (which is, after all, an empirical question), it may be objected to such a criticism that most of their members are authorised by some 'principal' to participate, and are thus subject to control regarding their actions. Also, it appears that the role of politicians may not be as marginal as might be feared, depending much on institutional configurations as shown by the em-

---

in that respect: 'politique d'opinion' on European matters is virtually absent, with the recent exception of referendums that are increasingly utilised on issues of European integration.

38   Lehmbruch, 'Verhandlungsdemokratie, Entscheidungsblockaden und Arenenverflechtung', in W. Merkel and A. Busch (eds.), *Demokratie in Ost und West* (Suhrkamp, 1999).

39   K. Strom et al. (eds.), *Delegation and Accountability in Parliamentary Democracies* (Oxford University Press, 2003).

pirical studies of Auel and Taiclet.[40] Yet even when politicians play a significant role in policy networks this is no guarantee for their responsive behaviour,
because they tend to instrumentalise them for their own strategic goals, or because of strong executive dominance over the parliament. For instance, according to a comparative study of three policy sectors in seven European democracies,[41] state actors remain the most powerful group in policy-making. If this
strongly qualifies the idea that 'governance' means a 'hollowing out' of the
state, this is not necessarily good news for accountability. Although it is not
clear from the study who these state actors are, their influence in the policy-
making process is higher than the influence of political parties, which are the
democratically legitimate actors for preference aggregation and policy formation.

Anyway, it should be considered that policy networks are largely composed
of top level bureaucrats, policy experts, and interest representatives. Some of
these actors are only indirectly accountable to the citizenry due to a lengthy
'chain of delegation' (administrators), or only to their peers (experts) or to limited constituencies (interest group negotiators). Therefore, several actors taking part in policy networks are not necessarily mandate holders, are not constrained by electoral pledges, and do not have to anticipate electoral sanctions.
With respect to accountability their presence raises however quite different
problems: public administrators and leaders of interest groups are present by
virtue of their representational properties (albeit remotely connected to the 'demos' in the case of administrators, or connected to a narrow part of it in the
case of leaders of interest groups), while others' presence is justified on quite
different grounds (experts on the grounds of knowledge, private firms on the
grounds of their blackmailing – i.e. 'exit' - power). All but experts are collective actors in the sense that individual persons implicated in policy networks
represent collective interests, be they those of the state, or of various societal
segments and sectors (those who have a reputation to veto policy, or those –
'stakeholders' – who manage to argue convincingly that their preferences must
be given weight because of their high intensity). They are delegates accountable to principals, but for none of them are citizens the direct principal.

High rank bureaucrats are accountable to their minister, but this is administrative, not political accountability, lacking the public dimension. Democratic
control is much attenuated by the long chain of delegation. Bovens[42] identifies
in that respect a series of principal-agent relations: from citizens to parliamen-

40 Auel, 'Multilevel governance, regional policy and democratic legitimacy in Germany', and
    Taiclet, 'Governance, expertise and competitive politics. The case of territorial development
    policies in France', in A. Benz and Y. Papadopoulos (eds.), above note 26.
41 Kriesi et al., 'Comparative analysis of policy networks in Europe', (2006) 13 *Journal of Eu-
    ropean Public Policy* 3, 354.
42 Bovens, above note 19.

tarians, then to the cabinet, then to civil servants (and in addition increasingly to independent agencies). Further, new public management techniques *en vogue* leave more leverage to administrators, so that the democratic 'answerability' of their decisions and activities is reduced, and democratic control through citizens' 'voice' is increasingly replaced by 'customisation' (reliance on feedback by individuals as 'clients' or 'service users': see also below). True, the problem of administrative discretion is not specific to governance networks. It has been on the agenda for several decades, since the first influential studies of bureaucracies inspired by organisational sociology. It acquires however a new dimension in network governance, where the administration pools considerable external expertise. I do not intend to resuscitate the old and simplistic theories of technocratic power: the influence of experts depends on administrations being receptive (after all science and politics are functionally differentiated spheres), and experts seldom share the same views (even less on highly controversial issues). But an intriguing thing is that to claim credibility, experts have to convince about their independence. They should not appear as the vehicles of the preferences of any 'principal' to which they would have to account[43]. Experts are only credible if they can demonstrate the autonomy of science from politics, and they must convince that their discourse rests on different premises than the discourse of politicians or interest groups.

Experts are of course subject to 'peer-review' within the scientific community, and risk loss of reputation. Control is here internalised by the profession, but again this soft and 'horizontal' form of accountability is not political or public accountability. And if experts are in a sense also 'authorised' to act (by virtue of their acknowledged intellectual capital), they are not delegated by any 'principal' whom they would represent, but usually selected by the administration. Therefore, there is no guarantee that those who are co-opted (perhaps the less critical) are also the most distinguished according to the self-referential criteria of the scientific system. The requirement of expertise combined with independence is very similar to the requirement that increasingly leads national and European policy-makers to deliberately insulate some decisional spheres from the arena of partisan politics and electoral competition. The delegation of power to various independent bodies and agencies ('agencification') has indeed been justified by the need to ensure the credibility of those entrusted with decision-making, and this credibility is deemed to be primarily safeguarded

---

43 This is complicated by the fact that experts' independence is often unrealistic. Empirical studies tend to show that the most competent on a field are also those who are related to the interests in competition in this field: see Barthe et al., 'Impuretés et compromis de l'expertise, une difficile reconnaissance', in L. Dumoulin et al. (eds.), *Le recours aux experts* (Presses universitaires de Grenoble, 2005), p 53.

through independence and expertise according to the 'fiduciary' principle.[44] And in the EU system there are connections between IRAs and network governance: regulation by national agencies is influenced by mutual learning and the diffusion of recipes that take place at European level in informal networks of national regulators.[45]

Network governance also implies the cooperation of political power holders with non-public actors. One should distinguish between two sorts of them: interest groups and NGOs, or private firms. Although it is hard to disentangle the rationales behind these two forms of cooperation, partnerships with NGOs can be mostly attributed to a 'community' orientation of policy-making, while partnerships with (and outsourcing of public tasks to) private actors can be attributed for their part to the influence of neo-liberal thought and new public management doctrines. Accountability problems differ: interest groups and NGOs are accountable to their members ('internal' accountability[46]), and sometimes also to donors. This is partial accountability, neither to the general public, nor to the populations affected by their actions ('external' accountability[47]). It is also argued that these organisations do not escape problems of elitism (such as in the neo-corporatist model). This is no privilege of NGOs: the same was repeatedly said about parties ('iron law of oligarchy', 'cartelisation'). However, partisan representation is regulated by electoral competition, whereas pressures from public authorities to deal with a small number of interlocutors representing encompassing social segments reinforce monopolistic trends in interest representation.[48] Large private corporations for their part are primarily accountable to their shareholders, but even this form of capitalist accountability is not always well-developed in corporate governance. More fundamentally, this poses again the problem of partiality and lack of external accountability, as these firms are not accountable to those who can be subject to their externalities (workers, residents in neighbouring areas, etc.), apart through the market (NGOs for instance threaten with boycotts firms reluctant

---

44 Majone, 'Two Logics of Delegation. Agency and Fiduciary Relations in EU Governance', (2001) 2 *European Union Politics* 1; Majone, 'Delegation of Regulatory Powers in a Mixed Polity', (2002) 8 *European Law Journal* 3.

45 Eberlein and Grande, 'Beyond delegation: transnational regulatory regimes and the EU regulatory state', (2005) 12 *Journal of European Public Policy* 1; Maria Martens, Run-away bureaucracy? Exploring the role of National Regulatory Agencies in the EU, *Arena working paper* no. 30, November 2005.

46 Koenig-Archibugi, above note 18, 236-237.

47 The distinction between internal and external accountability partly overlaps with the distinction between what Gutmann and Thompson call respectively 'electoral' and 'moral' constituents: see A. Gutmann and D. Thompson, *Why Deliberative Democracy?* (Princeton University Press, 2004), p 39.

48 Offe, 'The Attribution of Public Status to Interest Groups', in S. Berger (ed.), *Organized Interests in Western Europe* (Cambridge University Press, 1981).

to apply social and environmental standards), but again this is not political accountability.

The 'multilevel' aspect of governance

In addition, network governance can be 'multilevel', consisting of complex structures cutting across decisional levels. This is the case of policy-making in federal states, but more centralised states are affected too: from 'below' social differentiation renders policy implementation contingent on compliance by policy addressees, and from 'above' internationalisation (think about WTO regulations) and Europeanisation require multilevel cooperation. Accountability is further inhibited by this multilevel aspect of governance.

Multilevel governance entails cooperative intergovernmental relations between subnational and national authorities, or between national and supranational organs: multilevel govern*ment*. The interdependence of decisional levels requires their cooperation notwithstanding the formal division of competencies between them (that may be accompanied by vertical accountability of lower to upper levels), and this cooperation often takes place in weakly visible policy-making structures. Federal – or quasi-federal systems like the EU (for a recent discussion see Thorlakson[49]) – are characterised by a formal division of decisional competencies across levels, often justified on the grounds of subsidiarity. But problems of scale caused by the need to produce efficient decisions, or the fragmentation of power resources between actors have led to a 'competence mix' and to cooperation schemes even in pure systems of dual federalism.[50] This occurs for instance in the phase of policy implementation when the latter comes to depend much on the resources of the constituent units (leading to a dialogue in the EU between the Commission services, national and possibly also regional administrations). Formal verticality becomes thus 'Politikverflechtung', generating several accountability problems.

First, negotiations across levels are often deemed to be more successful if they take place under conditions of informality that impede accountability. Further, as "Politikverflechtung" rests on mechanisms operating along an intergovernmentalist logic and implicating sometimes multiparty executives, it can exacerbate problems of dilution of responsibility ('many hands'). Decisions are taken by representatives of collective bodies in processes involving a

49 Thorlakson, 'Building Firewalls or Floodgates? Constitutional Design for the European Union', (2006) 44 *Journal of Common Market Studies* 1.
50 Thorlakson, 'Comparing Federal Institutions: Power and Representation in Six Federations', (2003) 26 *West European Politics* 2.

multitude of them. The problem of shared responsibility is amplified in cases such as that of EU structural funds policy, where to cooperation of public actors across levels is added cooperation with non-public actors in partnership forms.[51] Besides, even in principle democratically accountable actors are only fictitiously accountable because of lack of information on their positions. The accountability problem has to do with the lengthy 'chain of delegation' making the policy processes visible only to those principals who are closer to network members. In addition, multilevel negotiations tend to involve actors who are subject to administrative rather than democratic accountability, such as national and subnational bureaucracies who can enjoy considerable discretion.[52] Accountability problems are even more acute in the case of the EU administration: the Commission is itself more weakly accountable than national governments, and individual Commissioners do not have the same hierarchical relation to the administration as national ministers.[53] Moreover, even actors who are directly subject to the control of their electorates are subject to a 'two-level' accountability: they must account for their actions not only to their constituencies, but also to their negotiation partners. Usually 'two-level' games have been perceived as opening strategic windows of opportunity for their participants. It is instead the constraints posed by such games that need to be emphasised here, participants having to satisfy in a sense multiple 'forums'.[54] In a context of 'deliberative supranationalism'[55] network participants are constrained to a 'two-level arguing'[56] too. 'Comitology' committees in the EU are exemplars of multilevel governance in its technocratic version, being compo-

---

51 Empirical scrutiny tends however to disconfirm the openness of partnerships. Schmidt maintains that 'EU-mandated pluralist consultation in regional policy – which expected "horizontal co-operation" or "partnership" with civil society in the structural funds process – produced little more than statist forms of consultation in French and in German regions as well as in the UK': see Schmidt, 'Procedural democracy in the EU: the Europeanization of national and sectoral policy-making processes', (2006) 13 *Journal of European Public Policy* 5, 680.

52 On the influence of European and national bureaucracies upon the Council, see Curtin, 'Delegation to EU Non-Majoritarian Agencies and Emerging Practices of Public Accountability', in D. Gerardinet et al. (eds.), *Regulation through Agencies in the EU. A New Paradigm of European Governance* (Edward Elgar, 2005).

53 L. Verhey, 'Political Accountability in a European Perspective. A position paper for comparative research'. Paper presented at the workshop 'Political accountability from a European and comparative perspective', Maastricht University, 8th. and 9th. February 2006, pp 19-20.

54 For reasons of trust-building accounts must be given to negotiation partners even though the latter have not mandated those who must give account to them (see also above on professional, and below on 'peer' accountability).

55 Joerges and Neyer, 'From Intergovernmental Bargaining to Deliberative Political Processes: The Constitutionalization of Comitology', (1997) *European Law Journal* 3.

56 Risse, 'Transnational Governance and Legitimacy', in Benz and Papadopoulos (eds.), in A. Benz and Y. Papadopoulos (eds.), in A. Benz and Y. Papadopoulos (eds.), above note 26.

sed of experts and of administrators attached to different levels and subject to this kind of 'two-level' accountability.[57]

'Peer' accountability in networks

Relations between participants in networks pose different problems with respect to public accountability, depending on the status of the actors involved. However, all forms of network governance are propitious to 'peer' accountability,[58] a sort of accountability through embeddedness, typical according to Goodin[59] for third-sector organisations, but which may apply more in general to network forms of governance: 'based on mutual monitoring of one another's performance within a network of groups, public and private, sharing common concerns'. Participants are then deemed to be also (and perhaps primarily) accountable to their negotiation partners, usually in a 'soft' sense.[60] Durable co-operative interactions between partners are expected to generate self-limitation, empathy, and mutual trust, according to a major assumption common to two distinct strands of research, strategic-oriented research on cooperation, and discourse-oriented research on deliberation. Peer accountability is part of a more general trend where 'principles of informal role/control have risen in importance in comparison to formal accountability (principles)':[61] the Open Method of Coordination in the EU is a good case in point (see Benz in this issue). This form of accountability is sustained by mutual interdependence that derives in a sense (even though this may sound too cynical) above all from mutual blackmailing capabilities, also regarding compliance with moral commitments. The sheer fear of 'naming and shaming' is deemed to yield disciplining effects because 'free riders' or unreliable actors risk loss of reputation on behalf of their partners, who will consider them as untrustworthy in the

---

57 Pollack, 'Control Mechanism or Deliberative Democracy? Two Images of Comitology', (2003) 36 *Comparative Political Studies* ½.

58 Benner et al., 'Multisectoral Networks in Global Governance: Towards a Pluralistic System of Accountability', (2004) 39 *Government and Opposition* 2, 199-200.

59 Goodin, above note 11, 378.

60 This also presents similarities with mechanisms of 'légitimation croisée' (cross-legitimation) between representatives of the central state and local notables at the periphery that have been observed by works of the *Centre de sociologie des organisations* in France. For a theoretical synthesis of this research tradition see M. Crozier and E. Friedberg, *L'acteur et le système* (Eds. du Seuil, 1981).

61 M. Saward, 'Authorisation and Authenticity: Does Democracy Really Need Political Parties', paper presented at the ECPR Joint Sessions, workshop 'Democracy and Political Parties', Granada, 14-19 April 2005, p 13.

future and, in a sense, will no longer agree to 'invest' on them.[62] The standard-
ising effects produced by the threat to lose credit present some similarities with
the effects expected from 'horizontal' accountability systems of checks and
balances. In parliamentary bicameralism for instance, institutional actors involved in 'nested games' are induced to anticipate each other's reactions, possibly to deliberate together, and thus more easily reach agreement. Yet soft
accountability mechanisms within networks are distinctive through the lack of
formal sanctions, the focalisation of accountability on individuals, and the frequently missing democratic or even simply 'bottom-up' legitimation of participants.

It can indeed be expected from policy networks to produce, through deliberation or bargaining and by virtue of peer accountability, Pareto-optimal outcomes. They can even prove to be more respectful of criteria of social justice
than majoritarian decision-making.[63] For peer accountability to function effectively however networks must be sufficiently representative and pluralist, i.e.
not exclude weaker interests, or actors whose preferences do not coincide with
the network's 'mainstream' orientation. Whether this is the rule seems questionable. And even if the network is pluralistic the diversity of perspectives
does not guarantee that these perspectives are representative of the society at
large. In order to be included in networks, actors must possess resources that
are unevenly distributed (expertise, blackmailing capacity, preferences considered as intense…). Further, interest selectivity is not only caused by inequalities, but also by imperatives of governability: the reluctance to include actors
who are themselves not willing to 'play the game'. Not only have deliberative
modes of governance been criticised by radical theorists for requiring superior
argumentative skills from their participants,[64] but anecdotal evidence suggests
that self-governing networks tend in addition to reduce associative pluralism
and intra-organisational diversity, either by imposing an official policy paradigm, or by failing to co-opt in networks actors who do not comply with it.[65]
This is not only a loss of social pluralism but can undermine policy efficiency
too. The lack of 'requisite variety' in policy networks can lead to the formation

62 Offe speaks about a 'Gesetz des Wiedersehens': see C. Offe, *Thesen zur öffentlichen Anhörung der gemeinsamen Verfassungskommission zum Thema Bürgerbeteiligung/Plebiszite*
(manuscript, 1992). 'Naming and shaming' is also expected to be an efficient mechanism of
mutual adjustment in 'soft' law. However, as in the case of the GSP, the most powerful countries do not seem much embarrassed by that, confirming that power is 'the ability to talk instead of listen, the ability to afford not to learn': K.W.D. Deutsch, *The Nerves of Government.
Models of Political Communication and Control* (The Free Press, 1963), p 11.

63 Papadopoulos, above note 26, 492-493.

64 Sanders, 'Against Deliberation', (1997) *Political Theory* 25, 349; I.M. Young, *Inclusion and
Democracy*, (Oxford University Press, 2000), pp 37-40.

65 Wälti and Kübler, ''New Governance' and Associative Pluralism: The Case of Drug Policy
in Swiss Cities', (2003) 31 *The Policy Studies Journal* 4.

of 'group-think' or to what Sunstein[66] calls 'enclave deliberation'. This impedes critical reflection, which is necessary to accountability. It is also detrimental to problem-solving because this kind of deliberation favours conformity with convictions that may rely on erroneous causal hypotheses. For ideological pluralism to be preserved an exit option must be available for network actors ('opting-out clauses'). On the other hand, it is well known that such clauses favour a bargaining game with threats based on each one's blackmailing power and also inhibit problem-solving deliberation (it is no accident that corporatist devices rely on a design that increases the costs of exit). A lack of pluralism may also limit the optimality of resource allocation. This may be due to deliberate strategic behaviour on the part of 'insiders', but it may simply result from the necessity for mutual trust-building which may end up in collusion. Lord[67] stresses the danger 'that instead of balancing and checking one another, networks or their members may collude to suspend competitiveness between themselves, to reduce prospects of challenge from the constituencies to which they are supposedly accountable and to freeze new entrants out of access to the benefits of engagement with the political system'. For instance, rational choice approaches inspired by the Olsonian paradigm, but also critical neo-Marxist approaches of corporatism, tend to emphasise the risk of rent-seeking within weakly pluralist networks ('iron triangles') at the expense of third parties. 'There is a very real risk that they (mutual accountability networks) will degenerate into a complacent "old boy network", their accountability function blunted by mutual interest', write Harlow and Rawlings in their contribution to this issue.[68]

In addition, the requirements of mutual accountability within peer-groups can weaken public accountability. There is a trade-off related to the presence of multiple 'controllers' with different demands:[69] peers on the one hand, reference groups on the other. The necessity to build mutual trust discredits actors who are prone to make a strategic use of 'two-level games' and who are likely to 'free ride', but in case of 'group-think' it may also marginalise those who simply manifest their scepticism about some of the network common goals. One has to prove one's loyalty to the network by demonstrating that one is a credible and committed interlocutor. This kind of 'peer' accountability can

---

66 C. Sunstein, *Republic.com* (Princeton University Press, 2001).

67 C. Lord, *A Democratic Audit of the European Union* (Palgrave, 2004), p 114.

68 Harlow and Rawlings in this issue, manuscript, 4.

69 This trade-off should be distinguished from 'redundancy accountability' described by Scott: see Scott, 'Accountability in the Regulatory State', (2000) 27 *Journal of Law and Society* 1, 52. The latter refers to the tendency to supplement traditional mechanisms of accountability by the horizontal mechanisms of the market, in which overlapping (and superfluous) accountability mechanisms reduce the centrality of any one of them. See also E. Vos (2005) 'Keeping Independent Agencies under Control', paper presented at the CONNEX Workshop 'Delegation and Multilevel Governance', Paris, 11 May 2005, p 14). Instead of a redundant extension we observe here a partial substitution of accountability mechanisms.

hardly be achieved without some loss of accountability 'at home'. The 'logic of influence' tending to prevail among elites involved in mutual deliberation and negotiation seldom coincides with the 'logic of membership' consisting in mirroring the preferences of their constituencies.[70] The narrowing of the preference gap between collective actors in 'summit' negotiations and deliberations implies (at least if no vertical learning processes occur) the widening of the preference gap between the leadership and the rank-and-file within the represented organisations. In supranational governance, such a loosening of control by 'principals' is amplified by the lengthy chain of delegation. We also noticed that for 'peer' monitoring to perform effectively some degree of intra-network variety is necessary. But on the other hand, the more difficult it becomes then for external publics to identify who is at the origin of network outputs, especially when the latter result from compromise. In addition, compromise-seeking and problem-solving may require 'legitimate confidentiality',[71] while democratic accountability may prevent solutions that cannot be 'sold' with populist justifications. Consequently, increased accountability can also lead to 'subterfuge' as blame-avoidance behaviour. Marcinkowski[72] for instance maintains that 'informalisation' strategies are decided in policy-making processes in order to avoid media scrutiny, Bovens[73] stresses risk-avoiding behaviour from actors perceiving to be the objects of 'excess accountability',[74] and Philp[75] asserts that accountability often generates only an appearance of conformity. Self-presentation strategies utilised by politicians with the help of marketing consultants ('spin doctors') in a context of an increasingly 'audience' democracy point in this direction. Therefore, there are good reasons – at least in policy makers' minds – not to favour genuine accountability in strongly mediatised public spaces.

---

70 P.C. Schmitter and W. Streeck (1999) 'The Organization of Business Interests. Studying the Associative Action of Business in Advanced Industrial Societies', Discussion paper 99/1, Cologne: Max-Planck-Institut für Gesellschaftsforschung.

71 Schedler, above note 7, p 21.

72 F. Marcinkowski, *Die Politik der Massenmedien* (van-Halem Verlag, 2001).

73 Bovens, above note 19.

74 Not to mention the propensity of 'watchdogs' to focus sometimes on 'scandals' rather than on 'normal' behaviour.

75 M. Philp, Against Accountability. Paper presented at the 3rd ECPR conference, Budapest, 2005, p 21.

Conclusion and prospects for accountability

This article suggests that network forms of governance entail a number of accountability problems. 'Shared responsibility' and lack of visibility are aggravated by the frequent 'multilevel' aspect of these forms of governance. The relations between actors involved in networks are weakly exposed to public scrutiny, or to the scrutiny of the legitimate, democratic, and representative bodies. This is not to say that actors involved in governance networks are not accountable at all. They are subject to 'peer' or professional accountability, to reputational and market accountability, to fiscal/financial, administrative or legal accountability.[76] There is no guarantee however that such 'diffuse' or 'composite' control mechanisms[77] can be effective, as they operate in a fragmentary and uncoordinated way without forming a coherent system. Also, the problem of political and democratic accountability remains: only some network actors are subject to it, and control over them can be merely indirect or partial. In sum, the following points should be stressed:

- In network and multilevel forms of governance the direct democratic accountability of policy-makers is weakened
- On the other hand, there is a 'multiplication of control mechanisms'[78]
- Actors in such accountability 'forums' may have a distinct agenda from democratic 'principals' with whom policy-makers are in a relation of delegation and representation
- Those who control ex-post are thus not necessarily the same as those who formulate mandates ex-ante
- The accountability forums are dispersed and do not form a coherent accountability system, so that the picture of a 'patchwork' might be an adequate description here
- Part of the accountability mechanisms at work are of the 'light' or 'soft' type (indirect, not institutionalised, through moral commitments and social pressure, exposure to the public sphere, etc.), with the risk of being 'toothless'[79]
- As a result, the efficiency of a (syncretic) 'marble cake' of accountability mechanisms including (perhaps too) 'many eyes' that operate in a 'soft' manner is questionable
- Finally, in network and multilevel forms of governance there may not only be a trade-off between democratic accountability and policy efficiency (the 'input-output' dilemma), but a trade-off between democratic accountability and other 'peer' forms of accountability too.

Some would argue that, given the increased complexity of contemporary decision-making procedures, democratic accountability has become illusory. Regarding the issue of transparency in transnational private governance for

---

76 Benner et al., above note 59, 199-200.
77 Costa et al., 'Introduction: Diffuse control mechanisms in the European Union: towards a new democracy?' (2003) 10 *Journal of European Public Policy* 5; Héritier, above note 30.
78 Costa et al. , ibid, p 670.
79 Schedler, above note 7, pp 16-17.

instance, Scholte[80] critically concludes that 'most people (including many democratically elected representatives) have not even heard of private sites of global governance'. However, there is no sufficient reason why multilevel governance networks should not be accountable to democratic institutions at different levels, which should be able to exert effective oversight over their operation. It may be argued that there is a need for a 'parliamentarisation' of multilevel governance systems.[81] However, such a (in principle welcome) reform strategy also faces limits and should by no means be seen as a sufficient condition to enhance accountability. This is particularly true for the EU multilevel governance system: [82] by contrast to national settings where governance can be conceived of as 'government plus', governance in the EU is best described as 'government minus'.[83] Even if the EP continues for instance to gain influence over EU policy-making, this will not automatically solve other problems that weaken the influence of party representatives in the exercise of their role as accountability holders (think about the relative weakness of European party federations), or that weaken their legitimacy to act in that respect (think about the 'second-order' character of European elections). Considering these limits, I would like to conclude my contribution by suggesting a model to improve democratic accountability in multilevel systems, borrowed from common work with Arthur Benz.[84] This should be seen as a complement to better accountability to institutions like courts or ombudsmen.

We envisage a decisional pattern characterised by a functional separation of power between policy formulation in networks, and by constituent and veto power dedicated to institutions that are authorised and accountable to citizens. Formally authorised institutions should first set the 'meta-governance' procedural rules for fair participation and for accountability in network forms of governance. Although it happens sometimes that the formalisation of networks (provisions about participants, mode of operation, etc.) becomes an open political issue, it would be innovative to assign explicitly the design function to the democratically authorised institutions (as we noticed such a function is

---

80 Scholte, 'Civil Society and Democracy in Global Governance', (2002) *Global Governance* 8, 292.

81 See for instance W. Van Gerwen, *The European Union. A Polity of States and Peoples* (Stanford University Press, 2005), pp 344-368, and the proposals made by K. Holzinger and C. Knill for the EU, 'Eine Verfassung für die Europäische Federation. Kontinuierliche Weiterentwicklung des Erreichten', European University Institute, JM WP 07/2000 ('Responses to Joschka Fischer'): http://www.jeanmonnetprogram.org/papers/00/00f1401.html.

82 Interestingly Majone, who does consider the democratic deficit of the EU as problematic (given the nature of European integration), finds that the 'accountability deficit' by contrast is a 'real problem' for the EU: see Majone, 'The common sense of European integration', (2006) 13 *Journal of European Public Policy* 5, 621.

83 A.M. Sbragia (2002) The Dilemma of Governance with Government. Jean Monnet Working Paper 3/02, NYU School of Law, p 6.

84 Benz and Papadopoulos, above note 26.

often delegated to members of the bureaucracy).[85] These institutions should also have the final say on policy outputs, by being an effective locus of critical scrutiny over proposals formulated by governance networks, which have for their part the advantage of pooling expertise and of facilitating acceptance by 'stakeholders'.[86] This is no institutional innovation *per se*: formally things do work according to this pattern in national settings, and increasingly so at EU level too. Yet in order to effectively perform their constituent and veto functions, democratically authorised institutions should acquire additional resources in terms of legal instruments, but also in terms of time, information, intelligence, professionalism, or organisation. In national, regional, international and multilevel governance, citizens (by referendum), national parliaments, or elected governments should fulfil the constituent and veto functions, even though delegation to governments would play a stronger role at the supra- and international level. Actors in networks should then have to convince in communicative processes the legitimised veto-players about their policy proposals, while veto-players would be forced to effectively supervise participation and policy-making in governance. At the same time, learning mechanisms should be developed in order to prevent policy blockades by veto players: to give an example, parliamentary committees should base more frequently their proposals on hearings of experts and interest representatives (that could be public and mediatised).

Such a pattern of decision-making can serve as a benchmark to be approximated for all network governance situations, in order to increase the chances for improving their democratic accountability, and thereby their legitimacy. It should replace the current uncoupling of network governance from legitimate representative structures not by a tight coupling, that might lead to vetoing and policy blockades, but by loose coupling creating interfaces that can be beneficial for mutual learning.[87] The creation of such interfaces would require institutional innovation. For instance, particularly in a context where representative politics are also increasingly delegitimised, it does not suffice to redress the imbalance between network and parliamentary governance. A further step is

---

85 Some scholars have reflected on principles for 'chartering' governance arrangements that meet the requirement of 'democratic anchorage': Sørensen, above note 12; Schmitter, 'Governance in the European Union: a viable mechanism for future legitimation?', in A. Benz and Y. Papadopoulos (eds.), above note 26.

86 We leave aside here the issue of the implementation of decisions, which can again be delegated to policy networks, but also requires oversight by formally authorised bodies.

87 Benz, above note 26. Other forms of loose coupling can be found in the linkages between 'governance councils', administrative agencies, parliaments, and the judiciary in the framework of 'democratic experimentalism': Dorf and Sabel, 'A Constitution of Democratic Experimentalism', (1998) 98 *Columbia Law Review* 2; see also Eberlein and Kerwer, above note 3, 132-133 for an application to the OMC in the EU.

required, which is a closer familiarity of the mass public with the realities of complex decision-making processes, and thereby an increase of its evaluative competence that would permit to reduce informational asymmetries. 'Deliberative opinion polls'[88] for instance on some major policy choices formulated by networks can be instrumental for such an empowerment, under the condition that they are not confined to the role of mere participatory experiments as it is the case today.[89] They should be combined for instance with petition rights such as those that were foreseen in article I-47.4 of the Constitutional Treaty. In sum, models of decision-making should be proposed and discussed that allow to:

- Redress the imbalance between network and parliamentary governance by making the former more accountable to the latter
- Empower on complex issues not only representatives but also ordinary citizens
- Avoid stalemates due to the lack of mechanisms of mutual learning between network members, political representatives, and voters.

As a matter of fact, introducing a higher dose of public, democratic and popular accountability without setting up at the same time mechanisms of mutual learning by the involved actors can yield unintended negative outcomes, such as a lack of policy efficiency, and therefore also problems of governability that may ultimately lead to a decrease of (output) legitimacy. Institutional design should be cautiously carried out so as to avoid such 'perverse' or 'boomerang' effects.

References

Andersen, S.S. and Burns, T.R. (1996). 'The European Union and the Erosion of Parliamentary Democracy: A Study of Post-Parliamentary Governance', in S.S. Andersen & K.J. Eliassen (eds.), The European Union: How Democratic Is It? London: Sage, 226-251.

Andersen, V.N. and K.M. Hansen (2007). "How Deliberation Makes Better Citizens: The Danish Deliberative Poll on the Euro", in Y. Papadopoulos and P. Warin (eds.), "Innovative, participatory, and deliberative procedures in policy-making: democratic and effective?", special issue of the European Journal of Political Research.

Andeweg, R. (2005). "De super and ex post? Political Representation and Europeanisation", paper prepared for the Leiden workshop of CONNEX Research Group 2, Leiden University, March 3-4.

---

88 J.S. Fishkin, *The Voice of the People* (Yale University Press, 1995).
89 See for instance an evaluation of the Danish deliberative opinion poll on the Euro: Andersen and Hansen (forthcoming), 'How Deliberation Makes Better Citizens: The Danish Deliberative Poll on the Euro', in Y. Papadopoulos and P. Warin (eds.), 'Innovative, participatory, and deliberative procedures in policy-making: democratic and effective?', special issue of the European Journal of Political Research (2007).

Auel, K. (2006) 'Multilevel governance, regional policy and democratic legitimacy in Germany', in A. Benz and Y. Papadopoulos (eds.) Governance and Democracy. Comparing National, European, and International Experiences, London: Routledge, pp.44-62.

Bache, I. And M. Flinders (2004). Multilevel Governance. Oxford, Oxford University Press.

Barthe, Y. et al. (2005). 'Impuretés et compromis de l'expertise, une difficile reconnaissance', in L. Dumoulin et al. (eds.), Le recours aux experts, Grenoble, Presses universitaires de Grenoble, 43-62.

Bartolini, S. (1999). Collusion, Competition, and Democracy, Part I, Journal of Theoretical Politics 11 (4), 435-470.

Behn, R. D. (2001). Rethinking Democratic Accountability. Washington: The Brookings Institution.

Bendor, J., Glazer, A. and Hammond, T. (2001) 'Theories of Delegation', Annual Review of Political Science IV, 235-269.

Benner, T. et al. (2004), Multisectoral Networks in Global Governance: Towards a Pluralistic System of Accountability, Government and Opposition, 39 (2), 191-210.

Benz, A. (1998). 'Postparlamentarische Demokratie? Demokrtische Legitimation im kooperativen Staat', in M. Th. Greven (ed.), Demokratie - eine Kultur des Westens? Opladen: Leske + Budrich, 201-222.

Benz, A. (2004) 'Path-dependent Institutions and Strategic Veto-Players - National Parliaments in the European Union', West European Politics, 29, 875-900.

Benz, A. and Y. Papadopoulos (2006) 'Actors, Institutions and Democratic Governance: Comparing Across Levels', in A. Benz and Y. Papadopoulos (eds.) Governance and Democracy. Comparing National, European, and International Experiences, London: Routledge.

Bevir, M. (2006) Democratic Governance: Systems and Radical Perspectives, Public Administration Review, 66 (3), 426-436.

Bovens, M. (1998) The Quest for Responsibility, Cambridge: Cambridge University Press.

Bovens, M. (2005). "Public Accountability", in E. Ferlie, L.E. Lynne Jr. & C. Pollitt (eds.), The Oxford Handbook of Public Management, Oxford: Oxford University Press, 182-208.

Costa et al. (2003), 'Introduction: Diffuse control mechanisms in the European Union: towards a new democracy?' 10 Journal of European Public Policy 5.

Crozier, M. and E. Friedberg (1981). L'acteur et le système. Paris: Eds. du Seuil.

Curtin, D. (2005), Delegation to EU Non-Majoritarian Agencies and Emerging Practices of Public Accountability, In: D Gerardinet al. (eds), Regulation through Agencies in the EU. A New Paradigm of European Governance, Cheltenham (UK): Edward Elgar, 88-119.

Deutsch, K.W.D. (1963). The Nerves of Government. Models of Political Communication and Control. New York: The Free Press.

Dorf, M.C. and C.F. Sabel (1998). "A Constitution of Democratic Experimentalism", Columbia Law Review 98 (2), 267-273.

Eberlein, B. and Grande, E. (2005) 'Beyond delegation: transnational regulatory regimes and the EU regulatory state`, Journal of European Public Policy 12 (1), 89-112.

Eberlein, B. and Kerwer, D. (2004) 'New Governance in the European Union: A Theoretical Perspective', Journal of Common Market Studies 42(1), 121-142.

Fishkin, J. S. (1995). The Voice of the People. New Haven: Yale University Press.

Flinders, M. (2005). "The Politics of Public-Private Partnerships », British Journal of Politics and International Relations 7, 215-239.

Goodin, Robert E. (2003). Democratic Accountability: The Distinctiveness of the Third Sector, European Journal of Sociology, 44 (3), 359-393.

Grant, R. and R.O. Keohane (2004), « Accountability and Abuses of Power in World Politics », American Political Science Review, 99 (1), 29-43.

Gutmann, A. and D. Thompson (2004). Why Deliberative Democracy? Princeton, Princeton University Press.

Héritier, A. (2003). "Composite democracy in Europe: the role of transparency and access to information ", Journal of European Public Policy 10 (5), 814-833.

Hirst, P. (1994). Associative Democracy. Cambridge: Polity Press.

Holzinger, K. and C. Knill (2000), 'Eine Verfassung für die Europäische Federation. Kontinuierliche Weiterentwicklung des Erreichten', European University Institute, JM WP 07/2000 ('Responses to Joschka Fischer'): http://www.jeanmonnetprogram.org/papers/00/00f1401.html

Hooghe, L. and Marks, G. (2003) 'Unraveling the Central State, but How? Types of Multilevel Governance', American Political Science Review 97(2), 233-243.

Idema, T. and Kelemen, R.D. (forthcoming), New Modes of Governance, the Open Method of Coordination, and other Fashionable Red Herring, forthcoming in Perspectives on European Politics and Society.

Joerges, C. and Neyer, J. (1997), "From Intergovernmental Bargaining to Deliberative Political Processes: The Constitutionalization of Comitology", European Law Journal (3), 274-300.

Koenig-Archibugi, M. (2004). „Transnational Corporations and Public Accountability „, Government and Opposition, 39 (2), 234-259.

Kohler-Koch, B. (2000). Framing: the bottleneck of constructing legitimate institutions, Journal of European Public Policy 7 (4), 513-531.

Kohler-Koch, B. (2006). Research on EU Governance: Insight from a Stock-Taking Exercise. Connex Newsletter 3: 4-6.

Kriesi, H. et al. (2006). Comparative analysis of policy networks in Europe, Journal of European Public Policy 13 (3), 341-361.

*Kübler, D. and B. Schwab (forthcoming), « New regionalism in five Swiss metropolitan areas. An assessment of inclusiveness, deliberation and democratic accountability", in Y. Papadopoulos and P. Warin (eds.), Innovative, participatory, and deliberative procedures in policymaking: democratic and effective?, special issue of the European Journal of Political Research, 2007.

Leca, J. (1996). 'La gouvernance" de la France sous la Cinquième République. Une perspective de sociologie comparative', in F. D'Arcy & L. Rouban (eds.). De la Ve République à l'Europe, Paris: Presses de Sciences Po., 329-365.

*Lehmbruch, G. (1977). Liberal Corporatism and Party Government, Comparative Political Studies 10 (1), 91-126.

Lehmbruch, G. (1999), 'Verhandlungsdemokratie, Entscheidungsblockaden und Arenenverflechtung', in W. Merkel and A. Busch (eds.), Demokratie in Ost und West (Suhrkamp).

Lord, C. (2004) A Democratic Audit of the European Union, London: Palgrave.

Mair, P. (2005). "Popular Democracy and the European Union Polity", EUROGOV.European Governance Papers, C-05-03.

Majone, G, (2001). Two Logics of Delegation. Agency and Fiduciary Relations in EU Governance, European Union Politics, 2 (1), 103-122.

Majone, G, (2002). Delegation of Regulatory Powers in a Mixed Polity, European Law Journal, 8 (3), 319-339.

Majone, G, (2006). The common sense of European integration, Journal of European Public Policy, 13 (5), 607-626.

Manin, B. (1997). The Principles of Representative Government. Cambridge: Cambridge University Press.

Mansbridge, J. (2005). Rethinking Representation, American Political Science Review, 97 (4), 515-528.

Marcinkowski, F. (2001), Die Politik der Massenmedien (van-Halem Verlag).

Martens, Maria (2005), Run-away bureaucracy? Exploring the role of National Regulatory Agencies in the EU, Arena working paper no. 30, November 2005.

Mayntz, R. (1997). Politische Steuerung: Aufstieg, Niedergang und Transformation einer Theorie', in R. Mayntz, Soziale Dynamik und Politische Steuerung. Theoretische und methodologische Ueberlegungen, Frankfurt-New York: Campus 263-292.

Offe, C. (1981) 'The Attribution of Public Status to Interest Groups', in S. Berger (ed.) Organized Interests in Western Europe. Cambridge: Cambridge University Press, 123-158.

Offe, C. (1992). Thesen zur öffentlichen Anhörung des gemeinsamen Verfassungskommission zum Thema Bürgerbeteiligung/Plebiszite. mimeo, Bonn.

Olsson, J. (2003). 'Democracy paradoxes in multilevel governance: theorizing on structural fund system research', Journal of European Public Policy, 10 (2), 283-300.

Papadopoulos, Y. (2002). 'Populism, the democratic question, and contemporary governance', in Y. Mény and Y. Surel (eds.), Democracies and the Populist Challenge, London: Palgrave-Macmillan, 45-61.

Papadopoulos, Y. (2003). 'Cooperative forms of governance: problems of democratic accountability in complex environments', European Journal of Political Research 42 (4), 473-501.

Papadopoulos, Y. (2005), 'Taking Stock of Multilevel Governance Networks', European Political Science, 4, 316-327.

Peters, B. Guy (2006), The Meta-Governance of Policy Networks: Steering at a Distance, but Still Steering, draft paper for the Conference on "Democratic Network Governance", Roskilde, 3 Nov. 2006.

Philp, M. (2005). Against Accountability. Paper presented at the 3rd ECPR conference, Budapest, 2005.

Pierre, J. (2000). Introduction: Understanding Governance, in J. Pierre (ed.), Debating Governance. Oxford: Oxford University Press, 1-10.

Pollack, M.A. (2003). Control Mechanism or Deliberative Democracy? Two Images of Comitology, Comparative Political Studies 36 (1/2), 125-155.

Randall, Ed. (2006), Not that soft or informal: a response to Eberlein and Grande's account of regulatory governance in the EU with special reference to the European Food Safety Authority (EFSA), Journal of European Public Policy 13 (3), 402-419.

Risse, T. (2006). 'Transnational Governance and Legitimacy', in A. Benz and Y. Papadopoulos (eds.) Governance and Democracy. Comparing National, European, and International Experiences, London: Routledge, 179-199.

Sanders, L. (1997). Against Deliberation, Political Theory (25), 347-376.

Saward, Michael (2005), „Authorisation and Authenticity: Does Democracy Really Need Political Parties", paper presented at the ECPR Joint Sessions, workshop „Democracy and Political Parties", Granada, 14-19 April.

Sbragia, Alberta M. (2002). The Dilemma of Governance with Government. Jean Monnet Working Paper 3/02, NYU School of Law.

Scharpf, F. W. (1970). Demokratietheorie zwischen Utopie und Anpassung. Konstanz: Universitätsverlag.

Scharpf, F. W. (2002). Legitimate Diversity: The New Challenge of European Integration, Cahiers européens de Sciences.Po, 1.

Schedler, A. (1999). « Conceptualizing Accountability », in A. Schedler et al. (eds.), The Self-Restraining State, Boulder, Lynne Rienner Publ, 13-28.

Schmidt, V. A. (2006), "Procedural democracy in the EU: the Europeanization of national and sectoral policy-making processes », Journal of European Public Policy 13 (5) : 670-691.

Schmitter, P.C. (2004). « The Ambiguous Virtues of Accountability », Journal of Democracy, 15 (4), 47-60.

Schmitter, P.C. (2006) "Governance in the European Union: a viable mechanism for future legitimation?", in A. Benz and Y. Papadopoulos (eds.) Governance and Democracy. Comparing
National, European, and International Experiences, London: Routledge, 158-175.
Schmitter, P.C. and Streeck, W. (1999) 'The Organization of Business Interests. Studying the Associative Action of Business in Advanced Industrial Societies', Discussion paper 99/1, Cologne: Max-Planck-Institut für Gesellschaftsforschung.
Schöni, A. (2005). "Le contrôle parlementaire des conventions intercantonales", IDHEAP working paper, 4.
Scholte, J.A. (2002). Civil Society and Democracy in Global Governance, Global Governance (8),
281-304.
Scott, C. (2000), 'Accountability in the Regulatory State', Journal of Law and Society, 27 (1), 38-
60.
Skelcher, C. (2005) 'Jurisdictional Integrity, Polycentrism, and the Design of Democratic Govern-
ance', Governance: An International Journal of Policy, Administration, and Institutions 18(1),
89-110.
Sørensen, E. (2005). The democratic problems and potentials of network governance, European
Political Science (4), 348-357.
Strom, K. et al. (eds.) (2003), Delegation and Accountability in Parliamentary Democracies, Ox-
ford: Oxford University Press.
Sunstein, C. (2001) Republic.com, Princeton: Princeton University Press.
Thorlakson, L. (2003), "Comparing Federal Institutions: Power and Representation in Six Feder-
ations", West European Politics, 26 (2), 1-22.
Thorlakson, L. (2006), "Building Firewalls or Floodgates? Constitutional Design for the European
Union", Journal of Common Market Studies, 44 (1), 139-159.
Taiclet, A.F. (2006) 'Governance, expertise and competitive politics. The case of territorial devel-
opment policies in France', in A. Benz and Y. Papadopoulos (eds.) Governance and Democ-
racy. Comparing National, European, and International Experiences, London: Routledge, 63-
80.
Trubek. D. M. (2005). "Soft Law", "Hard Law," and European Integration: Toward a Theory of
Hybridity, Jean Monnet Working Paper 02/05, NYU School of Law.
Van Gerwen, W. (2005). The European Union. A Polity of States and Peoples. Stanford (Cal.),
Stanford University Press.
Verhey, L. (2006). "Political Accountability in a European Perspective. A position paper for com-
parative research". Paper presented at the workshop « Political accountability from a European
and comparative perspective », Maastricht University, 8th. and 9th. February.
Voelzkow, H. (2000). Von der funktionalen Differenzierung zur Globalisierung: neue Herausfor-
derungen für die Demokratietheorie, in R. Werle & U. Schimank (eds.), Gesellschaftliche
Komplexität und kollektive Handlungsfähigkeit. Frankfurt/Main: Campus, 270-296.
Vos, E. (2005). "Keeping Independent Agencies under Control", paper presented at the CONNEX
Workshop "Delegation and Multilevel Governance", Paris, 11 May.
Wälti, S. and Kübler, D. (2003) '"New Governance" and Associative Pluralism: The Case of Drug
Policy in Swiss Cities', The Policy Studies Journal 31(4), 499-525.
Wolf, K.D. (2002). Contextualizing Normative Standards for Legitimate Governance beyond the
State', in B. Gbikpi & J.R. Grote (eds.). Participatory Governance. Political and Societal Im-
plications, Opladen: Leske+Budrich, 35-50.
Wright, E.O. (ed.) (1995) Associations and Democracy, London-New York: Verso.
Young, I.M. (2000). Inclusion and Democracy. Oxford: Oxford University Press.

Chapter 3
Multilevel Governance and the Reconfiguration of Political Space

Alain-G. Gagnon, UQÀM

Introduction

Several different approaches may be taken to the analysis of multilevel governance. Some authors focus on institutions and their capacity to adapt to the ebb and flow of the economy and political tensions in the medium and long term. They thus deal with issues of effectiveness, good management and the adaptive capabilities of existing regimes; for example, Canadian federalism[1] or the Italian political system[2]. For some of these analysts, what matters is not respect for the distribution of powers so much as the ability of political actors to put in place a rational, pragmatic, effective system of governance. They thus tend to favour the study of new power relationships that take shape in response to circumstances with no regard for the normative foundations that had originally led to the formation of these states or for the historical compromises that had made their establishment possible.

The interpretive frameworks adopted in the predominant analyses of what are termed "federal states" are similar in that they largely attach greater importance to the political stability of established regimes than to the quest for justice or the empowerment of national communities. In this paper, we shall seek to show that federal (and pluralistic) practices have tended to wither and wane as political actors in positions of hegemony have preferred that policies instead be patterned on the wishes of the centre and that the public policies of the different orders of government be harmonized with them. Ferran Requejo and Klaus-Jürgen Nagel's recent book, *Federalism beyond Federations,* on asymmetry and processes of "resymmetrisation" in Europe is of great interest

---

1   Herman Bakvis and Grace Skogstad, eds (2002). *Canadian Federalism: Performance, Effectiveness, and Legitimacy,* Toronto: Oxford University Press.
2   Ugo Amoretti (2011). "Italy: Increasing Decentralisation, Decreasing Asymmetry," in *Federalism beyond Federations: Asymmetry and Processes of Resymmetrisation in Europe,* eds. Ferran Requejo and Klaus-Jürgen Nagel Farnham: Ashgate, 61–79.

in this regard[3]. Practices of "resymmetrisation" predominate throughout Europe as well as in many other federations, including Canada.

Over the past number of years, several authors (Peter Kraus, Ramon Maiz, Guy Laforest, José Maria Sauca[4]) have underscored the point that the Westphalian, monistic vision has gained the ascendancy in many complex democratic states. This paradigmatic approach has been challenged by two main schools of thought.

First, there are the proponents of a school that calls for the implementation of multilevel policies to better reflect the needs of people and groups living together in a state. The promoters of this school are generally little inclined to explore the needs of cohabiting national communities; they are rather more likely to look for pragmatic policies. They tend not to take into account what are, nonetheless, such crucial issues as the responsible management of the state and the accountability of political actors. For the supporters of this school, the important point is the ability of the actors to provide meaningful outcomes in terms of the effective management of public policy.

Second, there are those who promote practices founded on a multinational federalism. This approach allows for consideration of claims for recognition and empowerment by political communities in polities in which national diversity is the primary determinant of cultural, economic and social relations. Proponents of this school contend that the effectiveness sought by the supporters of the multilevel approach can be imposed only by eroding the capacities of the states of the founding national communities and undermining the raison d'être of the nation states that have been established. From this perspective, it is important to institute practices that respect what were freely negotiated political agreements.

In the analysis presented here, we shall first seek to identify changes in governance that have occurred over the past number of years and the reasons political actors in positions of power cite for having implemented them. We shall then explore and evaluate the "multilevel" approach which has, to a great extent, gained clear ascendancy in the places of power over the past several years. Finally, we shall lay out what the multinational approach has to offer nationally diverse federations in terms of ways of governance that are both more democratic and respectful of underlying constitutional values.

---

3   Requejo and Nagel, eds., *Federalism beyond Federation, op.cit.*
4   Peter Kraus (2008) *A Union of Diversity: Language, Diversity and Polity Building in Europe* (Cambridge: Cambridge University Press); Guy Laforest (2010) "The Meaning of Canadian Federalism in Quebec: Critical Reflections," *Revista d'Estudis Autonomics i Federals*, no 11, 10–55; Ramon Maiz (2011) *The Inner Frontier: The Place of Nation in the Political Theory of Democracy and Federalism* (Brussels: Peter Lang/Presses interuniversitaires européennes; José Maria Sauca (2010) *Identidad y Derecho : nuevas perspectivas para viejos debates* (Valencia: Tirant lo blanch).

Background: political ambitions and pitfalls

The period from the late 1970s to the early 1990s gave rise to the articulation of many national-affirmation movements and to the introduction across Europe and in Canada of policies of varying scope to recognize them. These policies ultimately cleared the way for devolution in the United Kingdom (1977-79, 1997-), decentralization and federalization in Belgium, "deconcentration" in the Spanish autonomous regions, and what we shall call a policy of "renationalization" in Canada.

These instances are each related to a particular political dynamic, and together they reveal the range of competing political projects. For example, the United Kingdom's policy of devolution was tested by Labour in a 1979 referendum before the party's defeat in general elections that year. Devolution could not ultimately be implemented until Labour's return to power under Tony Blair in 1997.

In Belgium, institutional practices of another type were introduced: decentralized institutions were established to promote the regionalization of government policy. The Flemish and Walloon regions were set up in 1980; the Brussels-Capital Region was formed only in 1988. Each of them was given specific powers in the areas of transport, housing, industrial development, and environmental protection.

Spain presents a distinct case in that from the late 1970s on it endeavoured to establish a regime of differential autonomy throughout the country. Implementation of this system enabled Spain to respond, in part, to two major challenges. First, the country had to make the transition to democracy, which had been so long awaited and demanded by increasingly important stakeholders. Second, it had to put in place a meaningful model of "ethnoterritorial concurrence[5]" to respond to the expectations of the regions and nations that make up the polity.

The Canadian experience, too, is distinct in many ways. Although it inherited the British parliamentary system, Canada also opted for a federal structure as a means of managing tensions between its two main founding communities. Unlike Belgium, which gradually came to favour policies to segregate the communities and thus reduce conflict between them, Canada sought instead to impose "standardizing" policies in order to erode the traits that distinguish the linguistic communities from each other. Moreover, while Belgium sought to implement confederal practices, Canada opted for policies imposed by Ottawa in areas outside its purview; a non-exhaustive list includes health, infrastructure, transport, education, and labour-force training. Thus, as Belgium was

---

5   Luis Moreno (2001), "Ethnoterritorial Concurrence in Multinational Societies: the Spanish communidades autonomas," in *Multinational Democracies*, eds. Alain-G. Gagnon and James Tully, Cambridge: Cambridge University Press, 201–221.

gradually becoming a federation, Canada was defederalizing and recentraliz-
ing policy leadership in Ottawa[6].

The Canadian case also differs markedly from the Spanish one. Despite a
number of systemic defects—what Ronald Watts has dubbed the "pathologies
of federalism[7]"— Canada is nonetheless a "negotiated country[8]" rather than an
imposed one, like the United States. Canada can thus lay claim to greater re-
spectability in international institutions and is deemed more hospitable to im-
migrants seeking a new place to live and national minorities from states where
democratic practices are wanting.

The last thirty years (1981-2011)—since planning began for the patriation
of the Constitution from the United Kingdom—have been characterized by periods of great tension between Quebec, the First Nations and the central government[9]. During this period, the central government has employed a variety
of strategies to impose its will within the federation. Immediately after the
Quebec government's first referendum in May 1980, the government of Canada embarked on a major four-pronged constitutional initiative, which involved: (1) entrenching a Canadian Charter of Rights and Freedoms; (2) seeking recognition of equal status for each of the federation's member states; (3)
making the Supreme Court the final arbiter of jurisdictional disputes; and (4)
imposing significant limits on the member states in their own fields of jurisdiction through the "federal" spending power. As a result of this sweeping program, Canada has become more of a territorial federal system, and the charac-
teristic features of multinational federalism (respect for and promotion of national diversity, a quest for checks and balances, safeguards for minority nations) have been eroded.

Several factors are responsible for these changes, which have been so detrimental to the spirit of federalism. We shall note only four of the most critical
of these.

- A laissez-faire approach to the economy has resulted in political actors increasingly
being sidelined.
- Inter-regional solidarity (support for equalization policies) is at its lowest ebb ever,
as member states have competed to attract private investment (New Brunswick) or

6   For a comparison of the way federal practices have evolved in Belgium and Canada, see Dimitrios Karmis and Alain-G. Gagnon, "Federalism, Federation and Collective Identities in
Canada and Belgium: Different Routes, Similar Fragmentation," in *Multinational Democracies*, eds. Gagnon and Tully, *op.cit.* 137-175.

7   Ronald Watts (1998) "Federalism, Federal Political Systems. and Federations," *Annual Review of Political Science*, 1: 117–137.

8   See Alain-G. Gagnon and Richard Simeon (2010) "Canada," in *Diversity and Unity in Federal
Countries*, eds. Luis Moreno and César Colino, Montreal: McGill-Queen's University Press,
109–138.

9   See Alain-G. Gagnon (2011) *Le temps des incertitudes : essais sur le fédéralisme et la diversité nationale*, Quebec: Les Presses de l'Université Laval.

obtain favours from the central government for new economic initiatives (Newfoundland, Nova Scotia).

- The accumulated of deficits of most of the member states have kept them from introducing public policies that would allow them to respond adequately and rapidly to
changed economic conditions.
- The member states (apart from Quebec) have tended to tolerate non-constitutional
policy changes and thus helped consolidate central institutions while they weakened
themselves.

In 2003, the member states set up a Council of the Federation to make common
cause and develop joint strategies to take on the central government. However,
they have proven unable to present a common front in making demands on
Ottawa because of conflicts among themselves, conflicts sometimes fanned by
the central government (competing development of hydroelectric basins, exploration of tar sands vs. development of clean energy, a single vs. a polycentric financial market, etc.).

The government of Canada has thus engaged in putting in place a policy of
renationalization rather than one responsive to the needs of each major region
and each national community.

This policy of renationalization and reterritorialization has proceeded on
several fronts. In the area of the economy, it was imposed through a policy of
free-trade for all of Canada and all of the North American economic area that
culminated in the plan for a North American Free Trade Agreement (NAFTA)
(Macdonald Commission, 1982-1985). In the constitutional sphere, it was imposed through patriation in 1982 and the erection of the Supreme Court as a
symbol of prime importance. In terms of identity, it was imposed on new arri-
vals to the country by demanding allegiance to Canadian institutions above all
others. It was also imposed through a wide range of government programs on
matters to which citizens are most sensitive (health and social services, pen-
sions, education, labour-market access, etc.).

Drawing inspiration from the policies of the *new public management,* the
central government throughout the 1990s also sought to have the member
states do what it could not do by imposing conditions and standards for strategic projects in exchange for financial assistance.

The multilevel approach seems, in a way, to be a more sophisticated version
of the new public management. It involves monitoring the various political
actors' activities in order to manage them more effectively with no regard either for the societal structures that underpin the functioning of the polity or for
cultural issues. This is the subject we shall explore more thoroughly in the next
section.

The "multilevel" approach

The proponents of the multilevel approach state as a general observation that the Westphalian system is no longer able to manage the diversity that characterizes complex states; a system is needed that better reflects institutional practices that buttress and sustain the democratic process. These authors have attempted to identify the different forms of institutionalized power by focussing on the various sites where power is exercised. They have thus helped highlight the role of actors who are often overlooked in the implementation of government programs and policies. However, their work reveals very little about the objectives that actors in positions of dominance pursue in their decision making. These authors have used the terms "inclusive democracy" and "integrative democracy" to indicate that what is involved is the notion that, on the one hand, all demands made by all actors must be taken into account when decisions are made and, on the other, all individuals are interchangeable.

The standard bearers of the multilevel approach generally declare that they wish to extend and enrich democratic practices by making room in the decision-making process for all actors without discrimination. Their endeavour involves, as it were, mapping the political actors at different intervention levels (municipal, regional, provincial, overarching state, international, etc.) in order to give them a say. However, no regard is paid to the communities behind the compact that may have led to the creation of a constituted nation state in the first place.

Many researchers are currently attempting to reconcile the notions of multilevel governance and federalism. Most of them, though, rarely take the time to distinguish between territorial (mononational) federal systems and multinational ones. This fundamental distinction is generally reduced to an issue of mere semantic variation (related to form) rather than dealt with as an existential difference (related to content).

Such distinctions matter, however, for they cast light on the nature and scope of the *demos*. Briefly, it is important to know if a polity is founded on a single *demos* or bases its legitimacy on a number of *demoi*. Ferran Requejo's and Ramon Maiz's examinations of the Spanish case in a comparative context are of great value on this score[10].

Discussion of multilevel governance tends (as does the new public management) to divert us from questions about the nature of the *demos* (by confirming and validating the established hierarchy of power relationships) and to ignore

---

10 Ferran Requejo (2011) *Fédéralisme multinational et pluralisme de valeurs* (Brussels: Peter Lang/Presses interuniversitaires européennes, 2009); Ramon Maiz, *The Inner Frontier: The Place of Nation in the Political Theory of Democracy and Federalism,* Brussels: Presses interuniversitaires européennes/Peter Lang.

issues of governmental autonomy: that is, the two main pillars of the notion of federalism[11].

There are at least five reasons why this situation should be of concern.

- The multilevel approach does not differentiate between federal and non-federal systems since both exhibit the same governance practices and the same sort of extension of powers.
- Nor—and this is a major weakness—does the multilevel approach distinguish between territorial (mononational) and multinational federations.
- In the multilevel approach, there is no concept of a fragmented sovereignty, yet this notion lies at the very basis of the federalist regime. Power is instead conceived as emerging from a single matrix, as if carried by a transmission belt from a single centre. The logic underlying the application of the multilevel approach thus rests on a vision of power relations that is hierarchical rather than community-based (and thus subject to territorialization).
- Nothing in the multilevel approach gives grounds to believe in the possibility of achieving a system that would be more representative of national communities in central institutions. Nor does anything in the approach guarantee the empowerment of national communities within overarching institutions or in particular territories. What we observe, rather, are sites for representation based on a variety of mobilizing principles (environmental groups, social movements of various types, political families, interest groups, the business world, municipalities, cities, and networks of all sorts).
- The principle of effectiveness, in this view, trumps the principle of legitimacy. In other words, there is no point in demanding respect for the distribution of powers since what matters above all else is the ability of the actors to put in place measures that meet the needs of citizens irrespective of the community they come from. Authors of this school thus tend to document the implementation of public policies rather than see whether the constitutional framework freely negotiated by the political communities is respected[12].

We would argue that the primary objective of the multilevel approach is not better representation of political actors and socioeconomic interests. Rather, it serves political and economic groups in a position of authority acting in the name of an actual *Staatsvolk*[13].

This approach allows the political centre to set itself up as the defender of a monolithic, integrated, flexible, and malleable system. In other words, far from contributing to the democratization of political practice in a nationally diverse environment, it is characterized by a bias in favour of the centre and its policies, often to the detriment of equally legitimate preferences voiced by

---

11 cf. Alain-G. Gagnon and Michael Keating, eds. (2012) *Autonomy: Imagining Democratic Alternatives in Complex Settings*, London: Palgrave Macmillan.

12 Three cases might be explored in this regard: the implementation of the Canadian social union, the merger of Canadian financial markets and agricultural policy. In each case, Canada's central government did not hesitate to try to impose its authority even though its constitutional role was disputed.

13 Brendan O'Leary stresses that the existence, authority and leadership of the *Staatsvolk* are necessary to guarantee the stability of the system.

community-based or regional authorities. Under cover of the multiplicity of channels of influence and spaces for mobilization, the introduction of the multilevel approach thus actually helps reinforce the centre's grip on all the instruments of governance and the machinery of government itself.

Furthermore, the multilevel approach fails to consider an important distinction: that between *constitutive power* and *constituted power*. The notion of constituted power refers back to the agreements negotiated at the time of the founding of the state to legitimate the basic rules setting out the powers of the different orders of government and the roles of the executive, legislature and judiciary. Constituted power is thus represented by all the rules and powers laid out in the Constitution. It consequently acts as a brake on the enthusiasm of political actors who might otherwise want to change the rules of the game in response to changing circumstances. The notion of constitutive power has to do with the way constitutional practices may change in accordance with the freely affirmed will of social, economic and political actors. It entails consideration of the repositioning of political families, citizens' expectations and shifting power relations over the long run[14].

These shortcomings have significant consequences. In plain terms, they enable political actors in positions of authority to dispense with making any sustained effort to seek democratic validation for non-constitutional changes[15]. The outcomes are policies all too often detrimental to minority nations in complex political entities.

Behind these issues lies another that is at least as—if not more—important: the undermining of democratic practices and the presumption that all the original partners in the constitutional compact accept changes to the system even without their having to give their consent.

The multilevel approach thus has many weaknesses, most particularly in nationally diverse settings; hence the urgency of correcting the deficiencies we have outlined. Achieving this goal in a context of national diversity entails implementing and respecting a federalism that is multinational in nature. This is the subject to which we shall turn in the next section.

---

14 For a more extensive discussion of the distinction between constitutive power and constituted power, see Maiz, *The Inner Frontier: The Place of Nation in the Political Theory of Democracy and Federalism*, 158–159.

15 Jennifer Smith (1995) "The Unsolvable Constitutional Crisis," in *New Trends in Canadian Federalism,* eds. François Rocher and Miriam Smith, Peterborough: Broadview Press, 1995, 67–90; Jennifer Smith (2002) "Informal Constitutional Development: Change by Other Means," in *Canadian Federalism: Performance, Effectiveness, and Legitimacy,* eds. Herman Bakvis and Grace Skogstad, Toronto: Oxford University Press.

The multinational approach to federalism

The idea of federalism makes it possible to contemplate the state and imagine the sharing of sovereignty[16]. The multilevel-governance approach (at least as presented in the literature) does not; rather, it presumes that power emanates from a single source of legitimacy, as in states, whether unitary or federal, pursuing a course of nation building[17].

In light of the preceding discussion, the lustre of classical federalism must be restored by taking as our point of departure the negotiated nature of inter-community relations. We cannot make do with a focus on questions of good governance, which evolves as a function of relationships of power, exercised through acquiescence in the right of might[18].

By accepting the premise that power must be shared and national communities provided with the tools essential to their emancipation as collectivities, multinational federations make it possible to achieve major advances in broadening and deepening democratic practice. It is on this basis that complex political regimes will be able to establish their legitimacy and thus guarantee the stability and durability of existing institutions[19].

As Ramon Maiz pointed out, a federal state is by definition a *constitutional state without a sovereign* considering that all its powers are distributed in different spheres and limited and subject to the constitution of the federation and the constitutions/statutes of its member states. Under the principle of *competence*, which stands in for *hierarchy*, there is no place for any supposedly originating or unlimited power of the state or of the federated states[20].

This approach leaves ample room for respect for founding entities, ongoing negotiation between political actors and empowerment of the various national communities aspiring to progress in circumstances in which they are not

---

16 See the papers published in Michael Burgess and Alain-G. Gagnon (2010) eds., *Federal Democracies*, London: Routledge.

17 Ferran Requejo devoted a major study to the subject of the democratic legitimacy of states; see *Fédéralisme multinational et pluralisme de valeurs : le cas espagnol* (2007), Brussels: PIE-Peter Lang, 2007, especially Chapter 2 "Légitimité démocratique et pluralisme national," 43–69.

18 André Leton and André Miroir (1999) *Les conflits communautaires en Belgique*, Paris, Les Presses universitaires de France; Alain-G. Gagnon (2008) *La raison du plus fort : plaidoyer pour le fédéralisme multinational*, Montreal: Québec Amérique.

19 See the studies by the Groupe de recherche sur les sociétés plurinationales (GRSP) including Alain-G. Gagnon and James Tully (2001) *Multinational Democracies*, Cambridge: Cambridge University Press, as well as A.-G. Gagnon, Montserrat Guibernau and François Rocher (2003) eds., *The Conditions of Diversity in Multinational Democracies*, Montreal: McGill-Queen's University Press.

20 Maiz, *The Inner Frontier: The Place of Nation in the Political Theory of Democracy and Federalism*, 191.

predominant. The realization of this objective remains a major challenge requiring the sustained raising of awareness and political alertness.

Territorial federalism does not take into consideration the possible presence of more than one *demos* in a federation since it seeks to impose a vision of a unified (if not unitary) state. The proponents of territorial federalism draw their inspiration from the American model, which was imposed on a very grand scale.

This observation leads us to point out the distinction between the sham federalism of the territorial or mononational type and the multinational federalism that is all too often ignored in the literature. This distinction ought to be a central concern for leaders in nationally diverse states.

A federation is a complex form of political system based on a constitution with formal and informal elements that links together different orders of government[21]. One particularity of federalism is that it simultaneously embodies both the *constitutive power* and the *constituted power;* it remains open to the test of deliberation and seeks to nourish the innovative capacities of political actors trying to change the regime through the democratic process. In these terms, multinational federalism is the most advanced form of complex, democratic political system.

Thinking about the multinational federal state means contemplating a federation of nations living side by side and, consequently, the coexistence of national sovereignties in one and the same state. It thus means thinking about federalism as divided and shared sovereignty.... By means of the division of sovereignty that is the specific feature of federalism, power will stand against power and offer protection from any abuse and any of the temptations of majority. National sovereignties coexisting within the federal state would consequently be limited[22].

The multinational approach opens the way to new considerations, particularly of the idea of a compact or agreement that can be updated by the original partners in the polity. In the late 1960s, Carl Friedrich (1968) dealt with the issue at length in *Trends of Federalism in Theory and Practice*[23]. The idea of an *open process* for the construction of a shared political project is worth noting here.

Multinational federalism is a far cry from the multilevel approach presented in the literature. In it, members of the different nations forming the multination are free to challenge the rules on behalf of their respective *demos* and to seek to institute new methods of accommodation that may evolve in time and space.

21 Michael Foley (1989) *The Silence of Constitutions: Gaps, Abeyances and Political Temperament in the Maintenance of Government*, London: Routledge.

22 Christophe Parent (2011) *Le concept d'État fédéral multinational: Essai sur l'union des peuples*, Brussels: PIE-Peter Lang, 26. [Translated from French]

23 Carl J. Friedrich (1968) *Trends of Federalism in Theory and Practice*, New York: Praeger.

However, many of the authors specializing in the study of federalism are opposed to multinational institutions. Their opposition is generally based on the preconception that leaders of minority nations tend to fight for the breakup of existing states for their own benefit rather than seek ways to resolve the conflicts inherent in federal systems.

Hudson Meadwell thus wrote, "Consociational federalism preserves differences and encourages substate nationalism, while providing nationalists with an embryonic state. It increases the political feasibility of secession and, at the same time, its institutional arrangements help to resolve problems of co-ordination and free riding in nationalist collective action[24]". This statement is more of a normative indictment of pluralistic federalism than an impartial view of the problems inherent in the establishment of federal regimes.

Similarly, Svante Cornell, who identified six factors (borders, national identity, existence of institutions, leaders, media, external support) to explain the rise of secessionist movements in the Caucasus, maintains that one should be wary of reserving powers or drawing up systems of autonomy for the benefit of ethnocultural minorities. Rather, he argues for establishing an overarching, standardizing state in order to maintain existing regimes[25].

Most of the authors opposed to multinational federalism cite the cases of Czechoslovakia, Yugoslavia and the Soviet Union. None of these federations was able to resist centrifugal forces. However, as John McGarry points out, "The multinational federations that have succeeded, including Canada and Belgium, were born out of voluntary agreements. Most of the federations that failed were, for their part, formed without the consent of their communities[26]". In other words, systems based on coercion are not appropriate examples.

In conclusion: Appropriate interpretive tools to deal with the democratic challenges of our time

Specialists on (territorial) federalism are responsible for much of the literature inspired by the multilevel approach. The literature indeed reflects a significant bias in favour of this approach, which claims to be open, dynamic, progressive,

24 Hudson Meadwell (2002) "When Voice Encourages Exit," in *Regionalism and Party Politics in Canada*, eds. Lisa Young and Keith Archer, Toronto: Oxford University Press, 198.

25 Svante E. Cornell (2001) "Autonomy as a Source of Conflict: Caucasian Conflicts in Theoretical Perspective," *World Politics*, 54, no 2: 253; and by the same author (2001) *Small Nations and Great Powers: A Study of Ethnopolitical Conflict in the Caucasus*, Richmond, UK: Curzon Press.

26 John McGarry (2004) "Le fédéralisme peut-il contribuer à concilier la diversité ethnique et nationale?" *Fédérations*, 4, no 1: 3–6. [Translated from French]

flexible, and effective. As this paper shows, a multilevel reading fails to take into account the foundations or traditions of a society; it ignores the social solidarity essential to the maintenance of social connectedness. In short, the multilevel approach ignores issues related to national diversity or the question of dual legitimacy in a multinational context.

The multilevel approach is not without merit in a standardized, unified society in which the only concerns deemed pertinent relate to efficiency, rationality, effectiveness, productivity, and the economy. Such societies are rather rare, though, for the world we live in is characterized by societal and ideological heterogeneity. We therefore have to imagine models that are better able to take into consideration national diversity and community pluralism. That is what we have tried to do here by suggesting implementation of a multinational federal state for countries trying to attain the federal ideal.

More cutting-edge scenarios must be imagined in order to respond to a threefold challenge. First, contrary to Harold Laski's suggestions in 1939 in an environment in which big business was already highly concentrated, the member states of federations generally have significant powers to meet the needs of their constituents; in our opinion, far from being obsolete, (pluralistic) federalism possesses intrinsic qualities that merit further development[27]. Second, the social, cultural, political, and economic leadership of the member states in multinational entities can help legitimate existing institutions and nurture solidarity between citizens, political actors and the institutions of civil society[28]. Third, multinational federalism would also help the societies behind the original constitutional compact make progress by allowing them to focus on fundamental preferences (content) rather than on merely defending more superficial ones (form).

In short, in contrast to the multilevel approach, the multinational approach makes it possible to imagine scenarios of sustained, continual democratic deliberation and debate, while offering individuals, groups and associated nations real societal choices.

27 Harold Laski (1939) "The Obsolescence of Federalism" *The New Republic: A Journal of Opinion*, no 3, 307–309.
28 Milton Esman, "State Sovereignty: Alive and Well" in *Sovereignty Under Challenge: How Governments Respond,* eds. John D. Montgomery and Nathan Glazer, New Brunswick, N.J.: Transaction.

References

Amoretti, Ugo (2011). "Italy: Increasing Decentralisation, Decreasing Asymmetry," in Federalism beyond Federations: Asymmetry and Processes of Resymmetrisation in Europe, eds. Ferran Requejo and Klaus-Jürgen Nagel, Farnham: Ashgate, 61–79.

Bakvis, Herman and Grace Skogstad, eds. (2002). Canadian Federalism: Performance, Effectiveness, and Legitimacy, Toronto: Oxford University Press.

Burgess, Michael and Alain-G. Gagnon. (2010) eds., Federal Democracies, London: Routledge.

Cornell, Svante E. (2001) "Autonomy as a Source of Conflict: Caucasian Conflicts in Theoretical Perspective," World Politics, 54 (2).

Cornell, Svante E. (2001) Small Nations and Great Powers: A Study of Ethnopolitical Conflict in the Caucasus, Richmond, UK: Curzon Press.

Esman, Milton, "State Sovereignty: Alive and Well" in Sovereignty Under Challenge: How Governments Respond, eds. John D. Montgomery and Nathan Glazer, New Brunswick, N.J.: Transaction.

Foley, Michael (1989). The Silence of Constitutions: Gaps, Abeyances and Political Temperament in the Maintenance of Government, London: Routledge.

Friedrich, Carl J. (1968), Trends of Federalism in Theory and Practice, New York: Praeger.

Gagnon, Alain-G. and Richard Simeon (2010) "Canada," in Diversity and Unity in Federal Countries, eds. Luis Moreno and César Colino, Montréal: McGill-Queen's University Press, 109–138.

Gagnon, Alain-G. (2011) Le temps des incertitudes : essais sur le fédéralisme et la diversité nationale, Québec: Les Presses de l'Université Laval.

Gagnon, Alain-G. and Michael Keating, eds. (2012) Autonomy: Imagining Democratic Alternatives in Complex Settings, London: Palgrave Macmillan.

Gagnon, Alain-G. (2008) La raison du plus fort : plaidoyer pour le fédéralisme multinational, Montréal: Québec Amérique.

Gagnon, Alain-G., Montserrat Guibernau and François Rocher (2003) eds., The Conditions of Diversity in Multinational Democracies, Montreal: McGill-Queen's University Press.

Karmis, Dimitrios and Alain-G. Gagnon (2001), "Federalism, Federation and Collective Identities in Canada and Belgium: Different Routes, Similar Fragmentation," in Multinational Democracies, eds. Gagnon and Tully, op.cit. 137-175.

Kraus, Peter (2008), A Union of Diversity: Language, Diversity and Polity Building in Europe (Cambridge: Cambridge University Press)

Laforest, Guy (2010) "The Meaning of Canadian Federalism in Quebec: Critical Reflections," Revista d'Estudis Autonomics i Federals, no 11, 10–55.

Laski, Harold (1939) "The Obsolescence of Federalism" The New Republic: A Journal of Opinion, no 3, 307–309.

Leton, André and André Miroir (1999) Les conflits communautaires en Belgique, Paris, Les Presses universitaires de France.

Maiz, Ramon (2011) The Inner Frontier: The Place of Nation in the Political Theory of Democracy and Federalism (Brussels: Peter Lang/Presses interuniversitaires européennes.

McGarry, John (2004) "Le fédéralisme peut-il contribuer à concilier la diversité ethnique et nationale?" Fédérations, 4, no 1: 3–6.

Meadwell, Hudson (2002) "When Voice Encourages Exit," in Regionalism and Party Politics in Canada, eds. Lisa Young and Keith Archer, Toronto: Oxford University Press, 198.

Moreno, Luis (2001), "Ethnotrerritorial Concurrence in Multinational Societies: the Spanish comunidades autonomas," in Multinational Democracies, eds. Alain-G. Gagnon and James Tully, Cambridge: Cambridge University Press, 201–221.

Parent, Christophe (2011) Le concept d'État fédéral multinational : Essai sur l'union des peuples, Brussels: PIE-Peter Lang.

Requejo, Ferran and Klaus-Jürgen Nagel, eds. (2011), Federalism beyond Federation, Franham, Ashgate.

Requejo, Ferran (2007), Fédéralisme multinational et pluralisme de valeurs : le cas espagnol, Brussels: PIE-Peter Lang, especially Chapter 2 "Légitimité démocratique et pluralisme national," 43–69.

Sauca, José Maria (2010) Identidad y Derecho : nuevas perspectivas para viejos debates (Valencia: Tirant lo blanch.

Smith, Jennifer (1995). "The Unsolvable Constitutional Crisis," in New Trends in Canadian Federalism, eds. François Rocher and Miriam Smith, Peterborough: Broadview Press, 67–90.

Smith, Jennifer (2002). "Informal Constitutional Development: Change by Other Means," in Canadian Federalism: Performance, Effectiveness, and Legitimacy, eds. Herman Bakvis and Grace Skogstad, Toronto: Oxford University Press.

Watts, Ronald. (1998). "Federalism, Federal Political Systems and Federations," Annual Review of Political Science (1), 117–137.

Part II
Trust and mistrust and how it shapes central-regional-local relationships

Chapter 4
The Rise and Fall of Institutional Trust in Spain

Francisco J. Llera Ramo*, Universidad del País Vasco

Introduction

Spain currently has the most long-lasting constitution in its history (passed in 1978) and since its exemplary transition (1976-1978) has been enjoying its longest and most successful period of democracy. The balance of the 30-year reign of Juan Carlos I, particularly since the country's entry into the EU, can be characterised by a modernising leap forward in Spanish society, its economy and politics. However, there have been symptoms of institutional fatigue in recent years. The successful, rapid and peaceful ending of a 40-yearlong dictatorship through a consensual transition, followed by Spain's institutional, social and economic performance, explain the satisfaction indicators in Spanish society during this first stage of democracy (McDonough, Barnes and Lopez Pina, 1994; Wert, 1996, and Montero, Gunther and Torcal, 1997). The Spanish people had recovered their collective self-esteem and regained international recognition: the "Spanish miracle" had taken place. However, the brutal onset of the global financial crisis in late 2007 and its subsequent impact throughout Europe came as a surprise to a society in the midst of a consumerist feast and unconcerned about the performance of its political class. A sign of too much trust[1]?

Thus, in the spring 2004 Eurobarometer[2], we find that the level of satisfaction with the functioning of democracy in Spain had reached a record high of 65% (compared to 31% who were dissatisfied), placing the Spanish among the Europeans most satisfied with their democratic system and well above the EU-15 average (54%). The level of satisfaction in Spain contrasted with that found

---

*   This paper includes some of the results of the research project, CSO2009-14381-C03-01; it has also been made possible thanks to the funding the research team received from the Basque Government (IT-323-07).

1   See Morlino's excellent study (2003) for a comparison of problems regarding quality, satisfaction and legitimacy in recent democracies.

2   It is important to remember that during the fieldwork in 2004 (between 20 February and 28 March) two important events occurred in Spain: the Islamist terrorist attack in Madrid resulting in 200 deaths and close to 2,000 wounded and the change in government after the general elections on 14 March.

in Portugal (31%) and Italy (35%), and was only surpassed by that of Denmark (90%), Luxembourg (80%) and Finland (77%). However, during this same period, the level of satisfaction in Spain with the democratic functioning of the EU was slightly lower (57% of the Spanish were satisfied), compared to Luxembourg (62%) and Ireland and Greece (both 61%), with the highest levels of dissatisfaction found in Finland and Sweden (53%). In the spring of 2007[3], Spain was still the second most Europeanist country, with 73% of the Spanish expressing satisfaction with the country's membership in the EU (following Ireland with 77%). Some months later, in the fall of that same year[4], the European averages for trust in national governments and national parliaments were 34% and 35% respectively, while in Spain they were 49% and 47%, respectively, with parallel levels of distrust of 45% and 43%.

Seven years later, according to the latest Eurobarometer in the autumn of 2011[5], the EU (now 27) average regarding satisfaction with the functioning of democracy in each country had changed little (52% satisfied vs. 46% dissatisfied), but in Spain the level of dissatisfaction was greater than the level of satisfaction (53% vs. 45%) – representing a 20-point decline in those who were satisfied and a parallel increase in the percentage that were dissatisfied. The countries where a majority was satisfied ranged from Malta with 50% satisfied to Denmark with a high of 92%, followed by Luxembourg (88%), Sweden (87%), Finland (77%), the Netherlands (75%), Austria (73%), Germany (68%), Belgium (61%), the United Kingdom (60%), Poland (59%), Ireland (57%) and France (53%). In contrast, the countries where a majority was dissatisfied ranged from the 52% dissatisfied in Estonia to the high of 83% in Greece, followed by Romania (76%), Lithuania (75%), Bulgaria (71%), Portugal, Hungary and Czech Republic (68%), Slovakia (66%), Italy (65%), Latvia (60%), Slovenia (58%), Cyprus (56%) and Spain (53%). This reveals a clear contrast between the old European democracies of central and northern Europe and the democracies of eastern and southern Europe. However, regarding satisfaction with the functioning of democracy within the EU, Spain with 43% satisfied and 44% dissatisfied still comes close to the European average regarding levels of satisfaction (45%) and dissatisfaction (43%) – following a less negative but parallel trend to that of the above indicator – and very similar to that of Ireland (43% satisfaction vs. 42% dissatisfaction), but in contrast to the very negative percentages for Greece (29% satisfaction vs. 66% dissatisfaction) or more positive percentages for Sweden (52% satisfaction vs. 40% dissatisfaction) and Finland (49% satisfaction vs. 48% dissatisfaction). Although we can see the impact of the global financial crisis, this does not seem to be the only explanatory factor, at least in the case of Spain.

---

3 *Eurobarometer* No. 67 (2007).
4 *Eurobarometer* No. 68 (2007).
5 *Eurobarometer* No. 76 (2011).

In the following pages, we will try to clarify the nature and degree of the erosion of institutional trust in Spain, explaining its relationship to the economic and social crisis of the country as well as to a potential crisis of the political regime (Easton, 1975).

Economic crisis or political crisis or both at the same time

Seventy years ago, Schumpeter, in his book Capitalism, Socialism and Democracy (1942), reflected on the balance that exists between democracy and the market. It is now more important than ever to address this seminal issue once again. If the current crisis reveals anything, it is the imbalance that exists in favour of the market and the clear retreat of democracy (Fitoussi, 2004), threatening the social contract, the foundation of our democracies. This is what some have called "state of economic emergency" (Beck, 2005) or the "quiet coup" (Johnson, 2009). Present-day globalisation (Rodrik, 2011) is changing our lives and, above all, our democracies and the relationship between the economy and politics. Today there is a crisis in our traditional political and ideological references, a growth of mistrust, insecurity, fear, doubt and scepticism regarding the ability of our political representatives and even our nation states to provide answers to the problems we face. This is because the centre of decision making is far removed from our parliaments and the institutional systems of our national democracies, where we, as citizens, have established and maintained our social contract. But paradoxically, the hypertrophy of the state is bringing about a re-evaluation of the role of local and regional institutions, which are closer to the citizenry; on the one hand, multiplying intergovernmental tensions and on the other, reshaping the role of actors in civil society.

The prolonged economic crisis[6] – involving among other aspects, the financial system, public debt, the productive model, unemployment and social cohesion – has only exacerbated the weaknesses of the Spanish political system, affecting institutions, attitudes and political culture, the party system, political representation, socio-economic actors, local elites and intergovernmental

---

6   The consequences of this economic crisis, which hit Spain in 2008 (unprecedented fall in GDP, increased public debt, banking crisis, business closures, declining confidence in the country risk, etc.), are alarming when you consider that at the end of 2011 the unemployment rate (21.6%) was the highest in the EU (with a youth unemployment rate over 50% and more than one million households with no members employed), 25.5% of the Spanish population is at risk of poverty (8th in the EU-27) and the country is on the threshold of its second recession in only three years.

relations, as can be seen in the evolution of Spanish public opinion over the last four years. But above all, the crisis is seriously affecting national cohesion and the model of decentralisation, exacerbating interregional and centre-periphery tensions. Among other indicators, we find a bias toward recentralisation in Spanish public opinion in contrast to the centrifugal dynamic and demand for greater autonomy from Catalonia (tensions over financial/ fiscal issues and identity) and the Basque Country (tensions over identity and the end of terrorism) and comparative grievances between regions together with a weakening of interregional solidarity (particularly in Catalonia).

It is not easy to talk about a political crisis (Lamo, 2011 and Llera 2011) in a period affected by an economic crisis and the enormous difficulties involved in responding to it[7]. However, the positions political actors are taking and the ways in which they are responding to the current crisis, as well as the shocks it is causing, are highly revealing of a deeper political crisis and one that has been long in coming in Spanish democracy. This political crisis is associated with the gradual decline of a consensual politics or a politics of agreement regarding basic issues or issues of state, which produced such good results during the democratic transition and 32 years ago led to the passage of the most long-lasting and broadly supported constitution in Spanish history. This conflictive dynamic among the main political actors complicates institutional relations, makes problem-solving difficult, weakens the performance of the political system and creates a sense of fatigue in the society toward politics. The dissatisfaction with democracy that is generated distorts the perception that citizens have of politics, breaks down their connections to it, weakens political representation and can have an impact on social harmony.

Thus, a more or less conjunctural political crisis could turn into one that is deeper and long-lasting. In this case, we would be talking about a crisis of political disaffection and, ultimately, of political legitimacy. A conjunctural crisis is linked to the image of and the support for key political actors or to levels of trust in certain key institutions, while a crisis of legitimacy would be systemic, affecting democracy itself and its constitutional stability. The very model of a multilevel and regional distribution of power, which has been our great institutional innovation, has been showing clear signs of fatigue, becoming a primary source of conflict. In this regard, it is highly revealing that, according to the latest barometer of the CIS (Centro de Investigaciones Socio-

---

7   The drastic adjustment policies in the most important public services provided by the welfare state (healthcare, education, etc.), the reduction of the workforce and salaries in the public sector, the reduction of labour and social rights and the dramatic decrease in public investment implemented starting in 2010 are among the causes of the defeat of the socialist government in the November 2011 elections.

lógicas)[8], the Spanish say that the political class is the third most important problem in Spain (22%), after unemployment (82.1%) and the economic crisis (50.4%) and well ahead of terrorism (4%). We may therefore be facing a crisis of political or institutional trust.

What is a crisis of political trust?

Political trust has two dimensions, organisational and individual, macro and micro. Organisational trust exists when citizens' expectations are met, when they consider institutions and the performance of government and political leaders to be effective, transparent and honest. This is, in reality, a question of how responsible institutions and policy makers are considered to be. Thus, as indicated by Newton and Norris (2000), political trust is a key indicator of citizens' underlying feelings about their political system. But as we said, political trust also has an individual dimension, which refers to the way authorities and political leaders carry out their public responsibilities. At the macro or organisational level, we can distinguish between diffuse trust, referring to the functioning of the institutional system in general and specific trust referring to specific institutions of a political regime itself. Finally, trust, both organisational and individual, is a question of the credibility of political performance at both levels.

"Trust, in this regard, emerges as one of the most important ingredients upon which the legitimacy and sustainability of political systems are built"; it is also key to citizens' delegation of power, based on their expectations about uncertain outcomes (Blind, 2006). Conversely, distrust can be generated by a lack of results, the frustration of expectations, the mishandling of the regulation of conflicts of interest, a lack of transparency in management by actors and institutions, inefficiency or corruption within the political class and other factors. However, just as too much trust in government tends to produce depoliticisation and apathy, a certain degree of distrust may be a necessary condition for the quality of a democracy. This deficit in trust tends to generate a greater political commitment on the part of the citizenry in certain circumstances and regarding certain political activities. As indicated by Norris (1999), a high degree of dissatisfaction with democracy and a low level of trust often go hand in hand, which means that while it is healthy to distrust the promises of

---

8   CIS study No. 2.923 from December 2011. The responses included were: "the political class and the political parties" (with 19.7%) and "the government, the politicians and the parties" (with another 2.3%), as well as "corruption and fraud" (6%).

politicians, lowering expectations about the results of their actions, chronic social and political distrust can be lethal for institutions and democratic governance.

Numerous survey studies (Cheema, 2005) – institutional and non-institutional[9] [9] – that for years have been measuring different aspects and levels of
both governmental and institutional trust, show that there has been a widespread and consistent decline in institutional trust since early 2004. For example, overall dissatisfaction with government in 2005[10] ranged from a low of
60% in North America to 61% in Africa, 65% in Western Europe and the Asian
Pacific, 69% in Latin America and 73% in Central and Eastern Europe. In addition, the longitudinal studies on levels of trust in institutions and political
leaders in different countries of the world carried out by Dalton (2005) show a
clear and consistent negative trend, with the exception of the Netherlands. The
multidimensional nature of political support in the new democracies should
also be emphasised (Gunther and Montero, 2006).

Figure 4.1: The evolution of political trust in Spain, 1996-2012

INDICADORES DE LA SITUACIÓN POLÍTICA. Series originales

Source: CIS, January 2012

---

9   Among others, the WEF, Eurobarometer, Asian Barometer, Latinobarometro, AGIMO,
    MORI, BBC and Gallup International, UNPAN, Transparency International, Pew Research
    Center and the Edelman Trust Barometer.
10 See BBC, Gallup International.

We will now look at the evolution of political trust in Spain, taking into account the time series for the synthetic indicator developed on the subject by the CIS[11]. Figure 4.1 shows very clearly the applicability of Dalton's findings to the Spanish case: There has been a nearly constant decline in trust from a high of 50% in 1996 to just over 40% today, after a rebound caused by the change in government last December, but in any case, much smaller than that found after the socialist victory in the 2004 general election, when levels of trust were over 60%. We can, therefore, state that there is a real crisis of political trust, at least in the Spanish case, which we will now try to decipher based on new empirical findings.

Symptoms of the crisis in political trust in Spain: political disaffection

Political disaffection (Torcal and Montero, 2006) can be understood as a set of attitudes that distance citizens from politics, institutions and politicians, and it arises from a loss of trust in the political – i.e. institutions and politicians – as a way to solve problems (a loss of expectations). It may also be due to a simple lack of understanding of the debates and relationships among political actors, without calling into question the legitimacy of the democratic regime. In any case, these factors generate a more or less chronic state of dissatisfaction with democracy, straining the relationship between citizens and politics.

In fact, according to our surveys, in 2007 only a third of the Spanish (33%) considered the political situation in Spain to be bad (compared to 26% who felt the opposite). However, after the outbreak of the crisis, in late 2010, over three quarters of Spanish citizens (78%) described the political situation as bad (compared to one in ten who thought the opposite)[12]. Responsibility for this was mainly attributed to current political leaders (56%), as well as to the institutional mechanisms of the political system (27%) or to both equally (13%). In late 2011, the situation had not improved and 85% had a negative perception of Spanish politics (versus only 5% with a positive opinion).

In this section, we will examine some of the most important indicators of political trust in Spain, taking into account their recent evolution[13] in the

---

11 The CIS (Centro de Investigaciones Sociológicas) is the governmental agency dedicated to opinion surveys in Spain and has an excellent database. The series was updated in January of 2012.

12 See the survey, "*Pulso de España*" [Pulse of Spain] carried out by the *Fundación Ortega-Marañón* and published in the *Biblioteca Nueva*, Madrid, 2011.

13 We primarily draw on data from the surveys carried out by our research team in 2007 and 2011 for the SEJ2006-15076-C03-01 and CSO2009-14381-C03-01 projects.

context of the current economic crisis. Specifically, we will look at politicisation, satisfaction with democracy, institutional trust, ties to parties, political representation and political leadership.

The politicisation of the Spanish

First, it should be noted that the overwhelming majority of the Spanish express negative feelings toward politics[14]: distrust (39.2%), indifference (15.7%), boredom (14.7%) and irritation (12.3%). In contrast to this, a small minority does express interest (8.7%), commitment (4.8%) and enthusiasm (1.9%), although the trend in recent years has clearly been negative.

However, despite the fact that the Spanish have predominantly negative feelings toward politics, the proportion who says they are very or quite interested in politics rose from 55% in 2007 to 60% in 2011, while the percentage of those who consider themselves very or quite well informed increased from 63% to 66% over the same period.

Dissatisfaction with democracy

According to our 2011 survey, there was a record high in the percentage of citizens dissatisfied with the functioning of democracy in Spain (62% dissatisfied vs. 32% satisfied): among voters of the right and voters for nationalist parties (65% and 57% respectively); among the electorate on the left (from 46% among voters for the Socialists to 65% among the voters for the Left United Party) and among those who abstain (59%); thus dissatisfaction was high, regardless of political or ideological affiliation. Most striking, however, has been the increase in dissatisfaction in recent years, as just four years ago, as seen in our own 2007 survey, the majority was still satisfied (55%), despite a slow decline. As shown in table 4.1 below, in just four years and due to the consequences of the political management of the crisis, satisfaction has fallen 23 points and dissatisfaction has risen 20, reversing the feelings of the majority of Spanish citizens toward the functioning of democracy. This trend sharpened in the last year of the socialist government due to their handling of the crisis, if we take into account that in the CIS barometer[15] [15] from November 2010, the majority was not dissatisfied (although the percentage of dissatisfaction did reach 47% of the population).

---

14 CIS Study No. 2.914 (October, 2011).
15 CIS Study No. 2.853 (November, 2010).

Table 4.1: Satisfaction with the functioning of democracy in Spain, 2007-2011

	2007	2011
Very satisfied	10%	6%
Quite satisfied	45%	26%
Neither satisfied or dissatisfied	–	6%
Not very satisfied	36%	43%
Not satisfied	6%	19%
DK/NA	3%	0%
Total	**100%**	**100%**

Source: F.J.Llera SEJ2006-15076 and CSO2009-14381

The decline in institutional trust

Opinion polls in Spain usually use a scale from 0 (low trust) to 10 (high trust) to measure the level of the public's trust in various institutions. Drawing on our surveys in 2007 and 2011 and using the same scale, we have created the following table (table 4.2), which shows the evolution of the Spanish public's trust in 20 public institutions and actors. The first thing that stands out is the nearly universal decline in trust toward most institutions, and in particular, toward the King. In 2007, the King obtained the highest score (7.2) but fell to fourth position in 2011 with a score of 5.79 (the same as the EU), although with the highest standard deviation (3.32). Only the police, the most highly rated institution in 2011 (7.01), the armed forces (6.83), NGOs (6.37) and NATO (5.17) maintained or improved their trust ratings. In 2007, 14 out of 19 institutions had scores over 5, whereas in 2011, this was the case for only 11 of the 20, after the collapse in trust toward national representative institutions (the Congress and Senate) and national and regional executives. Today, the police, the armed forces, NGOs, the King and the EU are followed in the ranking by municipal governments (5.29), NATO (5.17), the European Parliament (5.16), the regional parliaments (5.08), the media (5.05) and the Constitutional Court (5). Below them, the other 9 institutions do not reach the conventional level of approval (5): the Congress of Deputies (4.87), regional governments (4.83), business organisations (4.32), the justice system (4.28), the Senate (4.07), the Government of Spain (3.93), the Church (3.76), the political parties (3.38) and the unions (3.26).

Table 4.2: Trust in different institutions

	2007		2011	
	AVG	STAN DEV	AVG	STAN DEV
The King	7,20	2,83	5,79	3,32
The Constitutional Court	6,08	2,58	5,00	2,91
The Congress of Deputies	5,54	2,47	4,87	2,76
The Senate	5,45	2,49	4,07	2,78
The Spanish government	5,46	2,87	3,93	2,97
The justice system	4,79	2,58	4,28	2,81
The Armed Forces	6,72	2,66	6,83	2,67
The European Union	6,67	2,15	5,79	2,59
NATO	5,20	2,71	5,17	2,79
The parliaments of the autonomous regions	5,67	2,52	5,08	2,81
The autonomous regional governments	5,66	2,71	4,83	2,86
The European Parliament	6,06	2,24	5,16	2,56
Municipal governments	5,45	2,82	5,29	2,86
The church	4,19	3,25	3,76	3,30
The national police and the Guardia Civil	7,03	2,50	7,01	2,56
NGOs	6,17	2,53	6,37	2,64
The political parties	4,22	2,39	3,38	2,59
The unions	4,58	2,61	3,26	2,80
Business organisations	4,92	2,12	4,32	2,70
The media	–	—	5,05	2,58

Source: F.J.Llera SEJ2006-15076 and CSO2009-14381

Party politics fatigue and the crisis of representation

We have just seen that political parties and trade unions are the institutions that Spanish citizens trust the least[16]. Moreover, while party identification reached 47% in 2007, it had fallen to 38% in 2011. This decline in trust in political parties and party identification is related to a series of indicators that clearly compound party politics fatigue in Spain. Thus, although a majority of citizens[17] still consider the parties to be necessary for the functioning of demo-

---

16 The anti-party feeling in the democracies of southern Europe is well-known (Torcal, Gunther and Montero, 2001).

17 Data from our previously cited 2007 and 2011 surveys.

cracy (66% in 2011, an 11 point decline since 2007), defending the interests of different social groups and classes (70% in 2011, a 12 point decline from 2007) and for channelling citizen participation in political life (50% in 2011, a 25 point decline), the public sees the parties as too focused on their own particular interests and fights (77%, representing a 7 point increase since 2007), despite their dialectic of (more or less ritualistic) confrontation among each other.

The citizenry holds the political parties and the political class responsible for this disaffection because they see them as being overly concerned with power and party problems. Thus, in our survey, 95% think parties make too many promises that they cannot keep, and 83% believe that, increasingly, what is most important for the major parties is to remain in power, even if that means abandoning some of their ideals. As a result, 75% believe that the parties do not take the demands of ordinary people into account (an increase of 31 points since 2007); this is also related to the perception that their current way of operating prevents the parties from recruiting the most qualified and well-prepared persons (67%). In addition, the parties are seen as being too entangled in inter-party confrontations, despite there not being clear differences between them (77%, 7 points higher than in 2007). The public believes that the main reason for standing for election is the power and influence that is obtained from holding political office (78%, an increase of 27 points since 2007).

In our 2011 survey, 58% of respondents believed that Spanish political life, due to partisan conflicts typical of the politics of a system dominated by two parties, had become tenser than ever; 91% felt that these conflicts had an impact on daily life. But most importantly, the vast majority of Spanish citizens (84%) – with virtually no distinction by political affiliation – thought that the lack of any agreement on almost all issues between the governing party (PSOE) and the main opposition party (PP), during a time of grave crisis, was a clear factor in the deterioration of the quality of Spain's democracy, as can be seen in figure 4.2. This is without a doubt one of the main factors eroding the Spanish party system. The pragmatism and moderation of the Spanish population has reached the point where they are demanding, almost unanimously (84%), that when there are urgent problems to be solved, the political class must focus on seeking practical solutions as quickly as possible, even if this means sacrificing their ideological principles.

Hence, there is nearly unanimous agreement (88%) that the major parties have abandoned the spirit of consensus of the Transition and only think about their own party interests, regardless of what may be most beneficial for Spanish society as a whole. Similarly, a qualified majority of nearly three quarters (73%) thinks that Spain needs a "second transition", which, in the spirit of agreement and amity of the first, would undertake changes and update many aspects of the current political system: in particular, the reform of the constitution (93%), with greater (48%) or lesser (45%) scope, the electoral system to make it more proportional (69%), the naming of the highest judicial authorities

Francisco J. Llera Ramo

to give greater independence to the judiciary (83%) and the use of the referendum for the public to decide on issues of particular importance (82%).

Figure 4.2: Influence of the confrontation between the PSOE and the PP on the quality of democracy
in Spain in 2011

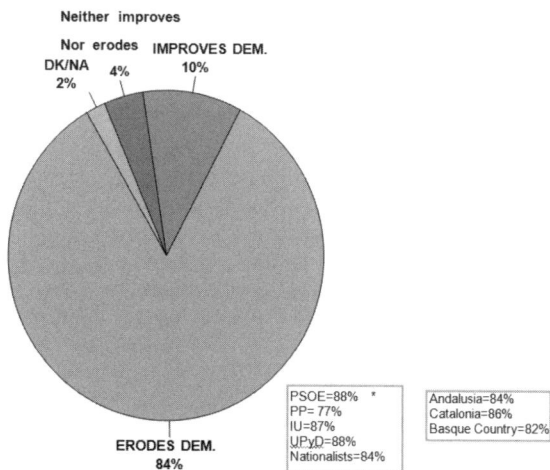

PSOE=88% *	Andalusia=84%
PP= 77%	Catalonia=86%
IU=87%	Basque Country=82%
UPyD=88%	
Nationalists=84%	

*PSOE (Spanish Socialist Workers Party); PP (Popular Party); IU (United Left); UPyD (Union, Progress and Democracy)

Source: F.J.LLera Survey CSO2009-14381

Crisis of leadership

In a democratic trajectory characterised by strong leadership in government
and opposition since 1977 (Suarez vs. Gonzalez and Gonzalez vs. Aznar), for
the first time, the declining evaluation of and confidence in the President of the
government at the end of his mandate has not been balanced by a positive perception of the leader of the main opposition party. Thus, in July 2011[18], the
President of the government and the leader of the PSOE (Zapatero) and the
leader of the main opposition party (PP) and now president of the government
(Mariano Rajoy) obtained a clear "failing" score (3.47 and 3.58) on a continuous scale from 0 (lowest rating) to 10 (highest rating) points, barely receiving
a passing score from their own respective constituencies (5.1 and 5.8, respectively). Moreover, neither of them obtained the trust of citizens, if we consider
that only 17% of the citizenry stated that they trusted José Rodríguez Zapatero

18 CIS study 2.909 (July, 2011).

(35% among Socialist voters) and only 20% trusted Mariano Rajoy (but reaching 60% among PP voters). However, Alfredo Perez Rubalcaba, who would be the Socialist candidate in the general election, replacing Zapatero as head of the party, obtained a 31% trust rating (57% among Socialist voters).

Thus, facing the final stage leading up to the November 2011 general election, both candidates (Rajoy and Perez Rubalcaba) competed in effectiveness (28% vs. 39%), capacity for dialogue (25% vs. 45%), better knowledge of Spain's problems (28% vs. 35%), ability to negotiate (25% vs. 42%), honesty (22% vs. 31%), vision (30% vs. 34%) and finally, who would make the best President of the Government (32% vs. 40%). However, on the latter question, while the opposition leader had the backing of 85% of his electorate, the governing party's candidate was supported by only 71% of Socialist voters. The deterioration of the Socialist party leadership in the past four years without a substantial improvement in the image of the leader of the main opposition party is striking, as shown in table 4.3 below. Thus, if before the general elections of 2008 and the outbreak of the economic crisis, President Rodriguez Zapatero stood out clearly in the preferences of voters in comparison to the leader of the main opposition party (50% vs. 23%, respectively), four years later preference for the opposition leader had improved by only 5 points, while the socialist candidate had dropped by 11 points compared to his predecessor.

Table 4.3: Preferred candidate for the president of the government

	2007	2011
José Luis Rodríguez Zapatero	50%	–
Alfredo Pérez Rubalcaba	–	39%
Mariano Rajoy	23%	28%
Both equally	4%	2%
Neither	21%	29%
DK/NA	2%	2%
Total	**100%**	**100%**

Source: F.J.Llera surveys SEJ2006-15076 and CSO2009-14381

The explosion of the "Spanish Revolution"

This is the term the Washington Post[19] used to label the protest movement that thousands of citizens began on 15 May 2011 (hence, referred to by its participants as the "15-M movement" or also as the "indignant") in the emblematic Puerta del Sol Square in Madrid. The protests were initially called for through the internet by the "Real Democracy Now" platform and spread to towns and cities throughout Spain. In part emulating the "Arab spring", they also spurred actions in all the capitals of the developed world in response to the consequences of the crisis and globalisation (perhaps the response having the greatest impact and continuity is the so-called "Occupy Wall Street" movement in New York). Without a well-defined ideological identity and taking the form of peaceful assembly, this movement brought political deliberation and participation into public squares, while simultaneously protesting the lack of prospects, the handling of the crisis, the rule of markets, party politics and the absence of channels for political participation. At a minimum, it expressed what had been hidden: a growing discontent in Spanish society. Hence, Spanish society identified en masse with its demands, as can be seen in figure 4.3 below.

Figure 4.3: Sympathy for 15-M and the extent to which its demands affect the majority of Spanish society

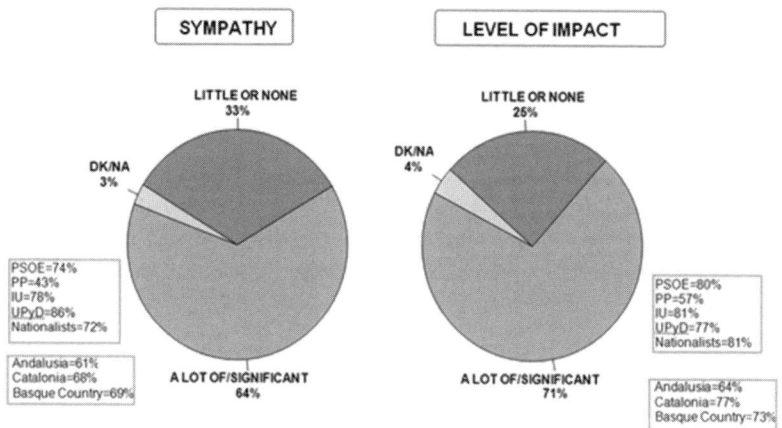

SYMPATHY

LITTLE OR NONE
33%

DK/NA
3%

PSOE=74%
PP=43%
IU=78%
UPyD=86%
Nationalists=72%

Andalusia=61%
Catalonia=68%
Basque Country=69%

A LOT OF/SIGNIFICANT
64%

LEVEL OF IMPACT

LITTLE OR NONE
25%

DK/NA
4%

PSOE=80%
PP=57%
IU=81%
UPyD=77%
Nationalists=81%

A LOT OF/SIGNIFICANT
71%

Andalusia=64%
Catalonia=77%
Basque Country=73%

Source: F J Llera survey CSO2009-14381

As can be seen, almost two out of three people are sympathetic to the 15-M movement, its form of peaceful protest and its demands; almost three quarters

---

19   *The Washington Post* (05/18/2011): Spanish 'revolution': Thousands gather in Madrid's Puerta del Sol Square.

of this group felt that it affected them. These are majority opinions, which, on the one hand, are found throughout the country and in its main regions, and on the other, they are found in all constituencies, though to a lesser extent among the conservative voters of the PP. In addition, 80% of the Spanish believed that institutions should establish channels of dialogue with the 15-M movement and try to respond to its demands, despite being sceptical (63%) about its future.

Conclusion

The institutional distrust and dissatisfaction with democracy among Spanish citizens is palpable on the street and in the media without having to resort to survey research; however, this research helps us to identify critical areas in the functioning of Spanish institutions and ultimately, to see possible courses of action for correcting the country's direction in the future. There can be little doubt that the lack of consensus between the major political parties and conflict among political elites are producing greater fatigue regarding the functioning of the democratic system in general and, above all, distorting what should be a smooth, satisfying relationship between the citizenry and politics.

As we have seen, this problem has been long in coming and is related to the way in which generational replacement within the Spanish political class has been redefining political competition in the last two decades. Spanish society – diverse, but clearly moderate and pragmatic – does not appear resigned to accepting that this change and direction cannot be reversed, as if it were historically determined. However, as a result of the economic crisis and the way in which political elites have responded, the political crisis has reached an alarming point, and unfortunately, without being too dramatic, could ultimately affect the proper functioning of Spain's constitutional system.

Although there have been repeated calls for democratic regeneration, they have not gone beyond good intentions and little political effort has been made in this direction. A solution will only be possible if political elites are willing to leave behind strategies of confrontation urbi et orbi and change direction toward concerted action in all that could most unite them politically. It is precisely at these historic crossroads when it is necessary to again find a moderate and legitimate leadership, especially considering that 60% of the Spanish believe that the state no longer has the tools needed to solve society's most urgent problems, demonstrating a clear crisis of sovereignty.

References

Beck, U. (2005) *Power in the Global Age,* Cambridge: Polity Press.

Blind, P.K. (2006) "Building Trust in Government in the Twenty-First Century: Review of Literature and Emerging Issues", in *7th Global Forum on Reinventing Government: Building Trust in Government,* Vienna: UNDESA.

Cheema, S. (2005) *Building Democratic Institutions: Governance Reform in Developing Countries,* Conn.: Kumarian Press.

Dalton, R.J.(2005) "The Social Transformation of Trust in Government", *International Review of Sociology,* 15(1), 135-154.

Easton,D. (1975) "A Re-assessment of the Concept of Political Support", *Bristish Journal of Political Science,* 5(4), 435-457.

Fitousi, J.-P. (2004) *La Démocratie et le Marché,* Paris: Grasset.

Gunther, R. and Montero, J.R. (2006) "Multidimensionality of Political Support for New Democracies", in M. Torcal and J.R.Montero (eds.) *Political Disafecction in Contemporary Democracies, Social Capital, Institutions and Politics,* London: Routledge.

Johnson, S. (2009) "The Quiet Coup", *Atlantic Magazine.* May issue (7364), 1-13.

Lamo, E. (2011) « ¿La segunda Transición ? », in J.J. Toharia (ed) *Pulso de España 2010: un informe sociológico,* Madrid: Biblioteca Nueva, 47-68.

Llera, F. (2011) « La crisis política », in J.J. Toharia (ed) *Pulso de España 2010: un informe sociológico,* Madrid: Biblioteca Nueva, 69-83.

McDonough, P., Barnes, S.H. and López Pina, A., (1994) "The Nature of Political Support and Legitimacy in Spain", *Comparative Political Studies* 27(3), 349-380.

Montero, J.R., Torcal, M. and Gunther, R. (1997) "Democracy in Spain: Legitimacy, Discontent and Dissafection", *Working Paper, 100,* Madrid: Fundación Juan March/CEACS.

Morlino, L. (2003) *Democrazie e democratizzaioni,* Bologna: Il Mulino.

Newton, K. and Norris, P. (2000) "Confidence in Public Institutions: Faith, Culture, or Performance ?", in S.J.Pharr and R.D. Putnam (eds) *Disaffected Democracies: What's troubling the Trilateral Democracies?,* New Jersey: Princeton Univ. Press, 52-73.

Norris,P. (1999) "Institutional Explanations for Political Support", in *Critical Citizens: Global Support for Democratic Government,* Oxford: Oxford Univ. Press, 217-235.

Rodrik, D. (2011) *The Globalization Paradox,* NY: Norton & Company.

Schumpeter, J.A. (1942) *Capitalism, Socialism and Democracy,* NY: Harper Torchbooks.

Toharia, J.J., ed.(2011) *Pulso de España 2010,* Madrid: Biblioteca Nueva.

Torcal,M., Gunter, R. and Montero, J.R. (2001) "Anti-party sentiments in Southern Europe", *Working Paper, 170,* Madrid: Fundación Juan March/CEACS.

Torcal, M. and Montero, J.R. eds. (2006) *Political Disafecction in Contemporary Democracies: Social Capital, Institutions and Politics,* London: Routledge.

Wert, J.I. (1996) « Sobre cultura política: legitimidad, desafección y malestar », in various authors, *Entre dos siglos: Reflexiones sobre la democracia española,* Madrid: Alianza.

Chapter 5
Trust and Mistrust Between Harper and Québec

Guy Laforest, Université Laval
Camille Brunelle-Hamann, Université Laval

Introduction

We will explore in this paper the complex and evolving relationship of trust and mistrust between Stephen Harper and Québec. The former federal Prime Minister of Canada was first elected in 2004 and returned to power with a majority government on May 2nd, 2011, before being ultimately defeated by Justin Trudeau and the Liberals in mid-October, 2015. Trust and mistrust are already complex affairs for contemporary Political Science and federalism studies. We will make them even more complex by considering qualitatively and quantitatively different partners in the relationship: one human being, who happened to be for nine years the most important political leader of a sophisticated federal democracy, and on the other side a geographical entity which happens to be a distinct national society in this federation. Québec, here, for the purposes of this paper, will encompass the following realities: the province of Québec, Québec Francophones, Québec nationalism and Québec nationalists, and finally the political leaders of Québec –We will essentially refer here to the current Premier of Québec, Mr. Jean Charest, in power since 2003. Although trust is relational, and requires levels of reciprocity, I shall look at this phenomenon mostly from the perspective of Mr. Harper himself, exploring his political and intellectual trajectory. We will altogether not completely ignore the other perspective, which can be glimpsed for instance by the electoral fortunes of Mr. Harper in Québec at federal elections since 2004, but our focus will remain on the factual, historical and perceptual elements which, taken together, have shaped Mr. Harper's cognitive perspective on Québec, leading over time to various degrees of trust and mistrust.

The paper will start with an exploration of these two primary concepts, trust and mistrust, in contemporary Political Science literature. It will then proceed to critically assess Mr. Harper's intellectual and political trajectories, concentrating with the dimensions that relate to Québec, as previously and broadly characterized. This part will be further divided in three sub-sections: 1986-2005, 2005-2008, and 2008-2012. In the conclusion of the paper, we wish to explore some alternatives for the future concerning the relationship between

Harper and Québec, and we will adventure ourselves in comparative waters, particularly those of Spain, in the aftermath of the Spanish general elections of November 20, 2011, which led to the formation of a new majority Partido Popular government led by Mariano Rajoy.

Some reflections on trust and its derivatives

Until recently, Political Theorists have been rather neglectful of the concept of trust, although this very idea is quite central in John Locke's liberal philosophy of sovereignty, explaining the relationship between the people and their elected representatives. Trust, following Locke, is always a limited affair, it can never be blind; it is revisable and consequentialist, depending on how our representatives behave when we "entrust" them with power. Before exploring in greater detail the cognitive dimension of trust, we will show its relevance for our topic –Harper and Québec- by quoting two Canadian academics, Ronald Watts and Wayne Norman, who have respectively analysed the role of trust in the political culture of federal regimes, and its place in the context of multinational societies:

> "The necessary conditions for a federal solution: A first precondition is the existence of a will to federate. Federal political systems depend on consensual support and therefore are unlikely to succeed as imposed solutions. Second, since federal systems involve both self-rule and shared-rule, without some basic underlying shared values and objectives, the basis for long-run shared rule will in the end be impossible to achieve. Third, trust is necessary to make federal arrangements work. An essential condition is the development of mutual faith and trust among the different groups within a federation and an emphasis upon the spirit of mutual respect, tolerance and compromise." (Watts, 2010: p.339).

> "From the point of view of the majority, the collective assent of federal partners cuts both ways: it constitutes a form of commitment and loyalty to the federal project by the national minorities and the majority alike, one that cannot be easily shirked. If minorities want assurances that the fundamental terms of partnership will not be violated without their consent, majorities will expect no less from minorities. The language of loyalty or solidarity is also likely to figure in the wording of a fair multinational constitution…There are tremendous benefits to trust in a federal partnership and a demonstrated commitment to anti-assimilationism is essential to secure the trust of minorities." (Norman: 2006, 164-165).

Watts and Norman's combined perspectives provide us with insights about the complexity of trust and mistrust in multinational regimes. François Rocher, Alexandre Pelletier and Richard Simeon have attempted to build on these insights without neglecting the more general literature on trust in political sociology. The following remarks attempt to synthesize their main contributions. Rocher builds on the work of Russell Hardin and attempts to go beyond the confusion between trust and trustworthiness. He considers that trust is relational, whereas trustworthiness deals with the quality of the person, or group, to whom trust has been granted (Rocher 2012: 2) Trust comes from the positive evaluation that one makes of the trustworthiness of the other. Trust, for Rocher, is the result of a calculation, of an evaluation. We believe that this is very important to keep in mind when dealing with such a Cartesian political figure as Stephen Harper. If trust is about calculating and evaluating, it is endowed with a major cognitive dimension. This involves a stable relationship between partners, tested by experience and basing itself on a substantial knowledge of the Other or Others. Enriched by his survey of the political sociology literature, Rocher wonders about the challenges at hand whenever scholars attempt to apply to the dynamics of trust/mistrust in multinational contexts the insights of most of the work on trust that concentrates its emphasis on interpersonal dyadic relationships. In multinational contexts, social relations will involve a variety of actors, majority and minority national groups, political parties wishing to represent them, political leaders, intellectual communities, governments, state institutions. These various entities deal not only with those of the same social "family" (parties with parties, governments with governments, etc.), they also interact with other groups or entities in a cross-cutting way. Stephen Harper, for instance, as a political leader, has dealt and is currently dealing with the Province of Québec, with the Government of Québec, with Jean Charest as the Premier of Québec and key political interlocutor, but also, if less systematically, with Québec nationalism and Québec's intellectual community.

Trust, however, is not exclusively a cognitive affair. It has to translate into reality in a political space, which happens to involve in multinational federations asymmetrical power relationships between majorities and minorities. Alain Noël has written intelligently about this dimension, inviting scholars of multinational regimes, particularly political theorists, to integrate in their reflections "the arguments of power as well as the power of arguments" (Noël 2006: 438). The existence of a power disequilibrium means that, generally, as Rocher suggests, the most important or influential group does not require the same degree of trust in its relation with minorities than vice versa, because its interests are more easily preserved or safeguarded. The cognitive and power dimensions of trust, as well as some others, are summarized in table 5.1, reproduced at the end of this paper (taken directly from Rocher 2012).

In their own work on trust relations in civil society associations in multinational contexts, Pelletier and Simeon provide a nice supplement to Rocher's typology and reflections. With regards to types of trust, they also suggest four variations:

Rocher	Pelletier and Simeon
Unconditional trust	Substantial trust
Moderate trust	Instrumental trust
Moderate mistrust	Cooperation without trust
Radical mistrust	Absence of cooperation

Pelletier and Simeon also insist, like Rocher, on the need in such complex federal contexts for an equilibrium between autonomy and interdependence. They suggest that trust always involves a combination of strategic (instrumental) and moral dimensions requiring good faith and reciprocity (Pelletier and Simeon 2012: 4). The domain of trust is of course always, or almost always, the realm of uncertainty. Reflecting on the two typologies of trust offered by Rocher, on the one hand, Pelletier and Simeon on the other hand, I wonder if it is at all theoretically or empirically possible to find such a thing as unconditional trust in a multinational context. Therefore, we prefer, prima facie, a political sociology that places substantial trust at the apex. We doubt, however, that substantial trust, in multinational contexts, can be devoid of instrumental dimensions. The logic of interest, both Rocher and Noël have insisted on it, cannot be discarded. Therefore, we believe that Rocher's notion of moderate trust is, prima facie, more helpful than Pelletier and Simeon's category of instrumental trust. We now move to the consideration of the evolving relationships concerning trust and mistrust between Harper and Québec.

Harper and Québec

The contours of deep mistrust between 1986 and 2005

Stephen Harper has been, arguably, the most important figure in Canadian politics since the advent of the new millennium. In the Canadian federal elections of 2000, the Liberal Party, led by Mr. Jean Chrétien, won its third consecutive majority government. In the aftermath of the election, Mr. Stockwell Day, leader of the Canadian Alliance Party, resigned. Alongside the Canadian Alliance, another right-wing party, the Progressive Conservative Party of Canada, were roundly defeated. Consider the achievements of Stephen Harper since these events: in 2002, he became leader of the Canadian Alliance Party; in 2003, he was instrumental in the fusion of the two right-wing parties and he became leader of the New Conservative Party of Canada; in 2004, his party was successful in reducing the Liberal Party, now led by Paul Martin, to the status of a minority government following the federal elections held in June;

in January 2006, Mr. Harper became Prime Minister of Canada in the wake of the triumph of his party which formed a minority government; in October 2008 Mr. Harper returned as Prime Minister, winning a second mandate at the helm of a minority government. In May 2011, the day of his greatest triumph, Mr. Harper and his party won the Canadian federal election and formed their first majority government, while altogether thoroughly demolishing two opposition parties, the Liberals led by Michael Ignatieff and the Bloc Québécois led by Gilles Duceppe. Both leaders were defeated in their own ridings. As matters stood in the Spring of 2012, when the conference at the basis of this paper took place, the Bloc Québécois had a new leader, Daniel Paillé, but was relegated to the margins of Parliament without the status and the resources of a parliamentary group. The Liberals had an interim leader in the person of Bob Rae. And the New Democrats, fresh from taking most seats in Québec for the first time ever, were in the process of selecting a new leader following the death of the previous one, the much-esteemed Jack Layton. They finally ended up picking Thomas Mulcair. Stephen Harper, in this context, reigned supreme at the top of the sphere of power in Canadian politics.

Born in Ontario in 1959, Mr. Harper moved to Alberta and Western Canada in his early twenties. He got involved into federal politics at that time, supporting Jim Hawkes, his local Conservative candidate who got elected in 1984 when Brian Mulroney became Prime Minister of Canada. He became estranged with Mr. Mulroney's government and with the Progressive Conservative Party of Canada, becoming disappointed with their treatment of Western Canada, their conduct of federal-provincial relations and constitutional politics during the Meech Lake saga (1987-1990), and their support of interventionist, statist economic and social policies, over such matters as unemployment insurance. He sided with Preston Manning's Western populist movement, made a major speech at the founding congress of the Reform Party in late October 1987, and became soon thereafter senior policy advisor to Manning as the first leader. The contours of Mr. Harper's deep mistrust and suspicion of Québec were already well established at that time. We insisted in the previous section on the fact that trust is endowed with a major cognitive dimension. This is created over time, in a multiplicity of experiences. In the case of Mr. Harper, many of these experiences were shared with one major significant Other, John Weissenberger, with whom he developed a deep personal relationship in his first years in the West.

Weissenberger had spent the first part of his life in Québec, as part of the Anglophone minority in Montréal, during the eventful years between the October Crisis in 1970, the language laws of 1974 and 1977, culminating with the victory of René Lévesque's sovereigntist Parti Québécois in the elections of 1976. With Weissenberger, Harper came to develop a vision of Québec's language régime as curtailing freedom of expression and the primacy of individual rights. As William Johnson, Harper's biographer, argues, both developed a profoundly conservative understanding of Canada and of the world (Johnson 2005: 43). With regards with the philosophical understanding of modernity, they came to support a strongly individualistic liberal vision, considering the state as a mere instrument to support the goals and projects of individuals. Owing much to Friedrich Hayek's vision of spontaneous order, they sided with the free market and remained immensely suspicious of the State's interventions in economic and social affairs. This played a role in Harper's vision of Québec. Ever since the Quiet Revolution of the early sixties, the state had been used in Québec by an upper middle-class academic and intellectual political elite to serve the interests of the French-speaking majority. René Lévesque's Parti Québécois could be seen as pursuing this project. Ever since that time, Harper has sided with at least a soft libertarian approach in economic and social policies, attempting to limit as much as possible the interventions of the state (Johnson 2005: 47). Weissenberger and Harper were also at that time self-proclaimed conservatives in the Burkean sense, placing greater value on traditions and conventions following the British experience, emphasizing reformist gradualism and deeply suspicious of radical, revolutionary change. This dimension heightened Harper's distrust of Québec. During the Quiet Revolution, statist Québec elitism had opted for radical change, and in the mid-seventies it appeared to become even more revolutionary with the Parti Québécois' sovereigntist project aimed at securing Québec's secession from Canada. On language matters, Weissenberger and Harper considered Québec profoundly disloyal.

On the one hand, according to them, Québec and Francophones from Canada benefited from Pierre-Elliott Trudeau's symmetrical pan-Canadian language regime of official bilingualism, whereas Québec enforced within its borders a regime of official unilingualism detrimental to the rights of Anglophone Québecers. To make matters worse, Québec's political culture of interventionist statism was considered by them thoroughly entrenched in Canada, with the domination of the Liberal Party in general and with the vision of Pierre-Elliott Trudeau in particular. To make matters even worse, in the late seventies, Trudeau's federal government appeared embarked on a collision course with Alberta and other Western provinces over the control of natural resources. With his friend Weissenberger, Harper was profoundly ill at ease with Québec's perceived attacks on Hayekian economic and epistemological conservatism, on Burkean's political conservatism, on a principled conservative defence of the rule of law in the British tradition of which Canada is considered to be one of the most important heirs in the world. According to his biographer, Stephen Harper has always shown a lot of respect for Mr. Trudeau's 1982 vision of patriating the Canadian constitution, enriching it with a Charter of Rights and Nations and attempting to consolidate Canada as one nation. At the same time, philosophically, he was profoundly opposed to Mr. Trudeau's policies, over such issues as languages and resources, to impose to the whole of Canada

Québec's culture of nationalistic statism. Mr. Trudeau and his Liberal Party, according to Stephen Harper in the mid-1980s, were obsessed with the question of Québec and neglected the higher purposes of individual and regional justice for all Canadians.

Beyond Hayek and Burke, Weissenberger and Harper were also quite influenced in the 1980s by a book by Peter Brimelow, which looked strategically at the future of Canada in North America and in the world, from a rather Churchillian perspective strongly prejudiced in favour of the English-speaking peoples and their contribution to the history of humanity. Brimelow offered a view of Québec's importance and role in the history of Canada. Weissenberger and Harper read the following passage about a decade after Lévesque's first victory, five years after the failed sovereignty referendum of 1980, and just as Brian Mulroney, Robert Bourassa and other Canadian politicians were about to agree on the terms of the Meech Lake Accord, recognizing Québec as a distinct society within Canada, and granting the government and the National Assembly of Québec –the STATE of Québec, from Harper's perspective- constitutional authority to legislate to protect and promote Québec as a distinct society:

> "The history and politics of Québec are dominated by a single great reality: the emergence of the French-speaking nation. The process has been slow, complex and agonizing. There have been false starts, reversals and long periods of quiescence. But for over two hundred years its ultimate direction has been the same: towards ever greater self-expression, as the growing plant seeks the light (Brimelow 1986: 180)."

From the first signing of the Meech Lake Accord in 1987 to its demise in 1990 and to the Canadian and Québec referendums of 1992 over the Charlottetown Accord, Stephen Harper, in solidarity with Preston Manning and the Reform Party or by himself, acted on his principled conservatism and on the cognitive and normative dimensions of his mistrust of Québec to strongly oppose the constitutional transformations that these projects offered for Canada. In essence, Harper was strongly opposed to real or perceived special status for Québec, adhering to a vision of individual, provincial and regional equality under the umbrella of the Canadian rule of law. As a Westerner and as a Canadian historical conservative, he did develop an understanding of federalism that allowed for strong provinces and substantial decentralization. Meech Lake and its distinct society provisions were not only at odds with his vision of provincial equality, they also meant that the state of Québec could become even more interventionist, endowed with the constitutional authority to preserve and promote such a distinct society. Moreover, by granting Québec a right of veto, Meech Lake meant that the Reform Party's cherished project of a Triple-E Senate (equal, effective and elected), would probably never see the light of day because Québec would oppose it. Interestingly, it seems relevant while discussing trust and mistrust in multinational contexts to remark that Harper, during the Meech Lake era, thought that Québec was not asked or did not propose to grant a significant concession of its own, which could have been "surrendering a clean option to secede" (Johnson 2005: 83). Obviously, from opposite perspectives developed at the time in the Québec government or in Québec's political and intellectual circles, the Meech Lake Accord was of course interpreted in a substantially different light, linked to the substantial transformation of the Canadian constitution in 1982 without the consent of Québec, thus seen as necessary to reestablish trust in the Canadian federal project. However, our focus in this paper remains insisting on the significance of Harper's trajectory and of his perspective. His angle on the matters of trust and mistrust remains our primary concern.

From the Charlottetown Accord to the end of the decade including the fateful months before, and after, the 1995 Québec referendum, Stephen Harper was steadfast in attempting to maintain, coldly, analytically, precisely, the coherence of his vision of politics and of his vision of Canada. Harper had epistemological and philosophical misgivings about the conduct of politics in Québec –too much statism-. From Brimelow, he carried strong prejudices about the historical inevitability of Québec's quest for ever greater forms of political self-expression –too much Québec nationalism-; moreover, he did not like the ambiguities surrounding Québec's struggles for sovereignty and self-determination and their relationships with the rule of law in Canada, in other words, with the primacy of the Canadian constitution. With Manning and the Reform Party, but also acting on his own, he sought a greater commitment to Canada as one nation on the part of Québec, and he sought greater clarity with regards to the legality of any secessionist enterprise. After the 1995 Québec Referendum, the 1998 Supreme Court of Canada Reference Case on the Secession of Québec, and the law passed by the Canadian Parliament in early 2000 under the initiative of Jean Chrétien and Stéphane Dion, known as the Clarity Act, can together be regarded as offering substantial satisfaction to Harper, to his actions and vision of the early 1990s. Taken together, the Supreme Court judgment and the Clarity Act reiterated the underlying principles of the Canadian constitution –federalism, democracy, constitutionalism and the rule of law, respect for the rights of minorities-, established a legal framework for the secession of a Canadian province within the categories of the constitution –following a referendum on a clear question translated into a clear answer leading to negotiations where all parties should show good faith and respect for the principles of the constitution-, and specified under which conditions the Canadian federal Parliament would consider that the question would be clear and the answer, equally clear. The two excerpts that we are about to quote come from a motion submitted at a Reform Party Congress during the Charlottetown saga, and from an individual Member's Bill that Stephen Harper submitted to the Canadian House of Commons in 1996, in the aftermath of the second Québec referendum. These two excerpts reveal a lot about the context of the times, which was using the terms of Rocher's typology, characterized by radical mistrust (absence of cooperation according to Pelletier and Simeon), of Québec nationalists and secessionists from the perspective of Harper and a broad section of Canadian opinion. Taken together, these two excerpts are, for us, the intellectual predecessors of the Canadian central government "Plan B" in the Chrétien-Dion years, of the Supreme Court's Reference on Secession and of the Clarity Act itself. They contributed, possibly, to a transformation of the climate of politics in Canada in the late 1990s, from radical mistrust to moderate mistrust (Rocher), or from absence of cooperation to cooperation without trust (Pelletier and Simeon). This move from radical mistrust to moderate mistrust obviously characterizes here, if we are not mistaken, public opinion in the majority nation of a multinational federation. Beyond these excerpts, however, we believe nothing had really changed about Stephen Harper's deep mistrust of Québec.

> "Whereas concessions made on account of this separatist threat are, for many, proving to be costly, ineffective, a source of deepening friction between Quebec and the rest of Canada, and a barrier to the development of national purpose for the country as a whole... Be it resolved that the Reform Party state clearly its belief that Confederation should be maintained, but that it can only be maintained by a clear commitment to Canada as one nation, in which the demands and aspirations of all regions are entitled to equal status in constitutional negotiations and political debate, and in which freedom of expression is fully accepted as the basis for language policy across the country." (as quoted by Johnson 2005: p.147).

> "A unilateral declaration of independence by the government of Quebec or the legislature of Quebec, or the refusal of either to submit to any Canadian law that applies in Quebec is unlawful and of no force and effect with respect to the Constitution of Canada and the general laws of Canada and does not affect: (a) the jurisdiction of Parliament to pass laws that have effect in Québec; (b) the ability of the Government of Canada to govern Quebec as a province of Canada; (c) the jurisdiction of the courts to apply the law of Canada in Quebec; or (d) the continuance of Quebec as a part of Canada under Canadian law". (quoted by Johnson 2005: 255).

Evaluating Harper's relationship with Quebec, we believe nothing of substance really changed between 1996, the year Harper submitted this Member Bill to Parliament, and late 2004, sometime after his first federal electoral campaign as Leader of the reunited forces of the right and of the new Conservative Party of Canada. In 2004, struggling against the Liberal Party led by Paul Martin, Harper's Conservatives elected 99 members of Parliament, and reduced the Liberals to the status of minority government. However, their performance was dismal in Québec, with less than 9% of votes and no elected representatives. From 1996 to 2004, Harper remained adamant that Québec needed no form of special status, no new substantial or symbolic recognition, that it was legally fully integrated in Canada. In essence, the only fundamental difference between his group and their Liberal adversaries was that the Conservatives espoused a form of federalism that appeared more respectful of the powers of provinces. If nothing of substance really changed, some signs indicated that

Harper could reconsider, at least in part, his own vision, his approach to his
understanding of Québec and of Canada. We shall consider these signs in the
introduction of the next section, which deals with the period 2005-2008.

The promises of thin trust 2005-2008

Stephen Harper's conservative vision privileges market libertarian values over
the Welfare State and the political culture that supports it, it promotes individual rights and family values against the hedonism and nihilism of much of Late
Modernity in the West, it nurtures a politics of conflict that favors taxpayers
from the private sector over welfare recipients, it harbours huge suspicions as
we have seen vis-à-vis the nationalistic statism of Québec and its perceived
absence of commitment vis-à-vis Canada, and it promotes an understanding of
Canadian federalism that grants at least equal value, to federalism and the
founding of 1867 than to the refounding accomplished by Pierre Trudeau with
Patriation and the Charter of Rights and Freedoms in 1982. Harper's mind fully
integrates a vision of politics that sees it as primarily conflictual. In order,
therefore, to secure a lasting presence for his vision with all its elements in
twenty-first century Canada, he believes that the Conservative Party must attempt the Herculean task of displacing the Liberal Party as the dominant party
in the political system. From 1996 onwards, ever so gradually, Harper acted
on the premise that in order to secure a stable anchoring for his vision, in order
to displace the Liberals, the Conservatives had in a way to make their peace
with Québec. We use the expression thin trust to characterize the shift that
occurred in Harper's approach and which can be clearly seen at work in
speeches he made in Québec City in Montréal in December 2005 and January
2006 in the midst of the federal electoral campaign that led to the formation of
a Conservative minority government. In these speeches, and in some pro-
nouncements thereafter, Harper coined a new doctrine, "fédéralisme d'ouverture", which can be translated as "open federalism" or "federalism of openness" (Pelletier 2008 and Hébert 2007). It is clear in our minds that "fédéralisme d'ouverture" as a form of thin trust towards Québec corresponded to what
Pelletier and Simeon called instrumental trust. Once again, this is not necessarily negative or pejorative. Everybody has interests: political leaders, governments, nations. Thin or instrumental trust is a progress from the two inferior
categories in our two typologies, moderate mistrust (Rocher) or cooperation
without trust (Pelletier and Simeon). Over time, because trust is endowed with
a cognitive dimension which integrates the meaning and consequences of experiences, thin or instrumental trust can stabilize as moderate trust. We wish
to argue that however we interpret the promises of "fédéralisme d'ouverture"
between 2005 and 2008, they did not stabilize themselves as moderate trust,

therefore leading to our last, and possibly current moment in the relations between Harper and Québec, characterized by renewed mistrust from 2008 to 2012.

The seeds of thin or instrumental trust between Harper and Québec were already planted in 1996 when Harper evoked at a philosophically conservative policy convention in Calgary the conditions that would allow the Canadian political right to reestablish itself as a major force in order to compete with, and eventually to displace, the Liberal Party as the primary partisan group in the country. At that time, Harper believed that whenever conservative forces had coalesced to win an election, they included people from three groups: people from Ontario and Atlantic Canada who had traditionally supported the old Conservative Party; people from Western Canada who had supported historically various populist parties stemming from the West, in the late 1990s the Reform Party; and finally people linked with the nationalist tradition in Québec who had not completely abandoned the idea of a federal Canada as a political project (Johnson 2005: 264). In 1996, Harper had precious little to say about the ways in which such a coalition could be formed again in the future. In the ensuing years, events unfolded to create some preconditions for the realization of this project. Following three consecutive majority governments obtained by Jean Chrétien, the Liberal Party was becoming more and more engulfed in a fratricidal conflict involving the supporters of Mr. Chrétien and those of his internal arch-rival, Paul Martin. The latter would ultimately prevail and replace Mr. Chrétien in the Winter of 2004. In Québec, things began to change in 2003, when the Québec Liberal Party under the leadership of Mr. Jean Charest won the April 14 election and propelled the sovereigntist Parti Québécois in the Opposition.

Mr. Charest and his Liberals were committed federalists and sympathetic to Canadian nationalism while remaining autonomist nationalistic Québecers. They developed a coherent approach towards Canadian federalism, wishing to improve the quality of horizontal intergovernmental relations through the creation of a new institution of cooperation between provinces and territories, which rapidly saw the light of day as the Council of the Federation in late 2003. Rapidly, Mr. Charest and the Canadian Prime Minister were successful in changing the climate of federal-provincial relations by agreeing, with other provincial leaders, in the Fall of 2004, about a new ten-year deal to jointly finance the health system in Canada, completing this agreement with a parallel, asymmetrical accord between the central government and Québec. Mr. Martin and his government were less successful in Québec with the creation of a Commission of Enquiry, led by Mr. Justice John Gomery, which explored the ways in which regulations of many federal administrative departments were disrespected, while irregular means were employed to finance the federal Liberal Party, in a vast scheme to try to reinforce a sense of Canadian allegiance in Québec in the aftermath of the 1995 referendum. The electoral fortunes of the

Liberal Party in Québec, already weakened in 2004, could be fatally wounded if the situation was to be properly exploited by their adversaries. All in all, these events provided Mr. Harper with an opportunity that he began to seize during the early weeks of the federal electoral campaign in December 2005 and January 2006 when he expounded the major aspects of his new doctrine: "fédéralisme d'ouverture"

- aBeyond domineering and paternalistic federalism, show greater respect toward constitutional provincial jurisdiction and division of powers;
- Foster better collaboration and coordination with provinces and circumscribe Ottawa's spending power;
- Recognize the existence of a vertical fiscal imbalance between Ottawa and the provinces and willingness to act on this problem;
- Recognize the special cultural and institutional responsibilities of Québec and attributing a significant role to the government of Québec in the Canadian delegation at Unesco;
- In Canada-Québec relations, offer a noticeable change of tone: "we shall change the debate, change the programme and change the federation". (Harper's federalism of openness is discussed in Pelletier 2008, as well as in Caron and Laforest 2009).

It can be argued that Mr. Harper's surprising new flirt with Québec was the key element that led to the Conservative victory in 2006, thus enabling Mr. Harper to become Prime Minister of Canada (Hébert 2007:10). In 2006, Mr. Harper and his party made more than a modest breakthrough in Québec. They won ten seats in the province, whereas they had taken none in 2004, and garnered 24.6% of the votes, compared with 8.8% in 2004. Between Harper and Québec, between 2005 and 2007-2008, things were far from perfect. Mr. Harper was, and remains, far too conservative and anti-statist for Québec's left-of center mainstream public opinion and for its political elites. In the circumstances, it would have been totally unseemly to expect unconditional or substantial trust between Harper and Québec. However, for a while, at least for two years, it looked as if Harper and Québec were jointly navigating the waters of instrumental and moderate trust.

Although the Harper-led Conservative minority government has failed to deliver on its promise to elaborate a so-called "Charte du fédéralisme d'ouverture", we believe there is some consensus in Québec that Mr. Harper has made significant progress on most items of this agenda between 2006 and 2008. Considering, moreover, that Mr. Harper moved through the House of Commons in late 2006 a resolution recognizing that the Québécois form a nation in a united Canada, that he has shown tremendous respect for the French language, that he has highlighted here and abroad the role of Québec in general and of Québec City in particular, in the founding of Canada, it is somewhat surprising that he did not make substantial gains in Québec in the 2008 Fall federal election. In October 2008, Mr. Harper's Conservative won the election yet again, once more forming a minority government, once more with 10 seats in Québec, but with a reduced voter support of 21.7%. Any analysis of these matters must be careful. In truth, the engine of "fédéralisme d'ouverture" had been losing part of its energy from the start of 2007 on a variety of issues: statements about the need to circumscribe the spending power have been timid at best, some ambiguities remain concerning what Mr. Harper really meant in the nation resolution, senate reform projects, coupled with the desire to establish more provincial equality in the House of Commons by giving more seats to Ontario, Alberta and British Columbia (reform ideas met with resistance in Québec) and the idea of an Ottawa-based national securities regulator have met strong resistance in federalist Québec City. Moreover, Mr. Harper between 2006 and 2008 has shown no enthusiasm towards streamlining coordination through regular and more rational First Ministers Conferences, and he has generally stayed away from the idea of re-opening the constitutional file in order, among other matters, to formally recognize Québec's national identity. Add to this the rift between Mr. Harper and Québec Premier Jean Charest dating back to the latter's decision to reduce income taxes in the aftermath of a 2007 federal budget addressing the fiscal imbalance issue, and you get a more realistic portrait of the relationship between Mr. Harper's government and Québec. Somewhere between 2007 and 2008, the engine of thin or instrumental trust between Mr. Harper and Québec were derailed. We shall explore the psychological dimensions of this reality in the next section.

Renewed mistrust 2008-2012

In the Canadian federal elections of May 2, 2011, Stephen Harper saw his Conservative Party comfortably win the election, garnering 166 of 308 seats with 39.6% of voter support –see table 5.3- and in the days thereafter he formed the Cabinet of his first majority government. However, he did this with considerably reduced support in Québec, moving from 10 to 5 seats, from 21.7% to 16.5% of voter support –see table 5.2. During this election, seismic political changes did occur in Québec, with the New Democratic Party led by Jack Layton moving from 1 to 58 seats, garnering 42% of voter support, and with the collapse of both the sovereigntist Bloc Québécois led by Gilles Duceppe and the Liberal Party led by Michael Ignatieff. In the campaign leading to the election, it became clear that Mr. Harper and the Conservatives applied a different strategy than the one they had used in 2006 and 2008, placing much less emphasis on everything related to "fédéralisme d'ouverture". Creating jobs, supporting families, eliminating the deficit, providing increased security to Canadians, protecting Canada here and abroad by strengthening the Armed Forces and investing in the development and security of the North, those were the Conservative priorities in 2011, and they had nothing particular to offer to Québec. Clearly the richest and best organized political party in Canada, the

Harper-led Conservatives, attempted to secure a majority by making gains in Ontario, the Maritimes and British Columbia, strategically selecting potential seats and cleverly segmenting the electorate. In the months following the election, the new majority government made good of Mr. Harper's campaign promises.

The government's blueprint, as it appeared in the Throne Speech delivered by the Governor-General on June 3, 2011, included the following priorities: supporting growth and employment, eliminating the deficit, supporting hard-working families, protecting Canada, helping law-abiding Canadians, helping communities and industries, promoting integrity and responsibility. The latter priority included ideas such as a reform of the senate, more equitable representation in the House of Commons by granting more seats to Ontario, Alberta and British Columbia, and eliminating state support for the financing of political parties. All these elements bring Mr. Harper on a collision course with Mr. Charest's Liberal government in Québec and with mainstream public opinion in the province. Cooperation does exist between the governments of Mr. Harper and of Mr. Charest, as was demonstrated by the agreement on sales tax harmonization devolving two billion dollars to Québec on September 30, 2011, but I would argue that this is an example of cooperation without trust. Moreover, Mr. Harper was forced after the election to reshuffle personnel in the Prime Minister's Office with the resignation of his Press Secretary, Dimitri Soudas, who also happened to be his top Québec advisor. He replaced him with Angelo Persichillli, a veteran of the ethnic media in Toronto who does not speak French and made disparaging comments about Québec's role in Canada in the recent past. Considering all these events, the following question needs to be asked: what really went wrong between Mr. Harper and Québec in 2007-2008 to explain this change of course, this move from instrumental or thin trust to renewed mistrust?

Whenever partners in a relationship move from deep mistrust (radical mistrust, absence of cooperation, cooperation without trust, in the typologies I have used here) to instrumental or thin trust, the whole matter remains quite fragile. I believe that in the era of "fédéralisme d'ouverture" and thin trust, Mr. Harper's stance towards Québec started to change in the Spring of 2007, in the context of the Québec electoral campaign that ultimately saw Mr. Charest's Liberals reduced to the status of a minority government, with Mario Dumont's ADQ replacing the Parti Québécois as the Official Opposition. Prior to the election, Mr. Harper's government in Ottawa announced that in the settlement of the issue of the existence of a fiscal imbalance between the central government and the provinces, which had been for years a priority of Québec and of Mr. Charest's government, Québec would receive over one billion dollars. Mr. Charest had always said that Québec needed this money in order to face rising costs in its two most important jurisdictions, health and education. However, at the end of a difficult first mandate in government, Mr. Charest chose instead to use these subsidies to offer Québec voters substantial income tax reductions. Obviously, the Québec government is perfectly entitled to do whatever it wants, within the rule of law and within its jurisdictional ground in the federations, with its revenues. Mr. Harper, however, who had spent some political capital in the rest of Canada to recognize the legitimacy of the issue of a fiscal imbalance, must have been quite surprised and deeply disappointed by the move. Mr. Charest made matters worse, in 2007-2008, not only by disagreeing with Mr. Harper's government policy on environmental issues such as climate change, but also by vigorously expressing himself about this disagreement in a number of important international forums. "Fédéralisme d'ouverture" remained an important theme for the Conservative electoral platform leading to the elections of October 2008, and it figured among the elements that were mentioned in the Throne Speech which followed this election returning Mr. Harper's Conservatives with a minority government. Although the words remained there, the spirit did not happen to be. Mr. Harper's Conservatives did not lose seats in Québec in 2008, but they did not gain ground either. In levels of voter support, they suffered a marked loss, moving from 24.6% to 21.7 % after a lacklustre campaign where they were cleverly attacked by the Bloc Québécois, for intended federal reductions of governmental support for culture. By the end of 2008, in the weeks following the re-election of Mr. Charest with his third government and second majority one, with the electoral disaster suffered by the ADQ and Mario Dumont, with whom Mr. Harper had established good personal relations and with whom he shared some ideological traits –suspicion vis-à-vis Welfare statism, broad support for greater individual responsibility- the window of opportunity for "fédéralisme d'ouverture", for instrumental or thin trust between Mr. Harper and Québec appeared to be closing.

Conclusion

Trust and mistrust are cognitive affairs. They are experience-based, dynamic, fluid, evolving with changing historical and political circumstances. In multinational federations, between majorities and minorities at the level of civil societies, between political leaders and governmental representatives, trust will always be something fragile, inherently unstable. Majorities and minorities, and their respective leaders, do not exclusively seek the same objectives. Some objectives will be commonly shared: security, social peace, economic prosperity, the crafting and preserving of a liberal polity enhancing individual rights, the normal functioning of representative and deliberative institutions of democracy, the establishment of a pluralistic public sphere. Still, in a multinational democracy, the majority nation, as Simeon coherently showed, will put greater priority at national integration at the level of the state, at securing solidarity and interdependence for all individuals and groups throughout the state. On the other hand, minority nations will put greater focus on national empowerment for minorities, through increased powers, through expressions of distinctiveness and asymmetry, through securing forms of symbolic and substantial recognition by the majority nation and by the state.

In this general context, to come back to the categories explored in this paper, unconditional trust is unimaginable. At best, majorities, minorities and their respective leaders will reach a reasonably stabilized order hovering between what Rocher has called moderate trust and moderate mistrust, between the broader spectrum suggested by Pelletier and Simeon from cooperation without trust, to instrumental trust to substantial trust. As we have suggested in this paper, we believe an element of instrumentality will always exists.

In order to stabilize a form of moderate trust, we believe that two lessons can be learnt from an examination of the relationship between Harper and Québec. Harper's trajectory helps us understand that, when moderate or instrumental trust has been achieved, in a personal context steeped in historic mistrust and deeply-held prejudices, top elected leaders must act coherently and respect their promises. Jean Charest failed to do this in the Spring of 2007 when he used the money Québec had received as a form of compensation for vertical fiscal imbalance in the federation to reduce the income taxes of its citizens. Secondly, although they may have substantial policy differences, leaders of majorities and minorities should not act at the international level as if to widen these policy differences, without any appearance of communication on the matter with each other. On environmental issues, the Premier of Québec, Mr. Charest, showed a kind of lack of respect for Mr. Harper in a variety of international forums. What can be the meaning of all this for Spain, and particularly for the relationship between Mariano Rajoy, the freshly elected President of the Spanish government, and Artur Mas, the leader of CIU and President of the Catalan government? We should add that we believe our comments with regards to the relationship between Rajoy and Mas in 2011-2012, apply to the relationship between Rajoy and Carles Puigdemont in 2017.

Rajoy and Mas talked to each other at least twice between the November 20, 2011, Spanish elections, and the Christmas recess. They met formally at La Moncloa in Madrid for a formal work session on February 3rd, 2012. We believe the categories explored in this paper can be useful to understand the relationship between these two leaders, their respective governments, and the peoples-societies they represent. Unconditional trust should not be sought. Discussions should be frequent. Each side should understand the hierarchy of each other's objectives. Whenever possible, common speeches and deeds should be pronounced and accomplished to build up the edifice of relative trust. Promises, whenever expressed, should be kept at all costs. And whenever conflicts will be unavoidable –and considering the essence of politics in a multinational federation, this is bound to happen- channels of communication should be maintained as well as interpersonal respect. The rest, as ever, will be cognitive, experience-based and revisable.

Table 5.1: Trust-mistrust—Dynamics in a plurinational context marked by the asymmetry of communities

Type of Trust	Power relation	Institutional characteristics	Cognitive dimension	Normative dimension
Unconditional Trust	Symmetrical	Double majority	Fusion of interests	Trustworthiness predictability and general interest
Moderate Trust	Asymmetrical	Conventional/ constitutional veto	Divergent interests and common goals	Dialogue, compromise and general interest
Moderate mistrust	Asymmetrical	Political capacity to bloc	Divergent interests and disagreements concerning goals	Pressure, compromise and particular interests
Radical mistrust	Domination	Majoritarian uni-lateralism	Antagonical interests	Treason, Treachery and particular interests

Reproduced from Rocher 2012, with the permission of François Rocher

Table 5.2: Votes obtained by the Alliance-Reform-Progressive Conservatives, and later by the Conservative Party in Québec, 2000-2011

Year of the election	% of votes	No. of seats
2000	5,6	1
2004	8,8	0
2006	24,6	10
2008	21,7	10
2011	16,5	5

Guy Laforest and Camille Brunelle-Hamann

Table 5.3: Results of Canadian general elections, 2000-2011

Year	2000 % of valid votes	2000 Number of seats	2004 % of valid votes	2004 Number of seats	2006 % of valid votes	2006 Number of seats	2008 % of valid votes	2008 Number of seats	2011 % of valid votes	2011 Number of seats
Alliance-Reform	25,51	66								
Bloc Québécois	10,71	38	12,4	54	10,5	51	10	49	6,1	4
Liberal	40,8	172	36,7	135	30,2	103	26,3	77	18,9	34
New Democratic Party	8,5	13	15,7	19	17,5	29	18,2	37	30,6	103
Conservative Party*	12,2	12	29,6	99	36,3	124	37,7	143	39,6	166
Green Party			4,3	0	4,5	0	6,8	0	3,9	1
Independent			0,3	1	0,5	1	0,6	2	0,4	
Others	2,2	0	1	0	0,5	0	0,4		0,5	
Total **		301		308		308		308		308

* The Reform-Alliance Party fused with the Progressive-Conservative Party to form the new Conservative Party of Canada in 2003.

** In 2003 as well, the number of seats in the Canadian House of Commons, the Lower House of Parliament, moved from 301 to 308

References

Baier, Annette. (1986). "Trust and Antitrust", *Ethics,* 96(2), 231-260.

Banting, Keith ed. (2006). *Open Federalism: Interpretations, Significance.* Kingston: Institute of Intergovernmental Relations.

Caron, Jean-François and Guy Laforest. (2009). "Canada and Multinational Federalism: From the Spirit of 1982 to Stephen Harper's Open Federalism", *Nationalism and Ethnic Politics* 15(1), 27-55.

Cook, R. et al. (2005). *Cooperation without Trust?* New-York: Sage.

Dryzek, John. (2005). "Deliberative Democracy in Divided Societies: Alternatives to Agonism and Analgesia", *Political Theory* 33(2), 218-242.

Flanagan, Thomas. (2007). *Harper's Team: Behind the Scenes of the Conservative Rise to Power,* Montréal and Kingston: McGill-Queen's University Press.

Gagnon, Alain. (2011). *L'âge des incertitudes: Essais sur le fédéralisme canadien et la diversité nationale,* Québec: Presses de l'Université Laval.

Gagnon, Alain and Ferran Requejo, eds. (2011). *Nations en quête de reconnaissance: Regards croisés* Québec-Catalogne, Bruxelles : Peter Lang.

Gagnon, Alain, ed. (2009). *Contemporary Canadian Federalism: Foundations, Traditions, Institutions,* Toronto: University of Toronto Press.

Gagnon, Alain and Raffaele Iacovino (2007) *Federalism, Citizenship and Quebec: Debating Multinationalism.* Toronto: University of Toronto Press.

Gambetta, Diego. (2000). *Making and Breaking Cooperative Relations.* New-York: Basil Blackwell.

Hébert, Chantal. (2007). *French Kiss: Stephen Harper's Blind Date with Québec,* Toronto: A. Knopf Canada.

Hardin, Russell. (2006). *Trust,* Cambridge, U.K.: Polity Press.

Laforest, Guy. (2010). "The Meaning of Canadian Federalism in Québec: Critical Reflections" 11 (October 2010), 11-56.

Laforest, Guy. (2009). "The Internal Exile of Quebecers in the Canada of the Charter", in James B. Kelly and Christopher P. Manfredi, *Contested Constitutionalism: Reflections on the Canadian Charter of Rights and Freedoms,* Vancouver: UBC Press, 251-262.

Laforest, Guy. (2004). *Pour la liberté d'une société distincte,* Québec: Presses de l'Université Laval.

Markova, Ivana and Alex Gillespie. (2008). *Trust and Distrust: Sociocultural Perspectives,* Charlotte, North Carolina: Information Age Pub.

Martin, Lawrence. (2010). *Harperland: the Politics of Control,* Toronto: Viking Canada.

Möllering, Guido. (2001). "The Nature of Trust: from Georg Simmel to a Theory of Expectation", Interpretation and Suspension, *Sociology* 35(2), 403-420.

Montpetit, Eric. (2007). *Le fédéralisme d'ouverture: la recherche d'une légitimité canadienne au Québec,* Québec: Septentrion.

Nadeau, Christian. (2010). *Contre Harper: bref traité philosophique sur la révolution conservatrice,* Montréal : Boréal.

Noël, Alain. (2006). "Democratic Deliberation in a Multinational Federation", *Critical Review of International Social and Political Philosophy* 9(3), 410-444.

Norman, Wayne. (2006). *Negotiating Nationalism: Nation-Building, Federalism and Secession in the Multinational State,* Toronto: Oxford University Press.

Pelletier, Alexandre and Richard Simeon. (2012). « Groupes linguistiques et société civile: confiance, cooperation et accommodements au sein des associations volontaires au Canada », in

Dimitri Karmis and François Rocher eds., *La dynamique confiance-méfiance dans les fédérations multinationales,* Québec: Presses de l'Université Laval.

Pelletier, Réjean. (2008). *Le Québec et le fédéralisme canadien: un regard critique,* Québec: Presses de l'Université Laval.

Pratte, André ed. (2007). *Reconquérir le Canada: un nouveau projet pour la nation québécoise,* Montréal: Les Éditions Voix Parallèles.

Rocher, François. (2012). « La construction du Canada en perspective historique: de la vigilance (ou de la méfiance) comme élément consubstantiel des débats constitutionnels? » in Dimitri Karmis and François Rocher, eds. *La dynamique confiance-méfiance dans les fédérations multinationales,* Québec: Presses de l'Université Laval.

Russell, Peter H. (2010). "Trust and Distrust in Canada's Multinational Constitutional Politics", Workshop on Trust, Distrust and Mistrust in Multinational Societies, Montréal, June.

Sheppard, Blair H. and Dana M. Sherman. (1998). "The Grammars of Trust: A Model and General Implications", *Academy of Management Review* 23(3), 422-437.

Smith, David. (2010). *Federalism and the Constitution of Canada,* Toronto: University of Toronto Press.

Sztompka, Piotr. (1999). *Trust: A Sociological Theory,* Cambridge: Cambridge University Press.

Uslaner, Eric M. (2002). *The Moral Foundation of Trust,* Cambridge: Cambridge University Press.

Watts, Ronald. (2010). "Comparative Reflections on Federalism and Democracy", in Michael Burgess and Alain-G. Gagnon, *Federal Democracies,* London: Routledge, 325-346.

Weinstock, Daniel. (1999). "Building Trust in Divided Societies", *The Journal of Political Philosophy* 7(3), 287-307.

Part III
The increasing role of substate entities in world debates and trade regulations

Chapter 6
The Diplomatic Activities of Regional Substate Entities: Towards a Multilevel Diplomacy?

David Criekemans, University of Antwerp

A third wave in Regional Substate Diplomacy?

At the substate level, it is clear that substate actors – especially regions with legislative powers– are in relative terms becoming more relevant and are generating an increasing amount of diplomatic activities, both in quantitative and qualitative terms. One could even go further by stating that currently a "third wave" is developing in substate diplomacy, especially in Europe (Criekemans, Duran & Melissen, 2008). The *first wave* manifested itself from the 1980s onwards: a growing number of non-central governments tried to attract foreign direct investment through own initiatives (e.g. Catalonia's early efforts in Japan) or to use culture and identity as a lever to place oneself on the international map. Such initiatives often were of an ad hoc-nature, there existed only a minor integration of all the external activities that were generated. The *second wave* in the 1990s was characterized by the creation, within the substate entities of certain (European) countries, of a judicially grounded set of instruments for their own (parallel as well as complementary) diplomatic activities (e.g. the Belgian state reform in 1993, which awarded formal *ius tractacti* and *ius legationis* to the Regions and Communities within the country based upon the principle *"in foro interno, in foro externo"*). These instruments were supplemented by the gradual development of a "separate" foreign policy-apparatus (administration or policy-body) which started to horizontally coordinate the external activities of the different administrations in certain regions. The current *third wave* is characterized by steps in the direction of a 'verticalization' of the organisational structure of the administration or department of external/foreign affairs, a strategic re-orientation of the geopolitical and functional priorities *and* attempts to *integrate* the external instruments of a substate foreign policy into a well performing whole.

Zooming into the specific nature of substate diplomacy

Over the last decades, the international state system has increasingly been faced with other players entering in the global arena. Next to transnational corporations, NGOs, transnational civil society and international organizations, subnational (or substate) entities are coming more often to the fore. The reasons for this are twofold: on the one hand, important modifications have occurred on both national and international levels, while on the other hand important economic developments within subnational entities also have taken place (Keating, 1999: 1). "Paradiplomacy" can be defined as "the foreign policy of non-central governments" (Aldecoa & Keating, 1999), a term which is not always accepted with enthusiasm in parts of the academic community. According to some critics, the term seems to suggest an artificial separation between 'centralized diplomacy' and the 'diplomatic practice of substate entities', which is not always the case. Hence the prefix "para" (cf. parallel) is contested; the diplomacy of substate entities might also in some cases be part of a multilevel endeavor of central and non-central entities who together join diplomatic forces on the international scene...

The topic of substate diplomacy is a recent field of research. Although there is a high increase in the number of publications, it suffers from a lack of balance (Criekemans, 2007). Initially most of the studies concentrated on the problem of the distribution of responsibilities between central and regional governments. This resulted in a vast corpus of literature on the legal and internal-political framework within which substate entities develop their own foreign policy. A steadily increasing amount of empirical literature tries to gain insight into the phenomenon of substate diplomacy in an inductive manner, mostly by means of case studies (e.g. Catalonia: studied by Puig I Scotoni; Québec by Paquin; the Basque Country by Lecours & Moreno; Flanders by Criekemans, etc.). A second group of scholarship is also case-oriented, but in a comparative fashion. Here the domestic influence on the territorial division of power is studied from the bottom up. Finally, a third group of empirical scholarship starts from an International Relations perspective. Substate diplomacy is situated in ever changing international surroundings, or from the top down. One of the challenges in the academic study of substate diplomacy is to *gather comparable data* on the institutional mechanisms, the diplomatic instruments and the organizational structures which non-central governments utilize so as to develop a foreign policy, parallel, complementary or conflictual to those of their central state-colleagues. Gathering such data can help us to better evaluate the nature and width of substate diplomacy, and in a second move also to be able to appraise the relation between substate and small state diplomacy.

The dilution of the boundaries between traditional diplomacy and substate diplomacy

The central thesis of this chapter states that, within some dimensions, the boundaries between diplomacy (generated by states) and paradiplomacy (generated by regions with legislative powers) are visibly watering down. The dimensions which we will explore in this text are; (1°) definition of 'foreign policy', (2°) institutional context and intergovernmental relations in external relations, (3°) utilized 'diplomatic' instruments, (4°) character of the representations abroad.

The way in which regions define their respective 'foreign policy'

At the dimension of the way in which regions with legislative powers define their respective 'foreign policy', clear evidence exists of ever more all-encompassing conceptualisations and operationalisations – the 'foreign affairs' of regions with legislative powers sometimes closely emulates the activities of central governments, and becomes ever more sophisticated as time goes by.

It is interesting to observe that there often seems to be an *evolution through time* in the way in which regions focus on certain aspects of their international activities. In Flanders and Wallonia, the 'regional foreign policy', which was conducted before 1993 mainly focused on international cultural activities and some initiatives regarding cooperation in the educational field. In the Saint Michaels Agreement of 1993, the external activities of the Belgian regions were broadened to all their internal competences (ranging from 'hard' competences such as economy and the environment to 'soft' policy areas, such as youth policy and preventive health care). Yet, in the period 1995-99, the Flemish government still defined its 'foreign policy' very much in terms of 'image building' and public relations.[1] Today, after years of official competences in the international sphere, its 'foreign policy' has become multifaceted and is much more complex. This is also the case of Wallonia's external relations. Initially, its external relations were primarily cultural in nature, but they would soon encompass all other foreign policy domains: foreign trade,

---

1   In his 'Policy Letter Flanders International 1995-1999', the then minister-president Luc Van den Brande–who was responsible for the external relations of the Flemish government–wrote that *"the diplomacy [of Flanders] entails in fact the public relations, the foreign relations of a federated entity."* To a certain extent, this strong focus upon PR is understandable; Flanders had to make its existence as a (modest) 'international player' clear to the world. In terms of policy-making the vision was held that a substantive foreign policy is only possible when one has an 'image'.

education exchanges, political agreements, development cooperation, etc. The Bavarian external relations started off as an elaborated cross-boundary policy in the Alpine region, primarily focused on economic, environmental, educational and cultural development. Parallel to this Alpine vocation, Bavaria sought economic cooperation in the Far East: from the mid-eighties onwards, it was involved in a number of cooperation projects with the Chinese province of Shandong. Since then, Bavaria stayed true to this double vocation of maintaining excellent relations with its neighbours and looking for opportunities in the emerging markets. The launch of Catalan external relations was largely influenced by the search for international recognition of the Catalan culture and nation. The Catalan president Jordi Pujol (1980-2003) showed remarkable energy in signing international agreements, developing cooperation programmes, travelling abroad, and receiving foreign dignitaries. The age of voluntarism now lies in the past and the Catalan government is clearly moving toward a more structured and coherent foreign policy. Québec has by far the longest history in pursuing foreign relations. From the start, Québec's foreign policy has been a multilayered, largely institutionalized one. In the course of the years, a slow geographical shift to the American hemisphere went hand in hand with economic and cultural realities on the American continent, especially after the North American Free Trade Agreement came into force in 1994. Scotland is the youngest pupil in the 'paradiplomatic classroom'. Although Scottish external relations saw the light as recently ago as 1997, since then, the Scottish government has elaborated a well-performing foreign policy instrument, which combines a clever use of its scarce resources and the even scarcer constitutional boundaries with an emphasis on cutting edge new diplomacy tools. Its external relations are largely focused on the European Union and the United States.

In absence of clear-cut attributed competences in 'foreign policy', some regions with legislative powers focus very much on 'image-building' and 'public relations' in conducting their external relations. Especially in the still quite 'young' paradiplomacies of Europe, such as for instance in Scotland, one can detect a quite similar picture when compared to Flanders and Wallonia in their 'early days'; a strong focus on image-building or sometimes even on public diplomacy [2], and a strategy to utilize 'culture' and 'tourism'

---

2 As Huijgh and Melissen recently argued, *"public diplomacy is not identical to 'imagebuilding', 'nation branding' and other marketing communication (such as propaganda, advertisement, direct mail and 'publicity' also called (marketing) public relations). Public diplomacy wants to work upon more familiarity with and an amelioration of the reputation (of a region or country) via strengthening relations abroad while at the same time elaborating domestic relations with an eye to a dialogue about foreign policy. By comparison, marketing communication is rather directed to the projection of the 'desired' identity or logo."* Read: Ellen Huijgh and Jan Melissen, *De publieksdiplomatie van Québec* (Antwerpen en Den Haag: Steunpunt Buitenlands Beleid & Nederlands Instituut voor Internationale Betrekkingen 'Clingendael', 2008), p. 8.

as instruments to place one's own 'nation' on the map. Often regions with a
strong identity or cultural tradition make such choices. Over time, other regions seem to make a *gradual transition* from an external relations in which
culture and economy play a central role in establishing contacts, to a more
advanced approach in which *also* policy-based dossiers form the core of their
external relations. The Québécois foreign relations on the other hand had a
distinct political character from the start on, although it used to change its
focus from time to time, e.g. in the 1990s when the core business shifted from
a more cultural approach to a more economic approach.[3]

Many regions with legislative powers have made different choices with regard to the (organizational) structuring of their external activities. One can
detect diverging models among the regions with legislative powers.

A first 'model' is Scotland and Bavaria[4]. Their respective departments engaged in international relations mostly focus on coordinating the external activities of all other functional departments in their government administrations, and this in a quite loose, pragmatic way. In the case of Bavaria, international trade, international cultural or educational policies, and even tourism
are seen as separate areas, which are managed by separate institutions[5]. In
Scotland, the manoeuvring room to conduct a 'foreign policy' is rather limited.[6] Therefore, much attention is being given to public diplomacy. Scotland
is *re-branded* as a traditional nation with a strong cultural identity, yet also
one which stands at the forefront of intellectual and economical innovations.
The international cultural policy of Scotland is tied into this effort. Although
its international trade, its international education and tourism is managed by
institutions separate from the 'official' external relations department, the
Scots have managed quite efficiently to get every governmental entity on
board of its (inter)national public diplomacy efforts. The Scottish *Directorate
'Europe, External Affairs and Culture'* has been upgraded under the current

---

3   Ministère des Relations Internationales de Québec (2007) *40 Ans au Coeur de l'action inter-
     nationale du Québec.*

4   Some regions with legislative powers like for instance the German regions do not think of
     their 'paradiplomacy' as being a 'foreign policy' as such. For instance, Bavaria, which can be
     regarded as a quite developed German region in terms of international contacts and initiatives,
     underlines that it rather conducts a 'foreign affairs' (FA) at best or more correctly an 'external
     relations', focused on technical cooperation, intensifying cross-border regional cooperation
     and 'Europe' (since the EU is seen as part of the 'domestic' reality, no longer a pure 'foreign
     policy'-matter). The real foreign policy is conducted by the *Bund* in Berlin.

5   In Bavaria, EU policy is considered 'domestic policy'. The State Chancellery is responsible
     for the coordination of Bavarian European policy. Representing Bavarian interests in Brussels
     and Strasbourg is considered just as important as the representation of interests at federal level
     in Berlin.

6   Read the Scotland Act of 1998, Schedule 5, part 1, 7: *"International relations, including re-
     lations with territories outside the United Kingdom, the European Communities (and their
     institutions) and other international organisations, regulation of international trade, and in-
     ternational development assistance & co-operation are reserved [UK] matters."*

136   David Criekemans

SNP-government. The Directorate itself has a **horizontal structure,** and co-ordinates all the international aspects of the other directorates. Due to their limited personnel, this coordination is of an ad hoc-nature; only there were it is deemed necessary. Also, strategic choices are made for pragmatic reasons. In complex dossiers, the *Directorate 'Europe, External Affairs and Culture'* creates ad hoc-working groups with other departments. Bavaria also shows a similar limited interpretation of external policy and horizontal structure of its international relations.[7]

A **second 'model'** could be seen in such cases as **Québec and Wallonia.** Interesting is the way in which both international cultural policy and initia-tives in the area of educational cooperation very much remain central in the paradiplomatic activities of these regions. In many cases, the French language and culture is considered as a way of reaching out to new potential partners. It is for instance not a coincidence that *Wallonie-Bruxelles International* (WBI), the department responsible for external affairs of the Walloon Region and French-speaking Community, has established a vast number of contacts and agreements with a number of French-speaking countries and territories in Africa and in the rest of the world, the *Francophonie.* In Québec one can de-tect similar policy choices, perhaps less intense as compared to *Wallonie-Bruxelles*, but nevertheless important. Looking at the way both Québec and Wallonia fill in their respective policies, it is clear that their foreign relations constitute more than culture & education; activities are also developed in quite a number of other policy areas. The **organisation form** which accompanies this more advanced type of substate diplomacy is **mixed; matrix-shaped** *in which* elements can be found of **both horizontal coordination and vertical integration of foreign policy-mechanisms.** In Québec, the number of staff working in foreign policy-dossiers far outnumbers the other regions with leg-islative powers. In that case, one could speak of a more matured matrix-like organisational structure. Since the beginning of 2009, Wallonia is developing a more integrated foreign policy; the two respective administrations for exter-nal relations of the Walloon Region and the French-speaking Community were *fused together* into one single foreign policy-body.

A **third 'model'** which can be distinguished is **Flanders**. In the re-evalua-tion of the activities of the Flemish Government (cf. the *Programme 'Better Governmental Policy'* during the period 2003-06), the fundamental option was taken to pull all external activities together into a more 'verticalized' or-ganisational structure. In the new approach, the Flemish Department of For-eign Affairs is responsible for the **coordination and integration** of the for-eign policy of the Flemish Government. It does a follow-up on both the 'con-tent' and the 'logistical support' of the foreign policy developed by the Min-ister-President, the Minister responsible for Foreign Policy, Development

---

7   In Bavaria and Scotland the minister of external relations reports directly to the Ministerpräsi-dent / First Minister.

Cooperation[8], and the international policy-activities of all other Flemish ministers. This includes also European affairs (thus; no separate Europe-minister). On the one hand, the Flemish Department of Foreign Affairs is responsible for the communication between the Flemish ministry, the federal Public Service Foreign Policy, and the foreign policy-institutions of all other Belgian governments. On the other hand, it also follows up on all foreign partners of the Flemish Government. The organisation of the official international representation of Flanders abroad constitutes also one of the permanent assignments of the Flemish Department of Foreign Affairs. This choice for a more 'verticalized' and integrated structure, is quite striking. When one compares it to the choices made in the organization of the foreign policy of some small states, the similarities are apparent.

Finally, there are also what could be called **'hybrid cases'**. **Catalan foreign policy**, which is currently undergoing an intensive overhauling, could be seen as organisationally being in transformation from model 1 in the direction of model 3. Similar to 'model 2' is the traditional focus within Catalan foreign policy upon culture. This case is based upon the so called 'double export'; the simultaneous promotion of Catalan identity and economy. The *Institut Català de les Indústries Culturals* (ICIC), which operates separately from Catalan foreign policy plays a pivotal role in the cultural promotion of Catalonia. Via its network abroad, ICIC actively promotes Catalan cultural products (audiovisual, music, performing arts). The same principle of the 'double export' is also being implemented by both the Walloon and the Scottish government. They both quite successfully emphasize the value of their own distinct culture as such, but also manage to do some heavy promotion of their cultural industries (e.g. the Walloon film industry or the Scottish gaming industry). Furthermore, the organisational structure of Catalan foreign policy used to be quite horizontal, but this is changing. The jury is however still out on the final choices that will be made; Catalonia, like Flanders, is very much busy with an intense programme of re-evaluation of its structures, policies and instruments.

In conclusion, the above-mentioned elements could be summarized as follows.

---

8   Between 2004 and 2008 the function of Foreign Affairs-minister was separate from the position of Minister-President. Since September 2008, it is again the Flemish Minister-President who is responsible for the coordination of all external activities conducted by the Flemish Government. With this change, Flanders has returned to the situation in the 1990s, under Luc Van den Brande and his successor Patrick Dewael.

Table 6.1: Some diverse 'models' with regard to the way in which foreign policy is defined, as operationalized by different regions with legislative powers

	Model 1	Model 2	Model 3	Hybrid Case
Policy accents within the external relations	Public diplomacy & image building Focus on relevant individual dossiers	Strong attention to role of culture and education Also activities in wider policy-areas	All policy domains have international dimension Recent; interest in public diplomacy	Strong attention to role of culture and education Growing number of policy domains
Type of coordination	Horizontal	Both vertical & horizontal	Rather vertical than horizontal	From horizontal towards vertical
Frequency of coordination	Mostly on an ad hoc basis	Orderly and where required	Structural and daily	From ad hoc towards structural
Organizational structure	Flat organizational structure	Matrix-like structure	Rather verticalized structure	Combination of models 1 & 3, moving to 3
Level of integration of foreign policy dossiers	Disparate	Quite integrated	Integrated (with some exceptions)	Depending on dossier & urgency
Key principle	Pragmatism	Adaptation	Coherence & refinement	Re-evaluation
Example	Scotland Bavaria	Wallonia Québec	Flanders	Catalonia

The dimension of institutional context and intergovernmental relations in external affairs

At the dimension of institutional context and intergovernmental relations in external affairs, one notices that a higher degree of institutional agreements & consultation among governments goes hand in hand with a more cooperative nature of the relation among central & non-central governments on 'foreign policy'-matters. Not in all of the cases studied can this cooperative relation be detected. However, as time passes by, some countries seem to devote attention to finding internal solutions so as to 'pacify' the intergovernmental relations. Sometimes such as process is going up and down, as the case of Québec and 'federal' Canada clearly demonstrates. Belgium a good example of a process whereby cooperation agreements in different domains of foreign policy have institutionalized the relationship between the federal and regional tiers of government. Cooperation agreements among the different Belgian governments can help *institutionalizing* the role of the different parties, but they are never fully complete. They often need to be *updated* due to new intra-Belgian state reforms or de facto-changes, or due to changes on the European or multilateral policy scene. If it is unclear what goals policy-levels in certain domains such as economic diplomacy want to achieve, and via which means they want to achieve them, then the multilevel governance of the Belgian federation as a whole can suffer. Similar patterns can be detected in other countries.

The dimension of the utilized 'diplomatic instruments

At the dimension of the utilized 'diplomatic instruments, one can state that without any doubt the picture of early 21ˢᵗ century 'paradiplomacy' has become quite diverse and lively; extra (political and other) representations abroad are opened and planned, even more cooperation agreements with third parties are concluded, and the domain of multilateral policy is no longer the monopoly of the central states. One also notices that regions with legislative powers are very active in developing formal and informal networks that try to tackle specific needs/problems in very diverse policy areas. It moreover seems that they are more eager to invest in additional, new forms of diplomacy, like e.g. in 'public diplomacy'. The conclusion in our opinion is that paradiplomacy and diplomacy have become enmeshed. When studying the data collected at the level of the categories of 'diplomatic' instruments, some interesting elements arise.

The **political representation**[9] **abroad** of regions with legislative powers still remains modest, certainly if one would compare it with the diplomatic networks set up by the respective central governments. The Belgian regions[10] far outnumber other regions with respect to the sending out of political representatives abroad; there thus exists a definite relationship between the formal powers that were granted and the network that is established. Québec also has an important, be it in quantitative terms lower level of political representation abroad. Nevertheless, from all the regions in our study, Québec has the most experience in this regard.[11] Catalonia now has five political representations

---

9 The proportion of the political representation in relation to the representation abroad in the areas of economic, cultural, educational, and immigration affairs will be discussed under point 5.

10 Flanders has political representatives in The Hague, Paris, Berlin, London, Geneva, Brussels (EU), Madrid, Warsaw, Pretoria, Vienna and a Director of a Flemish House in New York. Wallonia has political representatives in Québec, Paris, Berlin, Brussels (EU), Warsaw, Geneva, Bucharest, Prague, Baton Rouge, Hanoi, Tunis, Rabat, Dakar, Kinshasa, Algiers and Santiago de Chile.

11 The first representative of the Québec government abroad was sent out in 1882 to Paris, this office remained operational until the start of World War II. In 1940, Québec passed a law with regard to the establishment of *'agents généraux à l'étranger'*. These could develop activities in the area of export, immigration, tourism, foreign direct investment and the development of financial links. Based upon this law, Québec sent its first official *'agent général'* to New York in 1940. The office is still operational today. In 1961, a new Québec Delegation was set up in Paris. Today it has the highest personnel of all the Québec-offices abroad. The other *'délégations générales'* of Québec were established in New York, Brussels, London, Mexico, Munich & Tokyo.

abroad, and is planning one extra. The recent growth is thanks to the new Statute of 2006, which incorporated the possibility to establish political offices abroad[12]. Scotland and Bavaria do not devote much attention to political representation compared to the other regions in our study. Scotland is active in Washington, D.C., in Brussels (EU) and in Beijing. Further developing this political network is not on the agenda for the moment. Bavaria has an office in Brussels (EU), and one in Montréal. Interestingly, it also has a 'liaison office' with the *Bund* in Berlin. The instrument of political representation seems to be much related to the institutional-legal manoeuvring room that a region with legislative powers has. Furthermore, only in the cases of the Belgian regions Flanders and Wallonia do the political representatives have an official diplomatic statute; they are presented to the outside world as being diplomats who are functionally specialised in following up on the dossiers of their respective regional governments. They thus have a diplomatic passport. Also, the Belgian regions have installed a rotation system among their senior diplomatic staff, comparable to the ones states have. In Wallonia, it has existed already for a number of years. Flanders introduced this system in August 2008, when the first rotation took place. None of the other regions want to install such a system; they think it would not be efficient and also their network is too small.

With regard to the **concluding of ententes and/or formal treaties**, one can detect a similar correlation with the institutional-legal manoeuvring room that a region with legislative powers has. The 'champions' are clearly Québec and Wallonia. Next come Flanders[13] and Bavaria. Catalonia and Scotland do not have any formal competences in this area. Certainly, the concluding of ententes or treaties can be seen as instruments via which regions with legislative powers further want to 'build' their international-legal recognition. Although Québec does not have strict formal treaty power, its vast number of 635 *ententes* (of which 391 are still active) can nevertheless be considered as coming quite close. An interesting aspect with Wallonia and Flanders is that the treaties they conclude do not *only* cover bilateral partners, but *also* some multilateral issues (e.g. with regard to the joint-supervision of rivers). Also remarkable is that Québec, Flanders and Wallonia have *not only* concluded formal relationships with regions, but *also* with central governments in other

---

12 The Catalan Government counts an important amount of economic offices abroad, as well as offices devoted to the promotion of the Catalan culture and tourism. The main goal of the Catalan government is, however, to develop a network of Catalan Government delegations which unify these entities under a political umbrella. The *Generalitat* is currently present in Berlin (since 2008), Paris (since 2008), London (since 2008), New York (since 2009), Buenos Aires (since 2009). In the second half of 2009, a delegation will be opened in Mexico, followed by one in Asia (exact location not specified just yet).

13 Flanders concluded 'exclusive treaties' with almost all Central and Eastern European countries (all ten new EU-members, including Croatia), also with the Netherlands, Luxemburg, France and several with South Africa.

countries. Flanders for instance used the opportunity of the fall of the Iron Curtain to conclude treaties with the Baltic states, and with Poland and Hungary. In this way regions seem to try to transfer to a 'higher division' in the 'international pecking order', being as capable as small states, but not quite the same. Between 1993 and 2008, Flanders concluded 33 so-called 'exclusive' treaties (27 bilateral and 6 multilateral). By comparison, during the same period the Walloon Region concluded 67 'exclusive' treaties *and* the French-speaking Community concluded 51 'exclusive' treaties.[14] The *Land* of Bavaria[15] is traditionally very active in establishing and developing formal relations both with organizations and territories within the European Union as well as with different regions around the world.[16] Whereas the representation of the Bavarian government in the European Union is relatively strictly conditioned by the federal constitution and as such similar to activities of other states, the German basic law (*'Grundgesetz'*) provides for a significant freedom of action in terms of the establishment of formal ties with foreign countries and regions. As mentioned before, according to Article 32 (3) of the basic law, the states may conclude treaties with foreign countries with the consent of the federal government in areas in which they have the power to legislate. In addition, the *Länder* may also transfer (again with the consent of the federal government) legislative competences to new trans-border regional arrangements (Article 24 (1a) basic law).[17] *Länder* may thus conclude treaties with foreign states with the consent of the federal government if the *Länder* have the power to legislate in those specific policy fields that the treaty addresses.

---

14 These figures show that Flanders is more prudent with regard to the "inflationary dangers" that might go hand in hand with a high number of external treaty obligations. When comparing what regions actually do with their international treaty making power, one should therefore make a distinction between the quantitative and the qualitative. This is not to say that Wallonia is less effective or efficient, but just that it has made different choices. Again, it would take further in depth study to judge this.

15 The German Grundgesetz states that foreign policy is the exclusive domain of the German Bund. However, the German Länder have to be informed by the federal government whenever a treaty is negotiated by Berlin that might influence the specific position of the Länder.

16 Since the mid 1980s, Bavarian foreign policy can be characterized as a strategic attempt to develop specific bilateral partnerships which become partly integrated into a network of sub-national entities at a Global scale that share certain similarities in terms of economic power, technological performance, and cultural self-reliance. This strategy has been implemented first by the foundation of a number of bilateral cooperation agreements between Bavaria and Shandong (since 1987), and Québec (since 1989), and Western Cape and Gauteng (since 1995), and São Paulo (since 1997), and California (since 1998), and Guangdong (since 2004). Most of these bilateral arrangements have also been transferred into a multilateral intergovernmental network which, since 2002, encompasses Bavaria, Québec, Upper Austria, Shandong, Western Cape, and São Paulo (contribution of Dr. Kaiser, see next footnote).

17 Contribution of Dr. Kaiser, Professur für Regierungslehre (Vertretung), Institut für Politische Wissenschaft, Universität Hamburg to our research project and questionnaire. We are very appreciative for Dr. Kaiser's insights.

Bavaria concluded 32 bilateral treaties. To conclude, a last typical aspect of the 'Belgian solution' is that international treaties also have to be ratified by the regions if/when their content is considered to be touching upon competences of these last entities. *'Mixed' treaties* are treaties which apply to both the Belgian federal and the regional competences. Due to the fact that the Belgian state structure lacks *'homogeneous pockets of competences'*, the regions are involved in many treaties. This explains the high number of over 345 mixed treaties (data from Oct. 2008).[18]

With regard to **other agreements of a certain formalised nature,** the data are more difficult to gather. One notices that both Flanders and Wallonia often make use of the flexible instrument of *joint political declarations of intent* with third parties. Catalonia has no political declaration of intent, but concluded nine cooperation agreements since 1992.[19] Scotland concluded six such agreements[20]. Although raw, complete data on *political declarations* for Bavaria or Québec are hard to come by, these regions do often make use this instrument. Making a joint statement when regional ministers meet, is also 'harmless' (see also our earlier remark about the non-enforceable nature of such instruments). Flanders is quite active in the area of *transnational contracts*. With regard to *cultural treaties*, a number of interesting patterns arise. First of all, the concluding of formal cultural treaties –a practice which used to be commonplace up to the end of the 1980s– seems to get outdated; many consider them to be too rigid as instruments. Wallonia still actively works with cultural treaties (often it concerns treaties which were concluded before 1993 by the central government). In Flanders, the number of cultural treaties has rapidly gone down (from 39 in 2001 to a mere 9 in 2007). In many cases, the cultural cooperation has been included in broader Flemish *'exclusive' treaties* with third parties, in other cases the more flexible instrument of *partnerships* is favoured more. In Catalonia, Scotland and Bavaria, one can detect similar choices. Québec signed 147 so-called non-binding agreement so far (data from August 2009), including various declarations of intent, joint statements, etc.

---

18 In Canada, the scope of involvement in international matters by the *provinces* is a political controversy. In 2004, the *Bloc Québecois* proposed a private member's bill (Bill C-260) in the House of Commons on treaty negotiation and treaty making. The bill barred the Canadian government from negotiating or concluding a treaty *"without consulting the government of each province"* if the treaty dealt with an area within provincial jurisdiction or affected the legislative authority of the provinces. It was defeated in September 2005. In speaking against it, government MPs stated that consultation with the provinces was already sufficient… Read: Law Commission of Canada, *Discussion Paper – Crossing Borders: Law in a Globalized World* (Ottawa: Law Commission of Canada, 2006), p. 19.

19 The nine cooperation agreements which Catalonia signed up to, are with Québec, Flanders, Wales, Scotland, Chile, Gyeonggy, Guandong, Gävleborg, Wallonia and Uruguay.

20 The six cooperation agreements which **Scotland** signed up to, are with Victoria State, Shandong, Catalonia, Tuscany, Nordrhein-Westfalen and Bavaria.

What patterns can be discerned concerning **the development of own programmes of assistance and sharing of know-how?** *First,* with regard to **bilateral policy,** each region has developed specific programmes embedded within treaties or other agreements so as to further advance its geopolitical priorities. *Second,* with regard to **cross-border policy,** *Bavaria* is rather the reverse of Scotland; it mostly focuses upon programmes for extensive cross-border cooperation; in the Alps, in the Donau, and in the Bodensee-area. Via the ARGE ALP[21] (*Arbeitsgemeinschaft Alpenländer*) and the IBK[22] (*Internationale Bodenseekonferenz*), Bavaria is conducting a rather low profile but highly effective Alpine policy, together with a number of Swiss cantons, German and Austrian *Länder* and Italian regions in a whole range of policy domains: economic development, culture, environmental policies, urbanism, transport infrastructure, etc. From this extensive Alpine cross-border policy, as well as from the special bilateral relations that Bavaria holds with a great number of Central and Eastern European countries, it is clear that the Land is truly positioning itself as the *Herzland Europas*. Cross-border policy is, and always has been, important in *Catalonia* (although its relative importance seems to have fluctuated over time); there, the *Pyrenees Mediterranean Euroregion*[23] is central & also the *Working Group of the Pyrenees* (CTP). *Flanders* and *Wallonia* both invest in various cross-border projects with areas in the Netherlands, France & Germany. Wallonia is especially active in the so-called *Grande Région*, consisting of a number of German *Länder*, the Grand Duchy of Luxemburg, the French department of Lorraine, the Walloon region together with the Belgian Francophone and germanophone Communities. The constant flux of frontier commuters is an important indicator of the success of this '*Grande Région*'. For *Québec*, the region of the Great Lakes is quite important, and also the economic trade with e.g. New York State. *Third,* with regard to **additional European programmes of assistance and sharing of knowledge (outside of the EU framework),** especially Bavaria and Flanders seem to be front-runners. Already in the 1970s, Bavaria started to extend its hand towards the countries of Central and Eastern Europe. Programmes were developed for the training of local administration officials (mayors, judges, police officers). Later on, the programme was encapsulated within the broader EU-policies on the implementation of the Copenhagen-criteria and the structural funds. Via this programme, Bavaria was able to extend its influence in a

---

21 Consisting of the German Land of Bavaria, the Austrian Länder of Salzburg, Tirol and Vorarlberg, the Swiss cantons of St. Gallen, Tessin and Graubünden and the Italian provinces of Lombardy, Trentino and Südtirol.

22 Consisting of the German Länder of Bavaria and Baden-Württemberg, the Austrian Land of Vorarlberg, Liechtenstein and the Swiss cantons of Appenzell, St. Gallen, Thurgau, Zürich and Schaffhausen.

23 The *Pyrenees Mediterranean Euroregion* was constituted in October 2004 by Aragon, Catalonia, the Balearic Islands, and the regional councils of Languedoc-Roussillon and Midi-Pyrénées; they coordinate regional policies.

144   David Criekemans

region which was historically and economically important for them (something which probably was initially more difficult for the German *Bund* to do
because of history). The Bavarian government was also successful in 'exporting' its values and policy-solutions towards these countries.[24] A quite similar
programme can be found in Flanders. Already in April 1992 (also before Flanders officially became an international actor with treaty making-power), the
Flemish Government had decided to make relations with Central and Eastern
Europe a priority. A new policy-instrument was created for this; the *'Programme Central and Eastern Europe'*.[25] In 1992, 10.68 million euros were
earmarked in order to support the transition process in Central & Eastern Europe, and the development of strong and healthy market economies.[26] With
this annual budget (which gradually decreased over the course of the 1990s),
projects were financed in such areas as economy, environment, infrastructure,
education, vocational training, socio-economic matters and judicial assistance. The final goal of this Programme was however political in nature; to
bring the countries of Central and Eastern Europe in contact with Flanders, an
equally young but reliable foreign partner.[27] None of the other regions studied
have similar extensive programmes compared to Bavaria and Flanders.
Fourth, with regard to **multilateral programmes**[28] **(see also: international
networks, below)**, the Belgian regions seem to be very advanced, and apparently are a model for other regions. Flanders seems to tower over the other
regions with regard to the development of this instrument, and is often seen
as an example which other regions partly want to emulate. Looking at the
multilateral schemes in which the other regions with legislative powers have
invested, it is clear that they are less focussed on traditional multilateral organizations and are more embedded within the frameworks and networks,
which they themselves have developed.
       **'Other forms of participation in multilateral frameworks and pro-
grammes'** are interesting examples to demonstrate the dilution between

24 These countries are a part of the Bavarian Central- & Eastern Europe-programme; Serbia
    (since 1970), Croatia (since 1972), Slovenia (since 1975), Czech Republic (since 1991), Hun-
    gary (since 1991), Ukraine (since 1991), Bulgaria (since 1995), Poland (since 1996), Rumania
    (since 2000), FYROM (since 2000) and Moscow (since 2000).
25 David Criekemans, 'The case of Flanders (1993-2005): how subnational entities develop their
    own 'paradiplomacy'', Kishan S. Rana (ed.), Foreign ministries: managing diplomatic net-
    works and optimizing value (Geneva, DiploFoundation, 2007), 118-156.
26 Yvan Vanden Berghe, Maarten Van Alstein, 'Flemish Foreign Policy with regard to Central
    and Eastern Europe (1992-2003)', *UNU-CRIS Occasional Papers*, n°3, 2004.
27 David Criekemans, 'Nieuwe dynamiek in Vlaams buitenlands beleid?' (translation: 'A New
    Dynamic in Flemish Foreign Policy?'), Internationale Spectator, vol. 59, no. 5, May 2005,
    248-254.
28 These are multilateral programmes or networks that are developed by the regions themselves.
    These are not to be confused with the multilateral programmes that are set up by international
    organizations, such as the United Nations.

traditional and substate diplomacy. Flanders is a front-runner on this front. Soon after the Flemish Government received its international competences, Flanders developed an interest to collaborate with and within multilateral organisations on concrete issues of policy.[29] Flanders developed its first initial multilateral steps vis-à-vis the International Labour Organisation (ILO), UNESCO and the European Bank for Reconstruction and Development (EBRD). It contributed also financially to certain projects of these organisations. Some interviewees underline that at that time –during the 1990s– the Belgian federal government had to cut back its participation in some of these projects (e.g. within UNESCO). Flanders thus seized the opportunity which presented itself to enter the multilateral stage.[30] Later on, the Flemish Government broadened its multilateral 'scope'. Its competency with regard to preventive health care led to an interest into the work of the World Health Organisation (WHO) & UN-AIDS. Because of its educational and cultural work, also the Council of Europe was selected. Within the OECD, Flanders promoted the development of more 'regional' statistical data and studies. Also, the WTO has become an important organisation for Flemish foreign policy, certainly regarding the negotiations in the liberalization of services (the Flemish economy is mainly services-based). Flanders thus contributes to the Belgian/European position in these matters (e.g. via the concept of 'cultural diversity'). In other words, one can detect a wide dispersal of Flemish multilateral activities; from a limited number of organisations and programmes into a much wider spectrum, in which all Flemish administrations are involved. Coordinating this effort therefore becomes a much more daunting task. Flanders finds itself today in a process in which the original project-based approach is less prominent, in favour of the development of a much more 'structural approach'.[31] In the last couple of years, Québec and later Catalonia seem to have developed an interest in the way in which Flanders advanced its 'multilateral position'. The debate

---

29 Before 1993, Flanders had already contributed to the Belgian multilateral position on its 'classical' Community-competences such as language, culture & education within organisations as UNESCO & the Council of Europe. Read: David Criekemans, 'The case of Flanders (1993-2005): how subnational entities develop their own 'paradiplomacy'', Kishan S. Rana (ed.), *Foreign ministries: managing diplomatic networks and optimizing value* (Geneva, Diplo-Foundation, 2007), 118-156.
30 Yvan Vanden Berghe, David Criekemans, Conclusions and policy recommendations on the further potential and opportunities for Flanders in multilateral organisations (Antwerp: Section International Politics, University of Antwerp, 2002).
31 Yvan Vanden Berghe (ed.), Timon Salomonson, David Criekemans, *Mogelijkheden en groeikansen voor Vlaanderen in intergouvernementele multilaterale organisaties* (translation: 'Possibilities and opportunities for growth for Flanders in intergovernmental multilateral organisations') (Antwerpen: Universiteit Antwerpen, Onderzoeksgroep Internationale Politiek, 2001).

within UNESCO about the *Convention on Cultural Diversity*[32] also foster a
cooperation among different regions. Québec has received special status as part
of Canada's delegation to UNESCO, and now also Catalonia is very interested.
Catalonia observed during the *33rd and 34th UNESCO General Conference*
(compare with Flanders & Wallonia, who 'rotate' so as to *"represent & speak
on behalf of the Belgian federation"* in this body), and participated at the *1st
Intergovernmental Committee 'Convention diversity cultural expressions'*
within UNESCO (as a member within the Spanish delegation). Nor Québec or
Catalonia have considered to create funds such as Flanders has within some
multilateral organisations, but this could well become a possibility in the near
future. By contrast, Scotland and Bavaria exclude such a possibility. In the case
of Catalonia, it should also be mentioned that the *Generalitat* has participated
in the multilateral proceedings of such programmes and gatherings as UNFPA,
the Global Fund, the Millennium Campaign and an UNRWA-donor meeting
(*'United Nations Relief & Works Agency for Palestine Refugees in the near
East'*).

Concerning the **participation of regions in other formal or informal networks,** a number of patterns can be detected. First, the regions with less formal
competences devote much more attention and efforts into *informal* networks
compared to formal ones. Scotland is the most apparent example, but to a large
extent this is also true for Bavaria. Second, *looking at the participation of the
European regions to REGLEG*, the Group of EU-Regions with Legislative
Powers, the picture is quite contrasted. Whereas some are very active (Flanders) and active (e.g. Catalonia, Bavaria), others such as Scotland have become
disinterested. This group of legislative regions is trying to find a new mission,
but is struggling. Third, *looking at the other networks in which the regions in
our study operate*, one is struck by the very diverse nature of the frameworks
in which they operate. Some regions are involved in single issue-networks (e.g.
Scotland on maritime issues), others focus on broader policy-issues (e.g. Wallonia and Québec via the *Francophonie*, or Catalonia within the *'Four Motors
for Europe'*), and yet others have established global networks to bring together
substate entities with a specific know-how (e.g. the *'Flanders Districts of Creativity'-network* on creativity and the economy, the last couple of years only
referred to as the *'DC-network'*). The fact that regions with legislative powers
are also very much interested in developing a 'network diplomacy', should not
be astonishing. As Jamie Metzl wrote in his attention-grabbing article *'Network Diplomacy'* in a 2001-issue of the *Georgetown Journal of International
Affairs*, globalization and the information revolution are empowering decentralized networks that challenge state-centred hierarchies. Networks distribute
influence and power across traditional boundaries, allowing powerful interest

---

32 The *'Convention for the Protection & Promotion of the Diversity of Cultural Expressions'*
(or: *'Convention on Cultural Diversity'*) was approved on October 20th, 2005. 148 countries
voted in favour, the USA and Israel opposed.

groups to form and re-shape rapidly. The network is flexible and agile, constantly able to reconfigure itself to address new challenges. Networks are able to bring together much broader communities to address problems in flexible ways that hierarchies often cannot, networks will make the non-competitive components of traditional hierarchies seem increasingly inefficient, ineffective, and ultimately irrelevant.[33] For regions with legislative powers, the development of networks is ideal to create a 'diplomatic level of activity' *next to* the traditional diplomacy of central governments. It might very well be that these networks are much more capable of dealing with the specific needs of post-industrial societies compared to the traditional diplomacies, which often were 'incorporated' at the time of the industrial 'national states' in the nineteenth century. Traditional state-diplomacy remains vigilant and resilient, but nevertheless the international networks that are woven by substate entities and other non-state entities seem to capture a part of the action that sometimes seems to elude central diplomacies. However, it remains quite *difficult to evaluate* the added value of some of the networks that have been developed. Some also are dissolved not long after they are created. Nevertheless, this instrument of 'networks' also allows for the regions with legislative powers to learn from each other's experiences, and hence in this way paradiplomacy advances further, and is being refined as the years pass by.

With regard to **public diplomacy efforts,** one can ask the question whether regions are not better at this than states. Part of the 'third wave' of substate diplomacy is that regions with legislative powers are investing quite a lot in public diplomacy initiatives. The region, which stands the farthest in developing this, is Québec. The Ministry responsible for international relations has in fact *institutionalized* it within a separate *'Direction'*, whose mission is focussed on developing an overarching strategy in public diplomacy. The ultimate aim is to give the broader domestic and international public a nuanced picture of the position and choices of the foreign policy of Québec, and to allow for debate and dialogue.[34] Scotland is also a very interesting case as public diplomacy is concerned. On July 1st, 2004, First Minister Salmond announced a long-term strategy to strengthen *Scotland's International Image* and outlined the Scottish government's plans for promoting Scotland more effectively overseas. Strengthening *Scotland's International Image* was considered a priority by the First Minister in order to bring economic, social and cultural benefits to the Scottish nation. The strategy to create greater awareness of, and interest in, modern Scotland consolidates the 'country's' position on the world stage. The Scottish Executive is aware that it will take a long time to change people's perceptions, but is resolute to create a public diplomacy in which a consistent pattern can be discerned. Scotland also wants to actively 'use' its own diaspora

---

33 Jamie Metzl, 'Network Diplomacy', *Georgetown Journal of International Affairs*, Winter/Spring 2001.
34 Ellen Huijgh and Jan Melissen, *De publieksdiplomatie van Québec.*

of Scottish people around the world to help this initiative (the so-called *'Diaspora Strategy'*, which was announced in October 2005 during a visit of First Minister Salmond to Canada). The developing of a 'brand' for Scotland also is seen as important, linking some of the traditional aspects of 'Scottishness' with aspects such as economic development.[35] The approach of Scotland is certainly less institutionalized compared to that of Québec. Nevertheless, it is very interesting indeed. In Catalonia, we can detect attention-grabbing developments in *re-branding*, in which tourism is given an important role. Catalonia also proves that city diplomacy can be an integral part of a public diplomacy strategy. The way in which the *Generalitat* is working together with the city council of Barcelona to put itself on the map via the well-known Catalan capital is an interesting example of this blend of 'public city diplomacy'. Their *tagline* is as follows: 'Everybody knows Barcelona, even those who do not know Catalonia'. Similarly, Wallonia takes advantage of Brussels' international charisma. It is not a coincidence that the department of foreign relations of Wallonia is called 'Wallonie-Bruxelles International', thus linking the city of Brussels to the region of Wallonia. In Bavaria, in turn, there are impulses in the direction of developing a public diplomacy. The Bavarians are branding their regions in a rather informal yet very effective marketing strategy. By promoting Bavaria as the region of *'Laptops und Lederhosen'*, they are combining the Bavarian benchmark of tradition (*Lederhosen*) with that of cutting-edge modernity (*Laptops*). Since 2004, the regional government of Flanders has shown an interest in public diplomacy, and has started some initiatives (e.g. an English newspaper *'Flanders Today'*, exchange projects for young influentials, etc.). Flanders also became interested in the public diplomacy-model of Québec.

With regard to the above overview, more and more regions realize that 'being active' is not the same as 'having impact'. The diplomatic instruments that are employed are thus critically analysed. Some governments, such as Québec and Flanders, have – under the influence the literature in New Public Management – set steps to 'measure' the effectiveness and efficiency of their activities. Québec is the most advanced in this, but at the same time also the most formal. Some argue that diplomacy is difficult to measure and to capture. Nevertheless, when one has limited resources, such an undertaking becomes more pressing. Increasingly, regions realize this. External pressures such as the international economic crisis since 2008 also heavily impacted these regions and forced them to make 'tabula rasa' to some extent. Many regions since then have identified 'economic diplomacy' as their top priority, and sometimes have reallocated resources in favour of this instrument.

35 Scottish Executive, *Scotland's International Image. Second Year Report* (Edinburgh: Scottish Executive, 2006).

The dimension of the character of the representations abroad

Regarding the character of the representations abroad, one notices that the external projection of many regions has many facets; political, economic, cultural, educational, and even such 'hard dossiers' such as immigration are followed. Although the foreign networks of regions are still modest in comparison to their respective central governments, they nevertheless do important work so as to further expand and deepen the existing cooperation with third parties *beyond the level of the "classical" diplomatic relations*. The table below offers a concise overview:

Table 6.2: Rough overview of the representations abroad of some regions with legislative powers, broken up by mission statement

	Catalonia	Flanders	Wallonia	Scotland	Bavaria	Québec[36]
Political	5 (+1) + EU	10 + EU	15 + EU	2 + EU	1 + EU [37]	6 (+ EU)
Economical (foreign trade & investments)	38	89 in 68 countries	107 in 73 countries	20	20	18
Cultural	9	3	(via Franco-phonie)	--	--	18
Tourism	11	12	--	--	--	--
Educational	--	--	12	--	--	10
Immigration	--	--	--	--	--	20
'Antenna'	--	--	--	--	--	4

From the data above, certain patterns can be distinguished. First, the political representation of regions abroad represents often only a fraction of the total 'outward' representation. The economic representation is also very important. All regions with legislative powers have set up their own agencies for foreign trade and investment. These are very active. There also exists a correlation with the *degree of openness* of the respective economies of the regions; in Flanders, more than 80% of the GDP is generated by exports, thus it is imperative to have a strong economic representation abroad. Also, Catalonia has a very active economic representation. Interestingly, in the cases of Catalonia, Flanders, Wallonia, Scotland and Bavaria, the economic network is between six and seven times larger than the political one. This gives an idea about the choices that are made. Cultural representation abroad is also quite important; Québec and Catalonia have very much focused on this. For Flanders, the cultural repre-

---

36 Because we have split up the Québec-representation abroad according to policy-domains, it might look as though it is vast. Québec has different kinds of representations (see also supra). Therefore, in practice, there are about 30 offices of Québec abroad.

37 Bavaria also has a liaison office with the federal government in Berlin.

sentation abroad is rather limited. Like Flanders, Bavaria and Scotland do not have any official cultural representative abroad. Looking at the more specific choices made by certain regions, one detects an importance being given by Catalonia and Flanders to attracting more tourism. Wallonia is very much engaged in having representatives abroad who foster cooperation and exchange programmes in the area of education. Québec possesses the most diverse external representation, with representatives in the area of foreign trade & investments, cultural, education, and even officers responsible for matters of immigration.[38]

In conclusion: towards a multilevel diplomacy?

It is still unclear whether a 'third wave' in substate diplomacy is currently materializing across the board. But, as happened in the past, the 'front runners' may today very well indicate where and how substate diplomacy will evolve tomorrow. An intriguing question is then whether this 'third wave' will lead to a multilevel diplomacy consisting of coordinated external activities between the central and regional policy levels. On the one hand, this chapter shows that one needs an institutionalization of the intergovernmental relations within a country for this to be achieved. Via cooperation agreements a joint ownership of dossiers in international relations can be realized. But this is not enough. Next to the formal, one also needs the informal; good contacts and working relationships between key people at the central and regional policy level, with a good understanding of the goals to be achieved in their respective foreign policies. The informal only works if trust exists between all key actors. But all this takes time. And that is what is often so difficult; diplomacy has become a real-time activity in a world where smart phones, email, social media, and the internet dictate the pace. This of course creates a field of tension; is a multilevel diplomacy possible in an era of space-time compression? The jury is thus still out on whether third wave—substate diplomacy also fosters a multilevel

---

38 Québec has seven *'délégations générales'* with a broad mandate and offering services in all policy-domains (Paris, New York, Brussels, London, Mexico, Munich, Tokyo), five *'delegations'* which offer services in specific pre-established policy-domains (Atlanta, Boston, Chicago, Los Angeles & Rome), ten *'bureaux'* which offer services in only one policy-area (e.g. immigration or tourism) (Barcelona, Beijing, Berlin, Buenos Aires, Damascus, Hong Kong, Miami, Shanghai, Vienna & Washington), four *'antennas'* which devote their activity to specific issues (Milan, Santiago, Seoul & Taipei), and one *'agent d'affaires'* (Hanoi). Data from: Nelson Michaud and Mark T. Boucher, *L'État québecois en perspective. Politiques Publiques: Les relations internationales du Québec comparée* (Québec City: Observatoire de l'administration publique, 2006), p. 20.

endeavour between central and regional players. Regional governments will continue to utilize *"let us in-strategies"* with *"leave us alone"*-approaches. Furthermore, each of the policy levels are still searching for their added value in the daily drama of international politics and the skilful application this requires of the diplomatic art.

References

Aldecoa, Francisco and Michael Keating (eds.). (1999). Paradiplomacy in Action: The Foreign Relations of Subnational Governments. London and New York: Routledge.

Criekemans, David. (2007). 'The case of Flanders (1993-2005): how subnational entities develop their own 'paradiplomacy'. In *Foreign ministries: managing diplomatic networks and optimizing value*, edited by Kishan S. Rana, Geneva: DiploFoundation.

Criekemans, David. (2005). 'Nieuwe dynamiek in Vlaams buitenlands beleid?' (translation: 'A New Dynamic in Flemish Foreign Policy?'), Internationale Spectator, 59(5), 248-254.

Criekemans David, Duran Manuel and Jan Melissen. (2008). 'Vlaanderen en Catalonië: voorhoedelopers in de Europese substatelijke diplomatie', Internationale Spectator, 62(7/8), 389-394.

Huijgh, Ellen and Jan Melissen. (2008). De publieksdiplomatie van Québec. Antwerpen en Den Haag: Steunpunt Buitenlands Beleid & Nederlands Instituut voor Internationale Betrekkingen 'Clingendael'.

Law Commission of Canada. (2006). Crossing Borders: Law in a Globalized World, Ottawa: Law Commission of Canada.

Metzl, Jamie. (2001). 'Network Diplomacy', Georgetown Journal of International Affairs, Winter/Spring.

Michaud, Nelson and Mark T. Boucher. (2006). L'État québécois en perspective. Politiques Publiques: Les relations internationales du Québec comparée, Québec City: Observatoire de l'administration publique.

Ministère des Relations Internationales de Québec. (2007). 40 Ans au coeur de l'action internationale du Québec.

Scottish Executive. (2006). Scotland's International Image. Second Year Report, Edinburgh: Scottish Executive.

UNESCO. (2005). The Convention on the Protection and Promotion of the Diversity of Cultural Expressions. Accessed from http://en.unesco.org/creativity/convention

United Kingdom. Scotland Act of 1998, Schedule 5, part 1, 7. Accessed from http://www.legislation.gov.uk/ukpga/1998/46/schedule/5

Vanden Berghe, Yvan and David Criekemans. (2002). Conclusions and policy recommendations on the further potential and opportunities for Flanders in multilateral organisations, Antwerp: Section International Politics, University of Antwerp.

Vanden Berghe, Yvan and Maarten Van Alstein. (2004). 'Flemish Foreign Policy with regard to Central and Eastern Europe (1992-2003)', UNU-CRIS Occasional Papers, n°3.

Vanden Berghe, Yvan, Timon Salomonson and David Criekemans. (2001). Mogelijkheden en groeikansen voor Vlaanderen in intergouvernementele multilaterale organisaties (translation: 'Possibilities and opportunities for growth for Flanders in intergovernmental multilateral organisations'), Antwerpen: Universiteit Antwerpen, Onderzoeksgroep Internationale Politiek.

Chapter 7
Multilevel Governance and International Trade Negotiations: The Case of Canada's Trade Agreements

Stéphane Paquin, ÉNAP

Introduction

The period since the end of the Second World War has witnessed increasing international multilateralism and negotiation. In the late nineteenth century, there were no more than one or two international conventions or conferences of official representatives a year. Today, some 9,000 such events are held annually (Union of International Associations, 2011). From 1946 to 2006, the number of international treaties rose from 6,351 to 158,000 according to United Nations figures (UN, 2011). Trade negotiations have followed the same upward trend. On the multilateral level, the General Agreement on Tariffs and Trade (GATT) originally comprised only 44 members; today the World Trade Organization (WTO) has 153. Since the 1990s, the number of preferential trade agreements (PTA) has risen consistently, quadrupling in a mere twenty years. In 2012 more than 300 PTAs are in force, and many more are under negotiation.

At the same time, the number of countries in the world with federal systems or decentralized structures has grown significantly. Of the countries in the European Union, only two had federal systems after the Second World War. Today, 19 of the 27, including Belgium, Spain, Italy, Great Britain, and France, have seen a significant increase in regional government, and some of these countries are now true federal systems. Since 1950, new levels of government have been established in 14 of the EU countries. In 1950, only 5 had elected regional governments; today 16 do. The Forum of Federations estimates that approximately 40% of the world's population lives in a country with a federal type of system (Forum of Federations, 2011; Paquin, 2010; Hooghe and Marx, 2001).

International negotiations and multilateralism are clearly not restricted to areas under the sole jurisdiction of central governments. All spheres of government activity, including matters under the jurisdiction of federated states and municipalities, come within the purview of at least one and often several intergovernmental organizations. International organizations and thematic conferences thus deal with such topics as free trade, the environment, government procurement, education, public health, cultural diversity, business subsidies, treatment of investors, removal of non-tariff barriers, agriculture, services, labour mobility; and the list goes on (Paquin, 2010; Devin and Smouts, 2011).

Federated states and municipalities are thus increasingly aware that their political power or sovereignty, that is, their ability to develop and implement policies, is the subject of negotiation in international bilateral talks and multilateral forums. In response, since the 1960s, the number of federated states actively engaged in international issues has risen considerably (Criekemans, 2010; Paquin, 2010 and 2004; Michelmann 2009; Aldecoa and Keating, 1999; Cornago, 2000; Michelmann and Soldatos, 1990).

In view of the growing impact on their fields of jurisdiction, federated states have taken to playing a greater role in international negotiations, leading the United Nations, for example, to formally recognize the important place of these actors in the talks on climate change. The United Nations Development Programme thus asserts that "most investments to reduce GHG [Greenhouse gas] emissions and adapt to climate change—50 to 80 percent for reductions and up to 100 percent for adaptation—must take place at the subnational level" (UNDP, 2010:3). The 16th Conference of the Parties to the United Nations Framework Convention on Climate Change in Cancún in December 2010 similarly acknowledged the importance of subnational actors in Article 7 of the Cancún Agreement.

The conjunction of all these trends has forced governments to reconsider how they deal with international negotiations. It has also obliged researchers to deploy different tools as they seek to understand the relationship between international negotiations and federalism. An approach framed in terms of multilevel governance is appropriate here, for it enables investigators to obtain a better grasp of the way decisions regarding international negotiations are made and applied when the fields of jurisdiction of federated states are involved. It allows for a better understanding of the role of federated states in the conclusion (negotiation, signature and ratification) and implementation (application) of international treaties when they affect matters within their jurisdiction.

To illustrate, we shall examine how international-trade negotiations are conducted in Canada. We shall see that the provinces are playing a greater role in them and that the multilevel governance approach has greater explanatory capacity than the rival centralized approach.

Theories of federalism and trade negotiations

The theoretical literature has dealt little with the relationship between international negotiations and federalism and has left the topic largely unexplored despite many case studies. Basically, we may say that there are two markedly different schools of thought in the approach to the question: the centralized school and the multilevel-governance school.

Among the proponents of the centralized approach, one of the first theoreticians of federalism, Professor Kenneth C. Wheare, maintained that the monopoly of international relations was a "minimal" power for any federal government (Wheare, 1967). In his major study, he set out the negative consequences of breaking down centralized control of foreign policy for the national interest and the operation of the international system. Robert Davis similarly affirmed that international-relations issues lie at the epicentre of federal systems (Davis, 1967). The centralization of foreign affairs is also, according to Bertrand Badie and Marie-Claude Smouts, required by international law, for the existence of a centralized political system is a necessary condition for a state to fulfil the role assigned to it under international law and practice. Indeed, absent a central government with authority over its territory in matters of international relations and the ability both to make binding international commitments and to impose them internally, inter-state relations are necessarily seriously compromised (Badie and Smouts, 1999). In this view, giving co-decision-making power over foreign policy to federated states risks paralyzing the foreign policy of the central state and damaging the country's image internationally (Scharpf, 1988).

Proponents of the multilevel-governance approach hold an opposing perspective (Bache and Flinders, 2004; Hooghe and Marx, 2003; Jeffery, 1995; Hocking, 1993). According to Brian Hocking, diplomacy and foreign policy cannot be considered a monopoly of the central state (Hocking, 1993). Federated states always have an important role to play, even if only in implementing international treaties that the central state has concluded. Moreover, a central-government monopoly over international relations in a federal system risks undermining the distribution of powers between the different orders of government to the benefit of the central authorities. According to these authors, there are many examples of federal states that must operate within constitutional limitations.

These authors consider that foreign policy must be conceived as a complex system in which the actors in a federal state structure are interlinked. They thus stress the existence of "imperatives of cooperation" between central governments and federated states. Implementation of a coherent foreign policy inevitably, they maintain, entails consulting with—and even according a significant role to—federated states through intergovernmental mechanisms, so that they may play an active part in the country's foreign policy. Regional integration, the rise of multilateralism and globalization have rendered the theses of the centralized approach obsolete.

The imperatives of cooperation between the different orders of government are, in this view, of ever greater importance; hence the considerable expansion in federal systems of executive federalism or intergovernmental relations with regard to international treaties (Meekison, 2004, Hocking, 1993). Canada is no exception to this trend, despite the still largely predominant temptation to govern from the centre (Savoie, 2004, 1999). Richard Simeon contends that intergovernmental relations are the weak link in Canadian federalism (Simeon, 2004); according to many experts (Smiley, Watts, Simeon, Gagnon, Rocher, Brown), the culture of intergovernmentalism in Canada is largely informal, intergovernmental arrangements are rarely binding, and they operate by flexible consensus.

Federalism and international negotiations in Canada

The *Constitution Act, 1867,* gives little mention to international negotiations. In fact, Canada's constitution does not provide for exclusive jurisdiction over foreign affairs. This omission should not be surprising; in 1867 Canada did not become sovereign; it became a dominion within the British Empire. Responsibility for international relations thus lay not with the Canadian government, but with London. The only part of the *Constitution Act, 1867,* concerned with international law is section 132, which deals with imperial treaties. It specifies that: "The Parliament and Government of Canada shall have all Powers necessary or proper for performing the Obligations of Canada or of any Province thereof, as Part of the British Empire, towards Foreign Countries, arising under Treaties between the Empire and such Foreign Countries." Under this provision, while the federal government could not conclude international treaties, it had the capacity to implement imperial treaties, even in provincial fields of jurisdiction.

Only with the passage of the *Statute of Westminster* of 1931 did Canada become sovereign in matters of foreign policy. The question then quickly arose: Does the federal government have the capacity to force the provinces to implement its treaties even in areas that, constitutionally, are under exclusive provincial jurisdiction?

In the *Labour Conventions Case,* the government of Ontario challenged the capacity of the Canadian government to legislate in provincial jurisdictions in order to fulfill its international commitments (Patry, 1980:155). After the 1930 election, Canada's Prime Minister, R. B. Bennett, had ratified three International Labour Organization conventions: one on working hours, a second on weekly rest and a third on the minimum wage. By imposing implementation of these conventions on the provinces, the Canadian government infringed on a provincial jurisdiction, labour.

The Judicial Committee of the Privy Council in London, which was still Canada's court of final appeal, rendered its judgment in 1937. This ruling is of fundamental importance for the legal capacity of the federal government and the rights of the provinces in international relations. The judges recalled that federalism constitutes the foundation of Canada. Furthermore, the principle of the sovereignty of Parliament means that the legislature is not obliged to pass measures that might be necessary to implement a treaty concluded by the federal executive. In this case then, it is up to the provinces, where the same principle of parliamentary sovereignty applies to provincial legislatures, to amend their respective laws and regulations to give effect to the said treaty in domestic law. In Canada, the power to implement treaties thus follows the distribution of powers.

As Jean-Maurice Arbour explains:

> "Since the legislatures are sovereign in their areas of jurisdiction, they cannot be compelled to give effect to the terms of an otherwise validly made treaty. The conclusion is thus that the provincial state, which in theory lacks any legal capacity to negotiate and conclude a treaty, has the entire authority required to implement a treaty dealing with matters reserved to provincial parliaments, and that the federal state, which possesses all the attributes of a sovereign state with respect to the conclusion of treaties, lacks some of the powers necessary to implement them throughout Canada. Perhaps nowhere more than here has Canadian federalism come up against so fundamental a problem, for it highlights the impediments both parties face in the field of international relations" (1997: 160-161) [Translated from French].

In the Gérin-Lajoie Doctrine, the government of Quebec expressed its concern, as had Ontario, over the effects of internationalization on provincial jurisdictions. In a speech in 1965, Quebec Vice Premier and Minister of Education Paul Gérin-Lajoie enunciated what would later become known as the "Gérin-Lajoie Doctrine of the international extension of Quebec's domestic jurisdictions" (Paquin, 2006 [Translated from French]). The doctrine asserts that Quebec itself must conclude any conventions in its fields of jurisdiction. Gérin-Lajoie declared:

There is not, I repeat, any reason for the right to apply an international convention to be separated from the right to conclude the convention. These are two essential stages of a single operation. Nor is it any longer acceptable that the federal state be able to exercise a sort of supervision or control over Quebec's international relations (Gérin-Lajoie, 1965) [Translated from French].

Gérin-Lajoie suggested overturning the approach then generally taken so that Quebec should itself negotiate and implement international agreements in its areas of jurisdiction. This doctrine is still topical. The most recent statement

of international policy by Quebec, in 2006, includes an argument along similar
lines:

> "The evolution of the international situation over the past decades has revealed issues
> that touch upon nearly every one of the government of Quebec's fields of jurisdiction,
> whether in the area of economic development, health, education, culture, or security.
> Most ministries are nowadays concerned with international questions, and carrying out
> the mandate of the Ministère des Relations internationales is based on close collaboration
> with the ministries and with other public sector partners, including the federal govern-
> ment of Canada" (MRI, 2006: 14) [Translated from French].

Furthermore, in 2002 Quebec's National Assembly unanimously passed an
amendment to the *Act Respecting the Ministère des Relations internationales*
requiring National Assembly approval for any important international agreement entered into by Canada that concerns Quebec's fields of jurisdiction. The
National Assembly has thus become the first parliament of the British model
to be so closely involved in the process by which a central government under-
takes international commitments. Quebec is the only province in this situation
(Paquin, 2006) and since then has set a number of precedents.

Treaty making in Canada

Treaty making in Canada is, in the main, a two-stage process, comprising: 1)
conclusion of a treaty, that is, negotiation, signature and ratification; and 2)
implementation. The first stage is the prerogative of the federal executive (a
monopoly which has nonetheless been contested by the government of Quebec
since the 1965 Gérin-Lajoie Doctrine) (Paquin, 2006). The second stage, the
passage of the necessary legislation to apply the treaty, is the prerogative of
the legislative branch, federal and provincial. Treaties must thus be incorporated into domestic law by legislative action at the appropriate level (Arbour,
1997:160). Armand de Mestral and Evan Fox-Decent (2008:617-622) cited
more than 13 different ways treaties may be incorporated into domestic law at
the federal level alone. In Canada, a treaty does not apply automatically over
existing laws. Judges base their rulings on Canadian laws, not treaties. The
issue is of fundamental significance in Canada, for as de Mestral and Fox-Decent point out, "roughly 40 per cent of federal statutes implement international
rules in whole or in part" (de Mestral and Fox-Decent, 2008:578).

Two examples illustrate the process. The United Nations Convention on the
Recognition and Enforcement of Foreign Arbitral Awards of 1958 was concluded by the federal executive (stage 1), but was implemented (stage 2) by
both the federal and provincial governments. The Hague Convention on the
Civil Aspects of International Child Abduction was concluded by the federal

government (stage 1), but was implemented (stage 2) exclusively by the provinces.

According to de Mestral and Fox-Decent, this situation has given rise to many problems.

> "From the federal perspective there are many frustrations and pitfalls. The federal government can commit Canada to a treaty, but it cannot guarantee that the treaty will be properly implemented if the subject matter falls within provincial jurisdiction. This fact can be a serious impediment to the rapid consolidation of a treaty relationship with other states" (de Mestral and Fox-Decent, 2008:644).

In Canada, trade negotiations are, according to the theory, typically led by the federal government. This is, in fact, generally so, even when negotiations deal with an exclusive provincial jurisdiction. There are many precedents, though, in which most notably the government of Quebec has been involved. Intergovernmental negotiations between senior bureaucrats and sometimes even ministers almost always take place. According to, De Mestral and Fox-Decent,

> "The policy-formation process relating to treaty negotiation is entirely in the hands of the federal public service, subject to political direction from the federal cabinet and other elected members of the federal government. In formal terms, provincial, territorial, and First Nations governments are not part of this process. They can be invited to participate, but the invitation is entirely subject to the discretion of the federal government and public service" (de Mestral and Fox-Decent, 2008:592).

The government of Canada here faces significant problems, for provincial collaboration is unavoidable when negotiations deal with the provinces' fields of jurisdiction. In Canada, there is no framework agreement providing for federal-provincial consultations, and there is very little consistency in the approach taken (de Mestral, 2005:319-322). In addition, and even more significantly in the case of trade accords, the effects of treaties on domestic policy do not end with their implementation because they usually include dispute-settlement clauses. For instance, since the North American Free Trade Agreement (NAFTA) does not apply directly in Canada, legislators amended Canadian law to conform to the treaty. Difficulties may emerge with respect to the dispute-settlement mechanism since judgments may require the offending state to amend its legislation or even revoke a past administrative decision. The question that then arises is whether the federal and provincial governments that implemented NAFTA committed themselves only with regard to the treaty or to future rulings by special bodies as well[1]. The issue of the democratic deficit is thus cast into very sharp relief and may cause many problems, both legal and political.

The Canadian government contends that ratification of international treaties is the sole prerogative of the federal executive. It may commit Canada internationally with no form of consent from federal or provincial legislatures, even if a treaty should require substantial changes to laws and regulations. To avoid foreseeable problems, some authors state, the federal government does not ratify international treaties that necessitate legislative changes by the provinces without prior provincial approval (de Mestral and Fox-Decent 2008:594). De Mestral and Fox-Decent state:

> "Generally, the federal government will not ratify a treaty until it is confident that Canada's domestic law is consistent with the treaty and that there are sufficient legal powers in place to comply with its obligations. If legislation is necessary, it is usually passed before the treaty is ratified. The same considerations apply when a treaty relates to matters falling within both federal and provincial jurisdiction, and a fortiori when the treaty relates to matters exclusively within provincial jurisdiction" (de Mestral and Fox-Decent 2008: 624).

In fact, though, a detailed examination of the legislative steps involved in concluding a treaty reveals a relatively long process that is often not completed before ratification by Canada (Paquin, 2010: 173-197). Take, for example, the two NAFTA side agreements on the environment and labour, which in Canada are exclusive (labour) or shared (environment) provincial fields of jurisdiction. Most of the provinces wished to take part in the negotiations on them, but the federal government wanted to act alone. The negotiations resulted in a clause that would permit provinces to withdraw from the side agreements (Kukucha, 2003:59-64). Only three provinces have since signed the environment agreement (Alberta in 1995, Quebec in 1996, and Manitoba in 1997)[1] and only four have signed the labour agreement (Alberta in 1995, Quebec and Manitoba in 1996, and Prince Edward Island in 1998)[1].

The NAFTA side agreements are not exceptional in this regard. Canada signed the Free Trade Agreement with Costa Rica on April 23, 2001. The implementation legislation was tabled on September 20, 2001; royal assent was given on December 18, 2001; and the treaty entered into force on November 1, 2002.[1] Quebec's National Assembly adopted the treaty only on June 2, 2004.

Similarly, the Government of Canada signed the Canada-Chile Free Trade Agreement on December 5, 1996. The House of Commons passed the implementation legislation on July 5, 1997. The treaty was not approved until June 3, 2004, seven years after it had come into effect.[1]

Not only trade agreements are subject to so lengthy a process. The Hague Convention on the Protection of Children and Co-operation in respect of Inter-Country Adoption of May 29, 1993, was ratified by Canada on December 19, 1996, and came into force in April 1997.[1] The treaty was adopted by the Quebec National Assembly on April 20, 2004, and implemented on February 1, 2006, nearly 13 years after it was originally agreed and eight years after ratification by Canada.

The United Nations Convention on Climate Change and the Kyoto Protocol followed a similar course. The convention was adopted on December 11, 1997. Canada signed it on April 28, 1998, and ratified it on December 17, 2002. It came into effect on February 16, 2005, but Canada withdrew from Kyoto on

December 12, 2011. Quebec passed a motion in support of Kyoto on November 28, 2006, and issued a decree adopting the accord on December 5, 2007.

As a final example, the World Health Organization's anti-smoking framework convention was adopted May 21, 2003. Canada signed it on July 15, 2003, and ratified it on November 26, 2004. It was adopted by the National Assembly on December 15, 2004, and the implementation legislation was passed on June 23, 2005, nearly two years after signature by Canada.

Intergovernmental trade mechanisms

Since multilateral and bilateral treaties on international trade increasingly affect the fields of jurisdiction of the provinces, they are increasingly consulted and involved in the negotiations even though international trade is the sole responsibility of the federal government. It is here that the adoption of a multilevel approach comes into its own. The provinces have gradually become key—indeed indispensable—actors in international trade negotiations, to the point that they are currently sitting at the negotiating table in the free-trade talks between Canada and the European Union.

After the Second World War, Canada's trade policy was structured essentially around its participation in the GATT negotiations. Until the 1970s, talks basically dealt with the reduction of tariffs, an exclusive federal responsibility. With the Kennedy Round (1964-1967) and even more clearly the Tokyo Round (1973-1979), multilateral negotiations would begin to have increasingly significant effects on provincial fields of jurisdiction, for they dealt particularly with non-tariff barriers. It was against this backdrop that the federal government developed consultative mechanisms for its international-trade initiatives. Since subsequent rounds of talks also involved provincial jurisdictions, the consultation mechanisms remained in place (Whinham, 1978-1979: 64-69). The Uruguay Round GATT negotiations, for example, considered such issues as subsidies, dumping, and phytosanitary measures, as well as agriculture, intellectual property and services.

Federal-provincial consultations have assumed even greater importance as domestic policies on business subsidies and trade-distorting or -obstructing provincial and local regulations have increasingly become the subject of international negotiations. Natural-resource-pricing and agricultural-support policies are but two of the many domestic issues touching on the provinces' constitutional jurisdictions that have been raised in international economic forums. Since 1980, the previous arrangements have come to be institutionalized through periodic federal-provincial consultations on trade policy (Fairley, 1988).

During the negotiations on the Canada-United States Free Trade Agreement (CUSTA) in the 1980s and the North American Free Trade Agreement (NAFTA) in the early 1990s, the provinces were active participants in the debates on the potential impact of the accords on their respective economies and fields of jurisdiction. CUSTA and then NAFTA included such subjects of provincial concern as rules of origin, technical standards, energy, financial services, and certification.

When Brian Mulroney's Conservative government launched free-trade talks in 1985, the provinces lost no time in making their respective positions known, not only through the first ministers' conference, but also by their representation on the preparatory committee for the talks established by Canada's chief negotiator (Doern and Tomlin, 1991: 126-151).

Quebec and Ontario retained the services of prominent counsellors to press their views in Ottawa. Ontario engaged Bob Latimer, a former federal public servant in the Department of External Affairs and the Department of Industry and Trade; and Quebec, recruited Jake Warren, Canada's negotiator at the Tokyo Round (Hart et al., 1994: 139).

During the CUSTA negotiations, the provincial premiers met for talks with Prime Minister Mulroney fourteen times in eighteen months. However, they met with opposition from the Mulroney government when they asked for seats at the table with the US (Hart et al., 1994: 139). A similar process was repeated during the negotiations on NAFTA in the early 1990s (Abelson and Lusztig, 1996: 681-698).

It was during these major talks that an intergovernmental mechanism was established to manage relations between the provinces and the federal government. The federal government subsequently made the meetings with the provinces regular events to seek technical advice and plan its arguments for the negotiations. This outcome was inevitable, for, as we have seen, the federal government does not have the constitutional capacity to impose treaties it concludes in provincial fields of jurisdiction. These intergovernmental-negotiation practices have continued in many forums, including the quarterly C-Trade gatherings of federal, provincial and territorial public servants to exchange information and plan the Canadian position on all trade-policy matters, including negotiations (Paquin, 2010).

When Canada launched trade negotiations with the European Union, the most important ones since NAFTA, the provinces' role in the process was expanded. To start the negotiations for a "new generation" free-trade deal, the EU insisted on the inclusion of the provinces in the Canadian delegation basically because the Europeans are particularly interested in accessing Canadian municipal and provincial public-procurement contracts. The EU judged that if the talks were to have any chance of success, provincial representatives had to be at the table since the provinces are not obliged to implement accords concluded by the federal government in their fields of jurisdiction.

For the first time in the history of Canadian trade negotiations, the provinces are represented at several negotiating tables. Twelve tables were established to deal with different issues, and the provinces have formally been given seats at seven of them. The provincial representatives also maintain informal relations with both the Canadian and European envoys. The government of Quebec's chief negotiator, Pierre Marc Johnson, for example, has had several bilateral meetings with the chief European negotiator, Mauro Petriccionne. The provinces are accordingly playing an increasingly important role. Provincial representatives accounted for 28 of the 50 members of the Canadian delegation at a January 2010 session of the talks in Brussels. In the opinion of the European negotiators interviewed by the author, the provinces will play a decisive role in determining the outcome of the talks.[1] Without a clear commitment on the part of the largest provinces, the negotiations stand only a slim chance of succeeding.

A comparison of the provinces' participation in Canada's free-trade negotiations with the US and the EU reveals their growing involvement. It is true that the provinces were not consulted on the selection of the chief negotiator or even of the chief negotiators for any of the negotiating tables. However, in the EU case, they were consulted at the crucial stage of defining the terms of reference; they are represented at the different negotiating tables, and they are directly involved in the negotiating process. Consequently, if concluded, this accord, unlike NAFTA, will have a very great impact in areas in the provinces' jurisdiction.

Conclusion

Today, the multilevel governance approach is a better method to use in studying trade issues than the centralized one. It is a major error to think of trade negotiations in federal systems as the sole responsibility of the federal executive. Such a view ignores the very intrusive nature of trade treaties, which are, indeed, proving intrusive in increasingly significant ways. Moreover, the centralized approach is all too often contradicted by the facts of the last thirty years. This situation is not unique to Canada; many countries, such as Belgium, Switzerland and Germany, have institutionalized mechanisms similar to those in this country.

The federal government must thus consult the provinces to obtain technical advice and plan its negotiating arguments and to ensure that the provinces fulfil their obligations and implement the treaty. In Canada, contrary to preconceptions, because the federal government's constitutional capacities are limited, it has been obliged to share some of its international prerogatives with the provinces. Since the 1970s, federalism and the negotiation of international treaties have necessitated ever greater federal-provincial cooperation.

References

Arbour, J.-M. (1997). *Droit international public.* 3rd ed. Cowansville: Les Éditions Yvon Blais Inc.

Abelson, D. E. and M. Lusztig. (1996). "The Consistency of Inconsistency: Tracing Ontario's Opposition to the NAFTA", *Canadian Journal of Political Science*, 29 (4), 681-698.

Aldecoa, F. and M. Keating (Eds.). (1999). *Paradiplomacy in Action. The Foreign Relations of Subnational Governments.* London: Frank Cass Publishers.

Badie, B. and M.-C. Smouts. (1999). *Le retournement du monde. Sociologie de la scène internationale*, 3rd ed. Paris: Presses de Sciences-po/Dalloz.

Bernier, I. (1979). "La Constitution canadienne et la réglementation des relations économiques internationales au sortir du 'Tokyo Round'", *Cahiers de Droit*, 20 : 673-694.

Conklin, D. (1997). "NAFTA: Regional Impacts", in M. Keating and J. Loughlin (Eds.), *The Political Economy of Regionalism,* London and Portland: Frank Cass Publisher.

Criekemans, D. (2010). "Regional Sub-State Diplomacy from a Comparative Perspective: Quebec, Scotland, Bavaria, Catalonia, Wallonia and Flanders", *The Hague Journal of Diplomacy*, 5, (1-2), 37-64.

De Mestral, A. and E. Fox-Decent. (2008). "Rethinking the Relationship Between International and Domestic Law", *McGill, L.J* (53), 576.

De Mestral, A. (2005). "The Provinces and International Relations in Canada" in Jean-François Gaudreau-DesBiens and Fabien Gélinas (Eds.) *The States and Moods of Federalism: Governance, Identity and Methodology,* Cowansville: Yvon Blais, 319-342.

Doern, B. G. and B. W. Tomlin. (1991). *Faith and Fear: The Free Trade Story,* Toronto: Stoddart.

Fairley, S. H. (1988). "Jurisdictional Limits on National Purpose: Ottawa, The Provinces and Free Trade with the United States", in M. Gold and D. Leyton-Brown (Eds.), *Trade-Offs on Free Trade: the Canada-US Free trade Agreement.* Toronto: Carswell.

Gérin-Lajoie, P. (1965). Texte de l'allocution prononcée par Monsieur Paul Gérin-Lajoie, vice-président du Conseil et ministre de l'Éducation, devant les membres du corps consulaire de Montréal, April 12.

Hart, M., B. Dymond and C. Robertson. (1994). *Decision at Midnight: Inside the Canada-US Free-Trade Negotiations.* Vancouver: University of British Columbia Press.

Karns, M. and K. Mingst. (2004). *International Organizations. The Politics and Processes of Global Governance.* Boulder: Lynne Rienner.

Kukucha, C. (2003). Domestic Politics and Canadian Foreign Trade Policy: Intrusive Interdependance, the WTO and NAFTA, *Canadian Foreign Policy*, 10 (2), 59-64.

Lubin, M. (1993). "The Routinization of Cross-Border Interactions: an Overview of the NEG/ECP Structures and Activities", in D. M. Brown and E. H. Fry (Eds.), *States and Provinces in the International Economy,* Berkeley: Institute of Government Studies Press.

Michaud, N. and I. Ramet. (2004). "Québec et politique étrangère : contradiction ou réalité? », *International Journal*, 59 (2), 303-324.

Michelmann, H. J. and P. Soldatos. (1990). *Federalism and International Relations, The Role of Subnational Units*, Oxford: Oxford Press.

Munton, D. and D. Castle. (1992). "Reducing Acid Rain, 1980s", in D. Munton and J. Kirton (Eds.), *Canadian foreign policy: Selected cases*, Scarborough: Prentice Hall Canada.

Palard, J. (1999). "Les régions européennes sur la scène internationale : condition d'accès et systèmes d'échanges", *Études internationales*, 30 (4), 657-678.

Paquin, S. (2004). *Paradiplomatie et relations internationales. Théorie des stratégies internationales des régions face à la mondialisation.* Brussels: Presses interuniversitaires européennes-Peter-Lang.

Paquin, S. (2006). "Le fédéralisme et les relations internationales du Canada depuis le jugement de 1937 sur les conventions de travail", in Stéphane Paquin (Ed.) *Le prolongement externe des compétences internes. Les relations internationales du Québec depuis la Doctrine Gérin-Lajoie (1965-2005),* Ste-Foy, Presses de l'Université Laval, 7-24

Paquin, S. (2008). "La paradiplomatie des États américains et la cohérence de la politique étrangère des États-Unis", in F. Massart-Piérard (Ed.). *L'action extérieure des entités subétatiques. Approche comparée. Europe – Amérique du Nord*, Louvain: Les Presses de l'Université Louvain-La-Neuve.

Paquin, S. (2010). "Federalism and Compliance with International Agreements: Belgium and Canada Compared", *The Hague Journal of Diplomacy*, 5 (1-2), 173-197.

Patry, A. (1980) *Le Québec dans le monde*, Montréal: Leméac.

Savoie, D. J. (2004). "Power at the Apex: Executive Dominance", in J. Bickerton and A.-G. Gagnon (Eds.), *Canadian Politics*, 4th ed. New York: Broadview Press.

Simeon, R. (2001). « Conclusion », in J. P. Meekison (Ed.), *Relations intergouvernementales dans les pays fédérés. Une série d'essais sur la pratique de la gouvernance fédérale*, Ottawa: Forum des fédérations.

Soldatos, P. (1990). "An Explanatory Framework for the Study of Federated States as Foreign-Policy Actors". In H. J. Michelmann and P. Soldatos (Eds.), *Federalism and International Relations, The Role of Subnational Units*. Oxford: Oxford Press.

Stevenson, G. (1982). *Unfulfilled Union: Canadian Federalism and National Unity*, Rev. ed. Toronto: Gage.

Whinham, G. R. (1978-1979). "Bureaucratic Politics and Canadian Trade Negotiation". *International Journal*, 34 (4), 64-89.

WTO (2011), *World Trade Report 2011*, Geneva.

Chapter 8
Business Associations and Multilevel Dynamics in Spain and the UK

Iván Medina, Autonomous University of Barcelona
Joaquim M. Molins, Autonomous University of Barcelona

Introduction

This chapter examines the adaptation of business associations to Multilevel governance in Spain and the United Kingdom. In a nutshell, previous studies stressed that: a) business associations copied market segmentation and state decentralisation, rather than the other way around; b) regional business associations were more oriented to providing services to members than were national associations; c) business associations contributed to the strengthening or defusing of regional forces; d) employers feared that political decentralisation was likely to generate market fragmentation; e) the appearance of meso-corporatist expressions was related to sectoral aspects of the market rather than a political necessity of the businesspeople; and f) in the case where a political mobilisation of employers at regional level took place, the region was so remote from the general interest of all employers that experimentation by regional actors were allowed as no one in other regions would be concerned about the failures of their colleagues elsewhere. This set of statements was forged in a time marked by a neocorporatist wave soaking Europe, including the United Kingdom. We should not forget to add to these considerations that during the heyday of Keynesianism local elites did not consider the right choice to relinquish to be present in the state governance even though it meant a weakening of regionalism. Only regions with salient cultural, economic, and political features opted for a strong regional model (see Medina 2012 for further discussion).

On the contrary, current territorial politics are influenced by global politico-economic processes that modify the state's traditional mechanisms of public intervention forging regions as 'spaces for politics'. The New Regional Development paradigm suggested that economic efficiency depends on local resources and dynamics, thus the various aspects shaping territory were incorporated into explanations of economic, social and even political change. Such accommodation between the market and the state should pave the way for a better government, achieve a more active democracy, and boost economic growth. The main result of this territorial move was the emergence of peripheral economies, regional institutions, regional elites, and regional cultures (Keating et al 2003), causing an increased interest to public agendas based on regional policies. Hence, nationalist aspirations will cease to be the only argument in support of the regional state; essential aspect of the old regionalism. In sum, the New Regionalism literature has mainly focused on the changing scale of public action caused by Globalisation, the European Union, the emergence of regional elites, and regional competitiveness. For obvious reasons, the gradual transformation of economic and political structures has implied adaptations and adjustments of the manifold actors that were interplaying with and within public institutions. In this way, business associations have faced alterations in the economic paradigm (from Keynesian macro-economies to neoliberal micro-economies) and adjustments in their traditional arenas of representation (collective bargaining, and social dialogue).

Business Associations and Territorial Politics

Globalisation challenges the state by transforming its forms. At stake is a profound deterritorialisation of state activities in terms of a steady involvement of private actors (e.g. interest groups) within representative institutions; a sharp loosening of national geographies when it comes to demarcate the scope of activity of various institutions; an increasing scope of goals and tasks of supra- and subnational institutions; and, last but not least, the spread of alternative visions and political movements aiming at empowering minorities, state-less nations, etc. As Globalisation marches on, the neoliberal approach to regional competitiveness challenges the very basic economic assumptions of regions. Swyngedouw (1992) argued that the economy was moving towards firms' competitiveness; then there is an ongoing necessity for relying on the productive capacity of the *meso* levels of governance. Theoretically, territories with large accumulations of value-added resources (human capital, innovation, technology...) are less exposed to the relocation of companies (Maillat 1995). It is worth mentioning that this neoliberal stance was severely criticised by Lovering (1999) who believed it was mere propaganda. In his contention, the well-sounding words underpinned by regional economists are not applicable to all sorts of regions, but only to a few ones that already showed conditions to internationalise their products.

There are regions that do better than others in mobilising resources, in developing strategies and in conditioning the intermediation of regional interests. Although regional authorities make strong efforts to cater resources and attract foreign investment, they cannot force any company to settle in its territory. The challenge for competitiveness and innovation can exclude those less privileged regions from the access to certain commercial networks, although many of them may offer other attractions linked to culture and tradition. Accordingly, Keating (2001: 219) highlighted that in no case economy will determine the process of regional construction. It is appropriate therefore not to focus solely on the search for economic development as the only objective of political and social actors in the region. Since territory is the main arena for mobilisation and political representation, regional elites deem necessary to consolidate regional autonomy relying on political, social, cultural, and fiscal issues (Keating 1996). Regional elites, in consequence, did attempt to 'skip' as much interactions as possible with state-wide actors, while seeking new complicities and compromises at the European arena.

Indeed, conflicts involving regional and national governments may be a source of permanent regional mobilisation in regions where language is a salient element, leading the regional elites to defend and, in turn, promote its usage as a way to 'construct' an own homeland. The empowerment of regional elites is strongly associated to the process of regional building: the more a region is differentiated from the state in terms of identity and policy-making, the more powerful and autonomous regional elites become. In this regard, there are expectations to shape regions, be it as 'imagined communities' or as systems of political action (Keating 2003). For instance, rich regions (that usually feature identity attributes) intend to secure their own economic and fiscal status by confronting poor regions (Caciagli 2006). Business actors may be interested in promoting the region as a fruitful economic arena (Molins et al 2010). Nevertheless, we think that it is important to remember that the very basic business associations' remit is to serve as experienced interlocutors when it comes to shape policies. If government vetoes business associations, or if regional institutions are incapable of meeting social interests, businesspeople would deem necessary not to get involved in the regional arena. In this way, we resort to Anderson's (1991: 70) caveat: 'Whether BIAs [business interest associations] become involved in politics about territory fought out across territory depends largely on their properties as interest groups. National, sectoral, and territorial BIAs are Janus-faced organizations that seek to intermediate between members and external actors, above all state agencies and trade unions'.

In this sense, the literature on industrial relations has pointed out that social dialogue occurs in less intensity than in previous decades, but it ultimately empowers lower organisational levels. As far as the relationships between levels of negotiation are concerned, Regalia (2007) assured, on the one hand, that autonomous and independent initiatives can take place at another level than the state, and, on the other hand, that the various levels encompass a variety of logic of actions, actors involved, and issues addressed. In this respect, regional/local concertation is likely to involve tripartite and multilateral negotiations extending participation to banks, labour market agencies, chambers of commerce, churches, environmental organisations, education and training institutes, and so forth. Whereas the national level usually tackles subjects such as curbing inflation, reducing the cost of labour, and reforming social policies, regional/local concertation mainly addresses territorial competition by accomplishing: (1) policies for local government, environmental policies, urban planning and regeneration; (2) policies for local development, industrial restructuring, innovation, technological transfer, and training; (3) policies on employment and labour markets; (4) local welfare policies, support for families, protection for weak groups; and (5) policies for social inclusion and support for the social economy.

The Territorial Logic of Business Associations in Spain

In Spain, the map of business associations has been structured around two main pillars: the sector and the territory. The combination of these two pillars forms a complex network of business associations in which the *Confederación Española de Organizaciones Empresariales* (CEOE) stands as the peak confederation since 1977. The CEOE embarked in a double duty during the early years: first, defending an open economy (that was not apparently a key issue concerning any political party); and, second, participating in social dialogue and in collective bargaining (Molins & Casademunt 1998). However, its main challenge was to integrate small and medium enterprises within its representative umbrella, assuming that this sort of firms abounded among the Spanish businesses. In 1980, the *Confederación Española de la Pequeña y Mediana Empresa* (CEPYME) was finally integrated within CEOE following a special status recognising its organisational singularity. Yet other SMEs associations did not join the CEOE and still claim for a more intense defence of small firms' needs. Therefore, the origins of CEOE's organisational structure are, on the one hand, large sectoral organisations at the national level with provincial branches following the francoist *Sindicato Vertical*'s model, and, on the other hand, inter-sectoral organisations at the provincial level emerging from the *Consejos Provinciales de Empresarios* (Martínez-Lucio 1992). A key factor determining the salience of the province for the organisation of sectoral business associations in Spain is the weight of such level within collective bargaining. As a consequence of this, and encouraged by the establishment of the *Comunidades Autónomas*, sectoral-provincial business associations began to deem necessary to talk with the new regional authorities.

The consolidation of regional business associations in the democratic re-gime has largely depended on power relations between state-wide leaders and local members, in that the former sought to define the broad guidelines of a cohesive business community throughout Spain, and the latter were seeking autonomy to participate in the governance of local community tensions. The result of these two intertwined trends has made the regional systems of busi-ness associability being charted by organisational complexity and a very in-tense struggle for institutional representation. The creation of an intermediate tier of government could have facilitated institutional experimentation to the extent that the regional governance could have opted for greater pluralism in the competition of interests. However, all of the *Comunidades Autónomas* have copied the neocorporatist model existing state-wide; probably showing that the Spanish political culture based on corporatist arrangements is thoroughly ex-tended throughout the territory. Generally speaking, one could say that Spanish regional business associations have gone through several stages over the last thirty years: they began prioritising organisational matters, then adapting to the economic needs, and ending up as highly institutionalised associations. Nonell et al (2011) summarised two trends charting the establishment of peak regional business associations in Spain. On the one hand, regional business associations emerged as cross-sectoral and intermediate organisations, whose membership is based on sectoral and local associations, as well as on some large firms di-rectly affiliated to them. In most of the regions, a single business association belonging to CEOE monopolises business representation. On the other hand, regional business associations set up as the result of the hierarchical integration of pre-existing local and provincial associations. This allowed business asso-ciations having wider cross-sectoral scope. Such a strategy is applied to Anda-lusia and Aragon, for instance.

To a greater extent, regions are becoming the most notable arena to allow competition between business associations in Spain (Nonell & Molins 2007). Whatever their typology, business associations have mainly a local landscape. In fact, local associations own legal status, thus the process of setting up a state-wide confederation proceeds *bottom-up* rather than *top-down*. In this sense, the region becomes a striking level of government for business associa-tions with scant resources to develop a solid logic of influence. As for small business, exerting influence on the regional government requires fewer efforts than monitoring the parliamentary activity and contacting the central govern-ment. None the less, peak regional business associations belonging to CEOE are not likely to diminish their power as a consequence of the establishment of independent associations. They are neither considering themselves as not rep-resenting SMEs nor willing to lose an important niche of potential members. All of these peak associations have fostered the creation of SMEs-related as-sociations as means of consolidating its dominance over the business spectrum. Very much as the CEOE-CEPYME relationship, these peak associations set up sister business associations, include them into their structure, and virtually endorsed them with representativeness (although they may be short of power).

As far as regional dynamics are concerned, it is worth mentioning the multilayered approach of social dialogue in Spain. Two trends are worth remarking: on the one hand, the onset of most agreements in the mid-1990s, and, on the other hand, a considerable increase of agreements from the 2000s onwards. The former trend is explained by the European Council's interest in promoting *Territorial Employment Pacts*. The latter is strongly associated with a bulky transfer of policy matters to the regions over the past fifteen years. In order to reach some sort of governability and economic coherence, regional governments have been cajoled to dialogue with social partners on health, education, industry, economy, and many other policy issues. According to Nonell (2010), the main consequence of having moved from partial agreements to real social pacts is the demand by social partners to reward their institutional participation.

Table 8.1: Corporatist Forums in Spain

	Economic and Social Councils	Labour Relations Council
CEOE	X	
Andalusia	X	X
Aragon	X	X
Asturias	X	X
Balearic Islands	X	
Basque Country	X	X
Canary Islands	X	X
Cantabria	X	X
Castile-La Mancha		X
Castile-Leon	X	X
Catalonia	X	X
Extremadura	X	X
Galicia	X	X
La Rioja	X	X
Madrid	X	X
Murcia	X	X
Navarra	X	X
Valencian Community	X	X

Source: Nonell et al (2011)

This is actually a recent demand seeking to imitate the model of representation that exists state-wide. Whereas recent social pacts have included a clause encouraging governments to enact a law on institutional representation, this concern was already mooted in the reforms of the regional Statutes of Autonomy. In this sense, the renewed statutes of autonomy of various regions do recognise explicitly the right of business associations and trade unions to carry out their very functions in the economic and social spheres. For instance, the Andalusia Statute acknowledges the Andalusian Economic and Social Council a striking salience because its 'primary purpose is to serve as a channel for participation and ongoing dialogue on socio-economic issues.'

All this has led to a new scenario in which business associations openly supported the attempts to renew the regional Statutes of Autonomy. There was a political motivation behind such a support, but the key factor explaining business associations' decision was that the new Statutes of Autonomy proposed a clear redistribution of public tasks in which regional governments could have enhanced their position within the provision of supply-side policies (innovation; research; infrastructures; energy, and so forth). Since the 2000s many of the regional business associations have been stressing the need for public investments in competitiveness and in internationalisation. For instance, the Catalan peak regional business association *Fomento del Trabajo Nacional* (FTN) stated in 2002 that the Catalan government's budget's main objectives for 2003 must have been focused on promoting competitiveness (human capital; internationalisation; innovation; infrastructure; and SMEs). Similarly, FTN continued to insist on public investments on these specific areas in consecutive years, not only to the regional government but also to the central government.

The Territorial Logic of Business Associations in the UK

Regardless the many goals achieved by the Confederation of the British Industry (CBI), the association has not been able to alter members' expectations on the grounds of firms' size, thus 'smaller firms in the CBI joined particularly because of the services it offered, whereas the larger industrial giants tended to join because of its position as a lobbying on behalf of industry' (Norton 1994: 155). Accordingly, the absence of a particular voice for small firms a few decades ago, whose problems are fairly different from those of large companies, was a powerful argument to constitute an independent SMEs employers' association to undertake both lobbying functions and membership assistance (McHugh 1979). The Federation of Small Business -previously the National Federation of the Self-Employed- was formed in 1974. The initial motivations for joining the FSB were 'political' in so far as its activity was aimed at modifying government policy (Jordan & Halpin 2004). The complexity of the UK business associations map increases with the presence of at least two more relevant associations: the Institute of Directors (IoD) and the Chambers of Commerce. The existence of four UK-wide business associations has led to several problems such as fragmentation, overlapping, limited resources, and difficulties in deciphering business interests (Greaves 2008). The government has carried out a couple of initiatives such as the Devlin Commission (1972) and the Heseltine initiatives (1993-1995), with which to simplify the business representation system by detecting problems and recommending changes. The two main problems detected in these reports were, on the one hand, the existence of many voices representing entrepreneurs at the state level, both in industry and institutions, making it difficult to engage in effective dialogue between business and the government; and, on the other hand, the problems of competition between the Chambers of Commerce and the CBI at the local level, which hinders the provision of services to members and the effective articulation of the demands of the local business community.

Unlike Spain, UK business associations are not set to undertake formal 'institutional representation', but act as mere business interest groups. Therefore, the UK is by far less institutionalised than Spain. There are no experiences of collective agreement at any level. Social concertation is virtually non-existent, just reduced to a few formal national tripartite or bipartite consultative advisory bodies and various informal bipartite and tripartite partnerships. Devolution has particularly affected, on the one hand, the provision of public services, with a major impetus in the creation of partnerships involving companies, sectoral organised groups, and the government, and, on the other hand, the increase in resources in hands of regional institutions. While regions have established neither regional economic councils nor 'Labour Arbitration Services', new regional services have been created to complement the programmes implemented by the various central government's agencies. For instance, the tripartite 'Advisory, Conciliation and Arbitration Service' (ACAS) endeavours itself to improve working life through training courses and conciliation services throughout the United Kingdom, whereas the Scottish government set up the *Skills Development Scotland* (SDS), an agency with which to provide careers services, as well as other specific business services such as 'P3' (People, Performance and Productivity) and the 'Labour Market Information and Intelligence'. Accordingly, the Welsh government also scheduled a number of initiatives to support companies such as the 'Welsh Economic Growth Fund' and the 'Regeneration Investment Fund for Wales'.

Table 8.2: Regional Social Dialogue in Spain

Region	Agreements by years (some years have produced more than one agreement)*
Andalusia	1993, 1995, 1997, 1999, 2001, 2005, 2009
Aragon	1996, 1998, 2001, 2004, 2008
Asturias	1988, 1998, 2000, 2004, 2008
Balearic Islands	1996, 2000, 2005, 2007, 2009
Basque Country	1996, 1999, 2003, 2007(2)
Canary Islands	1994(3), 1997, 1998, 2001, 2002, 2005, 2008, 2009, 2011
Cantabria	1998, 1999, 2000, 2001, 2003(2), 2005, 2007, 2008, 2010(2)
Castile-La Mancha	1995, 1996, 1998(2), 2004, 2005, 2007, 2008(2), 2009, 2010
Castile-Leon	1993, 1998, 2001(3), 2004, 2005(2), 2007, 2010
Catalonia	1998, 2005, 2008, 2009, 2011
Extremadura	1989, 1992, 1996, 2000, 2002, 2004, 2007, 2008(2), 2010
Galicia	1998, 1999(2), 2005, 2006, 2007, 2008
La Rioja	1994, 1996, 2001, 2005(2), 2006, 2009
Madrid	1995, 1997, 2002, 2004(2), 2008, 2009(2)
Murcia	1996, 1998, 2002, 2007(2), 2010
Navarra	1993, 1995, 1998, 2002, 2004, 2009
Valencian Community	1984, 1991, 1993, 1994, 1996, 1999, 2001, 2008

Source: Medina 2012

The Scottish parliament has had much more autonomy than that of the Welsh National Assembly in raising and scrutinising devolved matters, thus making the Scottish governance be more able to strengthen its functionality for the many actors involved in the Scottish arena. There was less speculation in Scotland regarding the legislative process – the existence of a more coherent institutional framework helped understand the legislative process. This fact has not blocked a permanent debate on how the devolved institutions can be enhanced both in Scotland and Wales. The Scots have sought to build stronger ties with civil society during the policy process by empowering consultation and transparency mechanisms, as well as considered the possibility of governing Scotland themselves independently from the United Kingdom's umbrella. Likewise, the Welsh have assessed the benefits of having a stronger parliament for a nation scoring poor economic figures. The regional governance in England attempted to develop better policy co-ordination and open new spaces for policy innovation. But to the extent that the English regions were ruled by quangos already, it was necessary to provide a political component to permit integration and democratic accountability (Tomaney 1999). The Regional Chambers should have incorporated a new democratic tier between the UK Parliament and municipalities, but in no case their creation and composition was meant to be mandatory and exclusive. In this vein, Regional institutions across England were formed by local councillors and to lesser extent welcome representatives from voluntary organisations, trade unions, business, and other interests.

However, devolution opened the door for many business associations to re-scale internal decision-making. As regards the CBI, a main feature is that the peak association geared internal devolution, so CBI regional branches' autonomy was conditioned by the permanent assessment of the overall membership. There is no room for ethnic or corporatist arguments when it comes to strengthen CBI's regional levels of governance. To the extent that the CBI seeks to influence public policy, decision over regional offices' autonomy will take into account the existence of legislative institutions and empowered governments. In general terms, three broad stages define the evolution of CBI regional business associations: first, a pre-devolution period in which they can be mostly labelled as regional branches of potent state-wide associations with a few, if not any, abilities to define the logic of influence of the businesspeople placed within the region. Second, a short period in which devolution emerged as an issue in British politics, thus CBI began to decentralise structures as well as assess the impact of the whole process in its internal division of labour. And, third, a post-devolution period in which CBI has been able to assess the degree of autonomy the entire association is likely to endorse the regional sub-units in Scotland, Wales, Northern Ireland, and the English regions. As regards the Federation of Small Businesses, it has long had a territorial approach so as to serve an increasing membership from 12 people in 1974 to over 200.000 members at present. In fact, the FSB regularly held meetings in several towns throughout the UK in the early days. In addition, the FSB soon discussed the need to establish a structure divided in Regions, posting Regional Organisers. Bettsworth (1999: 27) notes that in a meeting held on 12 December 1974 the FSB members 'decided to set up four sub-committees dealing with publicity, administration, finances and legal matters. More crucially, it was agreed that all Branch Chairmen should meet to formulate policy. Finally, plans for a Regional structure, including Northern Ireland, were submitted.' Thus, the main difference between the FSB and the CBI is that the FSB soon developed a territorial structure as a necessity and conviction. FSB's territorial profile resulted in the association giving a high degree of autonomy to its local branches in terms of new member recruitment, contacts with local governments, demands formation, and so forth.

However, CBI is no longer reluctant to devolution, but seems to be unlikely to cultivate regionalism in regions other than the nations. Not everyone in the United Kingdom agreed with the alleged benefits devolution was to bring before it came to reality. Employers were active in the *Scotland Says No* campaign against the 1979 Scottish devolution referendum. The only business association willing to take part in the pre-devolution process was the National Federation of Self-Employed and Small Business (Scottish section) (now Federation of Small Business in Scotland). The FSB participated in the Scottish Constitutional Convention (1989-1995), although its presence lasted only two years (1989-1990) (Lynch 1998). The CBI in Scotland was particularly active in confronting the devolution of powers to Scotland. As regards Wales, current economic figures are significantly worse than the UK average. According to David Rosser, director of the CBI Wales, speaking to the *Cardiffian* (March 1st 2011), 'poor economic performance was probably the greatest disappointment of devolved government so far.' At first glance, one might assure the CBI is no longer participating in the Welsh regional governance. However, such a harsh opinion does not suppose the CBI goes away from Wales. It is rather a reinforcement of CBI's economic function of warning about economic perils. In fact, CBI Wales' 2011 Manifesto (Energising the Welsh Economy) is a striking evidence of its regional commitment.

Despite the distinction drawn between nations and regions, it is evident that the development of regional alliances has occurred unevenly in Scotland and Wales. Scotland has relied on pluralism to shape 'government-interest groups' relationships, whereas Wales has enhanced its communitarian features to provide business associations a corporatist-friendly environment, really seeking inclusion, not promotion, of certain actors. Hence, the Scottish government is not willing to endorse business association with public status. This leads business groups to exert influence through three channels: a) official consultation; b) direct lobbying; and c) lobbying networks. Within these three possibilities, the CBI Scotland mainly uses the last two, while the FSB in Scotland prefers to stay out of the main coalition of business associations operating in Scotland, the so-called Group of 5. Certainly, the Welsh pattern of social dialogue has unfolded through many co-operative fora, supportive administrative bodies, and partnerships (Morgan & Rees 2001). Contrary to the Scottish experience, Welsh business associations (mainly the CBI Wales and the FSB in Wales) and trade unions (Wales TUC) undertake a wide number of advisory tasks, whether in governmental committees or in local economic forums. Employers can access the Welsh Executive's Departments through a series of Ministerial Advisory Groups and Advisory Boards such as the Wales Employment and Skill Board (WESB). Moreover, there exist four sub-regional Economic Forums, namely, North Wales Economic Forum (1996), South Wales Economic Forum (1997), Central Wales Economic Forum (1994), and South East Wales Economic Forum (1995), whose purpose is to create strategic agreements on various economic and social issues. Recently, Carwyn Jones, First Minister of Wales, announced the latest expression of public-private collaboration in Wales, the *Council for Economic Renewal*.

Conclusion

The aim of this chapter was to outline the various regional paths business associations take in two distinct, singular models of state territorialisation. Despite the initial Labour Party's plan attempted to set up regional institutions throughout the UK, regionalism has largely been appeased in England. On the contrary, Spain established regional governments all along its territory, although applying two different levels of self-autonomy. As devolution in both cases has been a political aspiration, business has not been in compliance with most of the regional claims so far. In fact, business has long shown little interest in supporting peripheral nationalism in Spain and the United Kingdom as supporting greater political decentralisation could generate market fragmentation.

However, we have witnessed a slightly (yet in some cases intense) change in the way business perceives the regions. Of course, employers are still against territorial secession, as the CBI Scotland has lively manifested. But it is widely believed by business that regions are functional arenas to boost economic growth when a competent institutional arrangement has been set up. Business associations have fruitfully worked together with trade unions and regional governments in order to shape territorial social dialogue in Spain. They have benefited from the decentralisation of public services in so far as regional governments have been granting business with access to a vast number of public administrations' advisory commissions, of which endorsing business associations with representative public status has become a big deal. To the extent that UK business associations do not operate in a corporatist environment, business does not seek formal participation in the devolved institutions, but exerting effective influence on them. In this respect, the CBI and the FSB have an intense activity in government's consultation regarding economic policy in Scotland and Wales. All in all, it seems reasonably to argue that business associations have accepted the functional value of the regional level of government (Medina 2012). In some cases, regional governments try to incorporate business associations within the regional governance by assuring them a privileged status. In other cases, business associations themselves adapt to devolution. In one way or another, this confirms that business associations' main goal, which becomes inalienable, is institutional representation. They first face an organisational adaptation and, then, seek the most efficient way to achieve their political objectives.

References

Anderson, J. (1991). Business Associations and the Decentralization of Penury: Functional Groups and Territorial Interests. Governance: An International Journal of Policy and Administration 4(1), 67-93.

Bettsworth, M. (1999). The Federation of Small Businesses. St Annes: FSB.

Caciagli, M. (2006). Regiones de Europa: Autogobierno, Regionalismos, Integración Europea. Valencia: Tirant lo Blanch.

Greaves, J. (2008). Continuity or Change in Business Representation in Britain? An Assessment of the Heseltine Initiatives of the 1990s. Environmental and Planning C: Government and Policy 26(5), 998-1015.

Jordan, G. & Halpin, D. (2004). Olson Triumphant? Recruitment Strategies and the Growth of a Small Business Association. Political Studies (52), 431-449.

Keating, M. (2001). Rethinking the Region. Culture, Institutions and Economic Development in Catalonia and Galicia. European Urban and Regional Studies 8(3), 217-234.

Keating, M. (2003). The Invention of Regions: Political Restructuring and Territorial Government in Western Europe. In N. Brenner, B. Jessop, M. Jones & G. Macleod (eds), State/Space: A Reader. Malden: Blackwell.

Keating, M., Loughlin, J. & Deschouwer, K. (2003). Culture, Institutions and Economic Development: A Study of Eight European Regions. Northhampton, MA: Edward Elgar.

Lovering, J. (1999). Theory Led by Policy: the Inadequacies of the ´New Regionalism´ (Illustrated from the Case of Wales). International Journal of Urban and Regional Research 23, 379-395.

Lynch, P. (1998). Reactive Capital: The Scottish Business Community and Devolution. In H. Elcock & M. Keating (eds), Remaking the Union. Devolution and British Politics in the 1990s. London, Portland, OR: Frank Cass.

Maillat, D. (1998). Innovative Milieux and New Generations of Regional Policies. Entrepreneurship & Regional Development 10: 1-16.

Martínez-Lucio, M. (1992). Spain. Constructing Institutions and Actors in a Context of Change. In A. Ferner & R. Hyman (eds), Industrial Relations in the New Europe. Cambridge: Blackwell.

McHugh, J. (1979). The Self-Employed and the Small Independent Entrepreneur. In R. King and N. Nugent (eds), Respectable Rebels: Middle Class Campaigns in Britain in the 1970s. London: Hodder and Stoughton.

Medina, I. (2012). Regional Business Associations in Spain and the United Kingdom. Unpublished Doctoral Dissertation. Department of Political Science and Public Law. Autonomous University of Barcelona, Spain.

Molins, J.M. & Casademunt, A. (1998). Pressure Groups and the Articulation of Interests. West European Politics 21(4), 124-146.

Molins, J.M., Nonell, R., Güell, C. & Medina, I. (2010). Business Associations Facing Regionalism. Pôle Sud 33: 83-101.

Morgan, K. & Rees, G. (2001). Learning by Doing. Devolution and the Governance of Economic Development in Wales. In P. Chaney, T. Hall & A. Pithouse (eds), New Wales – New Democracy?. Cardiff: University of Wales Press.

Nonell, R. (2010). Pactos Sociales y Crisis Económica en Europa. La Revista Online del CTESC. (http://www.ctesc.cat/scripts/larevista/article.asp?cat=26&art=762).

Nonell, R. & Molins, J.M. (2007). Spain. In F. Traxler & G. Huemer (eds), Handbook of Business Interest Associations, Firm Size and Governance. A comparative analytical approach. London: Routledge.

Nonell, R., Medina, I. & Molins, J.M. (2011). Social Pacts and the Institutionalisation of Social Actors in Spain. The Case of Employers Associations. In M. Baglioni & B. Brandl (eds), Changing Labour Relations between Path Dependency and Global Trends. Frankfurt: Peter Lang

Norton, P. (1994). The British Polity. New York and London: Longman (3rd ed.)

Regalia, I. (2007). Territorial Pacts and Local Level Concertation in Europe. A Multi-Level Governance Perspective. NEWGOV-New Modes of Governance Report, 18b/D05b, EUI

Swyngedouw, E. (1992). Territorial Organization and the Space/Technology Nexus. Transactions. Institute of British Geographers 17: 417-433

Tomaney, J. (1999). New Labour and the English Question. The Political Quarterly 70: 75–82

Part IV
The role and functions of political parties and party systems

Chapter 9
Political Parties and Party Systems in Multilevel Layered-out Systems: Canada

Lori Thorlakson, University of Alberta

Introduction

Canada is one of the most decentralized federations in the world in terms of the fiscal resources and range of policy areas controlled by provincial governments.

It is also a multilevel system in which the logic of the federal design is based both on a response to territorially defined linguistic cleavages (in the case of Quebec) as well as administrative expediency, when the boundaries of the western provinces were determined in the early stages of European settlement. Only in the case of one province can Canada be said to be an example of social federalism, with an underlying linguistic or ethnic cleavage. While Quebec's distinctive culture would lead us to expect the development of distinctive politics in this province, we in fact find such diversity much more widely in party competition across a number of provinces in the federation.

Provincial elections in Canada do not fit the model of 'second order' party competition, derivative of and conditioned by federal competition. Instead, federal and provincial political parties in Canada have long been said to occupy 'separate worlds' of political competition (Blake, 1982): provincial parties are highly autonomous and, in most cases, are organizationally independent of federal parties. Provincial party systems have long been distinctive and incongruent, and in terms of voter behaviour, evidence suggests that voters maintain separate party identifications at different territorial levels. This is balanced by the development at the federal level of integrative, state-wide political parties. The emergence of territorially concentrated or regional parties has been limited in scope and impact on the party system.

Party organization

Multilevel systems present political parties with multiple arenas of competition. This means that various territorial organizations of the party can face competing and sometimes conflicting interests, creating pressure for some autonomy for the regional organization of political parties. On the other hand, common party organizations that transcend territorial divisions can serve to integrate political life both horizontally across the units of a federation and vertically across its territorial tiers. Canada stands out among other parliamentary federations because many of its political parties have responded to this pressure by creating split organizations, where formal linkages between the provincial and federal party organizations are either weak or non-existent.

Conservative Party of Canada

The Conservative Party of Canada, formed in 2003 through the merger of the Canadian Reform Conservative Alliance and the Progressive Conservative Party, is a split party and has no organizational linkages with conservative parties in the provinces. The party's constitution explicitly rules out the establishment of provincial political parties and instead seeks to build relationships with the existing provincial conservative parties.

A similar organizational structure existed in both predecessors of the Conservative Party. In the Progressive Conservative Party, provincial parties existed as separate organizations alongside the provincial organization of the federal party in each province. In Atlantic Canada, where relations between conservative parties at the federal and provincial level were closest, the provincial and federal party organizations remained distinct yet occupied the same offices and shared personnel and resources (Dyck, 1991:134). The Canadian Alliance Party and its predecessor, the Reform Party of Canada, operated as truncated parties, without active provincial-level counterparts. Reform parties existed at the provincial level in Manitoba and British Columbia but were unaffiliated with the federal Reform Party. Without organizational linkages to provincial parties, the Reform and later, the Canadian Alliance party, were able to maintain alliances with other provincial right-wing parties such as the Progressive Conservative parties in Alberta and Ontario, the populist Saskatchewan Party and the British Columbia Liberal Party.

New Democratic Party

The New Democratic Party of Canada maintains a federal party structure that integrates its provincial organizations. Individual memberships are through provincial sections only and these provincial sections are responsible for setting the membership fees. The party's constitution provides that provincial parties will be autonomous, but requires the constitution and principles of these parties not conflict with those of the Federal Party. In the case of a conflict between the federal and provincial parties, the Federal Council retains the power the power of expulsion and can rule on whether or not the provincial organization is a member is good standing. This is similar to practice typically found in parties in Germany and Switzerland, where parties are integrated across territorial levels yet afford a high degree of autonomy to their state-level organizations. The exception to the party's vertically integrated organizational structure is the provincial party in Quebec where, a Quebec section of the party, New Democratic Party of Canada (Quebec), exists to organize for federal elections in constituencies in Quebec. The party constitution provides for an autonomous provincial party, the Nouveau parti démocratique-Québec, to exist alongside the Quebec section of the federal party, but the NDP do not have a presence in the provincial party system.

Liberal Party of Canada

The Liberal Party of Canada occupies a position somewhere between the New Democratic and Conservative party models. The party's constitution describes the Liberal Party of Canada as a 'federation' of provincial and territorial organizations. Membership in the party is through the provincial and territorial associations (PTAs). Only in Newfoundland and Labrador, Prince Edward Island, Nova Scotia and New Brunswick, the Western Arctic and Nunavut do we find integrated provincial and federal party associations. Nominations, leadership conventions, selection of delegates and membership rules in the integrated provincial party organizations are circumscribed by rules set by the federal party.

   The provincial Liberal parties in Quebec, Ontario, Alberta, British Columbia, Saskatchewan and Manitoba maintain separate organizations from the federal party. In these provinces, the provincial branches of the federal party concern themselves with federal party matters and federal campaigns, while the provincial party organizations concern themselves solely with provincial political activity. Quebec has maintained a separate provincial party since 1964; the parties in Ontario and Alberta split from the federal organization in the 1970s (Dyck, 1991:138-9).

What sets the Liberal party apart from the Conservative party is the emphasis the Liberal party places on its federal organization. While separate parties for federal and provincial elections operate in the six provinces with split organizations, the governance structure of the federal Liberal party nevertheless emphases the importance of these provincial organizational units in its governance structure. This has recently been scrutinized as the party sought ways to improve its operational efficiency. A 2006 report of a party task force on the party's operational and decision-making structure noted that the federal structure of the party had created an inefficient patchwork of policies that hampered the membership registration process and communication between the central party and its members—membership was only available through the PTAs and the organizational structure made it difficult for the central party to communicate directly with party members, rather than through the PTAs (Liberal Party of Canada, 2006:14-15). In response, the party created a national membership structure and a national membership database.

Green Party

The Green Party of Canada, which gained its first member of parliament with the election of leader Elizabeth May in Saanich-Gulf Islands in the 2011 federal election, is a minor party yet an interesting case because it illustrates the trade-offs between maintaining provincial party autonomy and reaping the benefits of coordination. The first provincial green parties emerged in Ontario and British Columbia in 1983.

Provincial green parties exist in every province except Newfoundland (Alberta's party, deregistered in 2009, was succeeded in 2011 by the EverGreen Party of Alberta). In keeping with the Greens' programmatic commitment to decentralization, local autonomy and grassroots democracy, the provincial parties are independent from the federal party. Despite this, there is a high degree of cooperation between the federal and provincial green parties, aided by high programmatic cohesion. It is not uncommon for candidates or party officials to be active in both the federal and provincial green parties. Many provincial parties feature endorsements from the federal party leader on their website.

Like the Liberals, the federal and provincial green parties in Canada have acknowledged that autonomy and independence of provincial organizations extract a price in terms of organizational efficiency. In December 2011, provincial green leaders and the national party director and national party leader met to develop a framework for cooperation and resource sharing.[1] Proposals

---

1 'Provincial Leaders Meeting', December 18, 2011, Green Party of Nova Scotia Website, accessed 7 January 2012 at http://greenparty.ns,ca/articles/3/144-provincial-leaders-meeting.

included the development of a common provincial and federal membership structure and shared databases and communication strategies.

Bloc Québécois

Finally, the nationalist Bloc Québécois organizes and competes only in the province of Quebec. It does not have an official provincial counterpart but maintains a strong natural alliance with the provincial Parti Québécois and the parties draw on a similar electoral base.

Cooperative linkages between parties

The loose organizational linkages between provincial and federal parties allow provincial parties the space to pursue their provincial interests when conflicts arise. In Canada, this has tended to occur over the resource allocation or sovereignty issues. The organizational divorce of the provincial parties in Quebec and British Columbia was accompanied by a severing of cooperative ties between the provincial and federal parties. In British Columbia, the federal Liberal party maintained a closer relationship with the provincial Social Credit party than with the provincial Liberals, who, by the late 1980s, had been relegated to minor party status. In Alberta, the Trudeau government's National Energy Program and multiculturalism policy were unpopular and made it difficult for a vote-seeking provincial party to closely identify with the federal party.

When Danny Williams was the Progressive Conservative premier of Newfoundland, he launched the 'ABC' (Anything But Conservative) campaign against the Conservative Party of Canada during the 2008 federal election after the federal Conservative government decided to include non-renewable resources into the federal equalization formula.

Compared to career paths in American and German politics, there is very little movement between the provincial and federal levels of competition in Canada (Filippov, Ordeshook and Shvetsova, 2004:210, 213). When movement across levels occurs, the loose organizational affiliations between provincial and federal parties as well as party system incongruence have meant that party labels do not necessarily govern career trajectories. Some politicians cross party lines when they move between provincial and federal politics (and vice versa). Bob Rae, the New Democratic Party premier of Ontario from 1990 to 1995, contested the leadership of the federal Liberal party in 2006 and in 2011 became the interim leader of the federal Liberal party. Changing affiliations from the federal to provincial level, Jean Charest was the leader of the federal Progressive Conservative Party from 1993 to 1998 and moved to provincial politics as the leader of the Quebec Liberal Party in 1998.

Party system incongruence

While Canada has statewide federal parties, the widespread occurrence of organizational separation between the federal and provincial parties is a contributing factor to a high degree of party system diversity, or incongruence, that we find across the Canadian provinces. Party system incongruence in a multi-level system refers to differences in the structures and patterns of competition, both horizontally across the units of the federation and vertically, between provincial and federal party systems. Party system incongruence can be assessed on different levels. One fundamental form is congruence of party label— whether the same parties compete at each level. In the case of Canada, we need to consider this form of party label congruence on two levels: first, whether unique parties exist in a provincial party system, and secondly, whether independent parties with similar labels maintain organizational linkages or are linked through the cognitive identifications or attachments of voters.

The party systems in Canada stand out in comparative perspective due to the widespread occurrence of party label incongruence. In Canada in the 1990s, the two major opposition parties at the federal level, the Reform Party and the Bloc Québécois, had no provincial counterparts (although the Bloc was closely affiliated with the sovereigntist Parti Québécois). In addition, the party system of Quebec has been incongruent in this fundamental sense during the entire post-war period. The parties unique to electoral competition in Quebec include the nationalist conservative party Union Nationale in the 1950s and 1960s, the Parti Québécois since the 1970s, Action Démocratique in the 1990s and, more recently, Coalition Avenir Québec, Québec Solidaire and Option nationale. In Saskatchewan, provincial Progressive Conservatives and Liberals joined forces in 1997 to form the Saskatchewan Party (initially led by a former federal Reform Party MP). It has formed the government since 2007.

Party system congruence can also take the form of similarity of the number of parties (a measure of the party system structure) and the similarity of parties' electoral strength across units of the federation. The party systems in Canada are relatively similar in structural terms (perhaps owing to the effects of the single member plurality electoral system used in all electoral arenas), with most systems converging around 2.5 effective electoral parties. One notable exception to this is the party system of Alberta, which has exhibited a pattern of one party dominance in most elections since the second world war. In contrast, there is significant dissimilarity in the levels of electoral support of parties across the party systems in Canada (Thorlakson, 2007:70).

In the Canadian case, party system congruence is the exception, rather than the rule. Party systems are most congruent across the maritime provinces, New Brunswick, Nova Scotia, Newfoundland and Prince Edward Island, where political competition has occurred as (usually) balanced, two-party competition, alternating between Liberal and Conservative parties. This largely mirrors the patterns of federal party competition before party system realignment in the early 1990s.

The party systems of the western provinces, and Quebec, have been most markedly out of sync with those of other provinces and with the federal party system. In British Columbia, provincial politics has been dominated by two federally minor parties, the Social Credit Party and the New Democratic Party. The Social Credit Party formed the government from 1953 until the 1975 election when the NDP formed the government. Today, the party system is a two-party contest between the Liberals on the right and the NDP on the left. The party system in Alberta features structural incongruence due to its one-party dominance, first of the Social Credit Party, and after 1975, by the Progressive Conservative Party. In Quebec, party system incongruence has stemmed from the party label incongruence: the Union Nationale displaced the Progressive Conservatives and the nationalist Parti Québécois became a major force in the 1970s.

Another source of party system dissimilarity has been the electoral success of the NDP in several provincial party systems, coupled with its minor status at the federal level until 2011, when it became the official opposition. The NDP have often been a major party in Manitoba (where the Liberals have been relegated to minor party status since the 1970s) and Saskatchewan, where its predecessor, the Cooperative Commonwealth Federation formed the government from 1952-1967. In Ontario, the strength of the NDP led to patterns of three party competition from the 1960s to the 1990s.

Considering congruence in terms of the similarity of the magnitude and direction of changes in support for a federal party in a federal election compared to the performance of its provincial counterparts in the nearest provincial elections can give us an indicator about the extent to which the forces that shape electoral outcomes are localized for each arena. High localization of the vote would occur if a federal party's vote share increased while the vote share of its provincial counterparts was decreasing. This tells us that changes in the provincial electoral arena differ from changes in the federal electoral arena during the same time period, suggesting that voters are making different decisions in their assessments of state and federal versions of the same parties, perhaps basing their decisions in the federal and provincial arenas on different factors. When localization scores are high, we can cautiously infer that different factors are driving provincial and federal voting decisions, and that voters' assessments of parties and vote choices at the provincial and federal levels are independent to a degree.

Comparing average vote localization scores since 1945 across six federations (Canada, the US, Germany, Austria, Switzerland, and Australia), only the United States, with its candidate-centered system, has higher localization scores than Canada (Thorlakson, 2007:84). Of all the provinces, Quebec has the highest localization score, followed closely by Saskatchewan.[2] Vote swing for parties in New Brunswick and Nova Scotia are most congruent with those of the federal parties. Comparing parties, the Progressive Conservatives and their provincial counterparts have the highest variation in electoral swing while the NDP parties have the most similar electoral change (Thorlakson, 2002). Not surprisingly, we find the strongest congruence in electoral swing among parties and in provinces where the party organizational linkages are the strongest and the party systems most congruent in terms of electoral strength of the parties.

Party system incongruence can create different competitive contexts at the provincial and federal electoral arenas and present voters with different party choices. The presence of parties with weak or absent organizational linkages can mean that voters are more likely to view their provincial party as an entity that is separate and distinct from the party in other provinces, or its federal counterpart, and so be more likely to develop separate and independent assessments of the party at the provincial and federal levels. There is evidence that such split identification, with partisan inconsistency between the federal and provincial levels occurs (Blake, 1982; Clarke and Stewart, 1987; Stewart and Clarke, 1998) and has increased since the early 1990s (Stewart and Clarke, 1998), when federal party system change increased party system incongruence.

The high degree of localization of the vote and partisan inconsistency suggests that Canada does not easily fit the 'second order election thesis'—the prediction that subnational electoral contests will be seen by voters to be less important than those determining the composition of a national government, and that as a result, voter turnout will be lower, the second order elections will be fought on national issues voting decisions taken to punish or reward the nationally incumbent party (Reif and Schmitt, 1980). In Canada, average voter turnout in provincial elections is close to levels for federal elections (Cutler, 2008:495), and voters report similar levels of interest in provincial and federal election campaigns (Cutler, 2008:495; Blake, 1982). There is evidence that the federal political context does not drive vote choice at the provincial level. Drawing from individual-level survey data, Cutler finds arena-specific factors drive vote choice in provincial elections in Ontario (Cutler, 2008:501).

---

2   This measurement compares the performance of the Union Nationale with the federal Progressive Conservatives.

Implications of organisational linkage and congruence

To summarize, in Canadian multilevel party competition, we find split or weakly integrated party organisations, a high level of party system incongruence with many parties that are unique to a single electoral arena and evidence that voters hold inconsistent partisanships. Elections in the Canadian provinces do not fit a model of second order party competition but instead take place in what Blake termed a 'separate political world' (Blake, 1982).

What explains these patterns of political development in Canada? The social cleavage basis of politics offers a limited explanation for high party system congruence, accounting for the rise of nationalist parties in Quebec and the resulting party system incongruence in that province, as well as for the emergence of populist parties in western Canada. It does not, however, provide a full and compelling explanation for incongruence or weak organizational linkages between federal and provincial parties. The institutional context of party competition may shed some light on Canada's political development. First, the strong fiscal and policy decentralization means that the provincial arena of competition, and winning provincial public office, is an important prize in its own right. There is significant policy autonomy and fiscal resources with which to shape public policies, creating an incentive for parties to respond to provincial policy priorities. This opens up potential for conflict between federal and provincial parties. Secondly, the existence of different federal and provincial constituency boundaries that are used in the provinces (with the exception of Ontario) encourage split organizations (or at least diminishes any efficiency gains from combined federal and provincial organizations).

The cause and effect of patterns of incongruence and party organizational linkage in Canada's multilevel political competition can be difficult to untangle. The structural separation of Canadian party organizations insulates federal and provincial politics. This can encourage voters to develop inconsistent partisanship and make provincial voting choices based on arena-specific assessments. Split partisanship can in turn reinforce party system incongruence. The high degree of incongruence across the Canadian party systems has meant that parties face different competitive pressures and different oppositions from one electoral arena to another, which can lead to a need to develop and emphasize different policy priorities. For example, provincial Progressive Conservatives in Alberta, a dominant party of the centre-right, face an emerging threat on their right from the populist Wildrose Party. Their federal counterparts face its key opposition on the left. This can increase a provincial party's need for autonomy in policy development in order to respond to local conditions, one pressure toward the creation or maintenance of a split organizational structure.

The nationalization of parties and party systems

One important issue in a multilevel party system is the extent to which the federal party system reinforces or cross-cuts territorial divisions. This is important because federal or multilevel systems are often created as a method for the territorial accommodation of plural societies. If federal parties draw their support from across the units of the federation, this forces the party to mediate potential territorial conflict within the party. When the geographic basis of party support mirrors the territorial divisions of the federation, territorial conflict is channelled into the federal legislative arena through inter-party competition.

When parties and party systems are 'nationalised', (as they are often referred to in the literature), they draw support from across the territory of the federation. This can play an important stability and integration function in a federation. Nationalized party systems develop when parties compete statewide (or polity-wide) and when these parties successfully secure statewide electoral support. This distinction is important because the term 'statewide party' is usually used as a designation reflecting a party's strategic decision to organize and contest seats across the polity. The nationalization of a party, by contrast, captures the electoral outcome and the party's success at achieving its goal. It is possible for a statewide party (or a party system with statewide parties) to have a low level of nationalization because its support remains territorially concentrated. Measuring nationalization is useful because it allows us to distinguish between parties that are statewide by design or by merit of their electoral success. Because it allows us to refer to degrees of nationalization, it is useful for discussing party system dynamics.

Most federal parties in Canada have operated as statewide (or polity-wide) parties, organizing and contesting elections across all provinces and serving as integrative brokerage parties. Throughout the twentieth century, federal party competition has been dominated by the Liberal and Conservative parties, both state-wide brokerage parties with broad national bases of support. The Bloc Québécois, a Quebec nationalist party that emerged in 1993, has been the main exception to this. It organizes as a non-statewide party contesting seats only in Quebec.

Compared to democracies in the Americas, Canada's party system is characterized both by having a relatively low level of party system nationalization and having a high degree of instability of its nationalization scores (Jones and Mainwaring, 2003). Canada's party system nationalization was highest and generally stable in the 1950s and 1960s. By the late 1970s, party system nationalization decreased as the unpopularity of the Liberals in the West and to an increasing territorial concentration of Progressive Conservative electoral support in the West. During these decades, the Liberal party had, on average, the highest degree of nationalization.

In the 1990s, fracturing on the right of the federal party system coupled with the emergence of the Bloc Québécois generated a sharp but temporary episode of high territorial concentration in the party system. Following the 1993 federal election, the BQ won a landslide victory in Quebec, with 54 of its 75 seats, earning it the role of the official opposition in parliament. On the right, the Progressive Conservative Party collapsed, winning only two seats. The Reform Party, a populist party on the right emerged to win 52 seats, concentrated in the western provinces of British Columbia and Alberta.

In Canada, a 'frontier' or centre-periphery cleavage has periodically provided a regional dimension to the party system. The Western provinces have, throughout Canadian history, produced populist political movements such as the Social Credit Party and the Cooperative Commonwealth Federation that have challenged the parties of the Eastern establishment. The election of the Reform Party in 1993 represented a replay of a familiar line of regional division. The election of the separatist Bloc Québécois, however, represented a new dimension of territorial concentration in Canadian federal politics and the politicization of an ethnolinguistic cleavage at the federal level. Until 1993, the majority of Québécois voters supported the Liberal party, and, in the 1980s, the Progressive Conservative Party, allowing the linguistic cleavage to be accommodated within parties, rather than expressed as a line of party-political competition.

While remaining a non-statewide party based in Quebec has been the intention of the Bloc Québécois from the outset, low nationalization was a developmental hurdle that the right fought to overcome. The Reform Party was succeeded by the Canadian Alliance Party and merged with the Progressive Conservative Party in 2003. The resulting creation of the Conservative Party of Canada mended the fracture of the right. The new Conservative party expanded its territorial support base eastward and in 2011 secured a majority government due to the electoral inroads the party made in Central Canada.

Conclusions

Multilevel politics in Canada is characterized by a low level of federal-provincial linkage in terms of party organization, party system congruence and voter behaviour. Evidence suggests that provincial elections in Canada are much more than merely 'second order' contests shaped by the federal political context. They are important contests in their own right and are shaped in important ways by factors specific to each provincial electoral arena. Canadian parties are organizationally unique compared to those in other federations, with a high incidence of parties that are organizationally split and of parties that are unique to a single arena. Following from these developments, the party systems across the federation have a high degree of incongruence. Finally, regional concentration of the vote has been limited in Canadian electoral history. While emerging parties have concentrated their efforts in particular regions, office-seeking parties have pursued a long-term strategy of building a territorially broad base of electoral support.

References

Blake, D. (1982). The consistency of inconsistency: party identification in federal and provincial politics. *Canadian Journal of Political Science* (15), 691-710.

Clarke, H and Stewart, M. (1987). Partisan Inconsistency and Partisan Change in Federal States: The Case of Canada. *American Journal of Political Science* (31), 383-407.

Cutler, F. (2008). One vote, two first-order elections? *Electoral Studies* (27), 492-504.

Dyck, R. (1991). 'Links Between Federal and Provincial Parties and Party Systems'. In Herman Bakvis (ed), *Representation, Integration and Political Parties in Canada*. Toronto: Dundern Press.

Filippov, M, Ordeshook, P. and Shvetsova, O. (2004). *Designing Federalism. A Theory of Self-Sustainable Federal Institutions*. Cambridge: Cambridge University Press.

Jones, M. and Mainwaring, S. (2003). The Nationalization of Parties and Party Systems: An Empirical Measure and an Application to the Americas. *Party Politics* (9), 139-166.

Liberal Party of Canada (2006). *A Party Built for Everyone: A Party Built to Win*. The Liberal Party of Canada's Red Ribbon Task Force Final Report. http://cdn.liberal.ca/files/2010/05/redribbon_e.pdf , accessed 7 January 2012.

Reif, K. and Schmitt, H. (1980). Nine second-order national elections: a conceptual framework for the analysis of European election results. *European Journal of Political Research* (8), 3-44.

Stewart, M. and Clarke, H. (1998). The Dynamics of Party Identification in Federal Systems: The Canadian Case. *American Journal of Political Science* (42), 97-116.

Thorlakson, L. (2002). Federalism and Party Competition: A Comparative Analysis of Canada, Australia, Switzerland, Austria, Germany and the United States. Unpublished PhD thesis, London School of Economics.

Thorlakson, L. (2007). 'An institutional explanation of party system congruence: Evidence from six federations'. European Journal of Political Research (46), 69-95.

Chapter 10
Political Parties as a Tool of Identity Paradiplomacy: The Case of the Parti Québécois and the UNESCO Convention on Cultural Diversity

Guy Lachapelle, Concordia University

Introduction

Over the years, much research has focused on the relations between substate entities – such as America's states, Canada's provinces and Spain's autonomous regions or communities – and their central governments. Many of these entities have assumed or claimed a place in the area of international relations and on the international stage, voicing their views in a variety of world forums. Over the years, we have witnessed continual growth in the practice of "identity paradiplomacy" (Lachapelle & Paquin, 2006; Lachapelle & Trent, 2000), "the fundamental objective [of which] is to reinforce or build a minority nation in a multinational country" (Paquin, 2005: 133).[1]

With this objective in mind, "national" or "regional" governments that wish to acquire an international personality must in large measure rely on a variety of nongovernmental groups, associations and organizations in civil society to assert their views on the international scene. These organizations are what we have called "identity entrepreneurs" (Lachapelle & Trent, 2000; Paquin, 2005). They are well aware that their participation in international forums in many ways helps legitimate their domestic demands, particularly in federal states. Such behaviour by these groups is not necessarily seen in regions that have a strong sense of nationhood or are claiming greater autonomy or independence: Scotland and Wales, for example, are often deemed to conduct "very weak identity paradiplomacy despite a strong sense of nationhood" (Paquin, 2005: 133).[2] However, globalization has led various other substate entities, even American states, to extend their networks of influence beyond their country's borders (Fry, 2000).

---

1   Translated from French.
2   Translated from French.

In the literature on paradiplomacy, international action by substate entities in federal states is generally viewed as possible only insofar as it is permitted by the existing federal legal framework and constitutional provisions and particularly concerns matters under their jurisdiction (Malone, 2011). Thus, Quebec governments have used what has come to be known as the "Gérin-Lajoie Doctrine" to justify their being able to transpose their fields of jurisdiction to the international level (Michaud, 2006). First enunciated in 1960s, the Doctrine has since been supported by all Quebec governments of every political stripe, whether federalist or sovereigntist, and has provided the framework for the development of a worldwide network of delegations, offices and agencies. However, recognition of the authority to undertake international activities is a necessary but not a sufficient condition for the development of such action for substate identities: rather, it will develop to the extent that the government in place displays an interest in pursuing it and that, in certain situations, the federal government concurs.

In the case of Quebec, the elected premier must, of course, display an interest for his government to play an active role on major international issues. The funds allocated to international relations are a good indicator of the government's desire to assert itself in this regard. Governments will also seek the backing of organizations of civil society to support their points of view on the international stage. In the current discussions on a Europe-Canada free-trade agreement, for example, economic interests, unions and organizations concerned by the issue can be valuable partners in legitimizing the entire process if the government keeps them informed about the ongoing negotiations. The new Quebec government elected in 2012 had just this purpose in mind when it asked for these groups to be updated about the status of the talks. The chief negotiator, former premier Pierre-Marc Johnson, acceded to the request and hold public meetings with civil society groups in the autumn of 2012.

The role of political parties on the international stage

Despite the foregoing, little research has been conducted on the role and function of political parties as incubators, actors or promoters of governmental international policy. Clearly, not all political parties in multilevel states "do" international relations; in some cases, though, whether in power or in opposition, their organizations may play an important role in supporting party foreign-policy positions. In the case of Quebec, it is rather paradoxical to find that a review of party platforms from 1960 to the late 1980s reveals little interest in international relations (Bernier, 1996; Beaudoin, Bélanger and Lavoie, 2002). The data are telling:

"From 1960 to 1989, on average only 2% of the platform planks dealt with international affairs; less than 1% did so in the 1960s; less than 2% between 1970 and 1981; 4.16% in 1985; and 3.06% in 1989. It is also noteworthy that, of the 171 planks enumerated that were international in nature, more than 90% came from Parti Québécois programs. The Liberal Party (7.6%) and the Union Nationale (1.2%) between them accounted for the smaller remainder. A glance at recent political platforms is sufficient to show that there has been little change in the situation" (Beaudoin, Bélanger & Lavoie, 2002: 41).[3]

The Parti Québécois thus stands alone in a way, giving rise to the question why some parties and their members pay more attention to international issues than others. In the case of the Parti Québécois, the fact that its historic leader and founder, René Lévesque, was a war correspondent with the American army during the Second World War and was later one of the first Francophone journalists to host a television program on international affairs, no doubt helped develop Quebecers' interest in international issues. Lévesque believed deeply that Quebec could play a role on the world scene and contribute in its own way to solving the problems of our times. Many Quebecers shared that belief in the 1960s without necessarily supporting the project Lévesque put forward or the party he created in 1968, the Parti Québécois.

More than in any other Quebec party, though, the members of the Parti Québécois have often raised and debated international political issues at their conferences. Many of them joined the party specifically because they knew it provided a public space where the major issues of the day could be debated. Quebec's intellectual avant-garde (artists, journalists, teachers, etc.) at various times flocked to the party in order to debate policy on free trade, security, the environment, and international cooperation. To properly understand the role of parties in the political process and their contribution to the development of the foreign policy of substate entities, one must ask how the opinions of political leaders and citizens and those advocated by political parties interact. Political parties help inform citizens about policy issues while also seeking to persuade electors of the validity of their program. Many international issues remain complex to voters, though. Political parties can play a useful role in this regard in mobilizing public opinion over certain issues in addition to fulfilling their fundamental role of producing new ideas, new ways of thinking and new arguments. As we shall see, while one must not minimize the decisive role of the government of Quebec in the matter, the Parti Québécois was a significant policy entrepreneur throughout the course of the debate on the Convention on the Protection and Promotion of the Diversity of Cultural Expressions.

---

3   Translated from French.

Guy Lachapelle

The Comité des Relations Internationales (CRI) of the Parti Québécois

The Parti Québécois is one of the few political parties to have included as part of its internal structure a committee primarily concerned with studying international issues and suggesting ideas for deliberation. The international relations committee, Comité des Relations Internationales (CRI), was established in 1979 and remained active until 2005. Its objectives were:

1. To suggest direction and policy with respect to Quebec's international relations before and after sovereignty to the party leadership and the government;
2. To establish and maintain relations for information and collaboration with foreign political parties or other bodies interested in the development of a sovereign Quebec;
3. To stimulate party life and educate members in view of the international dimension of the exercise of sovereignty;
4. To carry out, in conjunction with the Party leadership, any task involving information, education or foreign representation or in response to requests from the local diplomatic corps to explain the Party's viewpoint and defend its interests.

Party statutes also stated that the Comité des Relations Internationales works to ensure that respect for human rights, respect for languages and cultures and the development of new partnerships for international cooperation remain at the centre of all the Parti Québécois's undertakings. It also seeks to develop close ties with political parties pursuing objectives similar to its own (Parti Québécois, 1995; 1986)[4].

For example, in 2002, at a meeting of the members of the CRI and the office of the Minister of International Relations, it was agreed that the Committee should direct its efforts to four objectives: 1. developing a platform proposal on international relations in preparation for the 2005 national convention; 2. considering the actions that would have to be taken, in terms of international relations, to prepare Quebec to become sovereign; 3. developing relations with a number of political parties around the world; and 4. monitoring international current affairs and reacting as necessary.

Under party statutes, the Comité des Relations Internationales was headed by a chairperson elected by the National Council for a renewable two-year term. From 1979 to 2005 the CRI was chaired by six individuals. In chronological order they were: Michel Leduc, Nadia Assimopoulos, Anne Legaré, Paul-André Quintin, Daniel Turp, and Guy Lachapelle. The CRI chairperson also sat on the party's National Bureau and was an *ex officio* delegate to the National Convention with full speaking and voting rights. In terms of structure, the Committee was made up of at least nine members whose names the chairperson submitted to the National Executive Council. As well, the Committee

---

4 Translated from French.

could add additional members and set up working groups as necessary to fulfil its annual action plan. Over the years, members were recruited to the CRI on the basis of their expertise rather than their partisan activism.

After its defeat in the April 2003 elections, the Parti Québécois embarked on a program of modernizing its structures. Through these consultations with members in what was dubbed the "Saison des idées," party leader Bernard Landry wished to bring "together the innovative ideas and most dynamic streams" in Quebec society by restructuring the different committees. The idea of creating "political clubs" put into question the very raison d'être of the existing committees, including the one on international relations. As chairman of the CRI, I voiced my concerns in April 2004 in a presentation to the party's roving committee on modernization, the Commission Itinérante des Chantiers de Modernisation:

"The Comité de Relations Internationales of the Parti Québécois is an important element in the life and structure of the party. How can the Parti Québécois claim it wants [Quebec] to become a country if it shows no interest in matters of international politics? Not only must the committee stay in place, but its terms of reference must be expanded. It must have the means to realize its objectives" (Lachapelle, 2004).[5]

Since then, debates on international issues within the Parti Québécois have become less common. The party's recent victory in the fall 2012 elections may lead to a change should the Marois government choose to take another the direction on these questions.

The CRI's priorities evolved over the years depending on which international and continental issues were most critical. The debate on free trade between Canada and the United States was the focus of discussions in the period 1984–1989. After the failure of the Meech Lake and Charlottetown Accords and the election of the Parti Québécois in 1994, the Committee's attention centred on the referendum issue and Quebec's place on the international stage. In 1993, in the pre-referendum period, to better define the place of small nations like Quebec on the world scene, the CRI, then headed by Anne Legaré, published *Le Québec dans un monde nouveau* (Parti Québécois, 1993). After the 1995 referendum, globalization issues took centre stage, as the Parti Québécois engaged in efforts spearheaded by Paul-André Quintin to develop ties with South American political parties. The Committee followed closely the proceedings of the Parliamentary Conference of the Americas in Quebec City in September 1997 and Puerto Rico in 1998. The speaker of the National Assembly, Jean-Pierre Charbonneau, subsequently brought forward a policy on international activity for parliamentarians (Venne, 1999). Members of the CRI also took an active part in the first World Social Forum (WSF) in Porto Alegre, Brazil, in 2001 and engaged with members of various antiglobalization groups. Members of the Parti Québécois also attended the WSF in 2002 and 2003.

---

5 Translated from French.

Over the years, the CRI's work involved numerous meetings with foreign visitors, handling international correspondence and writing press releases. For example, in December 2003 the Comité des Relations Internationales welcomed the initiative by former Israeli Labour Party minister Yossi Beilin and former Palestinian negotiator Yasser Abed Rabbo to lay the basis for a framework that could lead to a lasting peace between their peoples. The Parti Québécois thus joined with the 58 other signatories to the declaration supporting the "Geneva Accord" to underscore the point that efforts aimed at constructive dialogue constitute the sole means to end the Israeli-Palestinian conflict. After the events of September 11, 2001, the question of Canada's participation in the war in Iraq was also high on the CRI's agenda and led the Committee to join in the citizen mobilization against the war and to support the National Assembly motion opposing Canadian military intervention in the conflict (Lachapelle, 2003).

The Convention on Cultural Diversity

The issue that engaged the members of the CRI and of the Parti Québécois in the Committee's last years was cultural diversity, a matter that in many respects stands at the core of the Parti Québécois's sovereigntist program. Indeed, quite recently, in February 2013, Jean-Francois Lisée, Quebec's new Minister for International Relations, La Francophonie and External Trade, underscored the ongoing importance for Quebec and Quebec society of the promotion of cultural and linguistic diversity:

"Québec's priority is to continuously create the conditions for its own development. For a [F]rancophone nation that makes up 2% of the North American population, that means working tirelessly on every stage to contribute, in an inventive and combative way, to a world that values cultural and linguistic diversity over uniformity, a world that acknowledges that nations can make their own linguistic and cultural choices that are not undermined by commercial considerations" (Lisée, 2013).

He also stressed that actions undertaken by Quebec and incarnated by a certain Louise Beaudoin, [were] instrumental in forging an international agreement protecting the right of States to support their national cultures—a convention first championed by Québec, France and Canada, then by the Francophonie and subsequently by every country in the world, except two (Lisée, 2013).

From the late the 1990s on, the Parti Québécois's international relations committee consistently supported Quebec government efforts in this regard by seeking to mobilize public opinion around what, for Quebec, was a vital issue.

As Daniel Turp, then the National Assembly member for Mercier and spokesman for the Official Opposition on International Relations, wrote in 2004, the Parti Québécois assumed:

"a leadership role on the issue of cultural diversity. It intends to continue to fight for adoption of an international instrument to preserve cultural diversity. The Parti Québécois has closely followed the work that UNESCO has undertaken on the matter since the General Conference of UNESCO's adoption of resolution 32C/34 on October 17, 2003" (Turp, 2004).[6]

It is against this backdrop that the Parti Québécois, in collaboration with the Bloc Québécois, held a symposium on October 2, 2004, on the Preliminary Draft of the Convention on the Protection of the Diversity of Cultural Contents and Artistic Expressions and the position of Quebec. The groundwork for this event, however, had been laid over many years by legal scholars, artists and politicians from Quebec and Europe through efforts meant to culminate in the establishment of a better framework to support cultural practices in the face of unbridled globalization (Beaudoin, 2006).

In this process, the CRI assumed what might be called a "supportive" role and held a watching and monitoring brief on the cultural-diversity question. At the 31st session of its General Conference in Paris in November 2001, UNESCO adopted its Universal Declaration on Cultural Diversity, the most complete and widely accepted statement setting the parameters for discussions on the issue. The Declaration proclaimed cultural diversity to be the "common heritage of humanity" and thus made its defence "an ethical imperative, inseparable from respect for human dignity" (UNESCO, 2002: 4).

However, even before the Declaration, cultural diversity had already become a major subject of international discussion by the late 1990s, when a number of regional and international organizations placed the issue on their agenda (Bernier, 2000; Bernier & Atkinson, 2000). For example, at the Intergovernmental Conference on Cultural Policies for Development held in Stockholm from March 30 to April 2, 1998, Betty Mould-Iddrisu of Ghana stated that it was absolutely essential to update international treaties and conventions in order to improve regulation and implement better protection for cultures. The aim of the conference was to provide government agencies and cultural stakeholders with a forum to discuss the principal reforms that would have to be undertaken.

A few months later, in June 1998, on the initiative of the Minister of Canadian Heritage, Sheila Copps, the ministers of culture of twenty countries decided on the creation of an "international network" with the purpose of protecting and promoting cultural diversity. The network was subsequently expanded to form the International Network on Cultural Policy (INCP) comprising the ministers of culture from more than 40 countries. In the year 2000, an

---

6   Translated from French.

international grouping of artists and cultural organizations, the International Network for Cultural Diversity (INCD), was established; its objective was to assess the effects of globalization on cultural practices. The Parti Québécois met with representatives of both organizations, which came to collaborate closely in mobilizing artists and decision makers around the issue.

In the same year, the governments of France and Quebec agreed that one of the priorities of their "strategic partnership" would be the defence of cultural diversity. The idea of drawing up binding international accords to protect and defend it had actually arisen in the alternating annual France-Quebec heads-of-government meetings held in Montreal and Quebec City from December 17 to 19, 1998, between Quebec's Premier Lucien Bouchard and France's Prime Minister Lionel Jospin. It was decided at the time to establish a bilateral working group on cultural diversity to be chaired jointly by Catherine Lalumière, a French member of the European Parliament, and Marie Malavoy, a member of Quebec's National Assembly. Members of the CRI attended the meeting and followed the discussions closely.

In February 1999, the Canadian government's Cultural Industries Sectoral Advisory Group on International Trade published a report titled *New Strategies for Culture and Trade-Canadian Culture in a Global World* in which it declared itself in favour of "a new international instrument, which would lay out the ground rules for cultural policies and trade, and allow Canada and other countries to maintain policies that promote their cultural industries" (International Trade Canada, 2004). The document provided a good explanation of the Canadian position and the overall conditions that justified regulations to guide cultural policies, but it did not explain how this objective might be attained.

In the end, the Organisation Internationale de la Francophonie (OIF) became the first international organization to pass a resolution in favour of cultural diversity at its 1999 summit in Moncton, New Brunswick (Beaudoin, 2004). The OIF had already approved a joint resolution in support of a "cultural exception" at the summit in Grand-Baie, Mauritius, in 1993; and the concept was favourably received six years later in Moncton when the fight to defend the diversity of cultures became a prime issue for the organization. The Parti Québécois, for its part, supported the efforts of the government of Quebec in this regard.

Subsequently, on November 2, 1999, during the 30th session of the General Conference of UNESCO, some forty ministers of culture held round table talks under the joint chairmanship of Canada and France. Quebec's Minister of Culture and Communications, Agnès Maltais, took advantage of the exceptional right to speak that she was given to explain Quebec's position on cultural diversity. In the name of the government of Quebec, she expressed the wish that

"UNESCO continue its formal consideration [with a view to arriving at] an international convention on culture, similar to that of the International Labour Organization, [which would be] recognized by the WTO [and] that, at the end of the deliberations of this session, a clear signal be sent, a signal about cultural diversity and the power essential to states and governments to implement their policies" (Gouvernement du Québec, 1999).[7]

In July 2000, the G8 foreign ministers "reaffirmed [their] commitment in Berlin in December 1999 to a sustained effort to promote a 'Culture of Prevention' throughout the global community and to develop conflict prevention initiatives." In September 2000, the International Network on Cultural Policy (INCP) studied "the draft international instrument for the promotion of cultural diversity." In December 2000, the Council of Europe adopted its own Declaration on Cultural Diversity.

In June 2002, the France-Quebec working group established by Lionel Jospin and Lucien Bouchard published its report under the title *Évaluation de la faisabilité juridique d'un instrument international sur la diversité culturelle (Assessment of the legal feasibility of an international instrument on cultural diversity)* (Bernier and Ruiz-Fabri, 2002). The study was to provide the basis for proposals, particularly in the Francophonie. Thus, at the OIF summit in Beirut in October 2002, the new Quebec premier, Bernard Landry, and Morocco's Crown Prince Moulay Rachid jointly introduced the issue. Their common desire to impress the member states of the Francophonie and UNESCO with the importance of bringing debate on the matter to a fruitful conclusion was taken up in the Official Declaration:

"We welcome the adoption of the UNESCO Declaration on Cultural Diversity. We support the principle of developing a universal regulatory framework, and we are consequently determined to contribute actively to the adoption by UNESCO of an international convention on cultural diversity that enshrines the right of states and governments to maintain, establish and develop policies to support culture and cultural diversity. Its aim must be to define the rights applicable in regard to cultural diversity. This convention must also stress openness to other cultures and cultural expressions" (Organisation de la francophonie, 2002).[8]

In the aftermath of the April 2003 election defeat of the Parti Québécois, the Comité des Relations Internationales had to take on a new role; it had to continue to mobilize public opinion and pressure the members of the new government to continue to give high priority to the issue of cultural diversity. These activities accorded with resolutions that emerged from the party's policy convention in March 2003 espousing the view that "fair" globalization cannot come about without the promotion of cultural diversity and affirming that the Parti Québécois intended to continue to champion the cause internationally. This position was expressed by, among others, the leader of the Bloc Québécois; in an address to the Montreal Council on Foreign Relations (CORIM) on June 3, 2004, he reiterated the main points of Quebec's policy on globalization and reasserted Quebec's desire for a seat at UNESCO (Cauchy, 2004).

In October 2003, former Quebec international relations minister Louise Beaudoin recalled that the Convention on Cultural Diversity would go down in the history of relations between France and Quebec as one of the rare cases in which a bilateral agreement was extended to the international level (Beaudoin, 2003). In November of that year, the CRI expressed its regret at the fact that the new Quebec government was letting the federal government take the lead on the matter and declared that the Parti Québécois had the duty to remain vigilant over the new government's activities (CRI, November 10, 2003).

Meeting in Paris, the heads of government of Quebec and France, Jean Charest and Jean-Pierre Raffarin, reaffirmed their continuing commitment to cooperating in actively pursuing the adoption of an international instrument on cultural diversity. They also emphasized the point that states must have the power to define their own cultural policies and use every tool at their disposal to support their national culture. While in France, Charest met with UNESCO Director-General Koichiro Matsuura. He stressed to him the importance that Quebec and Canada attached to the protection of cultural diversity and underscored his government's wish to see culture excluded from all trade-liberalization accords. He further expressed his satisfaction with UNESCO's efforts in preparing a draft Convention on the Protection of the Diversity of Cultural Contents and Artistic Expressions (Beauchamp and Gagnon-Tremblay, 2004).

Concerned by the negative impact of a loss of cultural diversity, Quebec civil society was also proactive on the matter. Indeed, Quebec was the first place to see the establishment of a coalition of associations of professionals in the cultural sector to protect and promote cultural diversity. Some twelve Quebec associations banded together in the spring of 1998 to join the fight against the planned Multilateral Agreement on Investment (MAI). The members of the Coalition pour la Diversité Culturelle recognized that "cultural diversity is a fundamental right that states must protect and promote"[9] (Coalition pour la diversité culturelle, 2004). They worked together with the aim of ensuring that international trade agreements not place restrictions on cultural policies and that "states and governments be completely free to adopt the policies needed to support the diversity of cultural expressions"[10] (Coalition pour la diversité culturelle, 2004). The Comité des Relations Internationales of the Parti Québécois sought to maintain relations with all these groups and in the spring of 2004 proposed holding a symposium on the topic "La diversité culturelle : l'engagement du Québec" (Cultural diversity: Quebec's Commitment) in the following autumn.

---

9   Translated from French.
10 Translated from French.

The coalition, with financial backing from the governments of Quebec and Canada, soon reached out to mobilize the cultural industry around the world. In September 2004, Pierre Curzi, one of the joint presidents of the coalition, voiced his regret that up to that point only Quebec and the government of Canada had shown an interest in the issue while the other provinces had shown very little. Quebec gave the coalition a subsidy of $100,000 a year from the time it was established (Baillargeon, 2004). Canadian creators, artists, producers, distributors, broadcasters, and publishers were quick to join with their Quebec colleagues in a cross-Canada coalition that now comprises 35 associations. At the same time, the group worked successfully to develop coalitions around the world: While the first meeting in Montreal in September 2001 drew representatives of professional associations from 11 countries, more than 400 delegates from 35 countries attended the last conference in South Korea in June 2004 (Baillargeon, 2004). It was against this backdrop that the CRI sought to maintain its relations with all these groupings even after the 2003 election. UNESCO's adoption in October 2005 of the Convention on the Protection and Promotion of the Diversity of Cultural Expressions thus marked the conclusion of an intensive cycle of discussions and efforts to obtain recognition of a fundamental principle: "The Convention recognises the rights of Parties to take measures to protect and promote the diversity of cultural expressions, and impose obligations at both domestic and international levels on Parties." (UNESCO, 2005)

Conclusion

In this chapter, we sought to explore the work of the Comité des Relations Internationales of the Parti Québécois in terms of a political party operating in a federal state in which there is recognized shared jurisdiction over areas of foreign policy. While the government of Quebec was able to voice its views on the protection of cultural diversity in various international forums, it is nonetheless true that the Parti Québécois stood at the forefront of the debate because, more than any other party, it sees itself as the guarantor of a developing and flourishing original culture in North America. The notable willingness of members of the party to play a role on the world stage is no doubt related to their desire to make Quebec a country, but that cannot be the reason the other political parties agree on Quebec's taking its place on the international scene. Indeed, as the history of the Convention on Cultural Diversity demonstrates, there may at times even be a convergence of interests between Quebec and federal political parties on certain issues.

The Parti Québécois doubtless remains a unique case, though, because, on the whole, few provincial parties in Canada aspire to play a similar a role. The Bloc Québécois followed up on the cultural diversity issue on numerous occasions by asking questions about it in the House of Commons. Still, the work of political parties in multilevel states often flies under analysts' radar. Quebec's bilateral and later multilateral collaborations were undeniably very helpful in driving the idea at the international level of creating an instrument to provide a legal framework for cultural practices at a time when, in the face of citizen demands, globalization had to be brought under control. The contribution of central and local governments must not be minimized, but political parties, just as much as other groups of civil societies, can play an important mobilizing role. This party function is sometimes underappreciated if not often overlooked.

References

Baillargeon, S. (2004, September 1). Diversité culturelle : les autres provinces manquent à l'appel. *Le Devoir* (Montréal), B8.

Beauchamp, L. & Gagnon-Tremblay, M. (2004, October 6). Diversité culturelle : une étape déterminante est franchie. *Le Devoir* (Montréal), A6.

Beaudoin, J.F., Bélanger, L., & Lavoie M. (2002). Les relations internationales du Québec : deux partis, deux visions. In F. Pétry (Ed.), *Le Parti québécois – Bilan des engagements électoraux, 1994-2000*. Québec: Presses de l'Université Laval.

Beaudoin, L. (2006). Le Québec et le combat pour la diversité culturelle. In S. Paquin & L. Beaudoin (Eds.), *Histoire des relations internationales du Québec*. Montréal: VLB, 232-238.

Beaudoin, L. (2004, March 16). Marchandisation et diversité culturelle. *Le Devoir* (Montréal), A7.

Beaudoin, L. (2003, October 22). La mémoire courte. *Le Devoir* (Montréal), A7.

Bernier, I. (2000). *Mondialisation de l'économie et diversité culturelle : les enjeux pour le Québec*, Québec: Assemblée nationale du Québec, Commission sur la culture.

Bernier, Y. & Ruiz-Fabri, H. (2002). *Évaluation de la faisabilité juridique d'un instrument international sur la diversité culturelle*. Québec: Groupe de travail franco-québécois sur la diversité culturelle.

Bernier, I. & Atkinson, D (2000). *Mondialisation de l'économie et diversité culturelle : Les arguments en faveur de la préservation de la diversité culturelle*. Paris: Agence intergouvernementale de la francophonie.

Cauchy, C. (2004). Bloquistes et libéraux partagent les mêmes valeurs, selon Graham. *Le Devoir* (Montréal), June 4, A2.

Coalition pour la diversité culturelle (2004): http://www.cdc-ccd.org/Francais/Liensenfrancais/framequi_sommes_nous.htm.Page viewed 12/09/04

Diouf, A. (2004). La diversité culturelle dans la francophonie *Participation*, 28 (2), 20.

Fry, E. (2000). Québec Confronts Globalization: A model for the future? *Québec Studies*, 30, 57-69.

Government of Canada – International Trade Canada (2004). New Strategies for Culture and Trade: Canadian Culture in a Global World. http://www.international.gc.ca/trade-agreements-accords-commerciaux/fo/canculture.aspx?lang=eng&view=d. Page viewed 26/11/2004.

Gouvernement du Québec (1999, November 2). Le Québec fait entendre sa voix à l'UNESCO. Press Release. Paris.

Hrbek, R. (Ed.). (2004). *Political Parties and Federalism – An International Comparison,* Baden-Baden: Nomos Verlagsgesellschaft.

Lachapelle, G. (Ed.). (2008). *Diversité culturelle, identités et mondialisation– De la ratification à la mise en œuvre de la Convention sur la diversité culturelle.* Québec: Presses de l'Université Laval.

Lachapelle, G. & Maltais, B. (2008). Diversité culturelle et stratégies subétatiques : le cas du Québec. In Guy Lachapelle (Ed.), *Diversité culturelle, identités et mondialisation – De la ratification à la mise en œuvre de la Convention sur la diversité culturelle,* Québec: Presses de l'Université Laval.

Lachapelle, G. & Paquin, S. (2005). *Mastering Globalization: New Sub-states' governance and strategies,* Routledge.

Lachapelle, G. (2004). *Présentation à la Commission itinérante des chantiers de modernisation du Parti québécois.* Mimeographed document, April 28.

Lachapelle, G. (2003). Pourquoi le gouvernement canadien a refusé de participer à la guerre en Irak? *Revue française de science politique,* 53, 911-927.

Lachapelle, G. & Trent, J. (Ed.). (2000). *Globalization, Governance and Identity The Emergence of New Partnerships.* Montréal: Presses de l'Université de Montréal.

Lachapelle, G. (2000).Identity, Integration and the Rise of Identity Economy: The Quebec Case in Comparison with Scotland, Wales and Catalonia. In Guy Lachapelle and John Trent (Eds.), *Globalization, Governance and Identity: The Emergence of New Partnerships.* Montréal: Presses de l'Université de Montréal, 211-231.

Lisée, J.-F. (2013). Québec's Global Ambitions, Address by the Minister of International Relations, La Francophonie and External Trade, Jean-François Lisée, to the Montreal Council on Foreign Relations (CORIM). http://www.mrifce.gouv.qc.ca/fr/salle-de-presse/allocutions/2013/2013_02_11. Page viewed February 13. 2013.

Malone, C. (2011). *Les entités non souveraines sur la scène internationale,* Cahier de recherche, 4 (2). Québec: École nationale d'administration publique.

Michaud, N. (2006), La doctrine Gérin-Lajoie. In S. Paquin & L. Beaudoin (Eds.), *Histoire des relations internationales du Québec.* Montréal: VLB, 263-277.

Organisation de la francophonie (2002). Déclaration de Beyrouth adoptée lors de la 9ième Conférence des chefs d'État et de gouvernement des pays ayant le français en partage les 18,19 et 20 octobre. http://www.francophonie.org/documents/word/declarations/Declaration_de_Beyrouth.doc Page viewed 12/09/04.

Parti québécois (1986). *Le Québec et la vie internationale,* Congrès 1987: document de réflexion.

Parti québécois (1993). *Le Québec dans un monde nouveau.* Montréal: VLB.

Parti québécois (1995). *Les avenues internationales d'un Québec souverain – Document d'orientation,* Comité des relations internationales.

Paquin, S. in collaboration with Beaudoin, L., Robert Comeau, R. & Lachapelle, G. (2006). *Les relations internationales du Québec depuis la Doctrine Gérin-Lajoie (1965-2005) – Le prolongement externe des compétences internes.* Québec: Les Presses de l'Université Laval.

Paquin, S. (2005). Les actions extérieures des entités subétatiques: quelle signification pour la politique compare et les relations internationales? *Revue internationale de politique comparée,* 12 (2), 129-142.

Stephanescu, A. (Ed.). (2008). *René Lévesque, mythes et réalités : L'état actuel des recherches.* Montréal: Québec/Amérique.

208   Guy Lachapelle

Stolz, K. (2009). *Towards a regional political class? Professional politicians and regional institutions in Catalonia and Scotland*. Manchester: Manchester University Press.

Turp, D. (2004), *Communiqué du 18 septembre 2004*. Québec: Assemblé nationale du Québec.

UNESCO (2005). *Convention on the Protection and Promotion of the Diversity of Cultural Expressions*. http://unesdoc.unesco.org/images/0014/001429/142919e.pdf

UNESCO (2002). *UNESCO Universal Declaration on Cultural Diversity*. France: UNESCO.

Venne, M. (1999). Nos députés et le monde. *Le Devoir* (Montréal), August 7, A8.

Chapter 11
Political Parties in Multilevel Spain: Organization, Influence and Strategies

Juan Rodríguez, Universidad de Valencia
Astrid Barrio, Universidad de Valencia

Introduction

The decentralization of former Unitarian states has led to a complex institutional setting in which political parties have had to adapt gradually. Spain is a major example of a multilevel party system (Swenden and Maddens, 2009), which asymmetrically overlaps different levels of government and electoral competition. It is therefore necessary to consider how these party systems and subsystems interact and how they shape party organization and behaviour. This dynamic of multilevel competition is mainly characterized by four features: an electoral system with regional variations and a mixed electoral calendar, the existence of regional cleavage with nationalist and regionalist demands in several regions, a challenging position of parties representing these demands both on the national and regional levels and, finally, the existence of electorates with different behaviors on each electoral level.

This decentralization dynamic has led to weak nationalization in the Spanish party system, due to the heterogeneous electoral performance of the People's Party (PP), the Spanish Socialist Party (PSOE) and United Left (IU) throughout the territory and also to the political competition fostered by non-statewide parties (NSWP)[1] (Lago and Montero, 2010). Although the nationalization trend has been strengthened over time, especially since the 90s, those parties aiming to compete in all regions face several constraints and challenges coming from the peripheral parties (electoral competition, policy proposals,

---

[1] There is an open controversy around the terms employed to distinguish the different political parties depending on the territorial basis of their representation. Following the more common use by scholars of multilevel party politics, we shall distinguish between statewide parties, those parties competing in every or almost every district across Spain, and non-statewide parties (NSWP) for those parties that only aim to compete in one or few districts (Molas, 1977; De Winter, 1994; Swenden y Maddens, 2009). However, we may refer in specific contexts to these parties also as nationalist or regionalist parties, according to the own definition expressed by each party.

elite recruitment...). This simultaneous shift of the party system towards nationalization and of electoral competition towards regionalization highlights the dynamic that has characterized the evolution of Spanish decentralization and feeds political controversy regarding territorial organization in Spain.

In this context, the statewide parties have set up gradual changes to adapt their discourse and organization in order to strengthen their electoral presence in the different territories and tighten their position in the newly devolved institutions. Following this process, parties have to define their strategies to compete against opponents by weighting and clarifying their long-term interests on the national and regional levels. To understand how this process has materialized, this chapter presents the coalitional strategies that the main statewide parties have employed in order to achieve the optimum electoral and institutional performance. The purpose is to show how political parties have interacted in the context of Spanish multilevel competition. First, we will provide a general view of how statewide parties have adapted to decentralization. Second, we will describe how NSWPs have accumulated strength in the national party system and, most particularly, in regional subsystems. Finally, we will classify the main statewide parties' coalitional strategies on the regional level.

The organisational adaptation of statewide parties

Spanish statewide parties seek to compete simultaneously on at least two levels of government (national and regional), which opens the door to possible risks in terms of disagreement and tension between the central office and the regional organization. The party's central office defends a national discourse based on centralized organization and decision-making rooted on the assumption of a common 'national' good. On the contrary, regional offices face several incentives and pressures to adapt their policy positions, their platforms and their leadership to the regional competition in each *Comunidad*, especially in those regions where other parties lead the defense of territorial interests. The success of this two-level competition will depend on how parties have adapted their organizational structures to the environment. This is not a challenge that NSWPs have to address, since they are implemented in just one or a few regions and the national level is a subordinate political arena. Although these also have to resolve strategic dilemmas concerning communication or coalitional politics, their organizational structure is much more homogeneous and the degree of territorial conflict is necessarily smaller.

In the academic literature, the organizational adaptation of parties in multi-level systems has been measured by three variables: vertical integration, influence and autonomy (Thorlakson, 2009). The first refers to the type of formal and informal links between the central office and the regional organizations. In general, Spanish statewide parties have a high degree of vertical integration, since the territorial units are strongly linked to central headquarters. This means that there is high interdependence between the national and regional levels, what has been labelled the model of integrated parties. Thus, the national executive formally plays an influential role in the organization and in the decisions that the party takes on the regional level. IU has the lowest degree of integration (Pérez-Nievas and Ramiro, 2005), while the PP is the most integrated party with, for instance, centralized management of its finance and data affiliation (Astudillo and Garcia-Guereta, 2006: 409-410). The PSOE also has high integration although it is self-defined as a federal party and recognizes some political entity for the territorial federations (Betanzo, 2006). However, the effects of vertical integration in the Spanish parties have been subject to the evolution of internal party life (Fabre, 2008).

The second indicator, the *influence* of regional organizations on the central party structure, shows the growing importance of regional leaders in national politics. This trend is particularly evident in the PSOE and the PP, parties that have ruled in most of the regions. In the territorial party branches, the regional presidents have become key actors in internal party life, because of their formal positions obtained on national boards and their major influence on strategic party decisions. The process for selecting party leaders is a good example of this growing influence, as occurred with the PSOE at the last competitive party conferences (1997, 2000 and 2012) when the territorial 'barons' (regional party leaders) conditioned the process of renewing the national leadership. This has sometimes led to conflicts between national and regional leaders in the former's attempt to limit the role of the latter. This was why the Territorial Council (PSOE) and Autonomous Council (PP) were created as national bodies to bring the regional leaders under the authority of the national executive (Fabre and Mendez, 2009: 112).

The limits on vertical integration can also be seen through the *autonomy* afforded to territorial organizations within their regional level. Although the autonomy of regional offices was very low in the 80s, the interference of the national organization in regional affairs has gradually been decreasing (Fabre and Mendez, 2009: 113). Indeed, regional leaders have tended to enjoy their autonomy by preventing it from endangering the stability of the party's national strategy, especially when the party comes to the national executive. The evolution of the PSOE clearly shows this dynamic. When the party has been in central government, national leaders have strengthened their authority over territorial federations. But when the party has formed the opposition in national parliament, regional leaders have increased their autonomy to make strategic decisions (Hopkin, 2009: 194). On the other hand, the existence of simultaneous local and regional elections in most of the *Comunidades* has facilitated the coordination of their strategies and platforms in electoral campaigns.

Neverthless, the main peculiarity in the organizational adaptation of Spanish statewide parties (and the major exception to the gradual process of vertical integration) is the existence of *permanent territorial alliances* between national parties and NSWPs. This is the case of the PSOE-PSC in Catalonia, the PP-UPN in Navarra and IU-ICV in Catalonia (Roller and van Houten, 2002; Barbera, 2009; Verge, 2009). In these cases, two formally independent organizations create a stable alliance by setting up a relationship typical of confederal or bifurcated parties. The specific nature of this party relationship makes informal practices sometimes more important than formal rules in explaining how they work.

The most relevant is the permanent territorial alliance between the PSOE and the PSC. It started in 1977 in the form of an electoral coalition and was institutionalized in July 1978 when the Catalan branch of the PSOE merged with two other Catalan socialist parties, leading to the creation of the Catalan Socialist Party (PSC) as an independent body. This formula was based on two major agreements: the PSOE would never present an electoral candidacy in Catalonia and would not interfere politically in Catalan affairs, while the PSC would respect and assume the position of the PSOE in Spanish politics (Roller and Van Houten, 2002). In organizational terms, this formula has not been recorded in any official document, other than some generic agreements adopted before the creation of the permanent alliance. The PSC has a seat in the central organs of the PSOE, participates in the Federal Congress like any other federation, Catalan socialist MPs have belonged to the PSOE parliamentary group in the national lower chamber since 1982 (although this is controversial issue for the PSC) and has always had ministers in national socialist cabinets (although it does not formally participate in the process of cabinet formation). In contrast, the PSC has a separate membership (dual membership of the PSC and PSOE is forbidden), manages its finances autonomously and participates separately in international party forums such as the Party of European Socialists. Since its creation, the alliance between the PSOE and PSC has been fairly successful electorally in Catalonia and has enabled relevant influence of Catalan socialists in national politics. However, this has not been without tensions and risks, which have always tended to be resolved in the informal sphere. The internal conflict in the alliance peaked in recent years when the PSOE and PSC simultaneously ruled the national and regional governments between 2004 and 2010 (Van Houten, 2009).

Non-statewide parties: representation and influence

One of the main features of the multilevel party system in Spain is the high number of NSWPs (Pallares, Montero and Llera, 1997). Most of these parties are not a product of the political decentralization process that started with the 1978 Constitution since there had already been NSWPs in the previous democratic periods in the regions with specific national identities (Catalonia, Galicia and the Basque Country). Neither can we confine NSWPs only to these regions, for the institutional characteristics of political competition after decentralization have acted as a source of political pluralism and have fostered the creation of new regionalist parties where they had not previously existed (Botella, 1989).

Decentralization has not produced a significant increase in the amount of NSWPs, but has favored the extension of their influence on political institutions. We need to establish a fundamental distinction between those NSWPs that have been influential only on the regional level and those that are also relevant on the national level. These have become key players in the system of political exchanges in Spanish multilevel politics, which has decisively shaped the strategies of the statewide parties. To check the relevance of this distinction between NSWPs, we will observe the electoral and institutional evolution of the NSWPs on both regional and national levels of political competition.

The strength of NSWPs on the regional level

The regional political arena is undoubtedly the priority for NSWPs. In most cases, these political parties were created during the transition to or in the early years of democracy, just before the autonomous institutions were constitutionally created. This means that most parties were regional political actors from the very beginning, although not all of them ultimately achieved the same political success. In fact, decentralization in Spain has fostered the political strength of the NSWPs rather than increasing the amount of new regional parties (Barrio *et al.*, 2010). During these years, the influence of NSWPs has grown substantially, so many of these actors that were initially *relevant* parties only in the parliamentary arena (as stated by Sartori, 1976) have become over time governmental parties (figure 11.1).

Figure 11.1: Evolution of the relevance of NSWP at the regional level

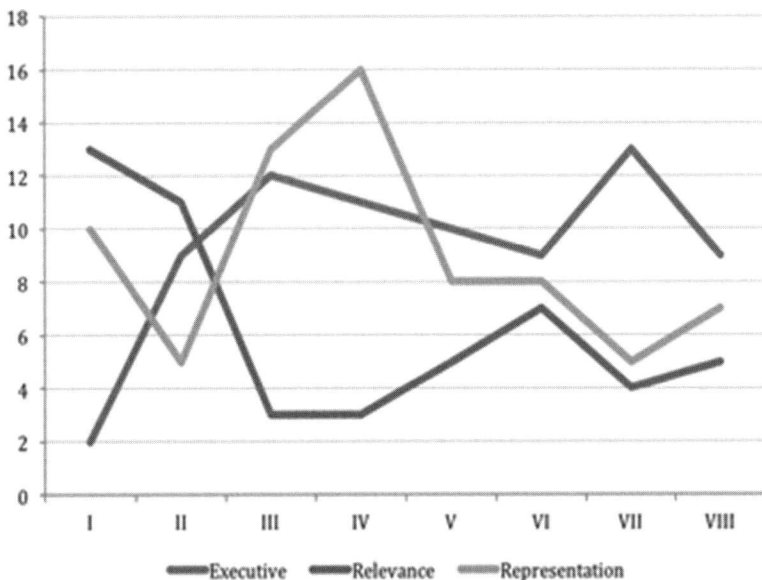

===Executive   ===Relevance   ===Representation

Sources: Own elaboration from our data published in Barrio et al. (2010).
Note: We employ Sartori's typology (1976): representation (the party only obtains a seat but without coalition potential); *relevance* (the party has coalition potential but without entering the cabinet); *executive* (the party enters the cabinet).

Behind this overall picture, the presence of NSWPs in the autonomous communities is much more diverse. Some communities have always had NSWPs in their regional parliaments while in others the presence of these parties has been discontinued. In the regions where regionalist and nationalist parties have been continuously present in parliament, we can find the most relevant examples of NSWPs.

Among these communities, Catalonia is the most prominent case, where all the parties in the regional cabinet and the winners of all elections have been NSWPs. The Catalan Parliament is quite an exceptional case, since the weight of statewide parties is very low - they have only ever managed to become the third party. This peculiarity is explained by the PSC's permanent territorial alliance with the PSOE, by which the latter does not compete directly in Catalonia, as explained in the previous section. The main Catalan NSWP is Convergence and Union (CiU), a bipartisan coalition of Catalan nationalists that have always competed as the same candidacy. CiU ruled the *Generalitat de Catalunya* (the regional government) between 1980 and 2003 and has done so again since 2010. Other relevant NSWPs with continuous presence in the Catalan parliament are, on the one hand, ICV (Green Initiative for Catalonia), which represents the greens and is the successor to the old Catalan communist party (United Socialist Party of Catalonia, PSUC), and on the other hand the pro-independence party (Republican Left of Catalonia, ERC). Both parties are smaller and their influence has been limited by periodical internal conflicts. In some cases, these crises have led to new parties. PSC, ERC and ICV ruled the Catalan government between 2003 and 2010, as a left-wing coalition government.

In the Basque Country, NSWPs have always been represented in the regional parliament. What they all have in common is that they compete not only in the Basque regional and local elections, but also in Navarre and the French Basque territory for they are demanding a Basque nation with larger territorial borders than the Autonomous Community, called Euskal Herria. The main NSWP has always been the Basque Nationalist Party (PNV), which is also stronger than the PSOE and the PP. The second NSWP has traditionally been Herri Batasuna (HB) or Sortu as it is now named after the banning of the original party. It represents the left-wing pro-independence electorate and has behaved as an anti-system party, allegedly being associated to ETA terrorist activity and therefore reluctant to accept the legitimacy of Spanish political institutions (including those of the regional decentralization). In recent years, the peace process and the decline in ETA's activism have created a new dynamic in the Basque party system that is fostering a realignment within the nationalist electorate and a reconfiguration of the balance between parties.

The NSWPs in Navarre have always been present in the regional assembly although in the early years the statewide parties were electorally stronger. The most relevant actor was the permanent territorial alliance between the Navarre People's Union (UPN) and the PP between 1991 and 2008, which allowed UPN to become the leading party and it has governed Navarre almost uninterruptedly since then. The alliance ended the division of the Navarre right in the 80s (Barberà, 2009). However, after the elections of 2007, the PSOE's support for the UPN minority government heightened the differences between the internal regionalist majority and pro-PP members of the UPN, which led to the PP's decision in 2008 to break the alliance and retrieve their own organization in Navarre. This has not prevented the PP and UPN from forming an electoral coalition for the 2011 general election.

While in Catalonia, the Basque Country and Navarre, several NSWPs have obtained an influential and continuous presence in parliaments, there are other communities with only one leading regionalist or nationalist organization. The presence of NSWPs in the Canary Islands has been continuous but has been of fluctuating influence, due to difficulties establishing a common organization. Until 1991, the regional parties were atomized in island-based organizations. The creation of the Canarian Coalition (CC), first as a federation of parties and later as a unitary party allowed them to become the leading political force in the region. The parties that did not join the CC, some of which were only implemented on one island, have been much less successful electorally. In Galicia, there has been a continued presence of NSWPs in the regional parliament, although the main parties in this community have always been statewide parties. The NSWPs have been consigned to a third party, with somewhat irregular results. The main NSWP is the Galician Nationalist Bloc (BNG), a federation of Galician nationalist organizations that has always obtained representation and reached government between 2005 and 2009 in coalition with the PSOE. In Aragon, the leading party has always been a statewide party, but there have been small NSWPs with permanent parliamentary representation that have often had a relevant influence on the formation of cabinets. This is the case with the main NSWP, the Aragon Party (PAR), which has successfully managed to become a hinge party, joining the cabinet when there are no single-party majority governments.

Finally, there are some communities where NSWPs have been continuously present, but which have rarely been able to participate in coalition governments and have never obtained representation on the national level. In the Balearic Islands, the Mallorca Union (UM) became the hinge party, despite its small representation, in the absence of absolute majorities. This is also the situation with the Cantabria Regionalist Party (PRC), although it joined the cabinet in the late 90s and won the regional prime-ministership. Finally, the Rioja Party (PR) has had a marginal influence after 1991, due to the continuous absolute majority of the PP since then.

A second group consists of those communities where the presence of autonomous NSWP parliaments has been discontinued, which has prevented them from being able to influence the institutions. And when any of these NSWPs has occasionally joined the cabinet for a short period, the result has been an internal crisis that has wiped out their parliamentary representation. A good example of this is to be found in Andalusia, where the Andalusian Party (PA) was present in the regional parliament from the first term, but its experience in the cabinet led to a crisis that split the party and caused it to lose its parliamentary status. A very similar case is that of the Valencian Union (UV), an influential political party during the 90s, but whose cabinet coalition with the PP weakened the organization and it eventually disappeared from parliament. In Asturias, Castilla-León and Extremadura, no NSWPs have ever managed to achieve any influential status because of their very weak representation in the regional parliament and strong majorities of the governing party.

There is a small group of regions (Madrid, Castilla la Mancha and Murcia) where NSWPs have never obtained parliamentary representation, though that does not mean that there are no such parties in these regions. The hegemony of statewide parties, the obstacles imposed by electoral law and the weakness of their electoral supporters have prevented these parties from entering regional parliamentary life.

The strength of NSWPs on the national level

The Spanish party system is organized around two main statewide parties (PSOE and PP), some small fluctuating national parties and several NSWPs of varying weight and degree of influence. The evolution of the party system has been characterized by increasing competition between and concentration of votes for PSOE and PP at the expense of the small statewide parties (Ocaña and Oñate, 2007), which in general are heavily penalized by the electoral system. However, the constant dominance of the major parties has not prevented a relevant presence of NSWPs in the lower chamber. In fact, they have often been partners in the creation of parliamentary majorities and have contributed to national governance.

Table 11.1: Amount of NSWP and its parliamentarians in the low chamber

| | Parliamentarians | | | | |
	NSWP	NSWP	PSC	CiU	Majority
1977	8	47	15	11	–
1979	11	53	17	8	–
1982	8	52	25	12	PSOE
1986	11	59	21	18	PSOE
1989	12	63	20	18	PSOE
1993	11	56	18	17	–
1996	11	56	19	16	–
2000	11	54	17	15	PP
2004	11	58	21	10	–
2008	9	53	25	10	–
2011	11	53	14	16	PP

Source: Congreso de los Diputados (www.congreso.es). 'Majority' indicates the party who got the absolute majority at each legislative term.

The presence of NSWPs in the Congress of Deputies (the lower chamber) has always been continuous and has remained stable. The number of parties has ranged between 8 and 12 and the number of seats between 47 and 63. However, behind this remarkable stability there is significant variation in both the composition of the group of NSWPs and in the political influence exerted by this representation.

In terms of composition, there is disparity in both the size and continuity of the NSWPs represented in the national parliament. The PSC (through the permanent territorial alliance with the PSOE) and CiU are the two most relevant parties in terms of size. Since both parties are electoral adversaries in Catalonia, their influence in parliamentary politics is akin to a zero-sum game, in that when one gains notoriety, this is usually at the expense of the other. Despite its electoral and parliamentary superiority, the strength of the PSC has often been conditioned by its participation in the PSOE's parliamentary group since 1982. Until then, the PSC had a separate group, but which was always coordinated alongside the PSOE. The elimination of its parliamentary group was a decision by the PSOE (in collaboration with the ruling party at that time, the UCD) to strengthen the cohesion and the image of unity of the socialist party in the lower chamber. This reduced thereafter the autonomy of the PSC and favored the protagonism of CiU's parliamentary group. In the 2012 elections, CiU managed to overcome the PSC's electoral support, becoming the leading NSWP in parliament. PSC and CiU are the only NSWPs that have always had national MPs, along with the PNV, which tends to win between 5 and 8 seats. Despite having significantly lower representation, PNV's political influence has enabled its parliamentary group to become an influential force in the absence of absolute majorities. Finally, Canarian centrist nationalism has been represented from 1982 through the Canarian Independent Group-Canarian Coalition (AIC, after CC), whose position has fluctuated between 1 and 4 seats. Although carrying much less weight than the Catalan NSWP, their willingness to offer parliamentary support to both the PP and PSOE has won them a very influential position.

Only PSC, CiU, PNV and CC (and to a lesser extent ERC and ICV) have become influential NSWPs on the national level. Some others with discontinuous representation have been less relevant in executive politics. The difficulty in obtaining representation in the national and European political arenas exposes one of the weakest features of these political parties. Aiming to overcome this obstacle, the NSWPs have implemented three types of strategy over the years.

The first is the building of a national political organization. In the mid 80s, there was an attempt to launch a successful statewide candidacy formed by various NSWPs and other parties. The Democratic Reform Party (PRD) was driven by the CDC and was supported by business interest groups and ex-leaders of the former Union of Democratic Centre (UCD), some of whom have become leaders of new regional parties seeking to build a coalition with different central, regional and liberal parties. However, the PRD's electoral failure put an end to the operation. Furthermore, although with much less impact, other NSWPs attempted to promote an alternative candidacy in parallel to the PRD: The Assembly of Regional Parties, which aimed to give voice to a set of regionalist parties in the national political arena. Following the 1989 European elections, this Assembly encouraged the creation of a Federation of Regionalist Parties (FPR). The FPR did not win any seats, but other candidates composed of NSWPs were more successful. Since then, NSWPs have continued to run for European Parliament but generally only those that join a coalition with stronger NSWPs (such as PNV and CC) manage to win any seats. Finally, some NSWPs have opted to join the AP-PP's candidacy in some general elections. However, this alternative has been considerably distrusted due to the high risk of absorption by the national party with which it is competing.

Of course, the influence of stronger NSWPs has mainly been exerted when neither the PSOE nor the PP have held a majority. The main feature of Spain in this regard is the absence of coalition governments, even though in most parliaments after 1977 the ruling parties have been in the minority. The impossibility of building cabinet coalitions only formed by national parties has increased the potential for coalitions with some NSWPs (usually CiU, PNV and CC) in the parliamentary arena. However, NSWPs have rejected offers to join the cabinet and have preferred to exert influence from outside, through parliamentary agreements (often on an *ad hoc* basis) based on parliamentary exchanges of support across levels, as well as obtaining some political benefits in national budget bargaining and regarding the most important policies (Reniu, 2002). Some have called these NSWPs *pressure parties* since this behavior is somewhat akin to that of lobbyists (Molas, 1977). This position of continuous bargaining between the nationalist parties and the PP or PSOE has generated a negative view of their role in Spanish public opinion, since the interpretation is usually that the NSWP's support is a general subordination to the particular interests of some regions (Lago and Montero, 2010: 310-11).

However, it should be noted that the ruling parties have always sought agreement with the main NSWPs even in parliaments with an absolute majority, seeking to enhance the political legitimacy of the main laws, due to the central position of these political parties. But this strategy of parliamentary bargaining does not necessarily guarantee political stability. Leaving aside the term from 1977-1979, due to its special characteristics, most minority governments supported by parliamentary agreements with NSWPs have not lasted to the end, as was the case with the UCD (1979-1982), with the last Gonzalez administration (1993-1996) and with the second Zapatero administration (2008-2011). However, both Aznar and Zapatero's first administrations (1996-2000 and 2004-2008) did complete their parliamentary terms, thanks to support from the NSWPs.

Statewide parties' coalitional strategies on the regional level

The challenge of NSWPs has shaped the behavior of statewide parties, which not only had to adapt to the new institutional framework but also to the characteristics of multilevel political competition (Maddens and Libbrecht, 2009; Alonso and Gómez, 2011). The PP and PSOE have faced similar dilemmas in regional party competition, and have tended to employ different strategies in different regions and legislatures. This means that one party has simultaneously employed several types of strategy in different regions and different strategies in the same region over time. These trade-offs may appear on the organizational level (as discussed in section 1), when it comes to defining party platforms and when the party decides on political agreements and alliances. One way to classify the third kind of strategy is based on two criteria: the types of coalition before elections (electoral coalitions) and those after elections (both parliamentary and cabinet coalitions), as shown in table 11.2 (Rodriguez *et al.*, 2010). This classification describes nine possible coalitional strategies that parties may adopt in order to collaborate with other parties in the absence of an absolute majority.

Table 11.2: Coalitional strategies in both electoral and parliamentary-executive arenas

		Parliament-Executive		
		Alone	Parliamentary coalition	Executive coalition
Elec-toral	Alone	The party runs alone for the election. It remains at opposition or in a one-party cabinet, with majority or minority (and without stable allies).	The party runs alone for the election and gives support to the majority but without entering the cabinet.	The party runs alone for the election and makes a coalition cabinet.
	Electoral coalition	The party runs in a coalition but it remains at the opposition.	The party runs in a coalition and gives support to the majority but without entering the cabinet.	The party runs in an electoral coalition that becomes a cabinet coalition.
	Permanent territorial alliance	The alliance remains at opposition or in a one-party cabinet, with majority or minority (and without stable allies).	The alliance gives parliamentary support to the majority but without entering the cabinet.	The alliance forms a cabinet coalition with other parties.

The degree of involvement of parties in collaborative strategies may range from a refusal to establish any kind of coalition at any time and opting instead run alone for an absolute majority, to the establishment of permanent territorial alliances that will enter coalition cabinets with other parties. This indicator seeks to capture the variety of responses that the parties have employed when competing in different territories.

Table 11.3 shows the frequencies of these types of strategy for the PSOE and the PP. It is no surprise to see that most of the time both parties prefer to compete and win on their own, and hence form a single-party majority cabinet. In the case of a minority, they will only seek stable parliamentary support from other parties. Otherwise, they remain in the opposition. However, this 'self-made party' strategy is employed less frequently than one might expect, only in half of the terms where there was a real choice. The PP has tended to apply this strategy more often than the PSOE.

When parties decide to collaborate with other parties, they prefer to form a coalition after the election. Electoral coalitions do not seem to be an attractive device, and when parties use them, this tends to be in the form of a permanent territorial alliance (with the PSC or the UPN). The PSOE has only established some kind of pre-electoral agreement in fifteen terms, nine of which corresponded to the permanent territorial alliance with the PSC in Catalonia. PP has only chosen the pre-electoral collaboration strategy in eleven terms, five of which corresponded to the alliance with UPN in Navarre. The PP has established various types of post-electoral coalition with other parties in nine regions, which has enabled it to rule and achieve the premiership in six of them. Sometimes, these alliances were preceded by pre-electoral coalitions. The PSOE has tried to form post-electoral coalitions with other parties in twelve regions. In half of them, it could only govern in coalition with NSWPs, which has often allowed the socialist party to achieve regional government despite losing the election. No pre-electoral coalitions were established in any of these cases[2].

The parties prefer to wait until the election is over before deciding which kind of collaborative approach to employ, when they will be able to make better informed decisions. When it comes to post-electoral alliances, the main dilemma for the PP and PSOE is whether they should remain in the opposition and reject any support or whether they should rule in coalition. However, exclusively parliamentary collaboration is very rare. The PSOE has established parliamentary cooperation with other parties in ten legislatures, while the PP has only done so in seven legislatures. None of these collaborations had any precedents in the form of pre-electoral coalitions, with the sole exception of Extremadura (where the PP and PSOE have formed pre-electoral coalitions with regionalist NSWPs). Consequently, the alternative strategy to standing alone is usually to join a coalition government with other parties, which happened in one out of three legislative terms where there was a real strategic

---

2   The only exception is the pre-electoral coalition set in the Ibiza-Formentera district, in Balearic Islands, in 2003, where the PSOE run in a candidacy with two leftist NSWP.

choice (42 terms for the PSOE and 20 terms for the PP). Coalition cabinets typically take place without any precedent of pre-electoral coalitions or permanent territorial alliance.

Table 11.3: Coalitional strategies implemented by PP and PSOE in both political arenas

		Parliamentary-Executive		
		Alone	Parliamentary coalition	Cabinet coalition
Electoral	Alone	PP 52,9 % (37) PSOE 45 % (36)	PP 8,6 % (6) PSOE 10 % (8)	PP 22,9 % (16) PSOE 26,3 % (21)
	Electoral coalition	PP 4,3 % (3) PSOE 3,8 % (3)	PP 1,4 % (1) PSOE 2,5 % (2)	PP 2,9 % (2) PSOE 1,3 % (1)
	Permanent territorial alliance	PP 4,3 % (3) PSOE 8,8 % (7)	PP 0 % (0) PSOE 0 % (0)	PP 2,9 % (2) PSOE 2,5 % (2)

Source: Own elaboration.
Note: Total amount of legislative terms (N): 138. We exclude the terms where a party obtained an absolute majority (PP=72; PSOE=62). The percentages are computed on the rest of the legislative terms for each party (PP N=70; PSOE N=80). The same party may implement two different strategies during the same term (which happens in 4 terms each party).

The decision to join coalition governments on the regional level does not necessarily follow a rational path of forming congruent executives or keeping policy coherent across levels (Stefuriuc, 2009). The main difference between the PSOE and PP is the parliamentary position from which they choose their coalition strategies. The PSOE tends to form coalition cabinets with NSWPs as a way of getting into the cabinet when they have not won the elections (16 out of the 24 legislatures where they formed coalitions) to a greater extent than PP (8 legislatures out of the 20). Moreover, in most of these cases, this strategy has enabled the PSOE to achieve the premiership of the regional government (Aragon, Balearic Islands, Catalonia, Galicia, Navarre, La Rioja and Basque Country) while the PP has never achieved the presidency through this route.

Conclusions

In this chapter, we have shown how the statewide political parties seek to adapt to the territorial decentralization and competition in a multilevel party system. The main challenge found in this process has been the important role of NSWPs, both in the national and in the regional arena. The number of regionalist and nationalist parties and their degree of influence on both levels means it is no longer possible to understand the dynamics of the Spanish political system without paying attention to these parties. In this sense, Spain is an unprecedented case for the study of such a situation.

Statewide parties have sought to maintain high vertical integration while generating increasing autonomy for regional organizations and giving them a growing role in their offices. We can find more traces of this influence in the PSOE than in the PP. This contradictory evolution has been conditioned to the relevance of territorial leaders, especially when they have become leaders of regional cabinets. In some cases, they have been key actors in maintaining internal party balance and in the election of new national leaders.

NSWPs have also played an important role since the beginning of democracy, despite many of them only achieving modest parliamentary representation. The establishment of the *Comunidades Autónomas* has created a better structure of opportunities for their political survival. Thus, most of these parties have been able to hold positions of influence, often within cabinets, despite a trend towards the concentration of the votes for the main statewide parties and the nationalization of the Spanish party system. From this perspective, as some scholars have suggested, it is not possible to understand the nationalization of party systems in decentralized states without considering what is happening on the regional level.

The result of this dynamic is that statewide parties must respond to multilevel competition by means of more flexible strategies in their organization, their platforms and coalitions, in order to adapt better to different competitive environments. Where there are strong NSWPs, national parties will have greater difficulties obtaining political success unless they adopt a more favourable attitude to decentralization. However, this also generates contradictions and trade-offs in their decisions regarding elections, government and accountability.

Acknowledgments

The authors are grateful with the support of the projects CSO2009-14381–C03–02 of the Spanish government and SGR 2009-1290 of the Catalan regional government.

References

Alonso, S. and B. Gómez. (2011). "Partidos nacionales en elecciones regionales: ¿coherencia territorial o programas a la carta?", *Revista de Estudios Políticos*, No. 152, 183-209.

Astudillo, J. (2010). "Una primera aproximación cuantitativa a la descentralización de los partidos de ámbito estatal en estados descentralizados: ¿Hay diferencias entre el PSOE y el PP?", *Revista d'Estudis Autonomics i Federals*, vol 10, 330-362.

Astudillo, J. and E. García-Guereta. (2006) "If it isn't broken, don't fix it: The Spanish Popular Party in power", *South European Society and Politics*, No. 11, 399-417.

Barberà, O. (2009). "Los orígenes de la Unión del Pueblo Navarro (1979-1991)", *Papers. Revista de Sociologia*, No. 92, 143-69.

Barrio, A., J. Rodríguez Teruel, O. Barberà and M. Baras. (2011). "La fuerza de los Partidos de Ámbito No Estatal en España (1977-2008)" en P. Biglino y C. Mapelli, dirs., *Garantías del pluralismo territorial*. Madrid: Centro de Estudios Políticos y Constitucionales.

Betanzo, A. (2006). "Los efectos de la transformación territorial del Estado español sobre el PSOE y el PP", *Revista d'Estudis Autonòmics i Federals*, Vol. 3.

Botella, J. (1989). "The Spanish New 'Regions': Territorial and Political Pluralism", *International Poltical Science Review*, No. 10, 263-271.

De Winter, L. (ed.). (1994). *Non-state wide parties in Europe*. Barcelona: Institut de Ciències Polítiques i Socials.

Fabre, E. (2008). "Party Organization in a Multi-level System: Party organiza- cional Change in Spain and the UK", *Regional & Federal Studies*, Vol. 18, No. 4, 309-29.

Fabre, E. and M. Méndez. (2009). "Decentralization and party organizationla change: the British and the Spanish statewide parties compared" en W. Swenden y B. Maddens, ed., *Territorial party politics in Western Europe,* Chippenham, Palgrave.

Hopkin, J. (2009). "Party matters. Devolution and Party Politics in Britain and Spain", *Party Politics*, Vol. 15, No. 2, 179-198.

Lago, I. and J.R. Montero. (2010). "La nacionalización del sistema de partidos en España: una perspectiva comparada" en J.R. Montero e I. Lago, (eds)., *Elecciones 2008*, Madrid: Centro de Estudios Sociológicos.

Maddens, B. and L. Libbrecht. (2009). "How statewide parties cope with the regionalist issue: the case of Spain. A directional approach" en W. Swenden y B. Maddens, ed., *Territorial party politics in Western Europe,* Chippenham, Palgrave

Méndez, M. (2006). "Turning the page: crisis and tranformation of the Spanish Socialist Party", *South European Society and Politics*, No. 11, 419-37.

Molas, I. (1977). "Los partidos de ámbito no estatal y los sistemas de par- tidos", en P. De Vega, ed., *Teoría y práctica de los partidos*. Madrid: Cuadernos para el Diálogo.

Ocaña, F. and P. Oñate. (2007). "Elecciones excepcionales, elecciones de continuidad y sistemas de partidos", J.R. Montero, I. Lago y M. Torcal, (eds)., *Elecciones generales 2004*, Madrid: Centro de Estudios Sociológicos.

Pallarés, F., Montero, J.R and Llera, F. (1997). "Non State-wide Parties in Spain: An Attitudinal Study of Nationalism and Regionalism", Publius, No. 27, 135-169.

Pérez-Nievas, S. and Luis Ramiro. (2005). "El impacto de los procesos de descentralización territorial en la organización de los partidos políticos: el caso del Izquierda Unida". Paper read at the *Congreso de la Asociación Española de Ciencia Política*, 21-24 September, Madrid, Spain.

Reniu, J.M. (2002). *La formación de gobiernos minoritarios en España 1977-1996*, Madrid: Centro de Investigaciones Sociológicas.

Rodríguez, J., A. Barrio, M. Baras and O. Barberà. (2010). *Las respuestas estratégicas de los partidos de ámbito estatal a los desafíos de la competición multinivel: la política de alianzas del PP y el PSOE en las Comunidades Autónomas de España (1980-2008)*, Working Paper No. 284, Barcelona: Institut de Ciències Polítiques i Socials.

Roller and L. Van Haute. (2003). "A national party in a regional party system: the PSC-PSOE in Catalonia", *Regional and Federal Studies*, Vol. 13, No. 3, 1-22.

Sartori, G. (1976). *Parties and Pary Systems. A Framework for Analysis*. Cambridge: Cambridge University Press.

Swenden, W. and B. Maddens. (2009). "Territorial party politics in Western Europe: a framework for analysis" en W. Swenden y B. Maddens, ed., *Territorial party politics in Western Europe,* Chippenham: Palgrave

Verge, T. (2009). "Las relaciones cambiantes de un NSWP con su partido hermano: el caso de Iniciativa per Catalunya Verds", *Papers. Revista de Sociologia,* No. 92, 227–245.

Chapter 12
The Organization and Functioning of Parties in Multilevel Belgium

Kris Deschouwer, Free University of Brussels

Introduction

The institutional architecture of the Belgian political system has been thoroughly transformed in the course of the last few decades. In 1970 Belgium was a unitary state with one single level of government. In 1995 and after four substantial revisions of the Constitution, Belgium had become a federal state. Since 1995 further constitutional reforms have increased the degree of autonomy of the substate level and have increased the complexity of the system. Belgium has indeed created two types of substates – regions and language communities – that partially overlap in an asymmetrical way (Deschouwer, 2009).

For the political parties this new institutional context has had far-reaching consequences. One must however not just assume that the political institutions have shaped the organization and strategies of the political parties. There has also been quite some adaptation of the institutional system to the form and organization of the political parties. One of the most striking features of the Belgian parties and party system is the absence of statewide parties. The original traditional political parties – Christian-democrats, Socialists and Liberals – have all fallen apart *before* the transformation of the unitary state into a federal state (Verleden, 2009). The breaking up of the parties occurred between 1968 and 1978, but in an earlier pre-war phase already the Catholic (later Christian-democratic) party had opted for an organization that clearly reflected the bipolar and bilingual structure of the country. The political institutions have thus also been adapted to the political parties that reflect divisions in the Belgian society.

In this chapter, we will first present the basic features of the Belgian political institutions. Next, we will zoom in on the peculiar characteristics of the split party system. The next part will discuss elections and patterns of electoral results since the direct election of the regional parliaments in 1995. After that we look at government (and thus coalition) formation at the different levels and that way in which the Belgian parties deal with (in)congruence and (as)sym-

metry. The last part of the chapter discusses career patters and the degree of
level hopping between the federal and the substate layers of government.

A double and asymmetric federation

The Belgian federal system is not the easiest to understand. The major reason
for that is the introduction of two different types of substates. The Belgian federation is indeed a double federation of regions and language communities.
The background against which this was done is a country divided from west to
east by a language border (McRae, 1986). North of the border (in Flanders) the
people speak Dutch, south of the border (in Wallonia) they speak French. Both
language groups are however not of an equal size: roughly 60% of the Belgians
speak Dutch (6.5 million) and 40% speak French (4.5 million). In the southern
and French speaking part, there is also a small community of some 70.000
German speakers, living close to the German border.

The capital city of Belgium is Brussels. Brussels is located north of the language border, which means that it used to be a city in which the population
spoke Dutch. Yet since the working language of the newly created Belgium in
1830 was French, Brussels was rapidly transformed into a (also much larger)
city in which French became the dominant language. The balance between the
two groups in Brussels – with 1.1 million inhabitants) is roughly 85% French-
speaking and 15% Dutch-speaking. It is the location of Brussels and the dominance of French in Brussels that explains the fairly complex institutional
setup.

Transforming the state from a unitary to a federal state could indeed be done
in two different ways. On the Dutch-speaking or Flemish side the preference
was for devolution to the language communities, based on the historical language border. That would include Brussels into the Flemish substate. The Francophone preference was for devolution to three regions, making Brussels a
separate substate next to Flanders (without Brussels) and Wallonia. The compromise reached in 1970 and subsequently implemented was to do both: to
create both language communities and territorial regions. These two types of
substates largely overlap. The Flemish community develops its policies
(mainly education and culture) in the Flemish region and in Brussels while the
French-speaking community develops its policies in the region Wallonia and
in Brussels. The German-speaking community belongs to the Walloon region
but can develop its own community policies (Deschouwer, 2005).

The complex institutional setup is thus the result of a different vision on
Belgium, on its internal boundaries and on its constituent parts between the
two major language groups. The division line between the two language groups

is also present in the rules for federal decision-making. All members of parliament belong to either the Dutch or the French language group. That membership is defined by the electoral district in which a member of parliament is elected. Only the members of parliament elected in the Brussels constituency (actually including the Brussels region and 35 municipalities of Flanders) can decide themselves to which language group they belong. Their choice is however never a surprise since they are elected on the lists of political parties that all belong to only one of the language groups.

The federal government – in which consensus is the rule for internal decision making – has to be composed of an equal number of Dutch-speaking and French speaking ministers (7 of each maximum), exception made for the Prime Minister (who is most often a Dutch speaker). For revisions of the constitution involving the functioning of the federal state a two thirds majority is needed in both houses of parliament and a majority in each language group. These hard rules of compulsory power sharing make the Belgian federation very much a consociational federation (Lijphart). Important for us here is that it is based on the linguistic bipolarity of the country. That is indeed also the way in which the parties and the party system are organized.

Parties and party system

Political parties in multilevel systems can be classified along two dimensions (Deschouwer, 2006). The first is the *scope* or *territorial pervasiveness* of the parties. That refers to the part of the territory on which they are active. For the Belgian political parties the scope is restricted to one of the two language groups. A Francophone party presents lists in the Walloon electoral districts and in Brussels. A Flemish party presents lists in the Flemish electoral districts and in Brussels. That means that all parties limit their activities to one of the two language communities and to two of the three regions.

Some of the Belgian parties used to have a wider and statewide scope. These are the so-called 'traditional' parties whose origin date back to the 19th century. The three traditional parties were a Catholic (later Christian democratic) party, a Socialist Party and a Liberal Party. A smaller Communist Party that was founded in 1920 also had a statewide scope but gradually declined and has today disappeared. These three traditional parties all fell apart along the language division and as a result of the tensions between the two language groups on the organization of the Belgian state.

In 1968, the Christian Democratic Party was split into a Flemish and a Francophone party. They are today called CD&V in Flanders (Christen Democratisch & Vlaams) and CDh in Francophone Belgium (Centre Démocrate

Humaniste). In 1971, the Liberal party split. Today there is a Flemish Liberal Party called Open VLD (Open Vlaamse Liberalen en Democraten) and a Francophone party called MR (Mouvement Réformateur). The Socialist party was the last to fall apart in 1978. Today the two parties are the SP.a on the Flemish side (Socialistische Partij Anders) and the PS (Parti Socialiste) on the Francophone side.

All parties created after 1978 immediately opted for only one of the language groups. The split of the parties and their limited scope has indeed also split the party system. The electoral competition is within each language group and therefore a party deciding to participate in the elections chooses for one or the other. In the late 1970s two Green parties were created – independently from each other. The Flemish Green party is called Groen! and the Francophone party is called Ecolo. Unlike the traditional parties who also sit in two separate party groups in the parliament, the two green parties form one single group in the federal parliament.

Regionalist parties obviously also limit their scope to the part of the country they want to defend. Since the 1920s there have been Flemish regionalist parties, defending a federal-type reform of the Belgian state. The current representative of that political line – and actually now defending a full independence of Flanders – is the N-VA (Nieuw-Vlaamse Alliantie). That party is active in Flanders and in Brussels. There used to be a Walloon regionalist party – with a scope limited to Wallonia only – but it has now disappeared. In Brussels, there is a party defending the rights of the Francophones in that region (that has to be officially bilingual). It is called FDF (Fédéralistes Démocrates Francophones).

And all other parties follow the logic of a scope limited to one language group only. There are two right wing extremist parties, one in Flanders (Vlaams Belang – also demanding Flemish independence) and Front National in Francophone Belgium. There are two liberal breakaway parties, one in each language group and thus created out of Open VLD and MR respectively.

The second dimension along which parties in multilevel systems can be classified is their *participation in elections at the different levels*. Parties can limit their presence to one level only – federal or substate – or participate in elections at both levels. For Belgium that picture is very clear: all parties are active on both levels. That means that they present lists for the election of the federal parliament and for the elections of the regional parliaments. Substate elections in Belgium are indeed only organized for the regional parliaments of Flanders, Wallonia and Brussels (but also for the language community parliament of the German speakers). The French Community parliament is composed of all members of the Wallloon regional parliament and of a delegation of Francophone members of the Brussels regional parliament. The parliament of the Flemish community is composed of all the members of the Flemish regional parliament and of six members elected by the Dutch speaking inhabitants of Brussels. The parliament of the Flemish region and of the Flemish community is actually one single institution that also has one single government. The members elected in Brussels do however not vote on matters devolved to the regions.

The split party system and the participation of all parties in elections at both the federal and the regional level have very important consequences. Federal elections are a competition among the Flemish and the Francophone parties in two different party systems. The result is the election of a federal parliament, but the results per party are seldom read at the statewide level. For a Flemish party the result is computed and interpreted within the Flemish party system only. In official election results for 2010 one can find that the largest party of the country was the Flemish regionalist N-VA with 17,3% of the votes. That figure has however no meaning in the political debates. More important and meaningful is the fact that N-VA polled 28% of the Flemish votes. That is the crucial point of reference. It can be compared to the result at the previous federal elections but also with the result of the previous regional elections. In both types of elections – regional or federal – the parties' electorate is the same. For the Flemish parties it is composed of the inhabitants of Flanders and the Dutch speaking inhabitants of Brussels. For the Francophone parties it is composed of the inhabitants of Wallonia and of the French speaking inhabitants of Brussels.

A split party system thus produces two results, one for each language group. Both language groups do indeed vote differently. The Francophone voters normally put the PS clearly in the first place (exception was 2007). Flemish voters used to put the Christian democrats in the number one position, but they have become more volatile. In 1999, the Christian democrats lost the position of largest party to the Liberals. They won it back in 2007, be it by forming an electoral alliance (common lists) with N-VA. And in 2010 N-VA was the largest party. The different election results in the north and the south of the country are not a new phenomenon. Both parts of the country have always voted differently, among others because the industrialization in the 19th century was very much concentrated in the south, while the north remained rural and traditional (and thus voted for the Catholic Party). The different electoral results in north and south are thus not different, but they have recently been increasing. The federal elections of 2007 and especially 2010 produced the largest differences between the two electorates since the introduction of universal suffrage in 1949. Figure 12.1 shows the evolution of the dissimilarity of the election results in Flanders and Wallonia[1].

---

1   That index is computed by summing up and dividing by two the absolute values of the differences between the parties of the same ideological family. This follows the same logic of the volatility index used to compare the degree of difference between two consecutive elections

Figure 12.1: The dissimilarity between election results per party family in Wallonia and Flanders, 1946-2014

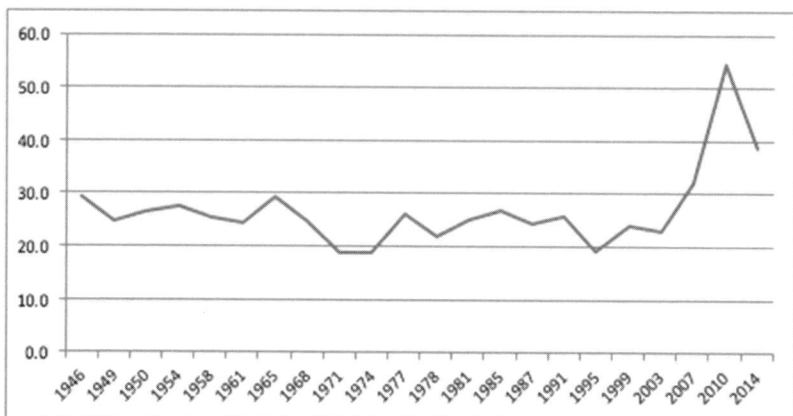

The split party system with two different election results and often also differ-ent electoral swings (parties or party families winning or losing votes) makes it fairly difficult to form a coalition government that is responsive to the moves of the electorate. Elections in the split party system produce two winners, one of which has not even tried to talk to the voters of the other language group. Suggestions have been made to increase the electoral relation between parties and the electorate as a whole, like electing some members of the Belgian fed-eral parliament in a statewide district (Van Parijs & Deschouwer, 2011). As a result of the split party system government formation in Belgium is a difficult and sometimes very time consuming affair (see section 4 below).

Elections: cycles and results

The Belgian federation is still fairly young. The first direct elections of the regional parliaments were organized in 1995. There have been so far only four regional elections. That makes it difficult to already find specific patterns. That is also related to the timing of the elections. In 1995 and in 1999 all elections were organized on the same day. From then on however the regional and the federal cycle has become different. Regional elections have a fixed rhythm: they are organized every five years in June, together with the elections to the European Parliament. The term of the federal parliament is four years. That means that in principle the two cycles only meet again after two decades. The federal term however is not fixed. Unlike the regional parliaments, the federal parliament can be dissolved before the end of the term. That happened in 2010 and early federal elections were held in June 2010. The following federal election date is then 2014, which is also the time for the regional elections.

When analyzing the relation between elections at two levels, the notion of first-order and second-order elections often proves to be useful (Reif & Schmitt, 1980). Second-order elections are elections for which the voters do not cast a vote that has a meaning at the level of the actual election, but rather cast a vote that is meant to send a signal to the other first-order level. European elections are typical second order elections, but regional elections can also be used by parties and voters to say something about federal politics.

In Belgium, the concept of first-order and second-order elections does not really work (except for European elections) because the elections at both levels are so similar. The same unilingual parties seek the votes of the same citizens at both levels. At both levels the result is read and given meaning at the substate level. Making a distinction between first and second-order against that background hardly makes sense. The two orders or the two levels are collapsed into one. Every election – regional or federal – is simply an election in Belgium.

One could wonder whether regional and regionalist parties score differently between the two levels of politics. That is a pattern that is quite strong in Spain. In Belgium though this question also loses a lot of its relevance since all parties are regional. Only for regionalist parties, that differ from the other parties not in their territorial scope but in their policy proposals, one might expect a higher score at the regional level. Yet since the reforms of the constitution are done in the federal parliament and do not formally involve the regional governments, the federal arena might be the better one to voice autonomist or separatist demands.

Table 12.1: Election results in the Flemish region

	Fed 1995	Reg 1995	Fed 1999	Reg 1999	Fed 2003	Reg 2004	Fed 2007	Reg 2009	Fed 2010
CD&V	27.4	26.8	22.4	22.1	21.2	26.1	29.6	22.9	17.0
Open VLD	21.6	20.2	23.3	22.0	25.1	19.8	18.7	15.0	14.0
SP.a	20.2	19.5	15.2	15.0	23.9	19.7	16.3	15.3	15.0
Vlaams Belang	12.3	12.3	15.4	15.5	17.9	24.2	18.9	15.3	12.6
Groen!	7.4	7.1	12.0	11.6	4.0	7.6	6.2	6.8	7.0
VU/ N-VA	7.4	9.0	8.8	9.3	4.8			13.1	28.0
LDD								7.6	3.7

Table 12.2: Election results in the Walloon region

	Fed 1995	Reg 1995	Fed 1999	Reg 1999	Fed 2003	Reg 2004	Fed 2007	Reg 2009	Fed 2010
PS	33.7	35.2	29.2	29.4	36.4	36.9	29.5	32.8	37.6
MR	23.9	23.7	24.7	24.7	28.4	24.3	31.1	23.4	22.2
CDh	22.5	21.6	16.8	17.7	15.4	17.6	15.7	16.1	14.6
Ecolo	10.3	10.4	18.3	18.2	7.4	8.5	12.7	18.5	12.3
FN	6.3	5.1	4.9	4.0	5.6	8.1	5.5	2.9	1.4

Table 12.3: Election results in the Brussels region

	Fed 1995	Reg 1995	Fed 1999	Reg 1999	Fed 2003	Reg 2004	Fed 2007	Reg 2009	Fed 2010
PS	18.2	21.4	16.5	16.9	24.6	28.8	21.5	23.3	26.6
MR	34.7	35.0	30.7	34.4	31.0	28.0	32.0	26.5	27.1
CDh	9.3	9.3	9.1	7.9	9.5	12.1	14.5	13.1	12.2
Ecolo	10.1	9.0	21.4	18.3	9.4	8.4	13.9	17.9	12.0
FN	7.6	7.5	2.6	2.6	3.5	4.7	2.9	1.7	
CD&V	3.3	3.3	2.5	3.4	1.8	2.3	2.0	1.7	1.6
Open VLD	3.0	2.7	2.8		3.1	2.7	2.7	2.6	2.3
SP.a	2.8	2.4	2.4		2.8	2.4	1.9	2.2	2.0
Vlaams Belang	3.7	3.0	4.1	4.5	5.9	4.7	3.1	2.0	1.7
Groen!	1.3	1.0	1.6		0.8	1.4	1.1	1.3	1.6
VU/N-VA	1.2	1.4	0.8		0.5			0.6	1.8
VLD-VU				3.2					
SP.a-Groen				3.1					

Tables 12.1 to 12.3 give the results of both regional and federal elections since 1995. With only four regional elections so far and only two regional elections that did not coincide with federal elections, it might just be too early to discern any clear patterns. But from the figures available one cannot conclude that there is a different dynamic between the two levels. In 1995 and 1999, when both elections were held on the same day, the results for each party were close to identical. Small fluctuations between the two levels can be attributed to the fact that different candidates figure on the lists and that some candidates might be able to bring a bit more votes to their party.

The results for the regionalist parties also do not confirm a stronger result at one level or the other. Vlaams Belang realized its best score ever at the regional elections of 2004. A few months earlier the party had been convicted in court for racism and it was able to fully play out its underdog position to attract almost 25% of the Flemish voters. After that high score, the party did however start to decline. And that decline has been going on irrespective of the level.

The other Flemish party that demands an increased autonomy and in the longer run full independence is N-VA. It is the successor of the Volksunie, a Flemish regionalist party that had fallen apart in 2001 (De Winter, 2006). The score for N-VA in 2003 was so low – below 5% of the Flemish votes – that it accepted the offer to put its candidates on joint lists with the Christian demo-cratic CD&V at the regional elections of 2004 and at the federal elections of 2007. After that the alliance was broken and N-VA went to the voters on its own. It scored a strong 13% at the regional elections of 2009 and reached more than 28% at the federal elections of 2010. Here also it is at this point impossible to see a pattern that might tell us something about voting behavior and party strategies at the different levels of the Belgian federation.

A basic feature of multilevel elections in Belgium is the strong overlap be-tween the two levels because all Belgian parties limit their electoral activities to one language group only. That overlap is however not identical for the two language groups. Here also the position of Brussels makes a difference. But on top of that comes the slightly different electoral system used in each of the regions.

In Flanders, the regional parliament is elected in five electoral districts. That is one per province. The federal level decided to enlarge the electoral districts to provinces from 2003 on and the Flemish authority decided to follow that move (Hooghe, Maddens & Noppe, 2006). The 5% threshold per province in-troduced for the federal level in 2003 was also copied to Flanders. The Walloon authorities however decided not to change the size of the electoral districts for the Walloon regional parliament. The Walloon parliament is elected in 13 dis-tricts with an average magnitude of 5.8. The Flemish parliament is elected in districts with an average magnitude of 20.7. This has two obvious conse-quences.

The first consequence is a varying degree of proportionality of the seat dis-tribution in Flanders and Wallonia. Although Flanders has a more fragmented party system and a 5% electoral threshold per district, the proportionality of the seat distribution in Flanders is higher. Table 12.4 presents the results in votes and seats for both the Flemish and the Walloon Parliament and computes the degree of proportionality (Gallagher's index – Gallagher, 1975) for both assemblies. The difference between the two is quite significant.

Table 12.4: Degree of proportionality (Gallaghers Least Square Index) in Flemish and Walloon regional elections (2009)

	Flanders			Wallonia	
	% Votes	% Seats		% Votes	% Seats
CD&V	22.9	25.0	PS	32.8	38.7
Open VLD	15.0	16.9	MR	23.4	25.3
SP.a	15.3	15.3	CDh	16.1	17.3
Vlaams Belang	15.3	16.9	Ecolo	18.5	18.7
Groen!	6.8	5.6	Others	9.2	0
VU / N-VA	13.1	12.9			
LDD	7.6	6.5			
Others	4.0	0.0			
Disproportionality	3.82			7.89	

The second consequence of this identical territorial organization of elections in Flanders and at the federal level is a strengthening of the provincial party level for the Flemish parties. The provincial level is the one at which the candidate selection is done for both elections. The provincial level is the place where the personnel of the party is selected and if possible or needed sent to one or the other parliamentary assembly). The provincial level is also the level where elections to the provincial councils are organized and the level at which the supervision over local elections is organized. Interestingly, the devolution to regions and communities has not strengthened the substate levels of the parties – since these are the highest levels and since they already existed before devolution – but has strengthened the provincial level in one of the regions.

For both the Flemish and the Francophone parties the Brussels region is a bit special. Parties are organized per language community and therefore cover two regions, always including Brussels. For regional elections though Brussels is a separate entity. And that is much more so for the Francophone parties than for the Flemish parties. On the Flemish side the importance of Brussels in the parties is extremely small. The number of valid votes cast in the Flemish region is 4,1 million (2009), while the number of voters choosing a Flemish party in Brussels is just over 50.000. Brussels accounts for only 1,3% of the votes for the Flemish parties. The number of votes cast in Wallonia is 2 million, while the number of Francophone votes cast in Brussels is just over 400.000. The weight of Brussels in the Francophone parties is thus a solid 20%.

The latter has always had consequences for the internal organization of the Francophone parties. They have a strong Brussels section that has the autonomy to deal with the specific Brussels situation. And that is one where the dominance of the Parti Socialiste is less evident. For elections to the Walloon government the PS has always won the race, while in Brussels the first-place alternates between the Socialist and the Liberal Party. For coalition formation though the Francophone parties do not let the Brussels sections really decide on their own. Since there must be a government for the Walloon region, for the Brussels region and for the French-speaking community, the Francophone parties prefer to keep all these executive under control of the same parties (see also section 4).

The Brussels region differs from the other regions because of the large number of seats available. While the Flemish parliament has 124 seats and the Walloon parliament 75 seats, the parliament of the smallest region has 89 seats. Of these 17 are reserved for the Flemish parties and 72 are reserved for the Francophone parties. This district magnitude of 72 for the Francophone parties allows them all to elect a fairly large number of candidates and to make a list that reflects all possible variations in the Brussels (francophone) electorate. The Brussels regional parliament is the most female parliament of all, but in general also the most 'mixed' of all, with a very visible presence of MPs from non-Belgian origin.

Government formation

Government formation at the federal level in Belgium is often a difficult task. The split party system produces different results in both language groups and – increasingly – swings going in different directions for the parties of the same ideological family. Furthermore, the Constitution requires a federal government that is composed of an equal number of Dutch-speaking and French-speaking ministers, which means that both language groups must be present in the federal government. There is no legal obligation to have a governmental majority in each language group of the parliament, but most often a federal government does control a majority in each language groups. Exceptions to that rule were the 1985-87 government and the governments formed in 2007 (after 194 days of negotiations) and in 2011 (after 541 days of negotiations).

Government formation in a multilevel system is always a multilevel game. Strategies at one level about the choice to govern or not to govern and about the choice of possible coalition partners are influenced by strategies at the other level. The analysis of coalition formation in multilevel systems has paid quite some attention to the *congruence* of coalitions. That is the degree in which a substate government has the same party composition as the statewide government (Stefuriuc, 2009). There are no general rules about what parties prefer. That very much depends on temporary the position of a party in the political system.

For Belgium, the split party system requires a slight adaptation of the notion of congruence. A full congruence between a regional and the federal government is indeed never possible, since the regional governments (but not in Brussels) are only composed of parties of one language group while the federal government has parties of both language groups. We therefore need to define congruence as the overlap between the composition of a regional government and the parties of the same language group in the federal government. The Tables 12.5, 12.6 and 12.7 compare the federal and the regional government composition for each of the three regions.

Table 12.5: The federal and regional coalitions compared: Flanders (shaded parties governing at one level only)

Elections	1995 Regional & federal	1999 Regional & federal	2003 Federal	2004 Regional	2007 Federal	2009 Regional	2010 Federal
Federal	CD&V – SPa – CDh - PS	Open VLD – Spa – Groen! – Ecolo MR - PS	Open VLD – SP.a – MR - PS	Open VLD – SP.a – MR - PS	CD&V – Open VLD – PS – MR - CDh	CD&V – Open VLD – PS – MR - CDh	PS – SP.a – Open VLD – MR - CD&V - CDh
Flanders	CD&V - SPa	Open VLD – SP.a – Groen! – VU	Open VLD – SP.a – Groen!	CD&V – N- VA – Open VLD – SP.a	CD&V – N- VA – Open VLD – SP.a	CD&V – N- VA – SP.a	CD&V – N- VA – SP.a

Table 12.6: The federal and regional coalitions compared: Wallonia (shaded parties governing at one level only)

Elections	1995 Regional & federal	1999 Regional & federal	2003 Federal	2004 Regional	2007 Federal	2009 Regional	2010 Federal
Federal	CD&V – SPa – CDh - PS	Open VLD – Spa – Groen! – Ecolo – MR PS	Open VLD – SP.a – MR - PS	Open VLD – SP.a – MR - PS	CD&V – Open VLD – PS – MR - CDh	CD&V – Open VLD – PS – MR - CDh	PS – SP.a VLD – MR - CD&V - CDh
Wallonia	PS– CDh	PS – MR - Ecolo	PS – MR - Ecolo	PS - CDh	PS- CDh	PS– CDh - Ecolo	PS– CDh - Ecolo

Table 12.7: The federal and regional coalitions compared: Brussels (shaded parties governing at one level only)

Elections	1995 Regional & federal	1999 Regional & federal	2003 Federal	2004 Regional	2007 Federal	2009 Regional	2010 Federal
Federal	*CD&V* – SPa – CDh - PS	*Open VLD* – Spa – Groen! – Ecolo – MR PS	*Open VLD* – SP.a – MR - PS	*Open VLD* – SP.a – MR - PS	*CD&V* – Open VLD – PS – MR - CDh	*CD&V* – Open VLD – PS – MR - CDh	*PS* – SP.a – Open VLD – MR - CD&V - CDh
Brussels	CD&V – SPa – CDh - *PS*	*MR* – PS – Spa – CD&V – Open VLD – VU - Groen	*MR* – PS – Spa – CD&V – Open VLD – VU - Groen	*PS* – CDh – Ecolo – CD&V – Open VLD – SP.a	*PS* – CDh – Ecolo – CD&V – Open VLD - SPa	*PS* – CDh – Ecolo – Open VLD – CD&V – Groen!	*PS* – CDh – Ecolo – Open VLD – CD&V – Groen!

Looking back to 1995 when the regional parliaments were elected for the first time (but in Brussels already in 1989) there are two time periods that can be clearly distinguished. The first is 1995-2003, the second is post 2003. During the first period the explicit aim of the governing parties was to form congruent coalitions. The first formation was in 1995 and the second in 1999. Both regional elections coincided with the federal elections and produces similar results for both levels. The formation of the federal and of the regional governments could thus easily be combined. In 1995, the outcome was simple: Christian democrats and socialists governed together at all levels.

In 1999, there was the same willingness to keep all levels congruent, but that resulted in a much more complex set of coalitions. The core of them was an alliance of liberals and socialists of both language groups. To reach a majority they did however also need the Greens. For a majority in the Flemish parliament that was however still not enough and therefore he Flemish nationalists were added to the Flemish coalition. In the Walloon region, the Greens were mathematically not needed, but to keep the congruence they were added to the – now oversized – Walloon coalition. At the end of the day only the Flemish nationalists governed at the Flemish level only. That double position is however one of the reasons why the party fell apart in 2001 in a more radical wing (later to become the N-VA) and a more moderate wing that joined the Flemish socialist party. When after the federal elections of 2003 the liberal and socialist parties went on governing without the greens, the green parties remained in the regional governments. The new rhythm of the elections had introduced incongruence.

The regional elections of 2004 were the real turning point. They put an end to the conscious search for congruence. The electoral victory of the Christian democrats and nationalists in Flanders put them at the head of the Flemish government while they remained in the opposition at the federal level. That did create some tensions and introduced into the Belgian federation a new type of conflict: the conflict between governments. In the (short) era of congruence the conflicts between governments were dealt with in a meeting with the leaders of the parties governing at all levels. After 2004, the intergovernmental relations have become one of the forums for the party competition.

Congruence was one of the early options after the federal elections of 2010. The idea was then to try to form the federal government by bringing together the parties governing the regions. That would have been a coalition of the two socialist parties, the two Christian democratic parties, the Flemish nationalists and the francophone Greens. The Green parties – having one single group in the federal parliament – did however make clear that they would either govern together or be together in the opposition. And that was the end of congruence again.

Congruence is however not only relevant between the federal and the regional level. On the Francophone side, where parties compete for power in the Walloon region, the Brussels region and the Francophone Community, they have very consciously tried to keep the coalitions nicely congruent. That is important because of the complex institutional setting. The government of the French Community has powers in Wallonia and in Brussels and having the same parties governing in the different institutions highly facilitates cooperation. That explains why in 2009 the largest party of Brussels – the MR (see table 12.3) did not join the government. The decision taken in Wallonia to go for a coalition of PS, CDh and Ecolo meant that the same coalition had to be formed in Brussels. Actually, since 2009 the even opted for a quite radical connection between the governments of the Walloon region and Francophone Community: they have the same Prime Minister.

The idea of keeping parties of the same family together in the federal government is referred to as the *symmetry* of the federal coalition. That symmetry has been respected in most governments. One exception was the 2007-2010 federal government in which only the Francophone socialists were present. That was for the Flemish socialists quite a difficult period. The party had indeed to oppose the government policies of a coalition in which the sister party PS played a prominent role. This was a one-time experience that is not likely to be repeated. Parties in Belgium have learned that they can live with incongruence and therefore easily accept a coalition at the federal or the regional level that is not congruent. Symmetry is more likely to remain a rule or at least an explicit preference of the parties that have an ideological partner on the other side of the language border.

Conclusion

The Belgian party system has a very peculiar form. There is actually no single party system but two party systems, organized per language groups. All parties compete in one language group only. That means that federal and substate elections are very similar. The same parties compete for the same subset of voters. There is no difference between first and second order elections.

The two party systems produce different results. That makes government formation at the federal level quite difficult. A coalition needs to respond to two different election results and to two different moves of the electorate. This split party system and the different results make it quite difficult to form congruent coalitions. As long as the elections at both levels were organized on the same day, the formation of congruent coalitions was an explicit goal of the parties. The disconnection of the electoral cycles since 2003 has however put an end to the search for congruence. Incongruent coalitions are now quite frequent, and intergovernmental relations have become a new arena for party competition.

References

De Winter, L. (2006). "In Memoriam the Volksunie 1954-2001: Death by Overdose of Success", in Lieven De Winter, Marga Gomez-Reion Cachafeiro and Peter Lynch (Eds), *Autonomist Parties in Europe: Identity Politics and the Revival of the Territorial Cleavage*, Barcelona: ICPS.

Deschouwer, K. (2005). "Kingdom of Belgium", in J. Kincaid & A. Tarr, eds. *Constitutional Origins, Structure, and Change in Federal Countries*, Montreal & Kingston: McGill-Queen's University Press, 48-75.

Deschouwer, Kris & Van Parijs, Philippe. (2011). "Electoral engineering for a stalled federation: a country-wide electoral district for Belgium's federal parliament", in Philippe Van Parijs, *Just democracy. The Rawls-Machiavelli programme*, Essex: ECPR Press, 123-142.

Deschouwer, Kris (2006). "Political parties as multi-level organizations", in Richard Katz & William Crotty (eds), *Handbook of party politics*, London: Sage Publications, 291-300.

Deschouwer, Kris (2009). *The politics of Belgium. Governing a divided society*, Palgrave, London.

Gallagher, M. (1975). "Disproportionality in a proportional representation system: the Irish experience", *Political Studies*, 4, 501-513.

Hooghe, M., Maddens, B. & Noppe, J. (2006) "Why parties adapt: Electoral reform, party finance and party strategy in Belgium", *Electoral Studies*, 25, 351-368.

Lijphart, A. (1981). "Introduction: the Belgian example of cultural coexistence in comparative perspective", in Lijphart A. ed, *Conflict and coexistence in Belgium. The dynamics of a culturally divided society*. Berkeley: Institute of international studies, University of California, 1-12.

McRae K. (1986). *Conflict and compromise in multilingual societies. Belgium*, Ontario, Canada: Wilfrid Laurier Press.

242   Kris Deschouwer

Reif, K.H. & Schmitt, M. (1980). "Nine second order elections. A conceptual framework for the analysis of European elections results", in *European Journal of Political Research*, 1980, 3-44.

Stefuriuc, Irina. (2009). "Introduction - Government coalitions in multi-level settings: Institutional determinants and party strategy", in *Regional and Federal Studies*, Special Issue on "Government coalitions in multi-level settings: Institutional determinants and party strategy" 19 (1), 1-12.

Verleden, F. (2009). "Splitting the difference: the radical approach of the Belgian parties", in W. Swenden & B. Maddens (ed), *Territorial party politics in Western Europe*, London: Palgrave, 145-166.

Part V
Toward a new system of governance

Chapter 13
Political Careers in Spain: Mobility Between Political Arenas in a Multilevel System

Pablo Oñate, University of Valencia

Introduction

Politics, in recent decades, has become a highly professionalized activity in many countries, more than Weber could ever have imagined almost a century ago. While many in office spend just a few years there before they return to private life, others view politics as a career and a way to earn a living. In his seminal book, Schlesinger (1966) distinguished between *discrete, static,* and *progressive* politicians, with discrete politicians erring in favour of short-term careers in office and not expecting to make it a long-term profession. Squire (1988 & 2007) and Moncrief (1988), among others, have studied in-depth what the professionalization of political careers means and how it can be measured. As a point of departure, we can state that Spanish politics was rapidly professionalized at about the same time that the new political system was institutionalized during the transition to democracy initiated in 1977.

As is well documented, a quick and intense process of democratization and decentralization took place in Spain, with 17 autonomous or regional[1] parliaments – the 17 self-governed Autonomous Communities – created in the early 1980s. The ensuing institutionalization of these regional bodies coincided with the professionalization of an elite political class. These elites were influenced and shaped by the political system that emerged in response to newly designed institutions (Borchert, 2003; Stolz, 2003, 2010 & 2011). The institution-building process spurred the rise of several different political arenas, within which various party systems, actors, competition dynamics and identities rose to prominence, establishing relationships with national institutions of government as part of a multilevel political system that included several "electoral Spains." (Oñate and Ocaña, 2008)

---

[1] For clarification I use the term *region*, regional or regionalization. People and political parties in some territorial substate entities prefer the term nationality or, even, nation. Article 2 of the Spanish 1978 Constitutions mentions "regions and nationalities" to denote these sub-state entities which turn into Autonomous Communities.

This proliferation of political positions, vested in legislatures as well as executive or agency offices, opened the door to an array of opportunities for political elites. As Schlesinger (1966: 118) points out: "Political careers do not proceed chaotically." While individual members of these elites have personal reasons and motives for aspiring to become career politicians, all do it within a structured institutional system of opportunity, which makes positions at all levels *attractive, available* and *accessible* (Borchert, 2011). Yet, formerly a political career would start at the local level before moving up to the regional level, and, later, the national stage (Francis and Kenny, 2000: 2-6). That path to political office does not necessarily work anymore. Regional arenas may be more appealing (the three A´s considered) than the national arena for some politicians. When considering the attractiveness of a given position in political office, several factors should be considered, including economic advantages or drawbacks, family ties, travel, social, political and institutional networking, and party-organization ties.

The structure of opportunity, for each politician, is conditioned to a large extent by the structure of the state and political institutions, the structure of representation itself, and that of political organizations. These institutional traits will have a determining effect on the kind of careers we find in a given system: unidirectional, alternative, or integrated (Borchert, 2011: 123 & 130). Stolz (2003 & 2010) considered four models; taking into account the degree of centripetal and centrifugal movement ratios, he/she identified four potential career patterns: unidirectional, alternative, integrated and inverse springboard.

In the following pages, my aim is to shed some light on this area of study, drawing on Stolz's four factors of influence in the structure of opportunity for politicians in Spain, each of which may be relevant to their political careers. In the third section, I describe some patterns specific to Spanish parliamentary elites from different regional parliaments in order to gauge whether there are significant differences between them. I also verify data on the careers of parliamentary elites to assess whether there is any mobility between levels, and in what proportion and direction. The objective, in this regard, is to determine whether political elites generally belong to a single type, or whether there are several such types. If the latter is true, what kind of political careers do they follow?

The Structure of Opportunity for Spanish Political Elites

As mentioned at the outset, Spanish political elites are highly professionalized. The 17 autonomous or regional parliaments conduct their activities in a professionalized, full-time manner, as does the national parliament, with staff, facilities and salaries that allow elites to earn a living, and the expectation that they will continue to do so in the future. Of course, there are many other official positions in the national and regional executive branches, and in other national and regional agencies through which politicians hone their professional skills. This spectrum of political positions at the local, regional and national levels allows them to plan their professional development as politicians.

Progressive and incremental decentralization has paved the way for a *de facto* federal system in Spain (Maiz, 2008), where regions (Autonomous Communities) enjoy a high level of autonomy to design their own institutions and exercise independent administrative, political and fiscal powers and to develop their own competencies. This process has created diverse political arenas, where statewide and non-statewide parties drive local and regional affairs, with considerable autonomy from the national state. The party system, in some of these territories, differs from the national party system, with different actors (parties), competition dynamics, and issues. Some non-statewide parties have held a majority in regional parliaments and formed long-standing regional governments, at times in coalition with statewide parties (SWP) or non-statewide parties (NSWP). In regions such as Catalonia and the Basque Country, a large proportion of the population does not identify as Spanish.[2]

Decentralization produced a devolution of power to the regions, with the result that Autonomous Governments developed large regional bureaucracies (larger, in some cases, than that of the national government).

The *de facto* federal institutional structure created a large pool of attractive official positions, paving the way for the emergence of an elite class of professional politicians at the regional level. Regional legislatures manage a larger proportion of public spending (51%) than the national government (30%), and local governments (19%). Moreover, all the regional institutional systems have created agencies across a wide spectrum of activities, run by professional politicians in a variety of official positions. And while inter-regional differences do persist in regards to institutions and the powers vested in the regional government / competency levels, most regional governments have attained a remarkably high level of self-government and power management.

Strong and cohesive political parties determine who holds positions in government. They compete in regular elections, under a system of proportional

---

2   According to data from the Centre de Estudis d`Opinió and Euskobarometro, 20% of the population of Catalonia identify solely as Catalan, while in the Basque Country 30% of people identify as Basque. The other options cited included identification as Spanish; more Spanish than Catalan (or Basque); Spanish as Catalan (or Basque); more Catalan (or Basque) than Spanish. The Basque Nationalist Party, it's important to remember, has governed the Basque Country for 30 years (since 1979); Convergencia i Unió (the main Catalan nationalist party) has governed Catalonia for 25 years since 1979. Both were the governing parties during the period of institution-building and consolidation, and they continue to govern to this day.

representation with closed lists, which allows the political party brass to hand-pick candidates to serve as gatekeepers in specific positions. There isn't much a single candidate or MP can achieve without his or her party, and that candidate will not be inclined to upset the status quo if he or she hopes to be re-elected (Oñate, 2000, 2008 & 2010). The work of selecting candidates for office is carried out largely by political parties, within a framework controlled by central party headquarters (even though regional organizations play a limited role). The parties recruit candidates, provide political action guidelines, and run electoral campaigns. They are well-managed organizations, and when it comes to organizing and shaping political institutions, they have no competitors (Oñate, 2000 & 2008).

Thus, structures of opportunity in institutions are quite similar across all 17 Autonomous Communities, irrespective of the non-statewide parties that may be present. They represent political arenas that offer a wide array of appealing and available official positions for politicians willing to lead professional careers and deal with the powerful gatekeepers who control access to those positions.

Career Trajectories in Multilevel Spain

When comparing the various regional (and national) parliaments, some differences emerge in regards to the presence of women in politics or parliament, for example, but also along the lines of age, level of study, job history, turnover/continuity rates, seniority rates, and prior experience as an elected or party official. There is no clear pattern for specific parties or parliaments, however. These differences apply regardless of such variables as strong/weak regional/national identity, regional population or geographic size, the existence of non-statewide parties in the region, and the scope of the powers vested in the regional government/competencies. Regardless of the characteristics specific to each Autonomous Community (and the institutional structure of political opportunity), no clear pattern emerges when we examine these traits among the political class in these regions. The clearest pattern among parliamentary parties or parliaments is *heterogeneity* (Oñate, 2010).

If we analyze the previous experience of national MPs as local or regional elected officials in the Autonomous Communities, the results differ widely for each Autonomous Community (Table 13.1; data are shown in percentages, regardless of the number of national MPs elected in each Autonomous Community, which is indicated beside its name).

Table 13.1: Percentage of national MPs elected in each Autonomous Community with previous experience al elected officials in Local or Regional Legislatures (9th term or Legislature)

	Experience at Local level	Experience at Regional level	No experience at any level
Andalusia (61)	36,1	22,9	49,1
Aragón (13)	30,8	30,8	53,8
Asturias (8)	62,5	12,5	25,0
Balear Islands (8)	75,0	25,0	25,0
Canary Island (15)	73,3	13,3	26,7
Cantabria (5)	40,0	40,0	40,0
Catalonia (47)	34,0	23,4	51,1
Castil-Leon (32)	40,6	25,0	46,9
Castil-Mancha (21)	61,9	28,6	28,6
Extremadura (23)	50,0	8,7	30,0
Galicia (35)	52,2	14,3	34,8
Madrid (35)	20,0	20,0	68,6
Murcia (10)	40,0	10,0	60,0
Navarra (5)	60,0	20,0	40,0
La Rioja (4)	75,0	50,0	25,0
Basque Contry (18	27,8	11,1	61,1
Valencia (33)	48,5	24,2	39,4

Table 13.1 shows heterogeneity to be that the most salient pattern among MPs with previous experience as local or regional elected officials. What's more, variety is the watchword when we look at the percentage of MPs with previous experience in local districts. Also worth nothing was the low percentage of elected MPs with previous experience in the Basque Country and Catalonia: they posted the second and fourth lowest percentages of MPs with representative experience at the local level, respectively, and the third and sixth lowest percentages of MPs with experience at the regional level. Looking at the final column in Table 13.1 (MPs with no experience as representatives at the local or regional level) we see that the Basque Country and Catalonia have some of the lowest percentages of MPs with local or regional experience, ranking second and fourth, respectively, out of 17 cases. There appears to be a lack of integration between national parliamentarian elites and their counterparts at the local or regional level, although they share this pattern with elites from other regions regardless of the distinct identities specific to Catalonia and the Basque Country.

We can delve a little deeper, however, by analyzing the levels of previous local or regional experience among national MPs and aggregating them according to political party (Table 13.2). Here again, the data confirm the same heterogeneity, regardless of the number of seats each holds in the *Congreso de los Diputados*. What's more, Table 13.2 shows that Catalan nationalist parties (CiU and ERC) have high percentages of MPs with previous local or regional experience, while levels of previous experience among MPs in the Basque Nationalist Party are quite low. These figures urge caution in establishing a direct link between differentiated national identity and an *alternative* model of political class.

Table 13.2: Previous experience of National MPs in Local Councils and Regional Parliaments (9th term or Legislature)

	Local Council		Regional Parliament	
	n	%	n	%
PSOE (169)	66	39,1	25	14,8
PP (154)	72	46,8	42	27,3
CiU (10)	3	30,0	5	50,0
PNV (6)	1	16,7	1	16,7
ERC (3)	1	33,3	1	33,3
CC (2)	2	100,0	1	50,0
IU (2)	0	0,0	1	50,0
BNG (2)	1	50,0	1	50,0
NaBa (1)	1	100,0	0	0,0
UPyD (1)	1	100,0	1	100,0

So, while data from the 9th term of the *Congreso de los Diputados* highlight some differences among regions and parties, there is no overriding pattern other than heterogeneity and a tendency on the part of national MPs from Catalan parties to have high rates of previous experience at other levels of government.

Finally, if, in addition to prior experience as an elected official, we also take into account prior experience as an appointed official in an executive position[3], a variation emerges. As stated in Section 2, the Spanish political class is highly professionalized. Even though an MPs' tenure in elected office might be temporary, for many it is a permanent profession. In most regions for which data were available, a high percentage of national MPs had prior experience in representative/elected or executive appointed positions (Table 13.3). Almost 50 percent of the national MPs had local experience when they acceded to the *Congreso de los Diputados*, and almost two-thirds had regional experience (in

---

3   Aside from representatives elected to local council or the regional parliament by appointed officials in executive positions, I understand top-ranking positions at the local or regional Public Administration (it has to be taken into account that many MPs have previous experience at both levels).

eight of the 12 regions considered, more than two- thirds of MPs had previous regional experience, including in Catalonia and the Basque Country. These data mitigate the importance of the data for the Basque Country shown in Table 13.2 (lack of previous regional experience among national Basque MPs). More than half of MPs from almost all regions (except those elected in Castile La Mancha, and by a small percentage) had previous experience as elected or executive appointed officials at the regional level. Moreover, in only three of the 12 regions for which information was available, fewer than half of their MPs had no prior experience at the local level.

About 80 percent of MPs had local or regional experience before becoming national MPs. They are politicians with extensive political and institutional management experience, and may be deemed specialists or professionalized politicians, therefore. Though considerable heterogeneity was observed among MPs in different regions, a common pattern emerged in all regions for which data was available, characterized by high levels of prior experience as elected representatives or executive appointed officials: more than half of MPs had political experience at a level different than that on which they were currently serving.

Table 13.3: Percentage of national MPs with previous experience in political positions (elected or appointed) at different territorial levels (9th term or Legislature)

	Local level	Regional level	Any level
Andalusia	54,1	61,5	81,6
Aragon	47,8	76,1	92,5
Asturias	43,2	72,3	81,8
Balearic Islands	10,2	61,0	61,0
Cantabria	61,5	69,2	89,7
Cast La Mancha	10,6	44,6	51,1
Castile Leon	46,9	78,1	92,2
Catalonia	54,5	68,6	83,5
La Rioja	60,5	54,5	87,9
Madrid	38,3	58,3	78,3
Murcia	72,7	63,6	72,7
Basque Country	45,3	69,3	81,3
Valencia	47,4	68,0	83,5

No data were available for Canary Islands, Extremadura and Navarra

Beyond this general pattern, we noted low levels of previous political experience at the local or regional level among MPs elected in Castile La Mancha. It also bears mentioning that MPs elected in Catalonia are not among those with the highest or lowest levels of previous political experience. They might be expected to register low levels of prior experience, if we assume that there is less integration between members of the Catalan political class and their national counterparts and, therefore, that they constitute an *alternative* political career model (Stolz, 2003, 2010 and 2011; Borchert, 2011). MPs elected in the Basque Country are among those with the lowest levels of prior local or regional experience in government (bearing in mind that the Basque National Party had ruled the Basque Country for almost 30 consecutive years before the start of the 9th Term of the *Congreso de los Diputados*).

But as Borchert (2011) points out, when studying the political careers of parliamentarians, it would be useful to analyze not just the scope of political mobility, but also its direction. For that purpose, we considered the regional parliament and the national lower chamber (*Congreso de los Diputados*)[4], leaving aside potential previous experience at the local level, given the complexity it would entail. In order to analyze the direction of mobility among MPs (i.e., between the regional and the national levels), I have taken into account data from 2012, a separate term for the respective legislatures than the one analyzed in previous tables (which explains why there may be different levels of mobility among the MPs cited above).

Political mobility means the MP had previous experience at the national or regional level, prior to the office that person held in 2012). As expected (Table 13.4), mobility is lower among regional MPs than it is among national MPs: there are significantly fewer seats at the national level (350) than at the regional level (939).[5] And while the *ladder, springboard* or *unidirectional* career model is not the only one, it is still the most popular. Taking a look at regional MPs (first column in Table 13.4) with no prior experience as national MPs, there are no major differences among the 12 regional parliaments considered. Again, the number of "single-level" MPs in the Catalan parliament is close to the mean, while the Basque parliament has the second highest percentage of "single-level" MPs (on par with that of other parliaments in this regard).

Percentages of "single-level" national MPs with no prior experience at other levels are lower (69,5) than they are among regional MPs (94.4); in other words, a significantly higher proportion of national MPs have prior experience in office compared to their regional counterparts, which was what we expected. That said, there is more variety from region to region: while the number of "single-level" national MPs is higher than 66 percent in eight of the 12 cases studied (or two-thirds of elected officials), the figures differ considerably from one region to the next. Most remarkable, perhaps, is that almost 79 percent of national MPs elected in Catalonia have not prior experience in the regional parliament. This data aligns well with previous findings concerning career

4   This analysis does not take into account the National Senate, since its members include a strong proportion of regional parliamentarians (appointed as senators by their parliament).

5   Data from 12 regional parliaments for which information on previous experience among MPs was available. There are five regional parliaments (totalling 279 regional MPs) for which it was not possible to collect the relevant information.

patterns in Catalonia (Stolz, 2003 & 2010). In the Basque Country, that figure (55.6 percent) is much lower, far from the mean. That means a high proportion (44.5 percent) of Basque national MPs have prior experience in the regional parliament. That reflects the highly integrated career patterns specific to national and regional parliaments[6] in the Basque Country, in sharp contrast to Catalonia, where that figure reaches only 21.3 percent.

Table 13.4: Political careers in Spanish National and Regional Legislatures, by type of movement (in %; data from 2012: 10th term or Legislature)

	No Move	Reg→ Nation	Nation→ Reg	Reg→ Nat→Reg	Nat→Reg→ Nat
Congreso Diputados (350)		69,5	27,4		3,1
Andalucía (109/60)	90,8	76,7	18,3	7,3	1,8	5,0
Aragón (67/13)	94,0	61,5	38,5	4,5	1,5	0,0
Cantabria (39/5)	95,0	100,0	0,0	2,5	2,5	0,0
Castilla-La Mancha (49/21)	93,9	66,6	23,8	6,1	0,0	9,5
Castilla y León (84/32)	97,6	75,0	25,0	1,2	1,2	3,5
Cataluña (135/47)	94,1	78,7	14,9	4,4	1,5	6,4
Galicia (75/23)	97,3	78,3	21,7	2,7	0,0	0,0
La Rioja (33/4)	97,0	0,0	100,0	3,0	0,0	0,0
Madrid (129/36)	92,2	69,4	30,6	7,8	0,0	0,0
Murcia (45/10)	91,1	40,0	60,0	2,2	6,7	0,0
País Vasco (75/18)	97,3	55,6	38,9	2,7	0,0	5,6
Valencia (99/33)	94,9	69,7	27,3	4,0	1,0	3,0
Total Regional Legislatures	94,4			4,5	1,2	
Cong Dips+Regional Leg.	87,6	87,6	27,4	3,3	0,9	0,9

The seats of National Congreso Diputados elected in each Region and the seats of each regional legislature are indicated in parentheses. Data for National Legislature are presented in red.

If we look at MPs with multilevel experience (final four columns in Table 13.4), it's clear that (proportionally) movement from the regional to the national level is the most common form of political mobility : 27.4 percent of national MPs had previously served as regional MPs. Again, there is a significant variation in the figures from one region to the next. As expected, Catalonia registers a low percentage of national MPs with previous experience in the Catalan parliament, whereas in the Basque Country that figure is almost three times higher.

Even though the amount of "multilevel" regional MPs (those with previous experience at the national level) is lower, heterogeneity remains the pattern

---

6   The significance of these figures is mitigated by the small number of MPs in the other two regions (La Rioja and Murcia) with significant numbers of multilevel national MPs.

among the different regions, with more significant differences noted in Madrid (7.8 percent) and Castile-Leon (1.2 percent). If we compare Catalan regional MPs with their Basque counterparts, we see that a higher percentage of Catalan MPs have multilevel experience. In fact, twice as many Catalan MPs had prior experience at the national level compared to Basque MPs, though the percentages, in both cases, remain quite low.

Finally, we found a few national MPs who had moved from one level to another and back (two jumps in either direction; see the two final columns in Table 13.4), whereas very few regional MPs had done to same. In some regions, however, the figures concerning national MPs with this dual mobility are not so insignificant: A relevant percentage (higher than five percent) of national MPs elected in Castile-La Mancha, Catalonia, the Basque Country and Andalucía have that dual multilevel experience. It is interesting that Catalonia and the Basque Country are among those regions, as these figures point to an integrated career model among political elites.

Given this heterogeneity (and notwithstanding the fact that no mobility remains the general pattern among MPs), it may be worth gauging career patterns among MPs in the main political parties to determine if any significant differences arise. As shown in Table 13.5, there are no significant differences in career pattern among regional or national MPs in the main political parties, though some differences are worth noting. In every instance, an overwhelming majority of regional MPs do not have prior experience as national MPs, but a higher percentage of regional MPs in the Socialist Party (PSOE) had multilevel experience, twice as many as MPs in other political parties. Still, the respective figures may not be considered high. It should also be noted that regional MPs from non-statewide parties register the highest percentages of "single-level" regional MPs.

Table 13.5: Political careers of Spanish National and Regional MPs, by political party (totals of National and Regional MPs; in %; data from 2012: 10th term or Legislature)

| | Reg. Parliaments | | Congreso Diputados |
	No Move	Move	No Move
PSOE	91,6	8,4	77,3
PP	95,6	4,4	65,6
IU	95,7	4,3	63,6
CIU*	96,8	3,2	68,8
PNV*	96,7	3,3	60,0

* Data for CIU and PNV refer only to Catalonia's and Basque Country's Legislatures

We found that more national MPs have multilevel experience than MPs in regional parliaments (30 percentage points higher, on average), reflecting the most common trend of unidirectional career mobility. The figures are similar across all the main political parties, though a smaller percentage of Socialist

Party MPs were found to have multilevel experience (regardless of direction). An opposite trend was observed among regional MPs. Again, we found highly significant differences in the percentages of MPs with multilevel experience in the Catalan CiU and Basque PNV, with a higher percentage in the later party.

This difference suggests that an alternative political career model is prevalent in Catalonia (Stolz, 2003 & 2011), and it would be interesting to determine whether there are differences among MPs with multilevel careers in territories where varying segments of the population identify as non-Spanish. In Table 13.6, I have aggregated data on MPs according to how strongly they identify as non-Spanish: weak, medium, strong.

Table 13.6: Political careers of Spanish MPs, by National identity/NSWP* (in %; data from 2012: 10h term or Legislature)

	Reg. Parliaments		Congreso Diputados	
	No Move	Move	No Move	Move
Weak national identity	94,1	5,9	65,0	35,0
Medium national identity	93,3	6,7	73,9	26,1
Strong national identity	95,8	4,2	73,9	26,1

* National identity or existence of non-statewide parties.

As expected, in both regional and national legislatures, the proportion of MPs with multilevel experience is higher in regions with weak or medium national identity. The differences are not really relevant in the regional arena, but the data for national MPs point to a clearer pattern. In regions with low levels of non-Spanish identification (or where non-statewide parties are not relevant or don't exist), the percentage of national MPs with multilevel experience is significantly higher than in other regions. As shown above, multilevel experience entails unidirectional political career patterns, from regional parliaments to the national parliament. And while these differences are not that significant (11 points), the data may reflect a different political career pattern at play among regional elites.

Conclusion

Over the past three decades, *de facto* Spanish federalism has paved the way for the institutionalization of professional politics in the regional sphere, spurring the emergence of a new class of political elites. These regional institutional systems created a considerable number of official positions for political elites to develop their careers in a professional manner. The current institutional structure of opportunity is quite similar across all 17 Autonomous Communities, with similar institutional designs and electoral systems, and hierarchical, cohesive and centralized political parties acting as the gatekeepers of positions in office and of fallback options.

The analysis conducted in these pages shows that career patterns among Spanish national and regional MPs are characterized by high levels of homogeneity and heterogeneity, and a general pattern of "single-level" representation among MPs in all legislatures. At the same time, there are relevant inter-regional variations as well as differences between levels of government, with a higher proportion of multilevel MPs in the national arena. We can conclude that a larger proportion of national MPs have previous multilevel experience (local or regional) compared to MPs in regional parliaments. And even though there are many *available*, *attractive* and *accessible* positions in regional arenas, a relevant number of local and regional politicians seem ready to move on to professional political careers on the national stage.

MPs, in many cases, are not newcomers to politics, and a significant number of national politicians do not stay put in prior positions at the local or regional level, but make the jump to the national arena in order to advance their political careers. I have not identified a clear pattern that would explain the differences in the respective rates across any of the variables considered (i.e., sex, age, education, previous profession, party, region, seniority, or experience as party officials). The findings related to these variables point to heterogeneity more than to any clear-cut pattern. We can conclude that most among the Spanish parliamentary class do not follow an alternative or integrated political career path, but are more likely to remain in their respective regional political arenas, which appear to offer appealing positions for the advancement of their political careers, without the potential costs of acceding to a different level of political office.

Nevertheless, a significant proportion of MPs are ready to make the leap to the national level after gaining experience at the local and/or regional level. When analyzing the incidence of mobility and its prevailing direction, no clear ladder model emerges in Spanish politics; rather, what we observe is an integrated political class whose members jump from one level to another or stay put at one level, depending on the opportunities that present themselves. And while "single-level" careers are the most common model, upward mobility to the national political stage is the most common form of movement observed. On the whole, there are (proportionally) more MPs with multilevel experience in national politics than in regional politics. Comparing patterns across different regions, we find significant homogeneity in regional parliaments (low rates of mobility), along with significant heterogeneity in the national legislature (with larger and varying figures for multilevel experience, even if more than 66 percent of MPs spend their parliamentary careers serving at only one level.

The latter figures are higher in Catalonia (79 percent) than in the Basque Country (56 percent).

Among MPs who move on to a different level, the most common pattern is unidirectional movement from the regional to the national political stage (approximately 30 percent). Again, Basque MPs tend to be three times more mobile than Catalan MPs.

Comparing mobility patterns between MPs from different parties in regional legislatures, the Socialist Party (PSOE) has (proportionally) more MPs who move to another level, whereas the opposite is true among national Socialist Party MPs. In regional parliaments, the percentage of Socialist Party MPs who moved to another level is lower than it is for MPs with a different party, particularly in Catalonia (10 percent fewer Socialist Party MPs move to a different level than in the Basque Country). These patterns are confirmed when differentiating regional MPs with a weak, medium or strong sense of non-Spanish national identity (where successful non-statewide parties exist). As expected, in both the regional and national legislatures, the proportion of regional MPs with multilevel experience is lower in regions where people identify more strongly with their own culture.

Therefore, above and beyond the tendency towards heterogeneity I have found, we can speak, in general, of an integrated parliamentary class in Spain, with some exceptions in regions marked by a strong sense of identification with a distinct local culture, especially in Catalonia (and to a lesser extent the Basque Country), confirming previous analyses (Stolz, 2003 and 2010). Further research (Oñate & Pérez-Comeche, 2012) is sure to provide a more in-depth understanding of these differences.

References

Borchert, J. (2003). "Professional Politicians: Towards a Comparative Perspective", in J. Borchert & J. Zeiss (eds.), *The Political Class in Advanced Democracies*, Oxford, Oxford University Press.

Borchert, J. (2011). "Individual Ambition and Institutional Opportunity: A Conceptual Approach to Political Careers in Multi-Level Systems", *Regional and Federal Studies*, 21, 2, 117-140.

Francis, W. & L. Kenny (2000). *Up the Political Ladder. Career Paths in the U.S. Politics*, Thousand Oaks, Sage.

Maiz, R. (2008). *La frontera interior. El lugar de la Nación en la Teoría de la democracia y el federalismo*, Murcia, Tres Fronteras.

Moncrief, G. F. (1988). "Dimensions of the Concept of Professionalism in State Legislatures: A Research Note", *State and Local Government Review*, 20 (3), 128-132.

Moncrief, G. F., R. G. Niemi, & L. V. Powell, "Turnover in State Legislatures: An Update", *Western Political Science Association Annual Meeting*, San Diego, California.

Oñate, P. (2000). "Congreso, grupos parlamentarios y partidos", en A. Martínez (ed.), *El Congreso de los Diputados en España: funciones y rendimiento*, Madrid, Tecnos, 95-140.

Oñate, P. (2008). "Los partidos politicos en la España democrática", en M. Jiménez de Parga y F. Vallespín (eds.), *La España del siglo XXI: La Política*, Sistema, Madrid, 2008, 617-643.

Oñate, P. (2010). "The Members of the Spanish Autonomic Parliaments: Some Features of a Regional Professionalized Elite", *Pôle Sud*, 33 (2), 27-46.

Oñate, P. & F. Ocaña (2008). "Las elecciones autonómicas de 2007 y los sistemas de partidos autonómicos en la España multinivel", in F. Pallarés (ed.), *Elecciones autonómicas y locales de 2007*, Madrid, Centro de Investigaciones Sociológicas, 133-164.

Oñate, P. & J. Pérez-Comeche (2012). "Political Careers in Spain: Movements between political arenas in a Multi-Level Political System", paper delivered at the *22nd IPSA Political Science World Congress*, Madrid, July, 2012.

Schlesinger, J. (1966). *Ambition and Politics*, Chicago, Rand McNally.

Squire, P. (1988). "Career Opportunities and Membership Stability in Legislatures", *Legislative Studies Quarterly*, 13, 65-82.

Squire, P. (2007). "Measuring State Legislative Professionalism. The Squire Index Revisited", *State Politics and Policy Quarterly*, 7, 211-227.

Stolz, K. (2003). "Moving Up, Moving Down. Political Careers Across Territorial Levels, *European Journal of Political Research*, 42, 223-248.

Stolz, K. (2010). *Towards a Regional Political Class. Professional Politicians and Regional Institutions in Catalonia and Scotland*, London.

Stolz, K. (2011). "The regionalization of Political Careers in Spain and the UK", *Regional and Federal Studies*, 21 (2), 223-243.

Chapter 14
Bringing Politicians Back in: Political Careers and Political Class in Multilevel Systems

Klaus Stolz, Chemnitz University of Technology

Political careers and their repercussions: a gap in the study of territorial politics

In the last decades, the study of territorial politics has developed into various sub-disciplines, covering a whole range of different aspects and approaching them from multiple perspectives. Recent research efforts are increasingly fo-cussing on the concrete interplay between institutions and political actors on various territorial levels. The emphasis in these studies has shifted from the formal structures of *government* to more complex and informal forms of polit-ical regulation that are currently subsumed under the term of multilevel gov-ernance (Marks 1993). In the field of regional studies this turn towards regional *governance* (Le Galés 1998) has produced studies concerned with a variety of important regional actors and processes, among them regionalist parties (De Winter & Türsan 1998), coalition-building in regional governments (Downs 2002), various segments of regional elites (Christopoulos 2001) as well as their co-operation in regional development coalitions (Keating *et al.* 2003). What has rarely featured in regional studies and other studies of territorial politics, however, is the very social group that actually populates the formal representa-tive institutions: elected politicians and their careers.

In a similar vein, studies of political careers until recently have rarely taken the territorial dimension of politics seriously. Career studies used to be largely confined to the borders of one nation state (lacking any comparative dimen-sion) and – with the exception of the US – focussed on the national level only. Interested basically in questions of elite recruitment, scholars employed a fun-nel perspective, investigating the careers of those politicians who have made it into an institutionally defined national political elite (usually the national par-liament or national government) (see for example Norris 1997, Best & Cotta 2000, Siavelis & Morgenstern 2008). This approach obviously neglects careers pursued on other territorial levels completely. Furthermore, even with regard to the careers under investigation existing territorial aspects are often blanked out by stripping careers of their territorial properties. The question is generally not *where* people come from, but *what kind* of office they held previously. Thus, other territorial levels of government might be acknowledged as recruitment pool for the national political elite, yet differences in career patterns of politicians from different regions and localities are hardly ever recognised.[1]

This chapter is trying to bring studies of territorial politics and career studies together by contemplating on how new regionalism and the emergence and expansion of multilevel systems might affect political careers, and how, in turn, newly emerging career patterns might affect the structure and mechanics of multilevel systems. Its relevance for the analysis of multilevel governance is derived from a neo-institutional understanding of the making of political careers based on Schlesinger's (1966) theory of ambition. From this perspective political careers may be seen as closely interrelated with the institutional context in which they occur: shaped by selective incentives and obstacles provided by an institutional "structure of opportunities" individual political careers tend to consolidate into recurrent career patterns. However, this perspective also allows us to see the potential impact of career experience and career expectations on political behaviour. Political career patterns might thus, in turn, also affect the mechanics and possibly the future development of the very institutional structures that have been shaping them. The relevance of the study of political careers in multilevel system is thus not confined to the identification of a great variety of career patterns. In addition, it might also contribute to a better understanding of the developments and mechanics of multilevel systems themselves.[2]

In the following, the complex interrelations between political careers and multilevel systems will mainly be demonstrated with recourse to the relationship between regional and national level.[3] The first step consists of a typology of patterns of career movements between these two levels complemented by empirical illustrations of each type (section 2). The next part (3) elaborates more systematically on potential *causes* for particular career movements (or their absence). In section 4 the analytical focus is shifted to the other side of the causal interrelationship. Now we are dealing with the potential *consequences* of the depicted career patterns, by introducing the concept of political class, and discussing its capacity to form and reform its institutional opportunity structure. Finally, the last section (5) briefly sets out the political careers

---

1   For a critique of such an a-territorial approach see Stolz (2012).
2   Fortuntately, the study of political careers has recently undergone major qualitative and quantitative improvements. Compilations of papers on multilevel careers in different institutional settings (Borchert & Stolz 2011, Edinger & Jahr 2012) are complemented by detailed studies of particular countries, regions or territorial levels (Spain and Belgium seem to be the most "popular" objects of study).
3   This has mainly pragmatic and no theoretical reasons. It should by no means be seen as an argument to neglect the local or the supranational level.

and political class perspective as another new and fruitful approach to the study of territorial politics and multilevel governance.

Political Careers in Multilevel Systems: Conceptual Framework and Empirical Illustrations[4]

The traditional assumption in career studies has long been that professional politicians use local and regional political positions as mere stepping stones to national office.[5] Yet this unidirectional springboard-hypothesis, probably developed according to experience in the US (and a Congress-centred perspective), has never been empirically tested in a comparative way. Furthermore, such a model is currently challenged by three processes: First, state parliaments in many federal systems have lately undergone profound processes of professionalization. Second, many unitary systems have recently undergone substantial processes of regionalisation, often going hand in hand with a professionalization of regional politics. And third, the European integration process has offered new career opportunities on the supranational level. Given that all three of these processes profoundly affect the opportunity structure of professional politicians, it has to be questioned whether the federal/national level can really be seen as the sole apex of professional political careers in what can increasingly be seen as multilevel systems.

Conceptual Framework

Theoretically, career movements between the regional and the national arena can take four distinct forms (see figure 14.1). The first is the *"classical springboard"* pattern, where regional politicians move "up" to the national level (i.e. in a centripetal direction), but hardly any of them move "down" to the regional arena (i.e. in a centrifugal direction). This pattern suggests a clear hierarchy of preferences with the national centre widely accepted as the apex of political careers.

---

4   This part of the article draws largely from Stolz (2003).
5   Francis & Kenny (2000:3) explicitly state it as a general ambition principle, that politicians "seek to increase their territorial jurisdiction" and "seek to increase the size of their electoral constituency".

Figure 14.1: Career patterns in multi-level systems

	High Centripetal Movement	Low Centripetal Movement
Low Centrifugal Movement	**Classical Springboard**	**Alternative Careers**
High Centrifugal Movement	**Integrated Careers**	**Inverse Springboard**

A second pattern would consist of *"alternative careers"*, where regional politicians remain on the regional and national politicians remain on the national level. Such an overall pattern could be the result of a fairly equal evaluation of regional and national positions, where transaction costs restrict movement between arenas. However, such a pattern could also reflect the existence of two groups of politicians with opposing preferences, one with a clear regional orientation and the other with a national one, each following their particular ambition. Finally, this pattern could also be the result of the existence of distinct party system at each level.

In a third scenario, we may find frequent career movements between the two arenas in both directions. Such a pattern of *"integrated careers"* is the result of an integrated circuit of positions with no strong institutional boundaries and no clear-cut hierarchy between regional and national positions, which make up one single rather than two distinct career arenas. Such a pattern could be produced by politicians with no particular preference, moving between regional and national positions with no sense of territorial direction, or by politicians who are being moved by their political masters (usually in the party leadership) according to short term strategic deliberations.

The final theoretical possibility is represented by the *"inverse springboard"* pattern, defined by frequent centrifugal career movements from the national to the regional arena and more or less no movement from the regional level "up" to the national centre. Such a pattern is only conceivable in the context of a complete reversal of the traditional hierarchy of offices. In such a scenario, national positions might be regarded as an important asset or even a pre-requisite for politicians to take up higher office at the regional level.

Empirical illustrations

So, what do political careers in multilevel systems really look like? The most general finding in the scarce literature on this topic is the rejection of the ubiquitous springboard label in connection with the regional level of government. Empirical evidence clearly shows the pathway from the regional to national parliament to be far less well-trodden than generally believed. Furthermore, some studies show that the increased status of regional positions in political careers is not only manifested in low centripetal movements, but that some regional parliaments even exhibit quite significant numbers of parliamentarians that have been moving in on a centrifugal pathway from the national parliament. Taken together these studies show that centripetal and centrifugal career movements vary considerably between countries, yet also between regions within the same country. Career patterns in federal and regionalised systems are thus rather diverse.

The most clear-cut *springboard* pattern is still to be found in the US, where around half of all Congressmen have served on the state level before, while hardly any Senator or House Member is moving into the opposite direction (Copeland & Opheim 2011). A similar pattern with even higher centripetal ratios is to be found in Switzerland, another traditional federal system (Stolz 2003). Germany on the other hand, seems to be moving away from this pattern. Here centripetal movements seem to be decreasing since the 1960s, with the Länder level becoming a more important career arena in its own right. However, the rather low levels of centrifugal movement (national MPs seem to move only toward the Länder-level, if they can enter regional government) still make for a rather uneven, centripetal balance of movements. Germany seems thus to be located somewhere between the springboard and the alternative careers model (Borchert & Stolz 2011b).

The *integrated careers* model is perhaps best displayed in Brazil. There the federal parliament seems to play a central role in political careers. However, its position is not at the apex of the career ladder. Instead it seems to be a stepping stone towards more prestigious positions in the executive rather than the legislative branch. While passing through federal parliament at some point or other, political careers in Brazil seem to have no clear-cut territorial direction. High risk positions make for a high turnover, and careers move from federal to provincial and local level as well as vice versa (Santos & Pegurier 2011). A similar pattern of level-hopping can be detected in Belgium since the federalization of the state. (Partly) synchronised elections and quite liberal regulations of candidacy have produced frequent movements between territorial levels in both directions. In Flanders, the overall balance is even tipped towards the regional rather than the national/federal level (Fiers 2012, Vanlangenakker *et al.* 2010) This pattern of frequent movement and centrifugally tipped balance is also to be found in the Spanish Communidad Autónoma (region) of

Catalonia (Stolz 2010). The high frequency of what has been called "si-
erra"/mountain careers (individual career pathways that show upwards- as well
as downwards movements) (Real-Dato *et al.* 2011) among Spanish parliamentarians in general, suggests that this integrated pattern may also hold for politicians from other Spanish regions.

The classical case of *alternative careers* has long been Canada, where a
highly fragmented party system has led to very low levels of career movements
across territorial levels (Stolz 2003), especially for the western provinces. Similarly low figures have also been found for some of Australia's states (e.g. Victoria, Queensland) (Stolz 2003) and for the newly-devolved regional parliaments in Scotland and Wales (Stolz 2010). The role of Canada as role model,
however, seems to vanish. A recent study clearly shows that politicians are
increasingly overcoming the lack of institutional linkage via the party system,
simply by switching parties. This seems to blur the strong institutional boundaries, and move the Canadian case away from the alternative model. Interestingly, the move is not uniform. While Eastern provinces seem to drift towards
a more unidirectional model (the classical springboard) where provincial legislators move up into the federal parliament, the Western provinces are also
experiencing some movement into the opposite direction, and thus seem to
move towards a more integrated career pattern (Docherty 2011).

Not surprisingly, no real-world case comes close to the ideal type of an *inverse springboard* pattern. This does neither mean that individually no politician is pursuing a regional career ambition by taking up a political position on
the national/federal level (in fact there are quite prominent cases for such a
pathway), nor that there are no cases with an overall balance of movement
tipped towards the regional level (Wallonia and Catalonia are such cases).
What it does say, though, is that there is no region where there is considerable
movement from the national to the regional level, with no significant movement into the other direction. This has to do with traditional notions of hierarchy yet also with very specific aspects of availability and attractiveness at the
respective other territorial level (as can be seen in the next section)

Causes: Availability, Attractiveness, Accessibility

So far, this paper has remained largely descriptive. But now that we know that
career paths of politicians follow rather different patterns, we have to ask how
to account for these differences. One of the most fruitful attempts to break
down Schlesinger "structures of opportunity" into analytically distinct components is provided by Borchert (2001: 6/7, 2003a: 8). According to him career
opportunities of politicians are defined by the *availability*, *accessibility*, and

attractiveness of political positions in a political system. As we are dealing with career movements between two levels of government, it is the relative availability, attractiveness and accessibility of positions on the regional level vis-à-vis the national level that matters. In the following, I will thus go through some of the most important institutional and non-institutional features and ask how they affect the three A's.

Availability

To state that careers and career movements are heavily dependent on the number of available positions is to state the obvious, yet such a statement is far from superfluous. Thus, it is easy to see, that it was not until the regionalisation of state structures that the pursuit of a political career on the regional level has been made possible at all in many countries. What is more difficult to understand is, that the frequency of career movements between regional and national level and the balance of movement in each direction is also clearly related to the respective number of available positions on each level.

As multilevel political systems usually have a pyramidal structure there are generally more regional seats available for national MPs from a particular region who wants to move "down", than there are national seats available for a member of the respective region's parliament willing to move "up". This "bottleneck" situation has consequences for the frequency of career movements: A low number of national MPs from a region means that only few members of the regional parliament will have the chance to move up, but also that there are only a few that are in a position to move down. Thus, the smaller the regional contingent in the national parliament the more the overall frequency of movement in *absolute* terms will be restricted.

But differences with regard to the availability of positions also affect to a large degree the various *relative* measures that are used to make sense of career movements. In general, we have to distinguish between an *import* (or recruitment) and an *export* (or career) perspective. While the former puts the number of members with a particular career background in relation to the overall size of the importing (recruiting) institution, the latter relates the number of members leaving their institution into a particular direction to the overall size of the exporting institution. The import perspective tells us something about the background of the members of a certain institution (e.g. 50% of members have come from regional parliament), while the export perspective provides information about the likely career prospects of a member in a certain institution (e.g. 50% of a particular cohort in the regional parliament have made it into the national parliament). An extreme bottleneck situation between regional and national parliament (low number of regional seats in national parliament, high number of seats in regional parliament) thus inflates import ratios for centripetal movement into the national parliament and deflate import ratios for centrifugal movement into the regional parliament. Similarly, it inflates export ratios for centrifugal movement from the national to the regional parliament and deflates export ratios for centripetal movement from the regional parliament to the national parliament.[6]

In general, we might conclude that the more the availability of political position differs between territorial levels (or particular institutions), the less we can rely on one single measure (usually import/recruitment ratios) to understand the significance of career movements between them.

Attractiveness

The main factor for the territorial orientation of political careers may be seen in the degree of attractiveness political positions on the respective territorial level of government entail. In general, positions on the national level have been and are still seen to be better paid, more prestigious and more powerful. Therefore, it is expected that ambitious politicians would strive for national office, and the more successful of them will actually reach there. However, as the centrifugal movements to some regions and the lack of centripetal movement towards the national level in others clearly show: there are also regions where a considerable number of politicians strive towards a regional career.

What kind of institutional factors would make a regional polity attractive to career politicians? Clearly high levels of professionalization (including parliamentary salaries, but also infrastructural resources, staff etc.) and legislative competencies – in other words: money and power – can be seen as among the most important attractions. While nearly all regional parliaments fall short of their national counterparts with respect to these factors, the extent of this gap between regional and national parliament differ widely. The professionali-

---

6   In 2003 all 5 members from the city-state of Bremen in the German Bundestag have come from the regional parliament, making for an impressive centripetal import ratio of 100%. While this result clearly suggests that in Bremen a regional mandate is a necessary career step for politicians who strive for national office, this does not mean that the regional parliament functions mainly as a stepping stone to federal office. On the contrary, the fact that Bremen has only a small contingent in the federal parliament means that the opportunity for each of the 100 regional MPs to reach the national parliament is much lower than in other regions (to be reflected in quite low centripetal export ratios). Applied to centrifugal career movements, this extreme bottle neck situation means that Bremen (and similar cases) are highly unlikely to produce any significant centrifugal import ratios. Even if all of Bremen's current national MPs would decide to move back to the regional parliament, they would only make up five per cent of all regional MPs. Viewed from the national parliament, however, the same kind of career movement would be reflected in an export ratio of 100%.

zation argument is supported by the low centripetal ratios in the strongly professionalized German *Länder* parliaments as against the higher centripetal ratios in the Swiss cantons. It would also fit with the much higher centripetal
ratios in the less professionalized German city-states (Stolz 2003). The level
of competencies might help to explain the quite high centrifugal ratio of Catalonia compared to Spanish ACs with lower levels of autonomy (Asturia) and
the higher centrifugal ratio of Scotland vis-à-vis Wales (ibid.).

While levels of professionalization and legislative competencies are features that affect the general attractiveness of the regional vs. the national level
of government, other institutional features affect the relative attractiveness of
pursuing a career path that crosses over territorial boundaries (no matter which
direction) in contrast to a career that remains within one territorial arena. Two
of the more important factors in this respect are a) the inner-institutional structure of parliaments and their relation to the executive and b) party system and
the structure of party competition.

In a parliamentary system with a widely differentiated internal career structure, where the legislature is also the main (or only) recruitment pool for executive office, career prospects usually increase with seniority. This provides a
strong incentive to remain on the parliamentary career path once adopted. Any
cross-over would entail at least the partial loss of resources acquired in the old
system and is thus less attractive. On the other hand, parliaments that show
only little internal differentiation, or no seniority advantage, and parliaments
with restricted or no access to executive positions (e.g. in presidential systems)
would make a cross-over to another institution less costly and thus more attractive. This may be one of the reasons why Spain (where seniority does play
no role at all) shows rather frequent movements between the regional and the
national level.

Another factor affecting career prospects, though one that mainly explains
variation between parties rather than between regions, can be seen in potential
discrepancies between levels of government with regard to the party system
and the structure of party competition. Deputies of parties that are in permanent
minority positions on one level yet in a governing position (or at least with
government potential) on the other might be more inclined to move into the
former than into the latter direction. This is true in many cases, just think of
social democrats in Bavaria, conservatives in Scotland and Wales etc.

However, there are also some non-institutional factors that may be of interest here. The first one, geography, appears to be rather weak. Nevertheless, all
other things being equal, geography might indeed affect the attractiveness of
career paths. Generally speaking, the nearer a region is to the national capital
the less transaction costs arise from a crossover between levels of government.
Unlike their counterparts from the national centre deputies that move from a
peripheral region to the national parliament usually face a change of the place
of living, a change of life-style, a loss of friends, the separation from the family

etc. The fact that centripetal import ratios of capital regions in national parliaments such as Berlin (40 %), Vienna (29 %) and Lazio (16 %) (cf. Stolz 2003) are above the national average may be seen as support of this hypothesis.

A much stronger impact on careers is clearly coming from the existence of a strongly politicised regional identity, or regionalism. This is hardly surprising. In many regions with a strong and virulent regionalism the newly established regional parliaments are symbols of re-awakened political identity and democracy. For many regional deputies serving in these bodies the region and not its "host-state" represents the most meaningful political frame of reference. Holding a regional mandate in these cases also carries a high status with the general public. Often the media, too, tends to be strongly orientated towards the regional parliament securing its members high levels of publicity. The stronger the social and cultural dimension of the regional identity the more attractive it is for regional politicians to be able to stay in the region rather than move to the (alien) national capital. This high level of attractiveness of regional careers in cases with strong regionalism is sometimes reflected in high centrifugal ratios, often containing considerable numbers of deputies directly moving from a current national mandate to the regional parliament (such as in Flanders, Scotland, Catalonia etc.). In other cases (like the Basque Country, Galicia or perhaps even Piedmont) it is expressed by a rather low level of national ambitions reflected in low centripetal ratios.

Accessibility

While the availability and attractiveness of regional careers are necessary conditions for the existence of regionally (rather than nationally) directed career ambitions, they do neither determine individual career paths nor do they automatically produce particular collective career patterns. Whether regional MPs move to the national parliament or national MPs to the regional parliament depends not only on their individual ambition but also on the respective accessibility of such a path for them.

Competition for parliamentary seats is usually structured by two different mechanisms: inner party selection and public election. Together these mechanisms not only determine the amount of turnover in each institution, and thus the number of vacant seats, but also who will fill these vacancies. Thus the electoral systems, the structure of party competition and the inner-party selection system at work in each region produce widely varying chances for regional deputies to move up and for national deputies to move down one level.

This is not the place to formulate a coherent theory as to which particular configuration of these features allows for high or low movements between the territorial levels. As the examples of Switzerland (see above) and the United

States (see Stolz 2003) clearly show, a high centripetal ratio can be reached via an electoral system based on proportional representation but also via a plurality system. Nevertheless, I would argue, that a party list system with a centralised nomination process, where party leaders can place, replace and displace deputies according to their own strategic or personal criteria bears a higher potential for inter-parliamentary movement than a plurality system with its strong incumbency advantage.

Similarly, neither two-party nor multi-party systems as such have any affinity to high or low levels of movement. What clearly restricts movement, however, is the divergence of regional and national party system. The most extreme case in this respect is Canada, where often parties on the provincial level do not compete on the national level and vice versa. If leading parties of the regional parliament are not, or only weakly represented in the national parliament, pathways between the parliaments may become rather narrow.

However, seemingly small details with regard to the timing of elections, the eligibility for election and the replacement of members during a legislative period may have a much more important effect than the question of party or electoral systems. Thus, if regional and national elections are held at the same time, there should be a particularly smooth transition from the one to the other. This is even more so in a case like Belgium, where politicians may stand for election to different parliaments at the same time and decide only after the election, which body they will really join. Another mechanism that allows for easy movement between parliaments is to allow for double mandates. In Northern Ireland, this has produced high levels of movement in both directions.

On the other hand, systems that rely on a by-election to fill seats that have become vacant during the legislative period hamper inter-parliamentary movement. As there is always the possibility to lose such a mid-term contest, parties are generally reluctant to "promote" deputies to higher office, if that entails the potential of losing a seat (as it is now the case in Scotland, Wales and Westminster). A very strong deterrent to individual deputies is to be found in Canada. There, provincial deputies have to stand down from their mandate before they are even allowed to stand for the federal parliament in Ottawa. This high career risk asked of any regional deputy with national ambitions can be seen as another reason for the very low centripetal movements in Canada (Docherty 2011).

Consequences: Career Patterns, Political Class and Regional Institution-Building

But how do these career patterns, in turn, effect the shape and the working of institutions? The key to unravel this interdependent relationship is the concept of political class (as developed by von Beyme 1993, 1996 and in particular by Borchert & Golsch 1995 and Borchert 1999, 2003a, 2003b). The basic assumption of this theory is that professional politicians, once they start to live off politics rather than just for politics, will become conscious of their collective interest in the maintenance and advancement of their professional career (Borchert & Golsch 1995: 612). Furthermore, the "political class-hypothesis" states that these politicians try to form and reform democratic institutions according to their class interest, and thus constitute an often neglected, yet very powerful collective actor. Examples of the effectiveness of their collective action are seen in mechanisms to immunise members of this class against the unpredictable will of voters and against challengers from outside (Borchert 2003b: 50-55) and by their active colonialisation of wide parts of the state and society (Beyme 1993).

This concept, though, has been developed in the national context. It has no explicit territorial dimension. On the contrary, it is based on the unspecified assumption that the professionalization of politics is restricted to national institutions or at least that they remain the unquestioned focus of professional careers. In line with traditional modernisation theory, this interpretation sees the professionalization of politics as reflection of the functional differentiation of society that is eroding territorial cleavages. Regional variation does not sit easily with such a conception.

However, as the results of section two have clearly shown, such an assumption is hardly feasible. Career paths do not all follow the springboard model - they vary. Some are even directed towards the regional level. If career interests within one political system vary significantly, the internal coherence of the national political class is challenged. Typically, regional politicians might thus be classified in two different ways: The more they follow a national career pattern, i.e. a career path directed towards the national centre, the more they can be understood as integral part of a national political class, sharing a similar understanding of their profession and – most importantly – a common career interest. The more the regional level has become a career goal in its own right, though, the closer we get to a separate and distinct regional political class (cf Stolz 2001). As the many different patterns identified in recent studies of multilevel careers have shown, empirical cases hardly ever fall into one of the two categories. A completely distinct regional political class, with no career linkage between region and national centre is hardly conceivable, but so is a completely homogeneous national political class with no regional variation of career paths and career interests. However, this does not render such a perspective obsolete. Instead, the benefit of such a perspective is that it might help to reveal the potential consequences different career patterns and thus the different type of political class may have for the collective action of professional politicians in their attempt to institutionalise their career arena according to their own collective self-interest.

In general, the self-interest of professional politicians is largely status quo oriented. As a group of people who have successfully pursued their professional career in a particular institutional structure and whose career interest has been shaped by these institutions, they are more inclined to reinforce this institutional structure than to radically reform it. And even if there was such a collective self-interest for large scale institutional reform within the political class, their capacity to act according to such an interest is very limited. After all, in high politics decisions where the public is engaged and parties are pursuing different objectives, professional politicians have to be seen to represent their different social or territorial constituencies rather than any collective self-interest.

Thus major institutional reforms, like the regionalisation of a state, are much more likely to be caused by exogenous demands from social and economic forces. However, once the main decisions are taken, the situation changes. Constitutional rules do not determine completely how the profession of politics is to be conducted in multilevel systems. Instead, much of the mechanisms at work on different territorial levels as well as with regard to their interrelation are based on low key decisions as well as on informal rules and norms that emerge in a dynamic process of institutionalisation. This is where the collective self-interest of the politicians involved might make the difference.

This line of thought is fully compatible with the dominant approach in many of the more recent accounts of regionalisation processes, namely to bring politics back in. However, where Keating (see for example 1998: 59-61) and others rightly emphasise the self-interest of the many organisations involved in this process, a political class perspective, would ask whether there is also a collective interest of professional politicians. Parties, interest groups, local authorities, national governments etc. may be institutionally bounded, yet they are also linked to each other via the careers of their political personnel. From an institutionally centred perspective, it seems logical that local government or the national parliament may develop some form of hostility against the establishment of a regional tier of government (Keating 1998: 60) as they compete for the same competencies, resources and loyalties. However, from a career perspective, the attitude of local councillors and national parliamentarians towards the establishment (or even the strengthening) of a regional parliament will vary depending on their ambition and their opportunity to serve in such a legislature.

In general, I would assume that a political class with careers focussed towards the national centre will develop different institutional priorities than a highly self-contained regional political class. The former will take a keen interest in the uniformity and symmetry between regional and national institutions. At the very least, they should work towards a high degree of permeability of regional institutions as their upward mobility is not be restricted by institutional boundaries. The latter, on the other hand, would be much more interested in the maintenance and expansion of career opportunities, resources and competencies on the regional level, irrespective of their effect on linkages to the national level. Of course, these are only very crude assumptions as the collective interest of professional politicians in a region is not only dependent on their territorial orientation but also on the structural base of the political class, its concrete career pattern and its internal homogeneity.

Unfortunately, there is very little scholarly work done, that could serve as empirical evidence to underpin these theoretical deliberations. Nevertheless, some illustrations from a study (Stolz 2010) on two of the most clear-cut regional political classes – Catalonia and Scotland - might at least confirm the plausibility of my argument. In Catalonia, the strong regional career orientation within a highly integrated career pattern (see above) seems to correspond to a regional political class that has extended its territorial reach into the Spanish level of government. Driven by a common Catalanism (despite party political differences) but also fostered by a common career interest in institutions of Catalan self-government, this Catalan political class has successfully – and often unanimously - constructed and defended strong and resourceful Catalan institutions against a sometimes reluctant, sometimes hostile Spanish central government.[7] At times, the Catalan political class can also be seen to actively pursue its professional self-interest together with their Spanish colleagues at the central state level. However, failure to implement this interest might then result in a stand-alone strategy by the Catalan parties and thus in a conflict with the Spanish political class. Such a pattern can be observed in the wake of the so-called *Filesa* crisis. When Catalan (and other) attempts to revise the law on party finance were obstructed and finally abandoned on the Spanish level, Catalan parties reached their own voluntary *Acord* (2001). Explicitly defying the conventional reading of the Spanish party finance law, they granted themselves unconditional subsidies for the maintenance of ordinary party functions. As

---

7   Perhaps the best example for this largely successful form of consensual institutional politics in Catalonia are the laws that finally established a highly centralized and powerful Catalan Administration (Law 3/1982, 17/1985 and 13/1989). The consensual, cross-party character of the institutional politics (and thus at least potentially the collective class interest) vis-à-vis the Spanish state can be seen in the constant battle over competencies and autonomy (often litigated by the constitutional court) such as the transfer of power from provincial authorities to the regional government, the right to regulate local elections, Catalan representation in public enterprises owned and regulated by the Spanish state or the establishment of a Catalan public broadcasting company.

this advance was coupled with measures of extended self-limitation, control and transparency, the accord was serving two very different aims: first, it increased the public funds transferred to the political parties in Catalonia and thus the resource base of the Catalan political class. Secondly, however, it was meant to counter the increasingly eroding base of legitimacy of professional politician and political parties in Catalonia and to project Catalonia as a non-confrontational, consensus-based polity to the rest of Spain (for a more detailed account of this episode see Stolz 2010: 196-200). Reflecting their integrated career pattern Catalan politicians have thus been able to express (and sometimes to accomplish) their collective self-interest career both in Catalonia and at the central state level (often – but not always - in opposition other Spanish politicians)

In contrast to the Catalan political class, the regional political class in Scotland is based on the parliamentary rather than party realm and on patterns of alternative rather than integrated careers. As a consequence their efforts have been directed much more to the institutionalisation of their professional career interest in the Scottish parliamentary system, than in the party political colonialisation of state and society. Legislating for high levels of pay, infrastructure and staff support (almost equalling levels at Westminster), Members of the Scottish Parliament (MSPs) have established the parliamentary mandate in Scotland as an attractive professional career. Furthermore, their generous resource endowment together with some reforms in the intra-party candidate selection process (all parties now effectively practising a one-member-one-vote postal ballot for the regional lists) is placing incumbent MSPs quasi-naturally above any potential challenger, thus providing them with an important asset to secure and maintain their careers. Most revealing in terms of the career interests of the Scottish political class, though, was the conflict about the planned reduction of seats in the Scottish Parliament. When confronted with the choice of either accepting the automatic seat reduction that would keep Westminster and Scottish constituencies congruent or campaigning for a preservation of all 129 seats, yet accepting the divergence of constituency boundaries, MSPs opted unanimously for the latter. MSPs thus traded their most direct access route to a Westminster career (congruent constituencies offer MSPs a role as a kind of natural successor to an MP) for an increased job-security (a reduction would have cost the job of 20 MSPs, many more would have suffered high levels of insecurity in the process of candidate selection) and the preservation of career opportunities inside their own parliament's committee system (which would have been under pressure from reduced man-power). Scottish MPs in Westminster though were strongly in favour of maintaining the link between Westminster and the Scottish Parliament (for a more detailed account of this episode see Stolz 2010: 231-236). The divergence of career paths between the two sets of Scottish politicians seems to have informed their respective institutional politics pointing towards the formation of a distinct Scottish political class (with MSPs at its core), separate from the British political class (including Scottish Westminster MPs).

However, the correspondence between career interest and institutional politics (the core of the political class argument) is not always that obvious. In the German case, for example, the professionalization of regional parliaments seems to have shifted career patterns away from the classical springboard pattern and closer towards an alternative career models (see above). Paradoxically, this process has been accompanied by a transfer of legislative competencies away from the regional parliament towards the federal level. Why, one may ask, would regional politicians whose ambition to move up to the federal level seems to wane, accept such a degradation? The answer to this paradox may be located in the heterogeneity of regional parliamentarians and the complexities of multilevel systems (which, despite the focus of this paper, are not limited to two territorial levels only). Regional parliamentarians in Germany (*Landtagsabgeordnete*, MdL) do not follow a uniform career model. Unlike, for example, Scottish MSP most German MdL keep a local government office (local or provincial council or even mayor) after their entry into the regional parliament. Furthermore, additional party offices are often only acquired during the parliamentary mandate (Borchert & Stolz 2003). Within a regional parliament there are thus different groups of MdL. One group, ambitious parliamentarians who strive for cabinet office and/or a federal mandate,[8] actually benefits from the transfer of legislative competencies as MdL from this group either are or will be involved in federal decision making via the Bundesrat (regional governments) or the Bundestag. Many of the other MdL, though, compensate their low policy-making capacity in the regional parliament by an active participation in their party (at local and Land level) and in local government (Raff 2000). A lack of responsibility (and perhaps time demands) in their breadwinning office (the regional mandate) may thus be seen positive rather than negative by this group. Their heterogeneous career interests, the strong embeddedness in local politics (linking regional and federal level) together with the still unquestioned supremacy of the federal level are the reason, why regional politicians, in none of the 16 Bundesländer, can be seen as a distinct regional political class.

---

8   This can be seen as one group as regional cabinet ministers are far more likely to move into federal parliament than their backbench colleagues, Stolz & Fischer (2011: 13).

Conclusion

The multilevel governance perspective can be seen as part of wider, renewed interest in the territorialization of politics (Jeffery & Wincott: 2010). With its focus on non-state actors and informal processes of co-ordination it has further extended the territorial politics agenda. In this paper I have argued for another extension of this agenda, albeit within the confines of the formal framework of representative government. Major territorial re-organisations (i.e. decentralization and regionalization as well as supranational integration), it is argued, have not only occurred at the same time as processes of political professionalization, the two are also inextricably linked with each other. The emergence and strengthening of governmental levels beyond the nation state and the increasing professionalization of politics on these levels has induced a further differentiation of political career pathways, which had never really complied with the traditional springboard model in the first place. Scholarly efforts to identify and explain these newly emerging multilevel career patterns are currently on its way, although there is still a lot to be done in terms of comparative empirical studies as well as with regard to the sharpening of our theoretical and methodological tools.

But why should we be interested in political careers in the first place? While it seems straightforward that a variety of multilevel institutional arrangements may produce a variety of career patterns, the reversal of the causal link – the idea that collective career interests render professional politicians into a political class that is capable of shaping its own institutional surroundings – is much less obvious and much more contested. In this paper I have presented some examples where career patterns, and even the concrete territorial career orientation, seem to have made a difference for the institutional politics pursued. These are the fruits of a first study on the emergence of distinctive regional political classes in Catalonia and Scotland (Stolz 2010). While these results are clearly limited with regard to their potential for generalisation, they open up a research agenda that may focus on the causal linkage of institutional change and changes in career patterns (possibly by concentrating on critical junctures). Far from superseding traditional and current approaches, the political class perspective is meant to complement recent lines of research. Without a look at the professionalization of politics and the career patterns that link the different territorial levels, though, any analysis of multilevel governance will remain incomplete.

References

Acord de transparència I autolimitació de despeses electorals I de finançament dels partits politics (2001). Barcelona.

Best, H. & Cotta, M. (eds) (2000). *Parliamentary Representatives in Europe 1848-2000. Legislative Recruitment and Careers in Eleven European Countries*, Oxford: Oxford University Press.

Beyme, K. von (1993). *Die politische Klasse im Parteienstaat*, Frankfurt: Suhrkamp.

Beyme, K. von (1996). The Concept of Political Class: A New Dimension of Research on Elites?, *West European Politics (*19), 68-87.

Borchert, J. (1999). Politik als Beruf: Die politische Klasse in westlichen Demokratien, in J. Borchert (ed.), *Politik als Beruf*, pp.7-39. Opladen: Leske + Budrich.

Borchert, J. (2001). Movement and Linkage in Political Careers: Individual Ambition and Institution Repercussions in a Multi-Level Setting, Paper prepared for presentation at the ECPR Joint Sessions of Workshops, Grenoble April 6-11.

Borchert, J (2003a). Professional Politicians: Towards a Comparative Perspective. J. Borchert & J. Zeiss (eds). *The Political Class in Advanced Democracies*. Oxford: Oxford University Press, 1-25.

Borchert, J (2003b). *Die Professionalisierung der Politik. Zur Notwendigkeit eines Ärgernisses.* Frankfurt: Campus.

Borchert, J. & Golsch, L (1995). Die politische Klasse in westlichen Demokratien: Rekrutierung, Karriereinteressen und institutioneller Wandel, *Politische Vierteljahresschrift* 36(4), 609-29.

Borchert, J. & Golsch, L. (2003). Germany: From "Guilds of Notables" to Political Class. J. Borchert & J. Zeiss (eds). *The Political Class in Advanced Democracies*. Oxford: Oxford University Press, 142-163.

Borchert. J. & Stolz, K. (2003). Politikerkarrieren und Karrierepolitik in der Bundesrepublik Deutschland, Politische Vierteljahresschrift 44(2), 148-173.

Borchert, J. & Stolz, K. (eds) (2011a). *Moving through the Labyrinth. Political Careers in Multi-Level System,* Special Issue Regional and Federal Studies 21(2).

Borchert, J. & Stolz, K. (2011b). German Political Careers: The State Level as an Arena in its Own Right?, *Regional and Federal Studies 21(2),* Special Issue *Moving Through the Labyrinth: Political Careers in Multi-Level Systems (ed. by J. Borchert & K. Stolz),* 205-222.

Christopoulos, D.C. (2001). *Regional Behaviour. Political Values and Economic Growth in European Regions*. Ashgate: Aldershot.

Copeland, G. & Opheim, C. (2011). Multi-level Political Careers in the USA: The Cases of African Americans and Women, Regional and Federal Studies 21(2), Special Issue Moving Through the Labyrinth: Political Careers in Multi-Level Systems (ed. by J. Borchert & K. Stolz), 141-164.

De Winter, L. & Türsan, H. (eds) (1998). Regionalist Parties in Western Europe, London and New York: Routledge.

Docherty, D. (2011). The Canadian Political Career Structure: From Stability to Free Agency, Regional and Federal Studies 21(2), Special Issue Moving Through the Labyrinth: Political Careers in Multi-Level Systems (ed. by J. Borchert & K. Stolz), 185-203.

Downs, William (1998). Coalition Government, Subnational Style: Multiparty Politics in Europe's Regional Parliaments, Columbus: Ohio State University Press.

Fiers, S. (2012, forthcoming). Level-hopping in Belgium: a critical appraisal of 25 Years of Federalism, in Edinger, M. & and Jahr, S. (eds), Political careers in Europe: career patterns in multi-level systems, Baden-Baden, Nomos.

Francis, W.L. & Kenny; L.W. (2000). Up the Political Ladder. Career Paths in U.S. Politics, Thousand Oaks: Sage.

Hibbing, J.R. (1999). Legislative Careers: Why and How We Should Study Them, Legislative Studies Quarterly 24, 149-171.

Jeffery, Ch. & Wincott, D. (2010). The Challenge of Territorial Politics: Beyond Methodological Nationalism, in C. Hay (ed.), New Directions in Political Science. Responding to the Challenges of an Interdependent World, Houndmills/Basingstoke: Pelgrave Macmillan.

Keating, M. (1998). The New Regionalism in Western Europe. Territorial Restructuring and Political Change, Cheltenham: Edward Elgar.

Keating, M., Loughlin, J. & Kris Deschouwer (eds) (2003). Culture, Institutions and Economic Development. A Study of Eight European Regions. Cheltenham: Edward Elgar.

Le Galès, P. (1998). Conclusion – government and governance of regions: structural weaknesses and new mobilisations, in P. Le Galès & C. Lequesne (eds), Regions in Europe, London and New York: Routledge, 239-287.

Norris, P. (ed.) (1997). Passages to power. Legislative recruitment in advanced democracies, Cambridge: Cambridge University Press.

Raff, T. (2000). Abgeordnete im Niedersächsischen Landtag. Politische Ambitionen und Karrieremuster, MA thesis University of Goettingen, Germany.

Real-Dato, J., Rodriguez-Teruel, J. & Jerez-Mir, M. (2011). In Search of the 'Ladder Model': Career Paths of Spanish Diputados (1977-2010), Paper presented at ECPR General Conference, Reykjavic, Iceland.

Santos, F. & Pegurier, F. (2011). Political Careers in Brazil: Long-term Trends and Cross-sectional Variation, Regional and Federal Studies 21(2), Special Issue Moving Through the Labyrinth: Political Careers in Multi-Level Systems (ed. by J. Borchert & K. Stolz), 165-183.

Schlesinger, J. (1966). Ambition and Politics, Chicago: Rand McNally.

Siavelis, P. & Morgenstern, S. (eds.) (2008). Pathways to Power. Political Recruitment and Democracy in Latin America. University Place: Pennsylvania State University Press.

Stolz, K. (1999). Political Careers in Newly Established Regional Parliaments: Scotland and Catalonia, unpublished paper presented at APSA annual meeting, Atlanta, 2-5 September, 1999.

Stolz, K. (2001). The Political Class and Regional Institution-Building. A Conceptual Framework, Regional and Federal Studies 11(1), 80-100.

Stolz, K. (2003). Moving up, Moving down. Political careers across territorial levels. European Journal of Political Research 42 (2), 223-248.

Stolz, K. (2010). Towards a Regional Political Class. Professional Politicians and Regional Institutions in Catalonia and Scotland, Manchester: Manchester University Press.

Stolz, K. (2012, forthcoming). Legislative Careers in Multi-level Europe, in Edinger, M. & and Jahr, S. (eds), Political careers in Europe: career patterns in multi-level systems, Baden-Baden, Nomos.

Stolz, K. & Fischer, J. (2011). Patterns of Ministerial Careers in Germany, Paper presented for the 10th Annual Conference of the Asociación Española de Ciencia Política y de la Adminstración (AECPA), Murcia, Spain.

Vanlangenakker, I., Maddens, B. & Put, G-J. (2010). Political Careers in Belgium: An Example of the Integrated Career Model, Fédéralisme Régionalisme 10: Varia http://popuups.ulg.ac.be/federalisme/document.php?id=939.

Chapter 15
State Legislatures and the Policy Making Process in the United States

Peverill Squire, University of Missouri

Introduction

The United States has operated as a federal system since the Constitution went into effect in 1789. Prior to that, the country had been governed under the Articles of Confederation, a system that failed in large part because strong state governments dominated the weak national government. Indeed, the national government was so weak that it could not tax; instead it had to rely on voluntary contributions from the states, funds which usually never materialized. The Constitution was written to correct many of the flaws attributed to the Articles, notably by placing the national government and state governments on a more equal footing. Both were given constitutional standing.[1] Each level was allowed to engage in some shared powers. Importantly, both the national government and the state governments can tax and borrow, charter banks and corporations, and enforce laws and administer a judiciary. At the same time, each was also assigned certain exclusive powers—only the national government, for example, can coin money or regulate interstate and foreign commerce.

Although the Constitution established a federal system and in some instances allocated specific powers to each governmental level, there is sufficient ambiguity in the overall design that there has been an ongoing resorting of policy powers. The initial phase of the system, roughly from 1789 to the outbreak of the Civil War in 1861, is typically characterized as one of dual federalism, where the national government enjoyed supremacy within those areas specifically assigned to it in the Constitution, and the states were supreme in all other areas of public policy. At this point, each level enjoyed clear spheres of policy control. For instance, power over public education and law enforcement was left entirely to the states. From the end of the Civil War until the 1930s, a time period when the country industrialized and the economy nationalized with advent of the railroad and the telegraph, the first resorting of responsibilities took place, with the national government clearly establishing its

---

1 Local governments do not enjoy standing in the federal constitution; they are creations of state constitutions and state laws.

dominance over the regulation of commerce. Still, aspects of the initial dual federalism system maintained, with the states continuing to control education and law enforcement.

The fiscal pressures brought on by the Great Depression triggered another round of policy sorting, with the federal government, under the auspices of President Franklin Roosevelt's New Deal programs, asserting that it had a role to play in providing financial assistance to state and local governments. In 1932, the federal government provided only 3 percent of the money state and local governments spent. Under Roosevelt's new fiscal federalism approach, by 1940 that figure had increased to just over 10 percent, and it continued to rise until it peaked at 27 percent in 1980. As the states soon discovered, the money from Washington came with strings attached and the federal government began to involve itself in policy areas such as education, law enforcement, and public welfare that had traditionally been left to the states. Until the mid-1960s, fiscal federalism exhibited a strong element of cooperation between the levels of government. In more recent decades, however, fiscal federalism has taken on a less cooperative and more conflictual tone.

Another sorting of policy control was driven by President Ronald Reagan's agenda in the 1980s. Reagan wished to eliminate many federal aid programs. He was driven to do this by a desire to reduce how much the federal government spent on domestic programs and, in turn, diminish the federal government's influence over state and local policymaking. As a result, the federal government's contribution to state and local expenditures fell to 19 percent by 1990. But under President Bill Clinton federal aid began to grow again; by 1996, its share of state and local spending reached 25 percent. Over the next decade federal aid continued to grow even though Republicans controlled both houses of Congress during much of the time. In 2007, federal aid still constituted about 23 percent of state and local spending. Thus, federal aid continues to be a major source of funding for state and local governments[2].

Starting with President Reagan, however, there has been a strong trend toward policy devolution, with Washington returning some important policy powers back to the states. But this development has only occurred in fits and starts and not always in predictable ways. Generally speaking, Republicans have favored shifting policymaking powers to the states while Democrats have preferred to have the federal government retain control. But it was a Republican president, George W. Bush, and a Republican controlled Congress that passed the No Child Left Behind law that greatly expanded the federal government's role in education, while a Democratic President, Bill Clinton, signed a sweeping welfare reform measure that greatly increased state government

---

2   These data are take from *Historical Statistics of the United States: Colonial Times to 1970, Part 2* (Washington, D.C.: U.S. Bureau of the Census, 1975), 1125–28; and Office of Management and Budget, *Budget of the United States Government, Fiscal Year 2009, Analytical Perspectives* (Washington, D.C.: U.S. Government Printing Office, 2008), 113.

powers in that area. Consequently, it seems fair to say that although there continues to be debate over the appropriate policy powers each level of government should exercise neither the Republicans nor the Democrats have developed a consistent answer. Instead, each party determines the policy outcome it prefers and then works backward to the level of government that is more likely to produce their preferred outcome.

The design of governmental institutions in the United States

Although the creation of the original 13 states preceded the establishment of the federal government, in Article IV section 4 the Constitution states that, "The United States shall guarantee to every state in this union a republican form of government . . ." In truth, the newly created federal government looked much like the existing state governments, with separate legislative, executive, and judicial branches sharing powers. But the separation of powers was more pronounced in the new federal government, which gave the president greater powers than most state governors enjoyed. More importantly, the new Congress was not allowed to enjoy legislative supremacy to the extent that the existing state legislatures did. In a majority of the early states the legislature elected the governor to a one-year term. In some cases, they also elected the judges. Thus, when in 1784 the Rhode Island Supreme Court handed down an important decision contrary to the state legislature's wishes, legislators responded by voting to replace the judges. Legislative supremacy was largely dismantled during the first half of the nineteenth century as voters rebelled against what they perceived legislative abuse of powers, but it is worth noting that while separation of powers continues to be a hallmark of American governmental design, upon close inspection the demarcations between the branches continue to blur to differing degrees in different states (Squire and Hamm 2005, 39-40).

The current "republican form of government" found in each of the states exhibits the same basic framework. Each state has a governor, elected by the voters to a four-year term in 48 states and a two-year term in New Hampshire and Vermont. State judicial branches vary considerably in their details, but each has a court of last resort at its apex, usually but not always called the supreme court, with Oklahoma and Texas having separate courts of last resort for civil and criminal cases. In some states judges are appointed by the governor, in others they are elected by the voters—sometimes in partisan elections and sometimes in non-partisan elections—and in South Carolina and Virginia they are elected by the legislature.

State legislatures also vary greatly in their details. At the macro level, every state legislature, save for Nebraska, is bicameral. Importantly, like the two houses in Congress, both houses in the 49 bicameral state legislatures are powerful; both must pass bills for them to become law. One reason for the prevalence of bicameralism is a calculation that two houses allow for greater reflection in the policymaking process. Legislation that passes one house must still pass the other house, usually slowing down the lawmaking process by requiring a separate house of lawmakers, elected independently from the members in the first house, to render judgment on a measure's merits. Thus, having two houses makes it more difficult for bills to become law because it increases the number of obstacles a proposal must overcome. Only legislation enjoying broad support succeeds.

Nebraska's unicameral legislature is the great exception among current American legislatures. When the state entered the union in 1867, its legislature was a bicameral body, like every other state legislature at the time. But in 1934, Nebraska voters passed an initiative to change to a unicameral body. The idea had been pushed for years by U.S. Senator George W. Norris (R-NE), who argued that conference committees in bicameral legislatures were a source of corruption. Most Nebraskans, however, backed the change because they thought one house would be more economical, a powerful appeal at a time when the country was mired in the Great Depression.

But the Nebraska legislature is exceptional for an additional reason. At the same time unicameralism was adopted the legislature was also changed to become a nonpartisan body, meaning that party labels do not appear on the ballot attached to candidate names. Although most voters know which candidate for the Unicameral is a Republican and which is a Democrat, once elected Nebraska lawmakers downplay their partisanship. There are no party caucuses in the Unicameral; instead lawmakers are organized regionally with members assigned to the Omaha, Lincoln, or West caucus based on the district they represent. In recent years, Democrats have been elected committee chairs and speaker, even though they were in the minority. Importantly, party does not explain how Nebraska legislators vote on bills (Aldrich and Battista 2002; Schaffner, 2007; Wright and Schaffner 2002). Arguably, being nonpartisan has a greater impact on the behavior of Nebraska legislators than the fact that they operate in a single house system.

State legislative houses currently range in size from very small (20 members in the Alaska Senate) to very large (400 members in the New Hampshire House of Representatives). As has always been the case, in each state the lower house has more members than the upper house. None of the lower houses is as large as the 435 member U.S. House of Representatives and none of the 50 state senates is as large as the 100 member U.S. Senate—the largest is Minnesota with 67 members. Surprisingly, there is no statistically significant relationship between state population size and the number of legislators in a state (Squire and Hamm 2005, 48). The state with the largest population, California with 37 million residents, has 120 state legislators while New Hampshire, with 1 million residents, has 424 state legislators. The number of lawmakers in a house is important because it influences the way in which members interact. A study of decision making in the 99 state legislative houses found that party caucuses are more powerful in smaller houses while in larger houses party leaders are more important (Francis 1985a, 249). More generally, another legislative scholar observed that size influences "hierarchy, with more elaborate and orderly rules and procedures and greater leadership authority in larger bodies and informality and collegial authority in smaller ones; the conduct of business, with a more efficient flow and less debate in larger bodies and more leisurely deliberation and greater fluidity in smaller ones; the internal distribution of power, with more concentrated pockets possible in larger bodies and greater dispersion of power in smaller ones" (Rosenthal 1981, 132-34).

Differences in the size of state legislatures also have important implications for representation.[3] California state senators currently represent districts with 931,349 residents, while New Hampshire state representatives represent districts with 3,291 residents. Obviously, a California state senator cannot related to his or her constituents in the same way personalized way a New Hampshire representative can. More generally, contacts with lawmakers per constituent decline as district population size increases, suggesting that voters feel less connected to their legislators as the size of the legislative district increases (Squire 1993, 485).

Currently, most state legislators are elected from single-member districts. This has not always been the case. Earlier in American history multi-member districts was the norm. But by 2011, multi-member districts were found in just two upper houses and ten lower houses. Roughly 21 percent of lower house members and 3 percent of state senators in the country are elected from multi-member districts. This matters because lawmakers in multi-member districts are more likely than their single-district counterparts to think of themselves as "trustees," elected to act in the broader interests of their constituents rather than simply reflecting their preferences (Cooper and Richardson 2006, 174-94). Legislators from multi-member districts spend more time providing constituent services and they bring home more government funds (Freeman and Richardson 1996, 41-56; Snyder and Ueda 2007). There are also institutional effects. For example, political parties in the Illinois House were more ideologically diverse when the chamber was elected using multi-member districts than when single member district elections were used (Adams 1996).

Office terms in 30 states are for two years in the lower house and four years in the state senate. But in 12 states members of both houses are given two-year

3   Since the U.S. Supreme Court decision in *Reynolds v. Sims* (1964), all state legislative houses must be apportioned on the basis of equal population, meaning all districts in a house in a state must have the same population per legislator elected.

terms and in five states both houses get four-year terms. Nebraska legislators are given four-year terms. And in Illinois and New Jersey, state senators have shifting terms, with one two-year term and two four-year terms to accommodate redistricting every ten years.[4] Term length is thought to influence member behavior, with longer terms giving lawmakers greater freedom from electoral pressures and shorter terms providing less freedom.

Although term limits on member service have been debated since the country was formed, they did not become a serious possibility until the late 1980s and then they were adopted in 21 states with amazing speed. In 1990 voters in Colorado, Oklahoma, and California were the first to impose term limits on their state legislators. Two years later, term-limit measures passed in all twelve states in which they appeared on the ballot, and they were adopted in six more states by 1995. There were, however, some bumps along the way. Nebraska voters had to pass term limits three times—1992, 1994 and 2000—because the Nebraska Supreme Court tossed out the first two versions on legal technicalities. Voter passed term-limit laws were also overturned by state supreme courts in Massachusetts in 1997, Washington in 1998, Oregon in 2002, and Wyoming in 2004. It is important to note that term limits were pushed by voters, not legislators. Only in Utah and Louisiana did lawmakers place limits on themselves, and in Utah legislators were pressured by the threat that voters would use a ballot measure to impose more stringent limitations. In every other state that adopted them, voters, not legislators, made the decision. In 2002, the Idaho state legislature repealed the term limits voters had imposed eight years earlier (such a repeal option is afforded to legislatures in only a few states). In the general elections that fall, Idaho voters barely upheld the legislators' decision to remove term limits. Utah's legislature repealed term limits in 2003 without much public dissent. Elsewhere, voters have voted to maintain term limits when given the opportunity to revisit the question (Squire and Moncrief 2010, 22).

Currently there are 15 states that impose term limits, but the limits vary in regard to specifics. The differences revolve around the number of terms a legislator may serve and whether those term limits are life-time bans or simply limits on the number of consecutive terms. For example, Louisiana and Nevada have looser twelve-year limits in each house, while Arkansas, California and Michigan have more stringent limits of six years in the lower house and eight years in the upper house. Both Ohio and Missouri have eight year limits in each house, but Missouri's is a lifetime limit while Ohio's is simply a consecutive term limit. Therefore, in Ohio, a termed-out legislator is eligible to hold office again after sitting out for four years. In Missouri, once a legislator reaches the term limit his or her career in that house is finished.

---

4   A variety of other mechanisms are used to cope with redistricting in the other 37 states that
    have staggered electoral terms (Squire and Hamm 2005, 62-63).

What difference does term limits make? The most obvious consequence is greater membership turnover in most term-limited legislatures (Moncrief, Niemi, and. Powell 2004). Less obvious is that this turnover in personnel has led to instability in standing committee systems. Committees are a crucial element in the state legislative process and "the informational, deliberative and gatekeeping roles of the committees are undermined by term limits" (Cain and Wright 2007, 89). There also is evidence that term limits put legislatures at a disadvantage in their relations with the executive branch (Powell 2007).

Professionalization and legislative service

The most important development in American state legislatures over the last century has been their professionalization. In most states member pay has increased, sessions have become longer, and staff resources have greatly improved. Member pay, session length and staff support are the three characteristics commonly associated with legislative professionalization (King 2000; Squire 1988a; 1988b; 1992a; 1992b; 2000; 2007; Squire and Hamm 2005). Increases in each have been pursued in order to increase a legislatures' capacity to generate and digest information and are intended to make the institutions more capable policymakers along the lines of the modern U.S. Congress.

At the level of the individual, as we might anticipate, as legislative salaries increase legislators have greater incentive to continue service in the legislature. But increasing pay has an additional, less appreciated impact on lawmakers; it also allows them to focus their energies on their legislative responsibilities rather than having to juggle them with the demands of other occupations.

The implications of legislative time demands condition the impact of legislative pay on member behavior. On the one hand, when limited demands are made by legislative service, lawmakers do not need much salary to compensate for their time. Indeed, when legislatures meet for only a month or so each year, members may not have to sacrifice much time (and income) from their regular jobs to serve. On the other hand, when a legislature meets year-round, lawmakers must be paid enough to support themselves and their families, to compensate them for forgoing income from outside occupations. Thus, at the extremes of time demands, the implications of its relationship with salary are straightforward. But in the mid-range of time demands; where legislatures meet for several months each year as many state legislatures do, calculations get more complicated. In these states the point at which financial incentives are sufficient to compensate for lost income is not clear. Legislative time demands also have a second implication for legislators. The more days that a legislature meets each year, the better legislators come to understand the complexities of

Peverill Squire

the legislative and policymaking processes. Thus, longer sessions give members a better chance to master arcane rules and procedures, and to become educated about complicated policy matters.

The level of staff resources in a legislature has several clear-cut implications for legislators. First, more staff leads to better informed lawmakers, which allows each of them to exert greater influence in the policy making process. Second, as legislators enjoy making greater impact on policymaking, job satisfaction likely increases (Francis 1985b). Finally, more staff improves lawmakers' ability to provide constituent services.

The institutional implications of legislative professionalization are straightforward. First, higher salaries allow lawmakers to devote more time and energy to lawmaking, without the distraction of another occupation and thus can lead to longer serving, and therefore more informed and effective, legislators (Squire 1988b). Second, higher salaries attract better qualified legislators in terms of academic credentials and higher status occupations. Third, meeting for more days each year gives legislators more time to develop legislative proposals and more time to deliberate on them, thereby improving the quality of legislative output. Fourth, increased staff resources make the legislature a more equal partner with the executive branch in policymaking (Rosenthal 1996, 171-72).

Currently, state legislatures vary on each dimension of professionalization. Although a few states pay their legislators only a per diem, most states pay lawmakers a set wage, with the mean annual salary in 2009 being $28,230 and the median being $20,806. Because many states also supplement legislative salaries with per diems (which receive favorable federal tax treatment) and other sums, the actual income received by state lawmakers was slightly higher than these figures (Squire and Moncrief 2010, 79-88). The range of state legislative salaries, however, is remarkable. State lawmakers in California earn the highest annual salary, $95,291, down from $116,208 after having their wages cut 10 percent by the state's compensation commission in 2009. At the other end, New Hampshire state legislators are paid $100 a year, a sum set in the state constitution in 1889 and left unchanged ever since. Overall, American state legislative salaries pale in broader comparison; state or provincial legislators in Australia, Canada, and Germany make considerably more than their U.S. counterparts (Squire 2008).

All but four states currently meet in annual sessions; only Montana, Nevada, North Dakota, and Texas meet biennially. Most of the state legislatures that meet annually are not, however, full-time institutions. Only twelve states do not place any limit on the length of the regular legislative session; the rest restrict the number of days their legislatures can meet. Thus, the formal time demands made on state legislators by legislative sessions can vary dramatically by state. The Utah state legislature, for example, meets for relatively few days. The 2007 session started on January 15 and finished on February 28, covering

45 calendar days, the constitutional limit. Floor sessions were actually held on 33 days. In contrast, during the 2007 regular session members of the California Assembly met for 121 session days and members of the state Senate met for 130 session days over 272 calendar days. It is important to note that state legislators spend more time on matters related to their legislative service than the number of days spent in session might suggest. A survey of legislators in all 50 states reveals the median lawmaker considers his or her position as constituting two-thirds of a full-time job (Kurtz, Moncrief, Niemi, and Powell 2006).

Almost every state legislature provides professional and clerical staff to standing committees. Roughly half of the states provide members with year-round personal staff, but fewer than ten provide district staff and offices. Overall, a few states, such as California, Florida, New York, and Texas operate with staff and facilities comparable to the U.S. Congress. Many other states provide little in the way of assistance or facilities. Indeed, in a few states lawmakers are treated like elementary school students with little more than their own desk in which to keep their things.

Professionalization matters because it influences lawmaker behavior, the way a legislature operates, and the policy decisions it makes. In terms of member behavior, the most obvious impact is on membership turnover, which declines as professionalization levels increase (Berry, Berkman, and Schneiderman 2000; Moncrief, Niemi and Powell 2004). But there are additional behavioral differences. Lawmakers in more professional legislatures have more contact with their constituents, are more attentive to their concerns, and are more representative of their views than are their counterparts in less professional legislatures (Lax and Phillips 2009; Maestas 2003; Squire 1993; Wright 2007). Voting behavior is affected, with legislators in more professionalized legislatures asserting greater independence from their party (Jenkins 2010). Among institutional effects, legislative efficiency—the percentage of bills passed and the number of bills enacted per legislative day—goes up with professionalization (Squire 1998). Lawmakers invest their leaders with less power as professionalization increases (Richman 2010). And more professionalized legislatures are better able to counter gubernatorial influence in the budget process, to better resist a governor's policy agenda, and to more effectively constrain the bureaucracy (Huber, Shipan, and Pfahler 2001; Kousser and Phillips 2009).

Perhaps the greatest impact of professionalization is on the sorts of policy decisions state legislatures make. The inclination to reform government personnel and procurement practices increases with professionalization, as does the willingness to adopt complex regulatory policies and income tax systems (Coggburn 2003; Ka and Teske 2002; Kellough and Selden 2003; Slemrod 2005). Increased professionalization is associated with the adoption of more innovative e-government architectures and stronger environmental programs (Tolbert, Mossberger and McNeal 2008; Woods 2008). The stringency of lobbying regulations and the vigor with which they are enforced increases with professionalization, as does the propensity to adopt stricter campaign finance laws (Witko 2007). It also produces greater investments in higher education and better funded state pension systems (Coggburn and Kearney 2009; McLendon, Hearn, and Mokher 2009). As professionalization levels increase legislatures are more likely to increase the number of economic enterprise zones and to respond to local government pressures to adopt anti-smoking ordinances (Shipan and Volden 2006; Turner and Cassell 2007). More professionalized legislatures also are better able to mediate policy disputes, thereby reducing the motivation for interest groups to turn to citizen initiatives in the states that allow them (Boehmke 2005). More generally, professionalized legislatures are better able to learn from the policy successes of other states and to generate more innovative policies of their own (Kousser 2005, 197-98).

The increased analytical capacity produced by professionalization translates into a different set of policy choices. When compared with the U.S. Congress, in 2009 only a handful of state legislatures—New York, California, Michigan and Pennsylvania—approximated its professionalization level. Most states lagged well behind. A few states—New Hampshire, North Dakota, Wyoming and South Dakota—were so far from Congress in terms of pay, session lengths and staffing, that the bore only the faintest resemblance (Squire forthcoming).

Who serves in state legislatures?

Traditionally, the image of an American state legislator is a middle age, white male lawyer. That stereotype is less true today than in the past. The number of female lawmakers in the states has grown dramatically in recent decades. In 2011, 24.3 percent of all state legislative seats were held by women. But the percentages vary considerably by state. Women held a third or more of seats in four states (Colorado, Vermont, Arizona and Hawaii), but fewer than 15 percent of the seats in five other states (South Carolina, Oklahoma, Alabama, Mississippi, and North Dakota). In the past, legislative professionalization and the percentage of women serving in a state legislature were negatively related; in more recent years that relationship has disappeared. Instead, women now are less likely to be elected to legislatures in the South and in more conservative states (Squire and Moncrief 2010, 98-99). The number of African American state legislators has also grown noticeably over time, but is still largely driven by population distributions. In 2009, 9 percent of all state legislators were African American, with the largest contingents being found in Southern states: Mississippi (29 percent), Alabama (25 percent), and Maryland (23 percent). Similarly, although the percentage of state legislators who are Hispanic has increased across the nation to 3 percent, they too are still found in larger numbers in states with the largest Hispanic populations: New Mexico (44 percent), California (23 percent), and Texas (20 percent).[5] African Americans are more likely to be elected in more professionalized legislatures, but there is no relationship between the percentage of Hispanic state legislators and professionalization (Squire and Moncrief 2010, 98-99).

On average, American state legislators are better educated than the people they represent. In 2011, 75 percent held at least a bachelor's degree, and just over 40 percent had earned an advanced degree of some sort. Again, there is variation across the states, usually in predictable ways. California, for example, has the highest percentage of members with at least a bachelor's degree (90 percent), while New Hampshire had the lowest percentage (53 percent) (Smallwood and Richards 2011).

The number of state legislators claiming full-time legislator as their occupation has increased substantially over time. But those claiming to be full-time lawmakers are much more likely to be found in more professionalized legislatures than in less professionalized bodies. Currently, the largest occupational group listed by state legislators is business, which includes both those who own their own establishments and those who are employed by others. Lawyers continue to enjoy a prominent role in state legislatures, in large part because they develop skills that lend themselves to success in the legislative arena (Padró I Miquel and Snyder 2006). The percentage of lawyers varies considerably across the states, but even at the high-end attorneys represent at most only a third of a state's legislators. The percentage of legislators who are in farming or ranching is strongly related to the strength of agriculture's role in a state's economy. Thus, farmers and ranchers are found in much greater numbers in South Dakota and North Dakota than in Massachusetts or New Jersey. Finally, much larger percentages of lawmakers who are retired from their occupations are found in lower salary state legislatures, notably Idaho and Nebraska. It is not surprising that service in those bodies is attractive to retired people because they usually have other means of income to support themselves and more flexible schedules to accommodate legislative sessions (Squire and Moncrief 2010, 102).

---

5   These data are taken from the Center for American Women in Politics, http://www.cawp.rutgers.edu/fast_facts/levels_of_office/documents/stleg.pdf, as of September 2011. These data were gathered by the National Conference of State Legislatures, http://www.ncsl.org/default.aspx?tabid=14767; and http://www.ncsl.org/default.aspx?tabid=14776.

Legislative organization and decision making

The United States is a two-party system, a fact that is abundantly clear at the state legislative level. In 2011, of the 7,343 state legislators elected by partisan ballot, only 23, or .003 percent, were elected as something other than a Republican or a Democrat. This fact is central to understanding state legislatures because political parties organize every one of them, save, as noted above, for Nebraska. Typically, the majority party elects a house's leaders and organizes its committees. But, while this is what happens most of the time, the last 30 years has witnessed the occasional formation of bipartisan coalitions to elect state legislative leaders, something which has never happened in either house of the U.S. Congress. State legislative houses in at least 12 states have experienced one or more such coalitions in recent years. Why majority party unity occasionally disappears on leadership votes is not clear. An examination of such coalitions suggests strong issue differences within the majority party can be a potent source of friction, but the more common situation is one where deep dissatisfaction with the actions of an incumbent leader leads disaffected party members to seek an accommodation with opposition party members. Importantly, however, while some of these bipartisan coalitions last over a full session or two; more of them are, in the words of a Connecticut representative, only "one-day dates" (Squire and Moncrief 2010, 123).

Currently, both parties are represented in every state legislature, although each party has a few houses in which it enjoys large majorities. But it is important to note that party competition is not a constant in American state legislatures; at different points in time many states have been completely dominated by a single party. As recently as the early 1960s there were *no* Republican state legislators in Alabama, Arkansas, Georgia, Louisiana, Mississippi, South Carolina, and Texas, and only a handful in the other legislatures in the South. Over the course of the next 50 years, the situation changed, in some cases dramatically, with Republicans becoming the majority party in over half of the Southern state legislatures. The process of moving from a one-party house to a two-party house has had important consequences for legislative organization, with partisan structures such as caucuses developing after the minority party size reached roughly one-third of the seats in a chamber. At that point voting also became organized by partisanship rather than by factional allegiances (Hamm and Harmel 1993; Harmel 1986; Harmel and Hamm 1986).

State legislatures vary in the power exercised by party caucuses. In some houses party caucuses are powerful, even to the point of making votes binding on important issues (Rosenthal 1998, 281). In other houses caucuses are very weak or essentially non-existent. The importance of party caucuses varies over time in many legislatures. As many as one-quarter of the strong-party caucuses in the 1950s were not considered powerful by the 1980s (Hamm and Hedlund

1994, 968). It appears that the importance of party caucuses is a function of size and the degree of party competition in a house. The more evenly matched the parties and the smaller the house, the greater the importance of caucuses (Francis 1989, 45).

State constitutions provide for minimal legislative leadership, typically a speaker in the lower house and a president in the senate. Over time, however, most state legislatures have evolved much more elaborate leadership structures, with floor leaders and a host of whips, deputies, and assistants. State legislative leaders are not created the same. Some enjoy far more power than do others. One reason they differ is the leadership structures in which they operate. Among lower houses, Louisiana and Mississippi have just two leaders: a speaker and a speaker pro tempore, concentrating all power in their hands. The other extreme is anchored by the Connecticut House with 62 leadership posts, creating a situation where power becomes more diffused. (In the most extreme case the 36 member Connecticut senate has 36 leadership positions, meaning every Connecticut senator holds a leadership title!)

Regardless of the number of leadership posts, the top leader in every lower house is called the speaker. Universally, this is the most power position in the lower house. In contrast, state senate leadership structures are more complicated and confusing than those found in lower houses. Formally, the lieutenant governor is the president of the senate in 26 states, holding a position that is at least superficially similar to that of the U.S. vice president, who serves as president of the U.S. Senate. In the other 24 state senates, the president is elected by the membership. To further confound matters, in both Tennessee and West Virginia the senate elects one of its own members to serve simultaneously as the top leader—called the speaker in Tennessee and the president in West Virginia—and as lieutenant governor. Finally, although the members of the Nebraska Unicameral are referred to as senator, they are, like Tennessee, presided over by a speaker.

Looking across state senates, however, real leadership power is vested in the president or president pro tem in the vast majority of them. Although many lieutenant governors serve as senate president, they essentially perform a ceremonial role. Only a few, notably the lieutenant governors in Georgia and Texas, exercise significant power within their state senate, in those cases blurring the separation of powers between the executive branch and the legislative branch (Rosenthal 1998, 248).

How much power do legislative leaders really exercise? Typically, they have a number of formal powers at their disposal. Top legislative leaders make most committee assignments and usually name committee chairs. In a handful of state houses the top leader even selects his or her floor leader. Top leaders who also serve as a chamber's presiding officer can use the gavel to their advantage. Many leaders enjoy power over the referral of legislation to committees and over the flow of legislation to the floor. Both powers give a leader the opportunity to determine a bill's fate (Squire and Hamm 2005, 120). Finally, the authority to recognize speakers and make parliamentary rulings give a leader considerable opportunity to fashion debates and votes to his or her liking. Overall, legislative leaders use their powers in a carrot and stick fashion. The carrot is that leaders can greatly assist members by helping them get favorable committee assignments, progress up the legislative leadership ladder, and pass legislation. The stick is that members who fail to do the leadership's bidding can be punished in ways large and small, greatly limiting their prospects to achieve their personal and political preferences. But what is missing from American state legislative leaders' arsenals are any ability to prevent their party members from gaining renomination, a power their counterparts enjoy in many other legislatures around the world.

Standing committees

Every American state legislature operates with standing committees, bodies that exist from session to session and which have the power to recommend legislative proposals to the full house. Standing committees are mechanisms that allow legislatures to handle bills and other legislative matters efficiently by dividing the work load among lawmakers. Committees can be power centres in American legislatures because of the potential gate-keeping power they exercise in the legislative process. Legislation that is introduced is usually referred to a standing committee and the decision that committee makes on whether or not to pass bill or an amended version of it on to the full house may dictate the measure's ultimate fate.

It might be assumed that the power of standing committees is universally great because of the considerable influence such bodies exercise in the U.S. House and Senate. In reality, the power of standing committees varies considerably, both across state legislative houses and over time within a house (Hamm, Hedlund, and Martorano 2006). For example, committees in neither the Illinois House nor the California Assembly can be said to exercise significant gate-keeping powers. Instead, in both legislatures the real gate-keepers are party leaders.

Although American state legislative houses handle roughly the same set of policy decisions, they divide up the workload in very different ways. The Maryland House of Delegates, for example, has 141 members, but in 2011 it used only seven standing committees, all but one of which had at least 5 subcommittees. Delegates typically have only one standing committee assignment and one subcommittee assignment. In contrast, the Mississippi House, with 122 members, divides up its work very differently. It has 46 standing committees and 3 selected committees, only a few with subcommittees. Where Maryland has a single Judiciary Committee, Mississippi has three judiciary committees: Judiciary A, Judiciary B, and Judiciary En Banc, which as the name suggests incorporates all the members from Judiciary A and Judiciary B. In addition, there is a separate Juvenile Justice Committee. Mississippi House members typically serve on between four to six standing committees.

An altogether different standing committee system developed in Connecticut, Maine, and Massachusetts. The bicameral legislatures in those states rely almost exclusively on joint standing committees. Members from each house serve on the same committee, with a co-chair from each house. In practice, joint committees greatly reduce the need for conference committees to reconcile legislative differences between the two chambers, thus arguably making the legislative process more efficient (Moen, Palmer and Powell 2005, 94). With joint committees, however, the distinction between separate houses is to some extent unclear, raising questions about the rationale for their independent existence.

There are two questions about how standing committees are composed in state legislatures that merit special consideration. First, does the majority party stack committees with a greater percentage of its members than their representation in the chamber would warrant? In general, state legislatures usually follow proportional representation rules, although stacking of committees does occur with some frequency. An examination of legislative rules in the late 1990s revealed that in 25 of 91 houses an explicit rule mandated proportional representation while in another 45 houses the practice was usually followed even though it was not formally required (American Society of Legislative Clerks and Secretaries 1998, 4-4). Partisan committee stacking is more likely to happen when the majority party controls a chamber by only a slim margin (Hedlund, Coombs, Martorano, and Hamm 2009). Majority parties take particular care to stack committees that they want to ensure they control, such as rules committees that manage the legislative process and budget committees that determine how the government raises and spends money.

Committee assignments are handled in different ways in different legislative houses. Most assignments are made by the top legislative leader: the speaker in the lower house and the president, president pro tem, or majority leader in the senate. There are, however, some variations. In six lower houses and eleven senates a committee on committees gives out committee positions, although in several chambers the top leader chairs the committee and greatly influences the assignments it makes. A committee on rules acts as a committee on committees in three senates. Party caucuses make committee assignments in the Hawaii House, while caucuses organized around congressional districts do so in the Arkansas House. Rules allow the minority party a role in assigning its members to committees in about 40 percent of state legislative houses (American Society of Legislative Clerks and Secretaries 1998, 4-8).

Some chambers, however, do limit the appointing power's freedom to make committee appointments by requiring other considerations to be taken into account. One such constraint is a reliance on member seniority, where members who have served for longer have the opportunity to select the committees on which they serve. Assignment rules in most states do not mention seniority, but a few do. But seniority is the explicit basis for committee assignments in only a small handful of state legislative houses, and never along the exact same lines as in the U.S. House and Senate (Squire and Moncrief 2010, 146-47).

Decision making in American state legislatures

Potentially there are three competing sources of power in state legislatures: legislative leaders, party caucuses, or standing committees. In the early 1980s state legislators were surveyed and asked to identify the most important decision making entities in their house. Committees were thought to be an important decision-making centre in 81 of the 99 legislative houses. In only three states (California, Illinois and New Jersey) were committees deemed to be unimportant in both houses. Committees shared power with the leadership, the party caucus, or both in almost two-thirds of the houses. Committees, however, held dominant power in only about 15 percent of state legislative chambers (Francis 1985a). Importantly, however, a later study found that the locus of power with a legislature can change over time (Hamm and Hedlund 1994). Certainly, this appears to be the case for the power of committees in legislatures that have adopted term limits (Cain and Wright 2007).

Conclusion

The current configuration of policy responsibilities in the American federal system places considerable responsibilities in the hands of state legislatures. The capacity of those legislative institutions to handle those policy decisions varies across the states. A relatively small number of legislatures are professionalized along the lines of the U.S. Congress, with well paid, full-time lawmakers supported by staff resources. Most of the rest of the states provide their legislators much less in the way of financial incentives to serve for long, time to do their work, or informational assistance.

The mechanisms for policy making also vary across the state legislatures. Parties organize each house, but the role of leaders, committees, and caucuses differs. Who serves in each house and the qualifications and experiences they bring with them to their tasks also differs. It is no surprise, then, that the quality of policymaking decisions varies across the American states.

References

Adams, G.D. (1996). "Legislative Effects of Single-Member vs. Multi-Member Districts." *American Journal of Political Science* (40), 129-44.

Aldrich, J.H., and J.S. Coleman Battista. (2002). "Conditional Party Government in the States." *American Journal of Political Science* (46), 164-72.

American Society of Legislative Clerks and Secretaries in cooperation with the National Conference of State Legislatures. (1998). *Inside the Legislative Process.* Denver, CO: National Conference of State Legislatures.

Berry, W.D., M.B. Berkman, and S. Schneiderman. (2000). "Legislative Professionalism and Incumbent Reelection: The Development of Institutional Boundaries." *American Political Science Review* (94), 859-874.

Boehmke, F.J. (2005). "Sources of Variation in the Frequency of Statewide Initiatives: The Role of Interest Group Populations." *Political Research Quarterly* (58), 565–575.

Cain, B. and G. Wright. (2007). "Committees." In *Institutional Change in American Politics: The Case of Term Limits*, ed. K.T. Kurtz, B. Cain, and R.G. Niemi. Ann Arbor, MI: University of Michigan Press.

Coggburn, J.D. (2003). "Exploring Differences in the American States' Procurement Practices." *Journal of Public Procurement* (3), 3-28.

Coggburn, J.D., and R.C. Kearney. (2009). "Trouble Keeping Promises? An Analysis of Underfunding in State Retiree Benefits." *Public Administration Review* (70), 97-108.

Cooper, C.A. and L.E. Richardson, Jr. (2006). "Institutions and Representational Roles in American State Legislatures." *State Politics and Policy Quarterly* (6), 174-194.

Freeman, P.K. and L.E. Richardson, Jr. (1996). "Explaining Variations in Casework among State Legislators." *Legislative Studies Quarterly* (21), 41-56.

Francis, W.L. (1985a). "Leadership, Party Caucuses, and Committees in U.S. State Legislatures." *Legislative Studies Quarterly* (10), 243-257.

Francis, W.L. (1985b). "Costs and Benefits of Legislative Service in the American States." *American Journal of Political Science* (29), 626-642.

Francis, W.L. (1989). *The Legislative Committee Game: A Comparative Analysis of 50 States.* Columbus, OH: Ohio State University Press.

Hamm, K.E. and R. Harmel. (1993). "Legislative Party Development and the Speaker System: The Case of the Texas House." *Journal of Politics* (55), 1140-1151.

Hamm, K.E., and R.D. Hedlund. (1994). "Political Parties in State Legislatures." In *The Encyclopedia of the American Legislative System*, ed. J.J. Silbey. New York, NY: Scribner's.

Hamm, K.E., R.D. Hedlund, and N. Martorano. (2006). "Measuring State Legislative Committee Power: Change and Chamber Differences in the 20th Century." *State Politics and Policy Quarterly* (6), 88-111.

Harmel, R. (1986). "Minority Partisanship in One-Party Predominant Legislatures: A Five-State Study." *Journal of Politics* (48), 729-740.

Harmel, R. and K.E. Hamm. (1986). "Development of a Party Role in a No-Party Legislature." *Western Political Quarterly* (39), 79-92.

Huber, J.D., C.R. Shipan, and M. Pfahler. (2001). "Legislatures and Statutory Control of Bureaucracy." *American Journal of Political Science* (45), 330-345.

Jenkins, S. (2010). "Examining the Influences over Roll Call Voting in Multiple Issue Areas: A Comparative US State Analysis." *Journal of Legislative Studies* (16), 14-31.

Ka, S. and P. Teske. (2002). "Ideology and Professionalism—Electricity Regulation and Deregulation Over Time in the American States." *American Politics Research* (30), 323–343.

Kellough, J. E. and S. C. Selden. (2003). "The Reinvention of Public Personnel Administration: An Analysis of the Diffusion of Personnel Management Reforms in the States." *Public Administration Review* (63), 165–176.

King, J.D. (2000). "Changes in Professionalism in U.S. State Legislatures." *Legislative Studies Quarterly* (25), 327-343.

Kousser, T. (2005). *Term Limits and the Dismantling of State Legislative Professionalism*. New York, NY: Cambridge University Press.

Kousser, T. and J.H. Phillips. (2009). "Who Blinks First? Legislative Patience and Bargaining with Governors." *Legislative Studies Quarterly* (34), 55-86.

Kurtz, K.T., G. Moncrief, R.G. Niemi, and L.W. Powell. (2006). "Full-Time, Part-Time, and Real Time: Explaining State Legislators' Perceptions of Time on the Job." *State Politics and Policy Quarterly* (6), 322-338.

Lax, J.R. and J.H. Phillips. (2009). "Gay Rights in the States: Public Opinion and Public Responsiveness." *American Political Science Review* (103), 367-386.

Maestas, C. (2003). "The Incentive to Listen: Progressive Ambition, Resources, and Opinion Monitoring among State Legislators." *Journal of Politics* (65), 439-456.

McLendon, M.K., J.C. Hearn and C.G. Mokher.(2009). "Partisans, Professionals, and Power: The Role of Political Factors in State Higher Education Funding. *Journal of Higher Education* (80), 686–713.

Moen, M.C., K.T. Palmer, and R.J. Powell. (2005). *Changing Members: The Maine Legislature in the Era of Term Limits*, (Lanham, MD: Lexington).

Moncrief, G., R.G. Niemi, and L.W. Powell. (2004). "Time, Term Limits, and Turnover: Membership Stability in U.S. State Legislatures." *Legislative Studies Quarterly* (29), 357-381.

Padró I Miquel, G. and J.M. Snyder, Jr. (2006). "Legislative Effectiveness and Legislative Careers." *Legislative Studies Quarterly* (31), 347-381.

Powell, R. (2007). "Executive-Legislative Relations." In *Institutional Change in American Politics: The Case of Term Limits*, ed. K.T. Kurtz, B. Cain, and R.G. Niemi. Ann Arbor, MI: University of Michigan Press.

Richman, J. (2010). "The Logic of Legislative Leadership: Preferences, Challenges, and the Speaker's Powers." *Legislative Studies Quarterly* (35), 211-2233.

Rosenthal, A. (1981). *Legislative Life*. New York, NY: Harper & Row.

Rosenthal, A. (1996). "State Legislative Development: Observations from Three Perspectives." *Legislative Studies Quarterly* (21), 169-198.

Rosenthal, A. (1998). *The Decline of Representative Democracy: Process, Participation, and Power in State Legislatures*. Washington, DC: CQ Press.

Schaffner, B.F. (2007). "Political Parties and the Representativeness of Legislative Committees." *Legislative Studies Quarterly* (32), 475-497.

Shipan, C.R. and C. Volden. (2006). "Bottom-Up Federalism: The Diffusion of Antismoking Policies from U.S. Cities to States." *American Journal of Political Science* 50, 825–843.

Slemrod, J. (2005). "The Etiology of Tax Complexity: Evidence from U.S. State Income Tax Systems." *Public Finance Review* (33), 279–299.

Smallwood, S. and A. Richards. (2011). "How Educated Are State Legislators?" *Chronicle of Higher Education*, June 12.

Squire, P. (1988a). "Member Career Opportunities and the Internal Organization of Legislatures." *Journal of Politics* (50), 726-744.

Squire, P. (1988b). "Career Opportunities and Membership Stability in Legislatures." *Legislative Studies Quarterly* (13), 65-82.

Squire, P. (1992a). "The Theory of Legislative Institutionalization and the California Assembly." *Journal of Politics* (54), 1026-1054.

Squire, P. (1992b). "Legislative Professionalization and Membership Diversity in State Legislatures." *Legislative Studies Quarterly* (17), 69-79.

Squire, P. (1993). "Professionalization and Public Opinion of State Legislatures." *Journal of Politics* (55), 479-491.

Squire, P. (1998). "Membership Turnover and the Efficient Processing of Legislation." *Legislative Studies Quarterly* 23, 23–32.

Squire, P. (2000). "Uncontested Seats in State Legislative Elections." *Legislative Studies Quarterly* (25), 131-146.

Squire, P. (2007). "Measuring Legislative Professionalism: The Squire Index Revisited." *State Politics and Policy Quarterly* (7), 211-227.

Squire, P. (2008). "The State Wealth-Legislative Compensation Effect." *Canadian Journal of Political Science* (41), 1-18.

Squire, P. (forthcoming). *The Evolution of American Legislatures; Colonies, Territories, and States, 1619-2009*. Ann Arbor, MI: University of Michigan Press.

Squire, P. and K.E. Hamm. (2005). *101 Chambers: Congress, State Legislatures and the Future of Legislative Studies*. Columbus, OH: Ohio State University Press.

Squire, P. and G. Moncrief. (2010). *State Legislatures Today: Politics Under the Domes*. Boston, MA: Longman.

Tolbert, C.J., K. Mossberger and R. McNeal. (2008). "Institutions, Policy Innovation, and E-Government in the American States." *Public Administration Review* (68), 549-563.

Turner, R.C. and M.K. Cassell. (2007). "When Do States Pursue Targeted Economic Development Policies? The Adoption and Expansion of State Enterprise Zone Programs." *Social Science Quarterly* (88), 86–103.

Witko, C. 2007. "Explaining Increases in the Stringency of State Campaign Finance Regulation, 1993–2002." *State Politics and Policy Quarterly* (7), 369–393.

Woods, N.D. (2008). "The Policy Consequences of Political Corruption: Evidence from State Environmental Programs." *Social Science Quarterly* (89), 258–271.

Wright, G. 2007. "Do Term Limits Affect Legislative Roll Call Voting? Representation, Polarization, and Participation." *State Politics and Policy Quarterly* (7), 256–280.

Wright, G.C., and B.F. Schaffner. (2002). "The Influence of Party: Evidence from the State Legislatures," *American Political Science Review* (96), 367-379.

Index